THE PICKERING MASTERS

THE NOVELS AND SELECTED WORKS OF
MARY SHELLEY

Volume 3. *Valperga: or, the Life and Adventures of Castruccio, Prince of Lucca*

THE PICKERING MASTERS
THE NOVELS AND SELECTED WORKS OF
MARY SHELLEY

GENERAL EDITOR: NORA CROOK

WITH PAMELA CLEMIT

CONSULTING EDITOR: BETTY T. BENNETT

THE NOVELS AND SELECTED WORKS OF
MARY SHELLEY

VOLUME
3

EDITED BY
NORA CROOK

VALPERGA: OR, THE LIFE
AND ADVENTURES OF
CASTRUCCIO, PRINCE OF LUCCA

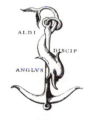

LONDON
WILLIAM PICKERING
1996

Published by Pickering & Chatto (Publishers) Limited

21 Bloomsbury Way, London, WC1A 2TH

Old Post Road, Brookfield, Vermont 05036, USA

BRITISH LIBRARY CATALOGUING IN PUBLICATION DATA
A catalogue record for this book is available from the British Library

ISBN 1–85196–076–7

LIBRARY OF CONGRESS CATALOGING-IN-PUBLICATION DATA
Shelley, Mary Wollstonecraft, 1797–1851.
    Valperga / edited by Nora Crook.
        p.   cm. –– (The novels and selected works of Mary Shelley ; v.
3) (The Pickering masters)
    Includes bibliographical references (p.   ).
    ISBN 1–85916–076–7 (set) –– ISBN 1–85196–079–1 (v. 3)
    Castracani, Castruccio, 1281–1328––Fiction.   1. Guelfs and
Ghibellines––History––Fiction.   3. Nobility––Italy––Fiction.
4. Condottieri––Fiction.   5. Italy––History––1268–1492––Fiction.
6. Lucca (Italy)––History––Fiction.   I. Title.   II. Series:
Shelley, Mary Wollstonecraft, 1797–1851.   Selections.   1996 ; v. 3.
PR5397.A1   1996 vol. 3
823'.7 s––dc20
[823'.7]   96–1537
                                                                   CIP

Typeset by Waveney Typesetters
Norwich

Printed and bound in Great Britain by
Biddles Limited
Guildford

CONTENTS

ABBREVIATIONS

Ab. Dep. e. 274	Bodleian Abinger MS Dep. e. 274.
adds. e. 17	Bodleian MS Shelley adds. e. 17.
Bennett (1978)	Betty T. Bennett, 'The Political Philosophy of Mary Shelley's Historical Novels' in *The Evidence of the Imagination*, eds D. H. Reiman, M. C. Jaye and B. T. Bennett (New York: New York University Press, 1978).
Cary	*The Vision; or Hell, Purgatory, and Paradise, of Dante Alighieri. Translated by the Rev. H. F. Cary* [etc.] (London, 1814).
CC Journals	*The Journals of Claire Clairmont*, ed. Marion Kingston Stocking, with the assistance of David Mackenzie Stocking (Cambridge, Mass.: Harvard University Press, 1968).
'Charles the First' Notebook	*The 'Charles the First' Draft Notebook; Bodleian MS Shelley adds. e. 17*, transcribed and edited by Nora Crook, vol. XII of *The Bodleian Shelley Manuscripts* (New York and London: Garland Publishing, 1991).
'Devils' Notebook	*Shelley's 'Devils' Notebook; Bodleian MS Shelley adds. e. 9*, transcribed and edited by P. M. S. Dawson and Timothy Webb, vol. XIV of *The Bodleian Shelley Manuscripts* (New York and London: Garland Press, 1993).
Forsyth	Joseph Forsyth, *Remarks on Antiquities, Arts, and Letters during an Excursion in Italy, in the Years 1802 and 1803* (1813), 2nd edn (London: John Murray, 1816).
Gisborne & Williams	*Maria Gisborne & Edward E. Williams, Shelley's Friends: Their Journals and Letters*, ed. Frederick L. Jones (Norman: University of Oklahoma Press, 1951).
Godwin, *Political Justice*	William Godwin, *An Enquiry Concerning Political Justice* (London: G. G. J. and G. Robinson, 1793), 3rd edn (1797).
Godwin, *Religious Writings*	William Godwin, *Religious Writings*, ed. Mark Philp, vol. 7 of *Political and Philosophical Writings of William Godwin* (London: Pickering & Chatto, 1994).
Green	Louis Green, *Castruccio Castracani* (Oxford: Clarendon Press, 1986).
Hellas Notebook	*The Hellas Notebook; Bodleian MS Shelley adds. e. 7*, transcribed and edited by Donald H. Rieman and Michael J.

	Neth, vol. XVI of *The Bodleian Shelley Manuscripts* (New York and London: Garland Publishing, 1994).
Lastri	Marco Lastri, *L'Osservatore Fiorentino* (1776–8), 3rd (enlarged) edn, 8 vols (Florence: Gaspero Ricci, 1821).
Lemprière	J[ohn]. Lemprière, *A Classical Dictionary* [etc.] (1788), 11th edn (London: T. Cadell and W. Davies, 1820).
Lyles	W. H. Lyles, *Mary Shelley: An Annotated Bibliography* (New York and London: Garland Publishing, 1975).
Marshall	Mrs Julian Marshall, *The Life and Letters of Mary Wollstonecraft Shelley*, 2 vols (London: Richard Bentley & Sons, 1889).
Medwin	Thomas Medwin, *The Life of Percy Bysshe Shelley* (1847), rev. edn, ed. H. Buxton Forman (London: Oxford University Press, Humphrey Milford, 1913).
Muratori	Lodovico Antonio Muratori, *Dissertazioni sopra le Antichità Italiane* (1751), new edn, ed. Gaetano Cenni, 3 vols (Monaco: Agostino Olzati, 1765–6).
Muratori, *Rerum*	Lodovico Antonio Muratori, *Rerum Italicarum Scriptores* [etc.], 25 vols (Milan, 1723–51).
MWSJ	*The Journals of Mary Shelley, 1814–1844*, eds Paula Feldman and Diana Scott-Kilvert, 2 vols (Oxford: Oxford University Press, 1987).
MWSL	*The Letters of Mary Wollstonecraft Shelley*, ed. Betty T. Bennett, 3 vols (Baltimore and London: Johns Hopkins University Press, 1980–88).
MWS Matilda etc	Mary Shelley, *Matilda, Dramas, Reviews & Essays, Prefaces & Notes*, ed. Pamela Clemit, vol. 2 in *The Novels and Selected Works of Mary Shelley* (London: Pickering & Chatto, 1996).
MWST	Mary Shelley, *Collected Tales and Stories*, ed. Charles E. Robinson (Baltimore and London: Johns Hopkins University Press, 1976).
Novellino	*Novellino e conti del duecento*, ed. Sebastiano lo Nigro (Turin: Unione Tipografico-Editrice Torinese, 1963).
OED	*Oxford English Dictionary*.
Palacio	Jean de Palacio, *Mary Shelley dans son œuvre: Contribution aux études shelleyennes* (Paris: Editions Klincksieck, 1969).
Paradise Lost	John Milton, *Paradise Lost, a Poem in Twelve Books* (1674).
PBSL	*The Letters of Percy Bysshe Shelley*, ed. F. L. Jones, 2 vols (Oxford: Oxford University Press, 1964).
PJV	*Political Justice Variants*, ed. Mark Philp, vol. 4 of *Political*

	and Philosophical Writings of William Godwin (London: Pickering & Chatto, 1994).
Robinson (1983)	Charles E. Robinson, 'Percy Bysshe Shelley, Charles Ollier and William Blackwood: the contexts of early nineteenth-century publishing' in *Shelley Revalued*, ed. Kelvin Everest (Leicester: Leicester University Press, 1983).
Romantics Reviewed	*The Romantics Reviewed: Contemporary Reviews of British Romantic Writers*, ed. D. H. Reiman, 9 vols (New York and London: Garland Publishing, 1972).
Sismondi	Jean-Charles-Leonard Simonde de Sismondi, *Histoire des républiques italiennes du moyen âge* (1807–9), 2nd edn, 16 vols (Paris, 1818).
Sunstein	Emily W. Sunstein, *Mary Shelley, Romance and Reality* (Boston and London: Little, Brown, 1989; 2nd edn, Baltimore and London: Johns Hopkins University Press, 1991).
Targioni	Giovanni Targioni-Tozzetti, *Relazioni d'alcuni viaggi fatti in diverse parti della Toscana* [etc.] (1751), 2nd edn, 12 vols (Florence, 1768–9).
Tegrimi	Niccolò Tegrimi, *Vita Castruccii Castracani* (1496); bilingual edn, *Vita Castruccii Antelminelli lucensis ducis auctore Nicolao Tegrimo equite jurisconsulto una cum Etrusca Versione Giorgii Dati* (Lucca: Sebastian Cappuri, 1742).
Villani	*Croniche di Messer Giovani Villani, Cittadino Fiorentino* [etc.], ed. Jacomo Fasolo (Venice: Bartholomeo Zanetti Casterzagense, 1537).
Walling	William A. Walling, *Mary Shelley* (New York: Twayne Publishers, 1972).
Ward	William S. Ward, *Literary Reviews in British Periodicals, 1821–26, A Bibliography* (New York and London: Garland Publishing, 1977).

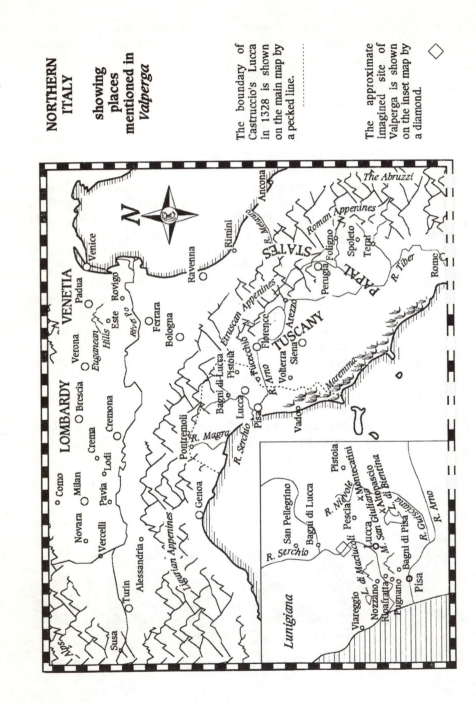

NORTHERN ITALY

showing places mentioned in *Valperga*

The boundary of Castruccio's Lucca in 1328 is shown on the main map by a pecked line. ⸳⸳⸳⸳⸳⸳⸳

The approximate imagined site of Valperga is shown on the inset map by a diamond. ◇

INTRODUCTORY NOTE

Valperga: or, the Life and Adventures of Castruccio, Prince of Lucca (3 vols, London: G. and W. B. Whittaker, 1823), Mary Wollstonecraft Shelley's second novel, was written at Pisa and the Bagni di Pisa. The present text is based on the first and only edition. Its genesis, writing and publication (1817–23) is in some respects better documented than that of *Frankenstein*. This 'child of mighty slow growth', she wrote on 30 June 1821, had been conceived 'in our library at Marlow'.[1] The idea took shape at Naples in early 1819 with the reading of Sismondi, but want of suitable books held her back until her move to Pisa (January 1820).[2] Journal entries 'Write' and 'read Machiavelli Hist. of Castruccio Castracani', for March 12 and 31 respectively, may signal the formal start.[3] After a summer hiatus at Leghorn she moved to the Bagni di Pisa in August and 'continued again'. She visited Lucca on 11–12 August 1820; a period of almost daily reading, note-taking and writing followed. This tailed off and virtually ceased during the winter of 1820–21. On 10 April 1821 it resumed, with writing quickly assuming primacy over reading. On 30 June the novel, she reported, was 'in a state of great forwardness': she had arrived at page 71 of the 'rough transcript' of Volume III. This she intended to finish within a month, allowing herself a further month for corrections, before fair-copying.[4]

She kept to her schedule; copying had begun by 31 August. On 11 November, P. B. Shelley told his publisher, Ollier, that *Castruccio, Prince of Lucca* (the first title) was ready; nevertheless, copying and late corrections, to which his cousin Thomas Medwin records him contributing by 'now and then altering in pencil' what Mary Shelley had written that day, continued until at least 3 December 1821.[5]

Mary Shelley described the novel as 'a work of some labour since I have read & consulted a great many books'.[6] This has been interpreted to mean that she exhaustively trawled through chronicles.[7] A study of her journal, working notebooks and *Valperga* itself, however, suggests that her research for the political and socio-historical background consisted, rather, of the judicious study and collation of a limited number of well-chosen primary and secondary sources, some of which are mentioned in *Valperga*'s Preface. Additionally, she used Muratori's *Dissertazioni sopra le Antichità Italiane*, Targioni-Tozzetti's *Viaggi in Toscana* and Lastri's *L'Osservatore Fiorentino* (first read in April 1821). These last two may be among the works she 'consulted' (i.e. did not read through from the first volume to the end). The editions used of Sismondi, Muratori, Villani, Targioni, Lastri and Tegrimi have been identified by the present editor, all except the last from information in Mary Shelley's research notebooks. (For full references, see Abbreviations, under the author's name.)[8] As with the later *Perkin Warbeck*, Mary Shelley follows her sources sometimes with rigorous fidelity, sometimes with great freedom, often taking contradictions between them as providing opportunities for invention.

The 'great many books' undoubtedly include imaginative works of Early Renaissance writers – Dante, Petrarch, Boccaccio, Chaucer, Tuscan *novellisti* and, perhaps, the thirteenth- and fourteenth-century *Novellino* ('The Hundred Old Tales').[9] Among contemporary writers, the most obvious influences are Godwin, Wollstonecraft, and P. B. Shelley, with Leigh Hunt, Scott, Byron, and de Staël contributing less overtly. However, the central story and much of the detail derive not from books, but from Mary Shelley's imagination and her exterior world: the abortive revolutions of Naples and Piedmont in 1820–21; the Tuscan landscape and its old towns; weather changes; people. Francesco Pacchiani (1772–1835), 'the Devil of Pisa', canon and ex-professor of chemistry, was said to be there 'drawn to the life',[10] while the *improvvisatore* Guarino is a fictional prototype in artistry, if not in personality, of Tommaso Sgricci (1789–1836), who so impressed the Shelleys in early 1821.

Valperga proved difficult to publish as Mary Shelley was concerned not to undersell it. An early (1819) approach to Lackington elicited no better terms than those the firm had exacted for *Frankenstein*. Charles Ollier expressed interest; active negotiations had begun (through P. B. Shelley) by July 1821.[11] However, they met an obstacle later that year, this apparently being not the sum Ollier offered (£300) but his unwillingness to pay £100 immediately, cash needed by Mary Shelley to discharge Godwin's most pressing debts.[12] By 11 January 1822 the manuscript had been shipped to Godwin, giving him the copyright to sell for his own benefit, while the Olliers pleaded for patience in the hope of keeping the commission. Mary Shelley awaited Godwin's reaction; as late as 2 June she had not even heard of the novel's arrival.[13]

It had, however, arrived. Godwin read 'Castruccio' between 18–27 April, during one of the major financial crises of his life, and with an eviction order impending. His business saved, he read it through again (2–10 July). On 11 July, and again on the 12th, he wrote 'Castruccio, abridge'.[14] According to Mrs Godwin, he postponed trying to sell it, fearing that knowledge of his financial distress would cheapen the price.[15] Eventually, on 1 August, he approached a publisher (unsuccessfully) and well into November was still trying others.[16] From 23 October–8 November he re-read 'Castruccio' once more almost daily, breaking off twice to revise; on completion of reading he revised on three subsequent days.[17] On 16 November he wrote to Mary Shelley to say that 'Castruccio' had more genius than *Frankenstein*, but too much 'proud flesh' (i.e. bulk).[18] Yet again he read it through, in shorter bursts, between 9 December and 10 January. Negotiations with Whittaker were now under way and by 18 February he was able to tell Mary Shelley that the novel was in print.[19] He had 'taken great liberties' but assured her that his intervention was 'nearly confined to the taking away things that must have prevented its success'. One was a 'long detail of battles and campaigning after the death of Beatrice, & when the reader is impatient for the conclusion'; he had scarcely ever seen 'anything more unfortunately out of taste'. But he praised the characterisation of Beatrice ('the jewel'), Euthanasia, Pepi, Bindo and Mandragola. His journal entry for 19 February says 'Valperga published'.[20]

Up to 10 January Godwin had been referring to 'Castruccio'; this is the first mention of a new title. According to Medwin Godwin chose it.[21] Conjecturally, Godwin's 'liberties' also cover such items as the excision of the final -l (as in 'waterfall') a possible spelling preference,[22] the kind of minor changes that he was to make to the 1823 *Frankenstein*, and the present form of the preface. The first paragraph of the latter is written in Mary Shelley's person and clearly derives from information supplied by her. But it is curiously ruled off from the remainder, which is taken from a reference book which she is not known ever to have used.[23]

For the rest, the available evidence supports Godwin's statement that his changes were mostly just cuts (i.e. not major rewritings or insertions), with, presumably, a few link phrases or sentences for continuity. 'Castruccio' is mentioned on fifty-seven days in Godwin's journal, but revision (without mention of recopying) figures on only seven of these. Moreover, while the tally *seems* to allow time for Godwin virtually to re-write the book, this would be an entirely misleading inference. Godwin gave up only a part of each day to 'Castruccio', keeping up his own routine of activities.

The manuscript Mary Shelley sent to Godwin is lost. Seventeen random pages of autograph manuscript of *Valperga* are extant, but these are 'rough transcript' or intermediate draft, which he did not see. What they do indicate, if imperfectly, is Mary Shelley's own process of correcting and excision; one omitted passage, the defrauding of Luparo, is of especial interest. These stray leaves are reproduced in transcript (see Endnotes and *Valperga* Draft Transcripts) by kind permission of the Pierpont Morgan library, New York.[24]

On 6 May 1823, still in Italy, Mary Shelley awaited her copy of *Valperga*, while Godwin learned from Whittaker that, of the print-run of 1000 copies, half had been sold.[25] But sales would then appear to have slumped; in 1826 Henry Colburn advertised *Valperga* as 'Just Published' (see vol. 1, Introductory Note, n. 22); he had bought up the unsold stock and was re-issuing it (with the 1823 price of 21s discounted to 18s).

Over twenty reviews dating from 1823–4 have been found;[26] most are favourable, but are not always reliable indicators of *Valperga*'s reception. Some are brief eulogies from friendly newspapers which Godwin had approached before publication.[27] The fashionable *La Belle Assemblée*, luke-warm towards

Scott's comparable *Quentin Durward* the month before, extolled *Valperga* as a work of 'extraordinary talent' displaying 'perfect knowledge' of the passions. The Whittakers acquired the magazine in 1823; the hyperbole and the timing of the review (August 1823, well past the first flush of notices) fuel suspicion of a sales puff. More discriminatingly, the *Literary Gazette* advised its readers to skim the 'sheer mummery' of the witch-scenes but assured them that they would find 'energetic language, landscapes worthy of a poet or a painter, feelings strong in their truth'; the *British Magazine*, won over despite disliking *Frankenstein*, treated *Valperga* approvingly as a revival of the older, pre-Walter Scott romance. *Valperga* was 'one of the best' of modern novels, admirable in its descriptions of elegant medieval dress and the sack of Cremona alike, in a class above most 'ladies' writing', though Mary Wollstonecraft's daughter might 'box our ears for saying so'. *Blackwood's*, the only one of the three 'Great Reviews' to notice *Valperga*, and one of the few to see contemporary political significance in it, offered barbed praise: 'It is impossible to read [Beatrice's anathema] without admiration of the eloquence with which it is written, or without sorrow, that any English lady should be capable of clothing such thoughts in such words'. Ignoring the Preface, it complained that the 'real' Castruccio (i.e. Machiavelli's) was a witty satirist, unlike hers; that she had succumbed to a new vogue for historical romances featuring a thinly disguised Napoleon (d. 1821); that she obtruded historical knowledge and fine writing ('we are mortally sick of "orange-tinted skies," "dirges," and "Dante"'). This mischievous piece (*Blackwood's* was at the height of its campaign against Leigh Hunt's *Liberal* and its contributors) was the longest, most widely-circulated and probably most challenging review of 1823–4.[28]

Medwin later (1847) ascribed *Valperga's* failure partly to the low tastes of 'readers of fiction' on whom its 'eloquence and beauty and poetry' were lost, and partly to 'Mrs Shelley's' shortcomings in dialogue and the delineation of character. But the reviews do not altogether bear him out. It was narrative structure that was most criticised, while eloquence, sentiment, painterly qualities and characterisation (except for Castruccio's) were praised. So was her ability to recreate the past, a dissenter being Anne Louise Swanton-Belloc, who, in the only Continental review so far found, preferred Scott. Predictably, most reviewers compared *Valperga* to *Frankenstein*; some were glad to find the stamp of the same 'wild imagination' (*Literary Gazette*), others relieved to find 'a more sober turn of feeling' (*Ladies' Monthly Museum*). *Blackwood's* apart, Beatrice's anathema drew little censure, contrary to Mary Shelley's own expectations. However, one critic, praising *Frankenstein* in the talented, short-lived *Knight's Quarterly*, confessed to throwing aside *Valperga* before finishing the first volume ('I do not think I ever was so disappointed in a work'), finding 'not one flash of imagination, not one spark of passion'. Perhaps, he conjectured, Mrs Shelley did write *Frankenstein*, 'but, knowing its fault was extravagance, determined to be careful and correct in her next work'. How damaging this late notice was is hard to assess, but it shows that the notion of Mary Shelley as a one-book author was already incipient.[29]

Mary Shelley hoped for a critique from Leigh Hunt, but it never material-ised; she wrote to him in August 1823 'If ever I write another novel it will be [...] more pleasing to you than this – After all, Valperga is merely a book of promise, another landing place in the staircase I am climbing'. But others tried to keep Valperga in the public eye. In 1825, John Watson Dalby wrote a laudatory 'Sonnet Written after reading "Valperga"' and in 1826 Thomas Jefferson Hogg wrote, with more gallantry than truth, of Lucca as famous for Castruccio 'who is known to many, because his life was described by Machiavelli, and to all as the hero of Valperga'. A systematic search of periodi-cals might well uncover more such. But, unlike Frankenstein, Valperga faded from view. The Bentley Archive records another Colburn remainder issue (1830), but that is all. Mary Shelley in 1837 wrote that it 'never had fair play; never being properly published' when trying (unsuccessfully) to suggest that Bentley reissue it in his Standard Novels.[30]

Had Mary Shelley read the proofs, Valperga's printing (by Richard Taylor of Shoe Lane) would have had fewer Italian errors (for instance 'agiolo' 'Teroretto' and 'Antichristà'). Most of these are here corrected but a few doubtful instances have been allowed to stand. Some inconsistency of names is ascribable to the mixture of medieval, modern, French, Latin and Italian texts that Mary Shelley used; these instances are left uncorrected, together with 'dei' where modern Italian would have 'degli'. Her factual sources, where traced, are (selectively) given in footnotes.[31] A guide to the general principles of textual treatment is found in volume 1 of this edition.

NOTES

[1] MWSL, I, p. 203; probably in the second half of 1817. Germs of Valperga may be found in her Marlow reading, e.g., Dante's Divina Commedia and Hume's Essays.

[2] See MWSL, I, pp. 120–21 and n.

[3] MWSJ, I, pp. 312–13. Valperga contains more of Machiavelli than the dismissive remark in the preface might suggest.

[4] 'All the winter I did not touch it' (MWSL, I, p. 203); for the journal record, see MWSJ, I, pp. 328–72.

[5] MWSJ, I, pp. 378–84; PBSL, II, p. 365; Medwin, p. 374. A single emendation by P. B. Shelley in ink to the 'rough transcript' has also survived. His interest is also shown by his translation 'If the good money which I lent to thee' (see Endnote 4); and possibly by (i) the first Canzone of Dante's Convito (Bodleian MS. Shelley adds. e. 9, pp. 337–9, 341, reproduced in the 'Devils' Notebook and dated c.January-February 1821 by the editors. Mary Shelley's transcript is in Bodleian MS. Shelley adds. c. 5. ff. 157–8); (ii) 'Love, Hope, Desire and Fear', his free version (composed ?July-November, 1821) from Brunetto Latini's Tesoretto (XIX. 81–154) (Bodleian MS. Shelley adds. e. 7 pp. 155–9; reproduced in the Hellas Notebook, and discussed pp. lv-lviii). The Canzones of Dante and the Tesoretto are mentioned together on p. 108.

[6] MWSL, I, p. 203; see, too, P. B. Shelley's semi-jocular remark of November 1820, that she had 'raked' Castruccio out of 'fifty old books' (PBSL, II, p. 245).

[7] Palacio (p. 48n.) inferred that at least another ten chronicles were read by her, having found various citations and authors' names in her research notebook (Ab. Dep. e. 274), originating in Muratori's twenty-five volume *Rerum Italicarum Scriptores* (1723–51). In fact they are all secondary references taken from Muratori's *Dissertazioni*, which drew on the *Rerum* for its illustrative material. Tegrimi's *Vita* of Castruccio is in volume XI of *Rerum*, but she used the 1742 bilingual edition. A reference for the latter is in Journal III (*MWSJ*, I, p. 427); it conveniently had a Latin chronology, unlike Muratori's edition. The titles of four chronicles included in the *Rerum* collection are listed, also in Journal III (*MWSJ*, I, p. 418), but they relate to Naples (tangential to *Valperga*). Position in the journal and subject-matter suggest that these were connected with the drama on Manfred which she projected in the autumn of 1822.

[8] Notes begin in Abinger MS. Dep. e. 274, pp. 26–97, and comprise, in order: (i) p. 26, some dated events relating to Manfred and Ezzelin from Sismondi, followed by two blanks; (ii) pp. 29–46, a chronology of selected events from 1300 to 1328, from Sismondi; (iii) pp. 46–7, transcripts of both monumental inscriptions to Castruccio in San Francesco, Lucca; (iv) pp. 49–97, brief notes, virtually in sequence, from Muratori, *Dissertazioni*, taken during August-September 1820, on (main topics) dowries, social rank, usurers, leprosy, laws, luxury, house-furnishings, dress, feasts, weddings, funerals, furs, shoes, overgarments, the *carroccios*, warfare, jousts, entertainments, trials, learning, seers, struggles for liberty, the law of reprisals, female visionaries, nunneries, fortune-telling, heresies, monasteries. When space ran out, she completed Muratori notes in another notebook, continuing straight on to Villani, Sismondi, Targioni, Lastri (Bodleian MS. Shelley adds. e. 17, pp. 234–21 rev.). A few short entries are untraced. Bodleian notebook notes are reproduced in the *'Charles the First' Notebook*, pp. 396–422, but those in Ab. Dep. e. 274 remain unpublished. No notes from the relatively brief works of Machiavelli or Tegrimi have been found. Notes are informational; the (sparse) comments never refer to her intentions for the novel. For the identified editions, see Abbreviations, under relevant names.

[9] For her reading of Dante, Boccaccio and Petrarch between 1817–21, see *MWSJ*, II, pp. 643, 637, 667; for a detailed treatment of Dante and Boccaccio in *Valperga* see Palacio, pp. 47–62, 69–70. *Novellisti* include Franco Sacchetti (c.1335–c.1400), read aloud by P. B. Shelley on 11 May 1821 (*MWSJ*, I, p. 366); novella 5 concerns Castruccio. For evidence that she read Ser Giovanni, Bandello and the *Novellino*, see pp. 44, 117, 177. The journal entry 'much Italian' (*MWSJ*, I. p. 347) possibly records these. Unknown inferred possible 'lost' sources include a collection of 13–14th-century Tuscan poetry containing Brunetto Latini's *Tesoretto* and a work on saints' lives.

[10] By Medwin (pp. 276–7), probably thinking of Pepi, but Tripalda also fits. 'One or two of the inferior characters are drawn from her own observation of Italians' (*PBSL*, I, p. 354); on Sgricci, see *MWSL*, I, pp. 176–7, 182.

[11] *PBSL*, II, pp. 117, 311 (fragment of 26 July letter to Ollier, in which P. B. Shelley evidently set out terms) and p. 312 (follow-up to the foregoing, asking that the novel not be announced as being by 'The Author of Frankenstein').

[12] According to Godwin's letter to Mary Shelley of 10 October, Ollier assented to P. B. Shelley's first set of terms around the beginning of September, making one stipulation (unspecified, but probably concerning the question of immediate payment). P. B. Shelley's letter of 25 September shows him insisting on immediate payment of a third of the copyright price, the rest to follow within eighteen months (*PBSL*, II, pp. 352–3; see also p. 365). Robinson points out that Godwin (unjustifiably) cautioned Mary Shelley against trusting Ollier in a letter of 10 October. According to P. B. Shelley, it was she who rejected Ollier's offer (*PBSL*, II, p. 424). Medwin (p. 374), possibly garbling P. B. Shelley's opinion that Godwin *might* get up to £400, reported that Ollier had actually offered that amount.

[13] See *PBSL*, II, pp. 372, 424; *MWSL*, I, pp. 218, 222; for the Olliers' reaction see Gisborne & Williams, pp. 73–4, 75, 80; *MWSL*, I, pp. 237 and n.

[14] Godwin, *Journal*, Ab. Dep. e. 219, entries for 18 April-1 May, 2–12 July; see also William St Clair, *The Godwins and the Shelleys* (London: Faber & Faber, 1989), pp. 465–9. Godwin's journal entries have enabled me to deduce that volume I of Mary Shelley's manuscript had 319 pages, volume II had 306 and volume III had 314. His page numbers record both where he broke off daily and the last page of each finished volume, sometimes by 'fin.'. Each of his four readings record all three numbers (the only numbers they have in common), except that his April reading of volume III has '304' where one would expect '314', an evident slip, since it is followed by 'fin.' (the end) as is '314' in his July reading. The record also shows that Godwin preserved Mary Shelley's pagination

throughout. See also P. B. Shelley's letter to Mrs Godwin of 29 May 1822 (*PBSL*, II, p. 428), which shows *his* awareness that Godwin had received *Valperga*, and his concern that Mary Shelley should retain ultimate control over any amendments that Godwin might wish. He was extremely averse to the part of Beatrice being cut.

[15] *MWSL*, I, p. 237 n.; *PBSL*, II, p. 428 and n.

[16] My inferences; he sent off 'Castruccio' on 1 August, received a visit from 'J. Ollier' and 'M. from Murray' on 18 September (Ab. Dep. e. 219). He was hoping (letter of 16 November to Mary Shelley) to make a deal with Longman. Whittaker is not mentioned in his journal until 31 December.

[17] Ab. Dep. e. 219; 'Castruccio, revise' entries occur on 31 October, the day after finishing volume I (i.e. p. 319); 7 November, having reached vol. III, p. 230 the day before, and on 9, 11, 17 November.

[18] Marshall, II, pp. 50–52.

[19] Godwin met Whittaker on 31 December 1822, 1 and 13 January and 10 and 11 February 1823 (Ab. Dep. e. 219).

[20] Ab. Dep. e. 219; *MWSL*, I, p. 322 and n.; in its published form, volume III is the shortest.

[21] Medwin, p. 374; Walling, p.152, n. 60. This is confirmed by Mary Shelley's letter of 10 April 1823: 'all alterations that have been made since I read it to you in my little room at Pisa have been made by my father.' She was displeased by the intrusion of '*The Life and Adventures of*' into the title, but what she thought of '*Valperga*' is not clear (*MWSL*, I, p. 331 and n.).

[22] See St Clair (p. 21–2) for Godwin's 'personal vendetta against unnecessary consonants' especially in proper names. Mary Shelley also prefers forms such as 'farewel' throughout her writing. But this was a common eighteenth-century practice.

[23] Godwin, though not Mary Shelley, used Moréri elsewhere, albeit much later, in a footnote to *Lives of the Necromancers* (London: F. J. Mason, 1834) and again in *The Genius of Christianity Unveiled* written c.1835 (Godwin, *Religious Writings*, pp. 195, 198).

[24] For a discussion of these leaves as evidencing Mary Shelley's essential Godwinism in *Valperga*, see Bennett (1978), pp. 361–2.

[25] 'I wish much to see it – as my father has made some curtailments' (*MWSL*, I, p. 336); Godwin to Mary Shelley, 6 May (Marshall, II, p. 84); Godwin visited Whittaker on 12, 15, 16, 22 and 23 of April and 6 and 21 May (Ab. Dep. e. 219).

[26] Listed in Palacio; Lyles; Ward.

[27] *Examiner*, no. 788 (3 March 1823), 154; *Morning Herald*, no. 13287 (12 March 1823), 3; see *MWSL*, I, pp. 323 n.

[28] *La Belle Assemblée*, n.s. XXVIII (August 1823), 82–5; for its ownership, see *Romantics Reviewed*, pt B, vol. I, p. 81. The *Quentin Durward* review appeared in the July number (pp. 32–3); *Literary Gazette*, no. 319 (1 March 1823), 132–3; *British Magazine*, I (March 1823), 33–41; *Blackwood's Edinburgh Magazine*, XIII (March 1823), 283–93; the reviewer, J. G. Lockhart, revealed his ignorance or hostility here. Witticisms attributed to Castruccio by Machiavelli are mostly borrowings from Diogenes Laertius, as Mary Shelley would have been aware.

[29] Medwin, p. 274; notices criticising plot while praising characterisation (especially of the heroines) include those of the *Monthly Review*, CI (May, 1823), 105, the *London Chronicle*, no. 10019 (8–10 March 1823), 240 and *The British Luminary and Weekly Intelligencer* (9 March, 1823), 74 (the last two taken from Palacio and Lyles; originals not seen); *Revue encyclopédique*, XX (October 1823), 132–3; *Ladies' Monthly Museum*, n.s. XVII (April 1823), 216–18; for Mary Shelley's surprise, see *MWSL*, I, p. 336; *Knight's Quarterly Magazine*, III (August–November 1824), 195, 199; reprinted in *Romantics Reviewed*, pt C, vol. II, p. 491; see also *Frankenstein*, vol. 1, Introductory Note.

[30] *MWSL*, I, p. 361; *Pocket Magazine of Classic and Polite Literature*, IV, n.s. (1826), 360, reprinted in Palacio, p. 657; 'Journal of a Traveller on the Continent: VII', *London Magazine*, VI (September–December, 1826), 23–4; *MWSL*, II, p. 332 and n.; see also Walling (pp. 56–7).

[31] Villani: referenced by book and 'cap.' (chapter/section), omitting folio numbers; this differs sometimes in text and section numbers from the version in Muratori, *Rerum*, vol. XIII, and others based on it. Sismondi: referenced by chapters only; these remain constant in major (perhaps all) editions. Machiavelli: edition used not ascertained, but it seems that the Shelleys had access to a collection of his chief works. Muratori, Tegrimi, Targioni and Lastri entries: volume, division, and page numbers are as in the editions used by Mary Shelley.

Valperga: or, the Life and Adventures of Castruccio, Prince of Lucca

VALPERGA:

OR, THE

LIFE AND ADVENTURES

OF

CASTRUCCIO,

PRINCE OF LUCCA.

BY THE AUTHOR OF "FRANKENSTEIN."

IN THREE VOLUMES.

VOL. I.

LONDON:

PRINTED FOR G. AND W. B. WHITTAKER,

AVE-MARIA-LANE.

1823.

PREFACE.[a]

The accounts of the Life of Castruccio known in England, are generally taken from Macchiavelli's romance concerning this chief. The reader may find a detail of his real adventures in Sismondi's delightful publication, *Histoire des Republiques Italiennes de l'Age Moyen*. In addition to this work, I have consulted Tegrino's Life of Castruccio, and Giovanni Villani's Florentine Annals.[b]

The following is a translation from the article respecting him in Moreri.[c]

"Castruccio Castracani, one of the most celebrated captains of his time, lived in the fourteenth century. He was of the family of the Antelminelli[d] of Lucca; and, having at a very early age borne arms in favour of the Ghibelines, he was exiled by the Guelphs.[e] He served not long after in the armies of Philip / king

[a] Probably by Godwin using some information supplied by Mary Shelley (see Introductory Note).

[b] Niccolò Machiavelli (1469–1527), Florentine political theorist, *La Vita di Castruccio Castracani da Lucca* (1532); Jean-Charles-Leonard Simonde de Sismondi (1773–1842), Swiss historian, economic theorist, liberal, *Histoire des républiques italiennes du moyen âge* (1807–9, 1818); Niccolò Tegrimi (d.1527), senator of Lucca, *Vita Castruccii Castracani* (1496, 1742). 'Tegrino' matches Mary Shelley's journal entry (*MWSJ*, I, p. 347); the 1742 edition contains four other variant spellings of his name (not counting Latin case endings): 'Nicolaus Tegrimus' 'Nicolaus Tigrinus' 'Nicoleus Tegrinius' and 'Nicolao Tegrimo' ('Nicalao Tegrimi' in *C C Journals*, p. 171). 'Tegrini' and 'Tygrini' have been found elsewhere; Giovanni Villani (1275–1348), Florentine historian, *Croniche Fiorentine* (1537).

[c] Louis Moréri (1643–80), *Grand dictionnaire historique* (1674), enlarged and republished several times after his death.

[d] Latinised form of 'Interminelli' found in Tegrimi, Machiavelli and Castruccio's tomb inscription.

[e] Italianised names of rival German ducal families, the Welfs (the Dukes of Saxony and Bavaria) and the Wuablingens (the Swabian house of Hohenstaufen), both candidates for the elective titles of Holy Roman Emperor and 'King of the Germans'. The feud, which had emerged in Germany by 1130, spread because the Emperor was also overlord of northern Italy, and, nominally, the temporal head of Christendom (the Empire in 1300 also comprised the Netherlands, Luxembourg, Burgundy and Provence). Conversely, the pope (usually based in Rome) combined the role of spiritual overlordship of the Empire with frequent support of the emperor's Italian subjects against German domination. When, to re-establish imperial authority, the Hohenstaufen Emperor Frederick Barbarossa invaded Lombardy, the cities of northern Italy formed the Lombard League to expel German influence (1167); this was supported by the pope and Barbarossa's Welfian enemies within Germany. In Florence, warfare broke out among the Guelph and Ghibelline nobility in 1215. By 1300 the original lines of the dispute had become complicated by the eclipse of the Hohenstaufens, the rise of the Hapsburgs, attempts of the French monarchy to supplant German influence in Italy, and, in Pistoia and Florence, the 'Bianchi' and 'Neri' factions, which split the Guelphs. Accounts are found in Villani (V, cap. 37), Muratori (III, diss. 51) and Sismondi (ch. vii, and ch. xiii).

5

of France, who made war on the Flemings. In the sequel he repassed the Alps; and, having joined Uguccione Faggiuola, chief of the Ghibelines of Tuscany, he reduced Lucca, Pistoia, and several other towns. He became the ally of the emperor Louis of Bavaria, against pope John XXII, Robert king of Naples, and the Florentines. Louis of Bavaria gave him the investiture of Lucca under the denomination of Duke, together with the title of Senator of Rome. Nothing seemed able to oppose his courage and good fortune, when he was taken off by a premature death in 1330, in the forty-seventh year of his age."[a]

The dates here given are somewhat different from those adopted in the following narrative.[b] /

---

[a] Philip IV (b.1268, reigned 1285–1314), Guelph-supporting, also known as 'le Bel' ('the Fair'). By his intrigues the papacy became French and moved in 1309 from Italy to Provence; Uguccione della Faggiuola (1250–1318), Ghibelline, Imperial Vicar (deputy of the emperor) in Genoa, lord of Pisa; Louis (Ludwig) IV, Ghibelline (c.1287–1347), Holy Roman Emperor-elect 1314–28, eventually crowned in 1328 after winning a civil war waged against his Hapsburg cousin, Frederick; John XXII, second of the 'French popes' (in office 1316–34), who sought to strengthen the papacy through allying himself with the French royal family; Robert of Anjou, King of Naples (b. 1275, reigned 1309–1343), leading supporter of the Guelphs in Italy, allied to the 'French popes' and to Philippe-le-Bel, his second cousin.

[b] Tegrimi, Villani, Sismondi give the historical Castruccio's dates as 1281–1328; Machiavelli gives c.1284–1328; Moréri 1284–1330; Mary Shelley gives her Castruccio the dates 1289–1328.

VALPERGA.

CHAPTER I.

Birth of Castruccio. – His family exiled from Lucca when he is eleven years of age.

The other nations of Europe were yet immersed in barbarism, when Italy, where the light of civilization had never been wholly eclipsed, began to emerge from the darkness of the ruin of the Western Empire, and to catch from the East the returning rays of literature and science. At the beginning of the fourteenth century Dante had already given a permanent form to the language which was the offspring of this revolution; he was personally engaged in those political struggles, in which the elements of the good and evil that have since assumed a more permanent form / were contending; his disappointment and exile gave him leisure to meditate, and produced his *Divina Comedia*.[a]

Lombardy and Tuscany, the most civilized districts of Italy, exhibited astonishing specimens of human genius; but at the same time they were torn to pieces by domestic faction, and almost destroyed by the fury of civil wars. The antient quarrels of the Guelphs and the Ghibelines were started with renovated zeal, under the new distinctions of *Bianchi* and *Neri**. The Ghibelines and the *Bianchi* were the friends of the emperor, asserting the supremacy and universality of his sway over all other dominion, ecclesiastical or civil: the Guelphs and the *Neri* were the partizans of liberty. Florence was at the head of the Guelphs, and employed, as they were employed by it in their turn, the Papal power as a pretext and an instrument.

The distinctions of *Bianchi* and *Neri* took their rise in Pistoia, a town of some moment between Florence and Lucca.[b] The *Neri* being / expelled from Pistoia,

---

* Black and White.

---

[a] Dante Alighieri (1265–1321); his *Vita Nuova* (c.1290–4) and the *Convito* (or *Convivio*), at that time believed to pre-date 1300, were written in the Tuscan dialect, which later became the official Italian language; a Ghibelline, he was expelled in 1302 with other leading 'Bianchi'. The date of composition of the *Divine Comedy*, with its tripartite division into the *Inferno*, *Purgatorio* and *Paradiso*, is still disputed; it was finished shortly before he died. Mary Shelley read it in Italian in November 1817, and many times thereafter; in December P. B. Shelley ordered H. F. Cary's translation (*MWSJ*, II, pp. 643–4; *PBSL*, I, pp. 575, 586).

[b] The Pistoian 'White' (Bianchi) and 'Black' (Neri) feud spread to Florence owing to the support given to each side by, respectively, the powerful Florentine Cerci and Donati families in c.1300.

7

the exiles fixed their residence in Lucca; where they so fortified and augmented their party, as to be able in the year 1301 to expel the *Bianchi*, among whom was Castruccio Castracani dei Antelminelli.

The family of the Antelminelli was one of the most distinguished in Lucca. They had followed the emperors in their Italian wars, and had received in recompense titles and reward. The father of Castruccio was the chief of his house; he had been a follower of the unfortunate Manfred, king of Naples,[a] and his party feelings as a Ghibeline derived new fervour from the adoration with which he regarded his noble master. Manfred was the natural son of the last emperor of the house of Swabia;[b] before the age of twenty he had performed the most brilliant exploits, and undergone the most romantic vicissitudes, in all of which the father of Castruccio had been his faithful page and companion. The unrelenting animosity with which the successive Popes pursued his royal master, gave rise in his bosom to a hatred, that was heightened by the / contempt with which he regarded their cowardly and artful policy.

When therefore the quarrels of the Guelphs and Ghibelines were revived in Lucca under the names of *Bianchi* and *Neri*, Ruggieri dei Antelminelli[c] was the chief opponent and principal victim of the machinations of the Papal party. Castruccio was then only eleven years of age; but his young imagination was deeply impressed by the scenes that passed around him. When the citizens of Lucca had assembled on the appointed day to choose their *Podestà*, or principal magistrate, the two parties dividing on the Piazza glared defiance at each other: the Guelphs had the majority in numbers; but the Ghibelines wishing, like Brennus, to throw the sword into the ascending scale,[d] assailed the stronger party with arms in their hands. They were repulsed; and, flying before their enemies, the Guelphs remained in possession of the field, where, under the

---

[a] Manfred (c.1232, King of Naples and Sicily 1258–66), used Saracen troops to defend his throne (which he had assumed, on behalf of his infant half-nephew, Conradin, to whom he intended that it should eventually revert). The pope excommunicated him and backed a rival French claimant, Charles of Anjou (b. 1220, King Charles I of Naples and Sicily, 1266–84). Manfred was killed at Benevento (1266) fighting the French. Mary Shelley's admiration for Manfred is seen in 'A Tale of the Passions' (*MWST*, pp. 1–23), 'Giovanni Villani' (*MWS Matilda etc*, pp. 136–8) and her attempt at a drama on him in 1822 and early 1824 (Marshall, II, pp. 51–2, 107).

[b] Emperor Frederick II, of the house of Hohenstaufen (sometimes called 'of Swabia').

[c] 'Geri' in Dati's Tegrimi. In Machiavelli, Castruccio is a foundling adopted by a celibate canon, Antonio Castracani and his childless widowed sister. Only Tegrimi and Machiavelli describe Castruccio's early life.

[d] In the *History of Rome from its Foundation*, V. xlviii. 48–9 of Livy (Titus Livius, 59 BC–AD 17). Brennus, the Gallic chief besieging Rome (387 BC), brought 'unequal weights' to weigh the ransom. To Roman protests, Brennus 'added his sword to the weights' saying 'Vae victis!' ('Woe to the conquered!'). Mary Shelley takes it that the weights were too light, and thus ascended when the Romans placed the correct amount of ransom gold in the other pan; Brennus's sword reversed the balance and made the gold appear light; another interpretation is that the weights were too heavy, and the sword was added to the weights as a further insult. (Camillus, champion of Rome, appeared on the scene at this moment and lifted the siege). Mary Shelley read systematically through Livy between June 1818 and July 1820 (*MWSJ*, II, p. 659).

guidance of their chiefs, they voted the perpetual banishment of the Ghibelines; and the summons was read by a herald, which commanded all the districts of Lucca to range themselves / the next morning under their respective banners, that they might attack and expel by force those of the contrary party who should refuse to obey the decree.

Ruggieri returned from the Piazza of the Podestà, accompanied by several of his principal friends. His wife, Madonna Dianora,[a] was anxiously waiting his return; while the young Castruccio stood at the casement, and, divining by his mother's countenance the cause of her inquietude, looked eagerly down the street that he might watch the approach of his father: he clapped his hands with joy, as he exclaimed, "They come!" Ruggieri entered; his wife observed him inquiringly and tenderly, but forbore to speak; yet her cheek became pale, when she heard her husband issue orders, that the palace should be barricadoed, and none permitted to enter, except those who brought the word which shewed that they belonged to the same party.

"Are we in danger?" – asked Madonna Dianora in a low voice of one of their most intimate friends. Her husband overheard her, and replied: "Keep up your courage, my / best girl; trust me, as you have ever trusted. I would that I dared send you to a place of safety, but it were not well that you traversed the streets of Lucca; so you must share my fortunes, Dianora."

"Have I not ever shared them?" replied his wife. His friends had retired to an adjoining hall, and she continued; – "There can be no dearer fate to me than to live or perish with you, Ruggieri; but cannot we save our son?"

Castruccio was sitting at the feet of his parents, and gazing on them with his soft, yet bright eyes. He had looked at his mother as she spoke; now he turned eagerly towards his father while he listened to his reply: – "We have been driven from the Piazza of the Podestà, and we can no longer entertain any hope of overcoming our enemies. The mildest fate that we may expect is confiscation and banishment; if they decree our death, the stones of this palace alone divide us from our fate. And Castruccio, – could any of our friends convey him hence, I should feel redoubled courage – but it is too much to risk."

"Father," said the boy, "I am only a / child, and can do no good; but I pray you do not send me away from you: indeed, dear, dearest mother, I will not leave you."

The trampling of horses was heard in the streets: Ruggieri started up; one of his friends entered: – "It is the guard going to the gates," said he; "the assembly of the people is broken up."

"And what is decreed?"

"No one ventures near to inquire out that; but courage, my noble lord."

---

[a] In Machiavelli, the name of Castruccio's foster-mother. The historical Castruccio's mother was named Puccia (Tegrimi, p. 15).

9

"That word to me, Ricciardo? – but it is well; my wife and child make a very woman of me."

"*Ave Maria* is now ringing," replied his companion; "soon night will set in, and, if you will trust me, I will endeavour to convey Madonna Dianora to some place of concealment."

"Many thanks, my good Ricciardo," answered the lady; "my safest post is at the side of Ruggieri. But our boy——— save him, and a mother's blessing, her warm, heartfelt thanks, all the treasure that I can give, shall be yours! You know Valperga?"[a] /

"Yes, the castle of Valperga. Is the Countess there now?"

"She is, – and she is our friend; if my Castruccio were once within the walls of that castle, I were happy."

While Madonna Dianora conversed thus with Ricciardo, Ruggieri held a consultation with his friends. The comfortable daylight had faded away, and night brought danger and double fear along with it. The companions of Ruggieri sat in the banqueting hall of his palace, debating their future conduct: they spoke in whispers, for they feared that a louder tone might overpower any sound in the streets; and they listened to every footfall, as if it were the tread of their coming destiny. Ricciardo joined them; and Madonna Dianora was left alone with her son: they were silent. Dianora wept, and held the hand of her child; while he tried to comfort her, and to show that fortitude he had often heard his father praise; but his little bosom swelled in despite of his mastery, until, the big tears rolling down his cheeks, he threw himself into his mother's arms, and sobbed aloud. At this moment / some one knocked violently at the palace-gate. The assembled Ghibelines started up, and drew their swords as they rushed towards the staircase; and they stood in fearful silence, while they listened to the answers which the stranger gave to him who guarded the door.

Ruggieri had embraced his wife he feared for the last time. She did not then weep; her high wrought feelings were fixed on one object alone, the safety of her child. – "If you escape," she cried, "Valperga is your refuge; you well know the road that leads to it."

The boy did not answer for a while; and then he whispered, while he clung round her neck, – "You, dear mother, shall shew it to me."

The voice of the man who had disturbed them by his knocking, had reassured the imprisoned Ghibelines, and he was admitted. It was Marco, the servant of Messer Antonio dei Adimari. A Florentine by birth, and a Guelph,

---

[a] The name has associations with Lucca, witchcraft and May-day. The body of the abbess St Walburga, a Wessex missionary, was said to be the source of a healing oil which flowed from her rock-tomb in Germany. The anniversary of her interment, 1 May, was celebrated with popular rites surviving from an older nature-religion, as depicted in the *Walpurgisnacht* scene (translated by P. B. Shelley in 1822 under the title 'May-Day Night') of Goethe's *Faust, Part One*, Her father, 'St Richard King of the English', or, according to another version, her brother St Willibald, was buried in the church of San Frediano at Lucca, and venerated there.

Antonio had retired from his native city while it continued under the jurisdiction of the opposite party, and had lived at the castle of Valperga, of which his wife was Countess / and Castellana.[a] He was bound to Ruggieri by the strongest ties of private friendship; and he now exerted himself to save his friend. Marco brought intelligence of the decree of the assembly of the people. "Our lives are then in safety," – cried Dianora, with a wild look of joy, – "and all the rest is as the seared leaves of autumn; they fall off lightly, and make no noise."

"The night wears apace," said Marco, "and before sunrise you must depart; will you accompany me to Valperga?"

"Not so," replied Ruggieri; "we may be beggars, but we will not burthen our friends. Thank your lord for his many kindnesses towards me. I leave it to him to save what he can for me from the ruins of my fortune. If his interest stand high enough with our rulers, intreat him to exert it to preserve the unoffending walls of this palace: it was the dwelling of my forefathers, my inheritance; I lived here during my boyish days; and once its hall was graced by the presence of Manfred. My boy may one day return; and I would not that he should find the palace of his father a / ruin. We cannot remain near Lucca, but shall retire to some town which adheres to our party, and there wait for better days."

Dianora made speedy preparations for their departure; the horses were brought to the door; and the stars were fading in the light of dawn, as the cavalcade proceeded through the high and narrow streets of Lucca. Their progress was unimpeded at the gates; Ruggieri felt a load taken from his heart, when he found himself, with his wife and child, safe in the open country. Yet the feeling of joy was repressed by the remembrance, that life was all that remained to them, and that poverty and obscurity were to be the hard-visaged nurses of their declining years, the harsh tutors of the young and aspiring Castruccio.

The exiles pursued their way slowly to Florence.

Florence was then in a frightful state of civil discord. The Ghibelines had the preponderance; but not a day passed without brawls and bloodshed. Our exiles found many of their townsmen on the same road, on the same sad errand of seeking protection from a foreign / state. Little Castruccio saw many of his dearest friends among them; and his young heart, moved by their tears and complaints, became inflamed with rage and desire of vengeance. It was by scenes such as these, that party spirit was generated, and became so strong in Italy. Children, while they were yet too young to feel their own disgrace, saw the misery of their parents, and took early vows of implacable hatred against their persecutors: these were remembered in after times; the wounds were

---

[a] Used in its original sense of a noblewoman who possessed a castle (Muratori, III, diss. 47, pp. 65–6).

never seared, but the fresh blood ever streaming kept alive the feelings of passion and anger which had given rise to the first blow.

When they arrived at Florence, they were welcomed with kindness by the chiefs of the *Bianchi* of that city. Charles of Valois had just sent ambassadors to the government, to offer his mediation in composing their differences; and on that very day the party of Ghibelines who composed the council assembled to deliberate on this insidious proposition.[a] It may be easily supposed therefore, that, entirely taken up with their own affairs, they could not bestow the attention they would / otherwise have done on the Lucchese exiles. On the following day Ruggieri left Florence.

The exiles proceeded to Ancona.[b] This was the native town of the Lady Dianora; and they were received with hospitality by her relations. But it was a heavy change for Ruggieri, to pass from the active life of the chief of a party, to the unmarked situation of an individual, who had no interest in the government under which he lived, and who had exchanged the distinctions of rank and wealth for that barren respect which an unblamed old age might claim. Ruggieri had been a man of undaunted courage; and this virtue, being no longer called into action, assumed the appearance of patience and fortitude. His dearest pleasure was the unceasing attention he paid to the education of his son. Castruccio was an apt and sprightly boy, bold in action, careless of consequences, and governed only by his affection for his parents. Ruggieri encouraged his adventurous disposition; and although he often sympathized in the fears of his anxious wife, when Castruccio would venture out to sea on a windy day in a little fair-weather skiff, or when he saw him, without / bridle or saddle, mount a horse, and, heading a band of his companions, ride off to the woods, yet he never permitted himself to express these fears, or check the daring of his son.

So Castruccio grew up active; light and graceful of limb, trusting that by his own powers he should always escape. Yet the boy was not without prudence; he seemed to perceive instinctively the limits of possibility, and would often repress the fool-hardiness of his companions, and shew his superior judgement and patience in surmounting the same difficulties by slower and safer means. Ruggieri disciplined him betimes in all the duties of a knight and a soldier; he wielded a lance adapted to his size, shot with bow and arrows, and the necessary studies to which he applied, became, on account of their active nature, the source of inexhaustible amusement to him. Accompanied by a troop of lads, they would feign some court surrounded by an old wall, or some ruined tower, to be Troy Town, or any other famous city of antient days, and then with mimic *balestri*,[c] and slings and arrows, and lances, they / attacked,

---

[a] This mediation of Charles of Valois (1270–1325), brother of Philippe-le-Bel of France, and thus, like him, second cousin to Robert, King of Naples, resulted in Dante's exile.
[b] The bare facts of Geri's exile to Ancona with his wife and son are in Tegrimi.
[c] Catapults (see p. 213).

and defended, and practised those lessons in tactics which their preceptors inculcated at an early age.

During the first year of their banishment his mother died; her weak frame was destroyed by hardship and disappointment. She recommended her son to his father in terms of tender love; and then closed her eyes in peace. This circumstance for a considerable time unhinged the young mind of Castruccio, and interrupted his studies. His father, who loved her tenderly, and who had found in her a friend to whom he could confide those regrets which pride forbade him to impart to any other hearer, now lamented her with excessive grief.

He did not dare check the silent tear that started into the eye of Castruccio, when, returning from his exercises with his companions, he was no longer embraced by his mother; he felt that his own sentiments would refute the lesson he wished to impress.

Ruggieri was consoled for all his past misfortunes by the promising talents and disposition of his son, and parental tenderness, the strongest of all passions, but often the most unfortunate, was to him the sunbeam, solitary, but bright, / which enlightened his years of exile and infirmity.

Yet at the moment that he most enjoyed this blessing, his security was suddenly disturbed. One morning Castruccio disappeared; and the following perplexing note addressed to his father, was the only trace that he left of his intentions: –

"Pardon me, dearest father; I will return in a very few days; I am quite safe, therefore do not disquiet yourself on my account. Do not be very angry with me; for, although I am indignant at my own weakness, I cannot resist! Be well assured that in less than a fortnight your unworthy son will be at your feet.

"CASTRUCCIO."

This was the year 1304, when Castruccio was fourteen years of age. Ruggieri hoped and trusted that he was safe, and that he would fulfil his promise and soon return; but he waited with inexpressible anxiety. The cause of Castruccio's flight was curious, shewing at once the manners of the age and country in which they lived, and the imagination and disposition of the boy. /

CHAPTER II.

Castruccio visits Florence. – Characters of Euthanasia dei Adimari and her father.
– The father of Castruccio dies.

A traveller had arrived at Ancona from Florence, and had diffused the intelligence that a strange and tremendous spectacle would be exhibited there on the first of May of that year. It had been proclaimed in the streets of the city, by a herald sent by the inhabitants of the quarter of San Frediano,[a] that all who wished to have news from the outer world, should repair on the first of May to the bridge of Carraia or to the quay of the Arno. And he added, that he believed that preparations were made to exhibit Hell, such as it had been described in a poem now writing by Dante Alighieri, a part of which had been read, and had given rise to the undertaking.[b]

This account raised the curiosity, and fired the imagination of Castruccio. The idea darted / into his head that he would see this wonderful exhibition; and no sooner had he conceived the possibility of doing so, than his determination was fixed. He dared not ask his father's permission, for he knew that he should be refused; and, like many others, he imagined that it was better to go, not having mentioned his design, than to break a positive command. He felt remorse at leaving his father; but curiosity was the stronger passion, and he was overcome: he left a billet for Ruggieri; and during the silence of a moonlight night, he mounted his steed, and left Ancona. While proceeding through the streets of the town, he several times repented, and thought that he would return; but no sooner had he passed the walls than he seemed to feel the joy of liberty descending on him; and he rode on with wild delight while the mountains and their forests slept under the yellow moon, and the murmur of the placid ocean was the only sound that he heard, except the trampling of his own horse's hoofs.

Riding hard, and changing his horse on the road, he arrived in five days at Florence. He experienced a peculiar sensation of pleasure, / as he descended from the mountains into Tuscany. Alone on the bare Apennines, over which

---

[a] 'Friano' in Villani; San Frediano (St Frigidian, an Irish missionary), venerated chiefly in Lucca, was reputed to have altered the course of the Serchio.

[b] The *festa* of 1 May 1304 figures in Villani (VIII, cap. 70), Muratori (II, diss. 29, p. 22) and Sismondi (ch. xxv); it is alluded to in *Inferno*, XXII. 8–9 as if in prophecy; for Sismondi this confirms Boccaccio's statement that Dante completed Cantos I-VII of the *Inferno* before his exile. (Modern scholarship places the start of composition no earlier than 1307.)

the fierce wind swept, he felt free; there was no one near him to control his
motions, to order him to stay or go; but his own will guided his progress, swift
or slow, as the various thoughts that arose in his mind impelled him. He felt as
if the air that quickly glided over him, was a part of his own nature, and bore
his soul along with it; impulses of affection mingled with these inexplicable
sensations; his thoughts wandered to his native town; he suffered his imagination to dwell upon the period when he might be recalled from exile, and to
luxuriate in dreams of power and distinction.

At length he arrived at the fair city of Florence. It was the first of May, and he
hastened from his inn to the scene of action. As he approached, he observed the
streets almost blocked up by the multitudes that poured to the same spot; and,
not being acquainted with the town, he found that he had better follow the
multitude, than seek a way of his own. Driven along by the crowd, he at length
came / in sight of the Arno. It was covered by boats, on which scaffoldings were
erected, hung with black cloth, whose accumulated drapery lent life to the
flames, which the glare of day would otherwise have eclipsed. In the midst of
these flames moved legions of ghastly and distorted shapes, some with horns of
fire, and hoofs, and horrible wings; others the naked representatives of the
souls in torment; mimic shrieks burst on the air, screams and demoniac
laughter. The infernal drama was acted to the life; and the terrible effect of
such a scene was enhanced, by the circumstance of its being no more than an
actual representation of what then existed in the imagination of the spectators,
endued with the vivid colours of a faith inconceivable in these lethargic days.

Castruccio felt a chill of horror run through his frame; the scene before him
appeared for a moment as a reality, rather than a representation; the Arno
seemed a yawning gulph, where the earth had opened to display the mysteries
of the infernal world; when suddenly a tremendous crash stamped with tenfold
horror the terrific mockery. The bridge of Carraia, on / which a countless
multitude stood, one above the other, looking on the river, fell. Castruccio saw
its props loosening, and the curved arch shake, and with a sudden shriek he
stretched out his arms, as if he could save those who stood on it. It fell in with
a report that was reverberated from the houses that lined the Arno; and even,
to the hills which close the valley, it rebellowed along the sky, accompanied by
fearful screams, and voices that called on the names of those whom they were
never more to behold. The confusion was beyond description terrible; some
flying, others pressing towards the banks of the river to help the sufferers; all,
as himself, seized with a superstitious dread, which rebuked them for having
mimicked the dreadful mysteries of their religion, and which burst forth in
clamorous exclamations and wild horror. The heroism of Castruccio failed; he
seized with eagerness the opportunity of an opening in the crowd; and, getting
into a by street, ran with what speed he could, while his knees still shook
beneath him, from the spot he in the morning as eagerly sought. The sound of
the shrieks began / to die away on his ear before he slackened his speed.

15

The first idea that struck him, as he recovered his breath, was – "I am escaped from Hell!" – And seeing a church open, he with an instinctive impulse entered its doors. He felt as if he fled from the powers of evil; and if he needed protection, where should he seek it with more confidence, than in the temple where the good God of the universe was worshipped? It was indeed as a change from Hell to Heaven, to have escaped from the jostling of the crowd, the dreadful spectacle of mimicked torments, the unearthly crash that bellowed like thunder along the sky, and the shrieks of the dying – to the silence of the empty church, the faint smell of incense, and the few quiet lights that burned on the high altar. Castruccio was seized with a feeling of awe as he walked up the aisle; and conscience, alive at that moment, reproached him bitterly for having quitted his father. When the idea struck him – "If I had been on that bridge," – he could no longer resist his emotions; tears ran fast down his cheeks, and he sobbed aloud. /

A man, whom he had not perceived before kneeling in a niche beside the altar, arose on hearing the voice of grief, and drew near the boy. "Why do you weep?" – he said. Castruccio, who had not heard his approach, looked up with surprise; for it was the voice of Marco, the servant of his father's friend, Messer Antonio dei Adimari. Marco instantly recognised him; for who that had once seen, could ever forget his dark eyes, shaded by long, pointed lashes, his sun-bright hair, and his countenance that beamed with sweet frankness and persuasion? The boy threw himself into the arms of his humble, but affectionate friend, and wept there for some time. When he had become more calm, his story was told in a few words. Marco was not inclined to find fault with an adventurous spirit, and soon consoled him. – "You are safe," – he said; "so there is no harm done. Come, this is rather a fortunate event than otherwise; my lord and lady are in Florence; you shall stay a night with them; and to-morrow morning we will send you home to your anxious father." /

The eyes of Castruccio sparkled with hope – "Euthanasia is here?"[a]

"She is."

"Quick then, dear Marco, let us go. – How fortunate it was that I came to Florence!"

The life of Messer Antonio dei Adimari had been spent in the military and civil service of his country; he had often been *Priore*;[b] and now, that age and

---

[a] From the Greek, with overtones of 'noble death', 'good death'; also so used by Godwin when urging that with the annihilation of ignorance and blind subservience would come the demise of the state and thus 'the true euthanasia of government' (*Political Justice*, I, III, vi, 'On Obedience'; *PJV*, p. 114. 281); Godwin here engaged against David Hume, to whom the 'true *Euthanasia* of the British constitution', would be its replacement by absolute monarchy (*Essays and Treatises on Several Subjects* (1753–6), pt I, vii); Hume's *Essays* were read by Mary Shelley 1817–20 (*MWSJ*, II, pp. 649, 654). The more common meaning 'easy death' appears in Byron's 'Euthanasia' (*Poems to Thyrza*, 1811–12); Mary Shelley's employment of the word as a first name appears to be original.

[b] One of the six elected members of the *signoria* or chief magistracy governing Florence. The system, dating from 1282, excluded aristocrats from holding office.

blindness had caused him to withdraw from the offices of the state, his counsels were sought and acted upon by his successors. He had married the only daughter of the Count of Valperga, a feudal chief who possessed large estates in the territory of Lucca. His castle was situated among the Apennines north of Lucca,[a] and his estates consisted of a few scattered villages, raised on the peaks of mountains, and rendered almost inaccessible by nature as well as art.

By the death of her father the wife of Adimari became Countess and Castellana of the district; and the duties which this government imposed upon her, often caused the removal of her whole family from Florence to the castle of Valperga. It was during these visits / that Adimari renewed a friendship that had before subsisted between him and Ruggieri del Antelminelli. Messer Antonio was a Guelph, and had fought against Manfred under the banners of the Pope: it happened during one campaign that Ruggieri fell wounded and a prisoner into his hands; he attended him with humanity; and, when he perceived that no care could restore him if separated from his prince, and that he languished to attend at the side of Manfred, he set him free; and this was the commencement of a friendship, which improved by mutual good offices, and more than all by the esteem that they bore one to the other, had long allied the two houses, though of different parties, in the strictest amity.

Adimari continued in the service of his country, until hs infirmities permitted him to withdraw from these active and harassing duties, and, giving up the idea of parties and wars, to apply himself exclusively to literature. The spirit of learning, after a long sleep, that seemed to be annihilation, awoke, and shook her wings over her favoured Italy. Inestimable / treasures of learning then existed in various monasteries, of the value of which their inhabitants were at length aware; and even laymen began to partake of that curiosity, which made Petrarch but a few years after travel round Europe to collect manuscripts, and to preserve those wonderful writings, now mutilated, but which would otherwise have been entirely lost.[b]

Antonio dei Adimari enjoyed repose in the bosom of his family, his solitude cheered by the converse which he held with the sages of Rome in ages long past. His family consisted of his wife, two boys, and a girl only two years younger than Castruccio. He and Euthanasia had been educated together almost from their cradle. They had wandered hand in hand among the wild mountains and chesnut woods that surrounded her mother's castle. Their studies, their amusements, were in common; and it was a terrible blow to each

---

[a] '[G]o to the top of the tower of the palace of Guinigi [in Lucca] an old tower as ancient as those times – look towards the opening of the hills, on the road to the Baths of Lucca, & on the banks of the Serchio & you will see the site of Valperga' (Mary Shelley to Leigh Hunt, 7 August, 1823, *MWSL*, I, p. 364).

[b] Francesco Petrarcha (1304–74), Florentine poet and humanist, in 1333 journeyed to Paris, Flanders and Cologne, copying the manuscripts of classical authors. He spent his final years in literary scholarship at Arquà in the Euganean hills.

when they were separated by the exile of the Antelminelli. Euthanasia, whose soul was a deep well of love, felt most, and her glistening eyes and infantine complaints told for many months / even years after, that she still remembered, and would never forget, the playmate of her childhood.

At the period of this separation Adimari was threatened by a misfortune, the worst that could befall a man of study and learning – blindness. The disease gained ground, and in a year he saw nothing of this fair world but an universal and impenetrable blank. In this dreadful state Euthanasia was his only consolation. Unable to attend to the education of his boys, he sent them to the court of Naples, to which he had before adhered, and in which he possessed many valued friends; and his girl alone remained to cheer him with her prattle; for the countess, his wife, a woman of high birth and party, did not sympathize in his sedentary occupations. – "I will not leave you," said Euthanasia to him one day, when he bade her go and amuse herself, – "I am most pleased while talking with you. You cannot read now, or occupy yourself with those old parchments in which you used to delight. But tell me, dear father, could you not teach me to read them to you? You know I can read very well, / and I am never so well pleased as when I can get some of the troubadour songs, or some old chronicle, to puzzle over. These to be sure are written in another language; but I am not totally unacquainted with it; and, if you would have a little patience with me, I think I should be able to understand these difficult authors."

The disabled student did not disdain so affectionate an offer. Every one in those days was acquainted with a rude and barbarous Latin, the knowledge of which Euthanasia now exchanged for the polished language of Cicero and Virgil. A priest of a neighbouring chapel was her tutor; and the desire of pleasing her father made her indefatigable in her exertions. The first difficulties being conquered, she passed whole days over these dusky manuscripts, reading to the old man, who found double pleasure in the antient poets, as he heard their verses pronounced by his beloved Euthanasia. The effect of this education on her mind was advantageous and memorable; she did not acquire that narrow idea of the present times, as if they and the world were the same, which characterizes the unlearned; she saw / and marked the revolutions that had been, and the present seemed to her only a point of rest, from which time was to renew his flight, scattering change as he went; and, if her voice or act could mingle aught of good in these changes, this it was to which her imagination most ardently aspired. She was deeply penetrated by the acts and thoughts of those men, who despised the spirit of party, and grasped the universe in their hopes of virtue and independence.

Liberty had never been more devotedly worshipped than in the republic of Florence: the Guelphs boasted that their attachment to the cause of freedom might rival what history records of the glorious days of antiquity. Adimari had allied himself to this party, because he thought he saw in the designs and

principles of its leaders the germ of future independence for Italy. He had ever
been a fervent advocate for the freedom of his fellow citizens: but he caught the
spirit with double fervour from the Roman writers; and often, not seeing the
little fairy form that sat at his feet, he forgot the age of his companion, and
talked in / high strains of that ennobling spirit which he felt in his inmost heart.
Euthanasia heard and understood; her soul, adapted for the reception of all
good, drained the cup of eloquent feeling that her father poured out before her,
and her eyes shone with the deep emotion. Her young thoughts darted into
futurity, to the hope of freedom for Italy, of revived learning and the reign of
peace for all the world: wild dreams, that still awake the minds of men to high
song and glorious action.

Such was the education of the friend of Castruccio, while he learned all
chivalrous accomplishments under the tuition of his noble father at Ancona;
and now, after three years absence, they met at Florence, neither having by
forgetfulness wronged the friendship they had vowed in infancy.

When Marco led his young friend to the palace of Adimari, he found his
master and the countess receiving the visits of some of the Guelph party; and
he knew that this was no time or place to introduce the young Ghibeline. But,
as they passed along the great hall, a sylph-like form came from a room
opposite, / appearing as a star from behind a cloud. – "I bring your exiled
friend," said Marco; "Castruccio dei Antelminelli is come to visit you."

"Castruccio in Florence!" cried Euthanasia; and she embraced him with
sisterly affection. "But how, dear friend, do you venture within these walls? – is
your father here? – but this is no place to ask all the questions that I must hear
resolved before you go. Come into this room; none but my father will enter
here; and now you shall tell me all that has passed since you quitted Lucca."

Castruccio gazed on Euthanasia: he could, he thought, feed for life on her
sweet looks, in which deep sensibility and lively thought were pictured, and a
judgement and reason beyond her years. Her eyes seemed to read his soul,
while they glistened with pleasure; he wished to hear her speak, but she insisted
that his tale should be first told, of how he had lived at Ancona, and how he
had ventured to Florence. She gently reproached him for having left his father;
and then said, – "But I must not play the hypocrite; I am glad you are come;
for it gives me more pleasure than I can express, to / see you again. But I hear
my father's step; I must go and lead him, and tell him of the stranger-visitor he
has got."

Castruccio enjoyed the most heartfelt pleasure, as he sat between Euthanasia
and her father. Their manners towards him were affectionate, and their conversation best calculated to fill an exile's bosom with hope and joy. He was told by
them, that if they now parted, he must look forward to the moment when he
and his father should be recalled with honour to their country. Adimari could
not see the bright eyes and ardent mien of the boy; but he heard with pleasure
the detail of his occupations at Ancona, and easily perceived that his young

mind slept not on the present, dreamless of the future. He encouraged his aspirations to honour, and exhorted him to be faithful to the lessons of his father.

The charmed hours flew past, and the following morning they were to separate. This consideration, as evening came on, threw more solemnity into their looks and talk. Castruccio became pensive, and gazed on his friend, as a treasure that he was about to lose, perhaps / for ever. Euthanasia was silent; her eyes were bent to earth; and the varying colour of her cheeks shewed that she was revolving some thought in her mind, to which she knew not how to give utterance. At length she raised her eyes, and said: – "We part to-morrow, Castruccio, as we have before parted, – for many years I fear. But there are two kinds of separation. One, during which we suffer time to obliterate the past, as we should if death, that parting to which no meeting succeeds, or a meeting in which all private ties are superseded, had been the cause of the separation. But there is another; when we cherish the memory of the absent, and act for them as if they were with us; when to remember is a paramount duty. This is alone practicable between friends, when each in his meditations is sure that the other thinks also of him: then, methinks to reflect on the words and looks of a friend, is as if one absolutely saw him. Let this be our separation. We are both familiar with the ideas of virtue and self-sacrifice; let friendship be joined to these, to make all sacrifice light, and virtue more delightful. / We are very young; we know not what misfortunes are in store for us; what losses, perhaps what calumnies, or even dishonour, may in after times taint our names. In calumny it is to the friends of our youth that we must turn; for they alone can know how pure the heart is, with which they were acquainted at the time when disguise could have no existence. They, if they are true, dare not leave us without consolation. Castruccio, I know that you will never dishonour yourself: and, remember, if in any hard struggle you want a friend who will console you by sympathy and confidence, and help you as far as her power will permit, I will always be that friend to you."

Euthanasia was yet a child, when she made this promise. But she saw Castruccio, the friend of her infancy, a youth of high birth and nobly bred, an outcast and an exile; she had heard and read how few friends the unfortunate find, and generosity prompted those sentiments, to which the frankness of her nature caused her to give utterance. She felt that Castruccio had a deep affection for her, and she hoped, that a promise thus voluntary / and solemn, would be a consolation to him during adversity. He felt the kindness of her motive, and replied earnestly: – "I am an exile, and can do no good to you who are prosperous; mine must be barren thanks. Yet not the less will I fulfil my promise, if our fortunes change, of being your friend, your knight, your rock, on whom you may build your hope and trust in every misfortune."

The next morning, accompanied by Marco, Castruccio quitted Florence. In his mind there was a mixture of grief at having left, and joy at having once more seen, Euthanasia. Every word that she had said, and every look of her lovely eyes, were treasured in his soul – to be a consolation and support in trouble, and an incentive to noble endeavour. Adimari had taken an affectionate leave of him, telling him, that, as far as a poor blind man could, he would promote his interests, and seize the first opportunity, if such should offer, of procuring a repeal for his exile. There was a kindness and distinction in the manner of his aged friend, that touched the heart of the boy; and in after times he thought he perceived a / hidden meaning in his last words, which he interpreted in a manner that gave a sober steadiness to what he would otherwise have considered as another airy bubble of the enchantress Hope. "Remember," said the venerable Florentine, "that I approve of, and love you; and if you become that which your talents and dawning virtues promise, you may in future be my elect favourite. Now, farewell; and do not forget me or mine!"

Thus cheered, thus buoyed up by hopes of future good fortune and advancement, which had before been too deeply mingled with fear, Castruccio returned with a light heart to his father, his soul more than ever bent upon improvement and the accomplishment of noble deeds. And now, forgiven by his anxious parent for the grief he had occasioned him, his days wore away, as they were wont, in delightful tasks.

Time passed on, while our young esquire was preparing himself for his future career; strengthening his mind by study, and his body by toil. His step assumed the firmness of one who does not fear, and who, with his eye fixed / on one point, will not be daunted by the shadows that flit between him and his desired sun. His eyes, before beaming with frankness and engaging sweetness, now sparkled with a profounder meaning. He entered his seventeenth year, and he was pondering upon the fit beginning to his life, and hoping that his father would not oppose his fervent desire to quit what he thought a lifeless solitude; when, as a young bather, peeping from a rock, is pushed into the sea, and forced to exert the powers of which he was before only dreaming, so chance threw Castruccio from his quiet nook into the wide sea of care, to sink or swim, as fate or his own good strength might aid him.

His father died. A malignant fever, brought by some trading vessels from the Levant, raged in the town of Ancona, and Ruggieri was one of its earliest victims.[a] As soon as he was attacked, he knew he must die, and he gazed upon his boy with deep tenderness and care. To be cast so young on life, with a mind burning with ardour, and adorned with every grace – the fair graces of youth, so easily and so / irretrievably tarnished! He had commanded him not to come near him during his illness, which was exceedingly contagious: but finding that Castruccio waited on him by stealth, he felt that it was in vain to oppose; and, only intreating him to use every imaginable precaution, they spent the last

---

[a] Geri's death from fever is in Tegrimi (p. 9), but the date given is seven months after the exile to Ancona in 1301.

21

hours of Ruggieri's life together. The fever was too violent to permit any regular conversation; but the dying father exhorted him to remember his former lessons, and lay them to his heart. "I have written a letter," said he, "which you will deliver to Francesco de' Guinigi.[a] He was one of my dearest friends, and of high birth and fortune, in Lucca; but now, like me, he is an exile, and has taken refuge at the town of Este in Lombardy. If he still preserves in adversity that generosity which before so highly distinguished him, you will less feel the loss of your father. Go to him, my Castruccio, and be guided by his advice: he will direct you how you can most usefully employ your time while an outcast from your country. Listen to him with the same deference that you have always shown to me, for he is one of the few / wise men who exist in this world, whose vanity and nothingness open upon me the more, now that I am about to quit it."

From time to time Ruggieri renewed his affectionate exhortations. His parental tenderness did not desert him in his last moments; and he died making a sign that in Heaven they should again meet. Castruccio was overwhelmed by grief at his loss. But grief was soon silenced by pain: he had inhaled the pestilential air from the dying breath of his father, and was speedily like him stretched on the bed of sickness. Yet not like him had he any tender nurse, to watch his fever, and administer to his wants: every one fled from the chance of death; and it was only the excellent constitution of the boy that enabled him to recover.

In a month after his father's death, himself in appearance more dead than alive, he crawled out from his apartment to breathe the enlivening air of the sea. A wind swept over it, and chilled his frame, while the dusky sky filled him with despondency. But this was a transient feeling: day by day he gained strength, and with strength and health returned / the buoyant spirits of youth. The first lively feeling that he experienced, was an ardent desire to remove from Ancona. During his illness he had bitterly felt the absence of many whom he considered dear and firm friends. When he was able to enquire for those whom he had inwardly reproached as false, he found that they were dead. The pestilence had visited them, and felled them to the ground, while he, bruised and half broken, raised his head when the deadly visitation was over. These disappointments and losses pressed on his soul; and he experienced that feeling which deceives us at every age, that by change of place, he could exchange his unhappy sensations for those of a more genial nature. The rainy season had begun; but he would not delay his departure; so, taking an agonizing farewell of the graves of his friends, and of those of his beloved parents whom he could never see more, he left Ancona.

The beauty of the mountains and the picturesque views for a while beguiled

---

[a] In Machiavelli (the only source of Guinigi's guardianship of Castruccio) Guinigi adopts the not-yet-exiled Castruccio in Lucca, and teaches him the arts of war.

his thoughts. He passed through the country where Asdrubal, the brother of Hannibal, was defeated and / slain on the mountain which still bears his name.[a] A river runs at the base; and it was clothed by trees now yellow and red, tinged thus by the winds of autumn, except where a cluster of ilexes gave life to the scenery. As he advanced, the rains poured down, and the hills, now more distant, were hid in mist; while towards the east the gloomy Adriatic filled the air with its restless murmurs. Castruccio had passed swiftly through this country before, when he went to the *Festa d'Inferno* at Florence. It was then adorned by the fresh spring; the sunbeams illuminated the various folds of the mountains, and the light waves coursed one another, dancing under the dazzling light. Castruccio remembered this; and he gazed sullenly on the sky obscured by a thick woof of black clouds, and reproached that with changing, as his fortune changed. Yet, reflecting on the chances that had occurred during his last journey, his imagination wandered to Euthanasia, and paused there, resting with delight on her beloved image.

He passed through many towns, among which he had no friends, and sought for none. / Yet, if he had desired protection, several of these were ruled by Ghibeline lords, who would have welcomed him with hospitality. Rimini was then governed by the husband of Francesca, whose hapless fate is immortalized by Dante.[b] She was dead; but the country people, with a mixture of pity and religious horror, still spoke of her as the loveliest creature that had ever dwelt on earth, yet for whose lost soul, condemned to eternal pains, they dared not even pray.

Castruccio journeyed slowly on. He was weak and unable to endure continued exercise. Yet his mind recovered by degrees its wonted strength; and imagination, ever at work, pictured his future life, brilliant with glowing love, transcendant with glory and success. Thus, in solitude, while no censuring eye could check the exuberant vanity, he would throw his arms to the north, the south, the east, and the west, crying, – "There – there – there, and there, shall my fame reach!" – and then, in gay defiance, casting his eager glance towards heaven: – "and even there, if man may climb the slippery sides of the arched / palace of eternal fame, there also will I be recorded."

He was yet a boy in his seventeenth year when he said this. His desires were

---

[a] Hasdrubal (d. 207 BC) and Hannibal (247–183 BC), Carthaginian generals, both invaded and threatened Italy in the second Punic War. Hasdrubal was cut off at the river Metaurus (Livy, XXVII. xlvii-xlix). Mary Shelley travelled along its banks and noted Monte Asdrubale on 15 November, 1818 (*MWSJ*, I, p. 236).

[b] Francesca da Polenta, married off to the deformed son (d. 1304) of Malatesta da Verrucchio (Lord of Rimini, 1293–1312), committed adultery with Paolo, younger brother of her husband, and in 1285 was executed with him (see Dante, *Inferno*, V. 73–142). Mary Shelley takes the husband to be the Lord of Rimini, perhaps following Leigh Hunt's ambiguous remark in the preface to *The Story of Rimini* (1816): 'All agree that the lady was in some measure beguiled into the match with the older Malatesta'.

afterwards to a considerable extent fulfilled: would he not have been happier, if they had failed, and he, in blameless obscurity, had sunk with the millions that compose the nations of the earth, into the vast ocean of oblivion? The sequel of his history must solve the riddle. /

CHAPTER III.

Francis Guinigi, the military Peasant. – Castruccio resides with him one Year.

Castruccio passed through Bologna, Ferrara and Rovigo, to arrive at Este. It was not the most favourable period for a visit to Lombardy. The beauty of that country consists in its exquisite vegetation: its fields of waving corn, planted with rows of trees to which vines are festooned, form prospects, ever varying in their combinations, that delight and refresh the eye; but autumn had nearly stript the landscape, and the low lands were overflowed by the inundation of various rivers. Castruccio's mind, fixed on the imagination of future events, found no amusement in the wintry scene; but he saw with delight the mountains that were the bourn of his journey, become more and more distinct. Este is situated nearly at the foot of the Euganean hills, on a declivity / overlooked by an extensive and picturesque castle, beyond which is a convent; the hills rise from behind, from whose heights you discover the vast plain of Lombardy, bounded to the west by the far Apennines of Bologna, and to the east by the sea and the towers of Venice.[a]

Castruccio ascended the hill immediately above the town, to seek for the habitation of Guinigi. The autumnal wind swept over it, scattering the fallen leaves of the chesnut wood; and the swift clouds, driven over the boundless plain, gave it the appearance, as their shadows came and went, of a heaving sea of dusky waters. Castruccio found Guinigi sitting at the door of his house; it was a low-roofed cottage, that seemed more fit for the habitation of a peasant, than of a man bred in camps and palaces. Guinigi himself was about forty years of age: the hardships of war had thinned the locks on his temples before their time, and drawn a few lines in his face, beaming as it was with benevolence. The sparkling intelligence of his eye was tempered by gentleness and wisdom; and the stately / mien of the soldier had yielded somewhat to his late rustic occupations; for, since his exile he had turned his sword to a ploughshare, and he dwelt with much complacency on the change.

---

[a] The Shelleys stayed at Este from September-November 1818 in Byron's villa, I Capuccini, built on the site of a Capuchin convent, from which they could see the ruins of the ancient castle of Este; for a description, see 'Note on Poems written in 1818' in *MWS Matilda etc* and *PBSL*, II, p. 43.

As Castruccio first saw him, he was gazing with the most heartfelt and benevolent pleasure on his boy, a child of seven years of age, who was busy with the peasants, drawing off wine from the vats; for it was just the time when the vintage was finished, and the last labours were bestowed on the crushed grapes. The youth paused: but for the air of dignity that was visible beneath his rustic dress, he could not have believed that this was his father's friend; his father, who in exile never forgot that he was a soldier and a knight. He gave the letter; and, when Guinigi had read it, he embraced the orphan son of his old comrade, and welcomed him with a cordiality that warmed the heart of Castruccio. The name of a stranger soon struck the ear of Arrigo,[a] his little son, who came with joy to greet him, bearing a large basket of grapes and figs. Guinigi was much amused by the evident astonishment / with which his guest regarded the appearance of the house and its master, and said: – "You come to the dwelling of a peasant who eats the bread his own hands have sown; this is a new scene for you, but you will not find it uninstructive. To my eyes, which do not now glance with the same fire as yours, the sight of the bounties of nature, and of the harmless peasants who cultivate the earth, is far more delightful than an army of knights hasting in brilliant array to deluge the fields with blood, and to destroy the beneficial hopes of the husbandman. But these are new doctrines to you; and you perhaps will never, like me, in the deep sincerity of your heart, prefer this lowly cottage to yonder majestic castle."

To say the truth, Castruccio was greatly disappointed. As he had ascended from the town, and saw a gay banner waving from the keep of the castle, as he heard the clash of armour, and beheld the sun-beams glitter on the arms of the centinel, he hoped that he should find his future protector a favourite with the happy chief. He would, he felt, have / accosted him with more respect, if he had found him a monk in the neighbouring monastery, than a contented farmer, a peasant whose narrow views soared not beyond the wine-vat and the ox's stall.

These were the first feelings that occurred to Castruccio; but he soon found that he was introduced to a new world in the society of Guinigi; a world with whose spring of action he could not sympathize, yet which he could not contemn. It was characterized by a simple yet sublime morality, which resting on natural bases, admitted no factitious colouring. Guinigi thought only of the duty of man to man, laying aside the distinctions of society, and with lovely humility recognized the affinity of the meanest peasant to his own noble mind. Exercising the most exalted virtues, he also cultivated a taste and imagination that dignified what the vulgar would term ignoble, as the common clouds of day become fields of purple and gold, painted by the sun at eve. His fancy only paused, when he would force it to adorn with beauty vice, death, and misery,

---

[a] According to Machiavelli, Guinigi's son was called Pagolo and was made Castruccio's heir.

when disguised by a kingly robe, by the trappings / of a victorious army, or the false halo of glory spread over the smoking ruins of a ravaged town. Then his heart sickened, and the banners of triumph or the song of victory could not drive from his recollection the varieties of death, and the groans of torture that occasion such exultation to the privileged murderers of the earth.

When Guinigi and Castruccio became intimate, the youth would reason with him, and endeavour to prove, that in the present distracted state of mankind, it was better that one man should get the upper hand, to rule the rest. "Yes," said Guinigi, "let one man, if it be forbidden to more than one, get the upper hand in wisdom, and let him teach the rest: teach them the valuable arts of peace and love."

Guinigi was a strange enthusiast. Men, like Alexander and other conquerors, have indulged the hope of subduing the world, and spreading by their triumphs refinement into its barbarous recesses. Guinigi hoped, how futilely! to lay a foundation-stone for the temple / of peace among the Euganean hills. He had an overflowing affection of soul, that could not confine itself to the person of his son, or the aggrandizement of his country, or be spiritualized into a metaphysical adoration of ideal beauty. It bestowed itself on his fellow-creatures; and to see them happy, warmed his heart with a pleasure experienced by few. This man, his imaginative flights, his glowing benevolence and his humble occupations, were an enigma that Castruccio could never solve. But, while he neither sympathized with nor understood him, he quickly loved him with the warmest affection.

Castruccio wished to speak to him of his future destination; Guinigi said, "Your father has recommended you to my counsels, and you must allow me to become acquainted with you, before I can give you advice. You are very young; and we need not hurry. Grant me six months; we will not be idle. We will ramble about the country: winter is the peasant's leisure time, so I am quite at your service. We shall be much together, and will / discuss many subjects; and by degrees I shall understand the foundations on which you are to build your future life."

They travelled to Padua, to lovely Venice, raising its head from the waves of ocean; they rambled about the coast for days together, having no other end than to enjoy the beauties of nature. Then, coming nearer home, they climbed the Euganean hills, and penetrated their recesses. Guinigi had an ultimate object in view; he wished to impress on the mind of his pupil a love of peace, and a taste for rural pleasures. One day they were on the summit of Monte Selice, a conical hill between Este and Padua, and Guinigi pointed to the country around. – "What a Paradise is this!" he said. "Now it is bare; but in the summer, when the corn waves among the trees, and the ripening grapes shade the roads; when on every side you see happy peasants leading the beautiful oxen to their light work, and the sun, and the air, and the earth are each labouring to produce for man all that is necessary for his support, and the ground is covered with vegetation, and the air quickened / into life, it is a spot, on which the Creator of the world might pause, and be pleased with his work. How different was this some years ago! You have heard of Ezzelino the tyrant of Padua, under whose auspices the rivers ran blood, and the unfortunate peasant found his harvests reaped by the sword of the invading soldier![a] Look at those peasants on yonder road, conducting their cattle crowned with flowers: habited in their holiday best, and moving in solemn procession; their oxen are going to be blest by St. Antonio, to ward from them the evils of the ensuing seasons.[b] A few years ago, instead of peasants, soldiers marched along that road: their close ranks shewed their excellent discipline; their instruments filled the air with triumphant sounds; the knights pricked their steeds forward, who arching their proud necks, seemed to exult in their destination. What were they about to do? to burn a town, to murder the old, and the helpless, the women, and the children; to destroy the dwellings of peace; so that, when they left their cruel work, the miserable wretches who survived had nothing to shelter them but the / bare, black walls, where before their neat cottages had stood."

Castruccio listened impatiently, and cried: – "Yet who would not rather be a knight, than one of those peasants, whose minds are as grovelling as their occupations?"

"That would not I," replied Guinigi fervently; "how must the human mind be distorted, which can delight in that which is ill, in preference to the cultivation of the earth, and the contemplation of its loveliness! What a strange mistake is it, that a peasant's life is incompatible with intellectual improvement! Alas! poor wretches; they are too hard-worked now to learn much, and their toil, uncheered by the applause of their fellow-creatures, appears a degradation; yet, when I would picture happiness upon earth, my imagination conjures up the family of a dweller among the fields, whose property is secure, and whose time is passed between labour and intellectual pleasures. Such now is my fate. The evening of my life steals gently on; and I have no regrets for the past, no wish for the future, but to continue as I am."[c] /

"Yes," cried Castruccio, "You have passed through life, and know what it is; but I would rather, while alive, enter my tomb, than live unknown and unheard of. Is it not fame that makes men gods? Do not urge me to pass my days in indolence; I must act, to be happy, – to be any thing. My father did not wish me to become a farmer and a vinedresser; but to tread in his steps, and go beyond them, and that is my purpose, which I would die to attain."

---

[a] Ezzelino da Romano (1194–1259), Ghibelline enemy of the Guelph Marquess of Este. His atrocities are detailed in Sismondi, chs xvii and xix.

[b] St Anthony of Padua (1195–1231), follower of St Francis of Assisi; a specific source for the ritual crowning of cattle has not been found.

[c] Guinigi, in contrasting the beauty of the Euganean landscape with the condition of the human inhabitants, fictively prefigures the P. B. Shelley of 'Lines Written among the Euganean Hills' (1818).

A year passed while Castruccio still lived under the low roof of Guinigi. He found that it was no vain boast, that this noble ate the bread that he had sown: for he saw him hold the plough, trim his vines, and enter into all the labours of the husbandman. There is something picturesque in the toil of an Italian peasant. It is not, as in more northern climates, where cold, and wet, and care are endured, to be scantily repaid; and their unceasing anxiety is often terminated by the destruction of their crops through the severity of their climate. Guinigi and his fellow-labourers rose with the sun, which, ascending from the / ocean, illumined the wide plain with its slant beams. The most beautiful vegetation luxuriated around them: the strips of land were planted with Indian corn, wheat and beans; they were divided, in some places by rows of olives, in others by elms or Lombardy poplars, to which the vines clung. The hedges were of myrtle, whose aromatic perfume weighed upon the sluggish air of noon, as the labourers reposed, sleeping under the trees, lulled by the rippling of the brooks that watered their grounds. In the evening they ate their meal under the open sky; the birds were asleep, but the ground was alive with innumerable glow-worms, and the air with the lightning-like fire-flies, small, humming crickets, and heavy beetles: the west had quickly lost its splendour, but in the fading beams of sunset sailed the boat-like moon, while Venus, as another satellite to earth, beamed just above the crescent hardly brighter than itself, and the outline of the rugged Apennines was marked darkly below.

Their harvests were plenteous and frequent. The mowing of the grass was quickly followed in June by the reaping, and the well-trodden / threshing floor, such as Virgil describes it, received the grain; then came the harvest of the Indian corn; and last the glorious vintage, when the beautiful dove-coloured oxen of Lombardy could hardly drag the creaking wains laden with the fruit.[a]

Castruccio attended Guinigi in his labours; and Guinigi, resting on his spade, would moralize on all around him, and win the ardent imagination of the youth to follow his flights. All in the country bore for him the immediate stamp of divine and eternal beauty; he knew every flower of the field, and could describe their various habits, and what insects best loved to suck their nectar. He knew the form and the life of every little being of that peopled region, where the sun seems to quicken every atom into life; and that which was insignificant to common eyes, appeared to him to be invested with strange attributes and uncommon loveliness.

Again Guinigi sat, Castruccio beside him, at the door of his cot, watching the evening work of the labourers, as the wine was drawn off from the last vat. Arrigo, now a year older, / was helping them: Castruccio said – "Instead of six

---

[a] Threshing-floors of Lombardy farms were, up to the nineteenth century, still kept uncovered and given a hard, flat surface with a cylindrical rolling stone, as described by Virgil (Publius Vergilius Maro, 70–19 BC) and observed by the Shelleys, who noticed the Virgilian oxen too (*Georgics*, II. 178–86; 'The English in Italy', *MWS Matilda etc*, p. 155; *PBSL*, II, p. 45).

months I have given you twelve, and I have not mentioned my future destiny; indeed we have been employed so pleasantly during the summer, that I almost forgot it. But I cannot live another year among these hills; you know not what bitterness I feel at heart, when I hear the clash of arms from that castle, I, who am wearing away an ignoble youth."

Guinigi smiled, and replied, "I have reflected for you, and I have dived into your secret thoughts, although you have not spoken. To-morrow we will make a journey; and you shall soon be introduced to a man who will bring you into that life whose promise of glory is so attractive to you. So bid farewel to these hills; you will not see them again for many years."

This hope stole sleep from the eyes of Castruccio that night. His imagination, which had lately rested on sickles, and wains, and vines, and the simple philosophy of Guinigi, now again fled to its wonted track, and entered upon what he conceived to be a more glorious world. Fleecy clouds hid the full moon, / and the world was invested by a faint light that gradually opened into day. Castruccio saw the horses led saddled to the door, and he hastened to join Guinigi. Before he departed he kissed affectionately the sleeping Arrigo, and said: "I fear those fair eyes will be dimmed with tears, when he hears that I am not to return. Sweet boy! I love you as a brother, and hope some future day to shew that love in something more than words."

Guinigi smiled at the aspiring spirit of Castruccio; he smiled to perceive that, still wanting protection, still a boy, his thoughts always dwelt on the power which he would one day acquire, and the protection he would then afford to others.

They rode silently along the well known road that led to Padua: after resting their horses at this town, they continued their way to Venice. Who knows not Venice? its streets paved with the eternal ocean, its beautiful domes and majestic palaces? It is not now as it was when Castruccio visited it; now the degenerate inhabitants go "crouching and crab-like through their sapping streets:"[a] then they / were at the height of their glory, just before the aristocratical government was fixed, and the people were struggling for what they lost – liberty.[b]

Guinigi and his young companion were silent during their long ride. Guinigi was on the eve of seeing the friends of his warlike youth; and perhaps his memory recalled those scenes. Castruccio dreamed of futurity; and the uncertainty of his destiny only gave more scope to his imagination, as he figured the glorious part which he flattered himself he was about to act on the great theatre. At length they arrived on the shore of the Laguna, and entered the

---

[a] George Gordon Byron, 6th Baron Byron (1788–1824), 'Ode on Venice' (1819), l. 13.

[b] Referring to the series of decrees enacted by Pietro Gradenigo (Sismondi, ch. xxviii), whereby, between 1297–1320, citizens were gradually stripped of their representative rights and the formerly elective council of Venice was transformed into an hereditary aristocracy.

gondola which was to convey them to the city. Guinigi then addressed the youth: –
"You trust your fate to me; and I must explain to you the plan that I have formed
concerning you, that you may judge whether I merit the entire confidence you
shew yourself inclined to repose in me. You know, my dear Castruccio, that poor
Italy is distracted by civil brawls, and how little honour one who is exiled as you
are from his native town, can acquire, to whatever party he may adhere. / His most
arduous exertions may be sacrificed to political intrigue, and assuredly he will be
repaid with ingratitude alone, whatever power he serves. In addition, a disgraceful
political craft now reigns in the palaces of the Italian princes, which renders them
ill schools for a youth, who, while he may, ought to preserve the innocence and
sincerity of which the world will but too quickly deprive him. You would inevit-
ably be disgusted by the narrow views, the treachery, and beggarly fraud, that
dwell in the hearts, and influence the actions of our proudest nobles.

"You must therefore begin your knightly career out of Italy. The honours
that you will obtain from a foreign sovereign, will ennoble you in the eyes of
your countrymen, and will enable you, when you return, to judge impartially of
the state of your country, and to choose, without being influenced by narrow
party-feeling, the course you will pursue. It is with this view that I am going to
introduce you to an old friend of mine, an Englishman, who is about to return
to his native soil. I knew him many years ago, when he accompanied / Charles
of Anjou to Italy.[a] A long time has elapsed since Sir Ethelbert Atawel returned
to England; but, upon the event of a new king's succession to the throne,[b] he
was chosen, as a person well acquainted with the customs of the holy court, to
be the chief of an embassy to the Pope. Having discharged his mission, he has
crossed the Alps to take a last farewell of his Italian friends, before he proceeds
to assume a distinguished part in his own country. I shall consign you, my
young friend, to the guidance of this noble gentleman. We have now been
separated for nearly twenty years; but our attachment did not arise from casual
intercourse alone; we esteemed one another, we bound ourselves one to the
other by vows; and, although at this distance of time, life has much changed its
appearance to both of us, yet I swear I would keep to the letter all that I vowed
to him, and I believe that he will do the same by me.

"Another motive influences me in sending you to England. You have a rich
relation there named Alderigo,[c] who requested Atawel to enquire for the

---

[a] In 1284 Charles I, King of Naples (grandfather of Robert, King of Naples), sailed for Naples
from Provence with an armed fleet in a last attempt to recapture his former kingdom of Sicily, lost
in 1282 (Sismondi, ch. xxiii).

[b] i.e. the accession (1307) of Edward II of England (1284–1327). 'Everard Atawel' has not been
traced. The name may be composed from 'Everardo' and 'Atawulfo', found in Muratori and
Villani, respectively.

[c] Taken from Tegrimi (pp. 9–13), the only source for Castruccio's sojourn in England; he
records Alderigo's wealth. Twentieth-century archive work has discovered an historical Alderigo
Antelminelli, a Lucchese merchant in Flanders living at a later date (Green, pp. 42–5).

various branches of the / exiled Antelminelli, and in particular for your father. It may well appear from the earnestness of his enquiries, that, if you go to England, you will find yourself neither friendless nor poor. I am an exile like you, and like you I am destitute of all resources, and am saved from embarrassment only by those labours in which I fortunately take a pride. I know that it would not be agreeable to you to be dependent on the favour of Atawel; but you are differently circumstanced with regard to your relation; and I believe him to have both the power and the will to serve you."

The gondola entered Canale Grande, and rested at the steps of a noble palace. Castruccio had no time to comment upon the relation of Guinigi; but followed him silently through the stately apartments, hung with silk and tapestry, and paved with marble, into the banquetting hall, where the owner of the palace sat surrounded by the aristocracy of Venice. The childish mind of Castruccio shrunk into itself, when he saw the satined and gold-laced state of these nobles, and then glanced his eye on the dignified form of his companion / clothed in the mean habiliments of an Italian peasant: but his shame was turned to pride and astonishment, when he found this homely-looking man received with reverence, and embraced with affection, by this lordly assembly. The most cordial salutes echoed from the ends of the hall, as they all pressed round to welcome their old friend and counsellor, to whose wisdom and calm courage many of them owed the most important obligations. There was a sweetness in the smile of Guinigi, that elevated him in appearance above other men, a sensibility beaming in his eye which added grace to his quick and expressive motions, and a gentleness that tempered the frankness of his manners. He introduced Castruccio to the nobles. The youth was beautiful to a wonder, and experienced a flattering reception from the friends of his protector.

"I shall remain but a few days in Venice," said Guinigi to his host; "but I will visit you again before I retire to my farm; at present you must tell me where I can find your English visitor, sir Ethelbert Atawel, for my business is with him." /

A man now arose, and advanced from a retired part of the room; his person formed a strange contrast to the sun-burnt faces and black eyes of the Italians who were around him. He had the round Saxon features, moulded with uncommon delicacy; his light hair slightly shaded his fair temples; and his slender person denoted elegance rather than power; his countenance bore the expression of much thought, of thoughts moulded by an enquiring, yet a gentle mind. He advanced towards Guinigi; his lips were almost convulsed; a tear stole into his eye, as he grasped his hand, and said: "You do not forget me?"

Guinigi replied with trembling emphasis, "Never!" – the hearts of the friends were full, they took leave of the company, and descended to the gondola, that without spectators they might express their remembered affection. /

CHAPTER IV.

Castruccio in England.

Castruccio spent several days with his friend at Venice. Guinigi and Atawel were constantly together, and Castruccio was thrown to a great degree into the society of the Venetian nobles. Having been for a year the constant companion of Guinigi, the contrast between him and these men struck him forcibly. The mind of the philosophical exile was fraught with a natural wisdom, a freedom from prejudice, and a boldness of thought, that suited the enthusiasm, while it corrected the narrow views of Castruccio. But these nobles were full of party spirit, and a never resting desire, to aggrandize first themselves, and secondly their native town, in opposition to the rest of the world. They were to them-selves the centre of the universe, and men and nations rose and set only for them. As Galileo was persecuted for saying that the earth moved attendant on / the sun, thus demonstrating the relative insignificance of our globe;[a] so they would have pursued with excessive hatred any one who should have pointed out to them their true station in relation to their fellow-creatures. They were in no danger of hearing such disagreeable truths from Guinigi: he was content not to be deceived himself by the false shadows thrown from society; but with that amenity which was his characteristic, he adapted his counsels to the ideas of others, and allowed those whom he could not hope to new mould, to sleep in their pleasant dreams.

Castruccio was presented to the doge, and partook of all the brilliant amusements of Venice. But at length the time arrived, when he was to depart with sir Ethelbert Atawel, and Guinigi to return to his farm among the hills. It was a sorrowful event for Atawel and Castruccio to separate from this kind and valued friend. Before he departed, Guinigi talked long with Castruccio, and vehemently urged him, when he should arrive in England, that he would put himself entirely under the guidance of Atawel. "You will be," he / said, "in a strange country, with unknown manners and customs; so that without a guide you would find it difficult to steer a right course among them. My dear Castruccio, God only knows what your future fortunes will be; but your father intrusted you to my care, and I feel the most earnest anxiety that you should enter life under good auspices, and enjoy, at least with untarnished pleasure,

---

[a] The studies of Galileo Galilei (1564–1642) were pursued near Florence. In 1633 he was forced by the Roman Inquisition to recant his belief in a heliocentric universe.

the years of youthful hope. Be towards Atawel as you ever have been to me; the natural ingenuousness of your character will discover to you the medium, which combines the graceful submission of youth, with that independence that is the dearest birthright of man. Atawel is gentle and unassuming; you must seek his counsels; for his best wisdom will be bestowed upon you, when you shew a desire to consult it."

They separated: Atawel and Castruccio departed with a few attendants towards Milan on their road to England.

Castruccio now found himself with a companion, different from him to whom he had just bade an affectionate farewel. Atawel was more a man of the world than Guinigi; nor did / he possess his genius and surpassing excellence. Entering into the common road of life, he was notwithstanding able to regulate his conduct by just principles, and to recommend himself by a sound judgement and a steady courage; but he was unable to strike into new paths, and become an adventurer in life and morals as Guinigi had been. He had great sensibility and warm affections; and various misfortunes in life had turned a constitutional gravity into melancholy. Yet he unveiled his spirit for a while from the clouds that obscured it, and entered with interest into the views and expectations of Castruccio.

They conversed together concerning his cousin Alderigo, who was a rich merchant in London, and who by his respectability and talents had acquired influence even among the nobles of England. Alderigo had been known and loved by Edward I:[a] for in those days kings did not disdain to seek friends among those classes of society from which ordinary etiquette would have excluded them. The merchant however had withdrawn from all communication with the court, since the accession / of Edward of Caernarvon;[b] for the childish amusements of this monarch ill accorded with the dispositions of one who had been the friend of his manly father. When the barons of England remonstrated with Edward, and insisted on the exile of Piers Gavaston,[c] Alderigo had however come forward to persuade the king to this necessary concession.

Atawel also was an enemy of Gavaston; and, as he sketched the political state of England to his young companion, he painted with indignation the change from the spirited counsels of the late sovereign, to the puerile amusements and weak inaction of his son. He described Gavaston as a man expert in feats of bodily activity, but destitute of judgement and manly enterprize. He said that he was vain-glorious, rapacious, and profuse. Insolent to his superiors and

---

[a] Edward I, 'Hammer of the Scots' (b. 1239, reigned 1272–1307).

[b] Edward II was born at Caernarvon Castle in Wales.

[c] Gavaston (or Gaveston), whose relationship with the king is the focus of Christopher Marlowe's *Edward II*, was murdered in 1312. His introduction into the narrative of Castruccio is Mary Shelley's invention.

equals, tyrannical to his inferiors, he deigned to use the arts of courtesy to the king alone: even the queen failed in obtaining from him the respect due to her sex and dignity. He had been raised to rank and wealth by the royal favour; but he conducted himself with an arrogance, that / would not have been tolerated in the first noble of the land. He was not content to overcome his adversary in the field of honour; but he endeavoured to add to his shame by sarcasm and ridicule. The barons exerted their utmost power for his destruction; Edward yielded to force; but on the first favourable opportunity he recalled his friend, who, untaught by adversity, again irritated his rivals to that hostility in which he was sure to be worsted.

The animated picture which Atawel drew of the discontent and turbulence of the English barons, although it would have excited terror in these quiet times, delighted Castruccio, as affording a hope of having now found a fitting stage on which he might commence his active career. The loss of Scotland to England,[a] and the inaction of the king and his favourite, easily induced him to sympathize in the indignation of Atawel; and he readily believed, that the insolence of the upstart and unworthy Gavaston demanded and justified the most rigorous measures to ensure his expulsion from the kingdom. /

Castruccio was now eighteen years of age. His converse with Guinigi had indued him with a manliness of thought and a firmness of judgement beyond his years; at the same time that the vivacity of his temper often made him appear rash, and the gaiety of his disposition led him to seek with ardour the common diversions of his age. He was bred as a young esquire in all those accomplishments which were deemed essential to a gentleman, and was expert in feats of horsemanship and arms, in the dance, and in other exercises peculiar to his country. His countenance, which was uncommonly beautiful, expressed frankness, benevolence and confidence; when animated, his eyes shone with fire; when silent, there was a deep seriousness in his expression, that commanded attention, combined at the same time with a modesty and grace which prepossessed every one in his favour. His slight, but active form never moved without displaying some new elegance of person; and his voice, whose modulated accents stole on the ear like sweetest music, forced the hearer to love him; his laugh, like that of a child, heartfelt / and joyous, was entirely distinct from the sneer of contempt, or the arrogance of superiority. He had read little; but he had conversed with those who had studied deeply, so that his conversation and manners were imbued with that refinement and superior sweetness, which are peculiar to those who unite the cultivation of the mind to exterior accomplishments. Gay, ambitious and beloved, there was little pride, and no insolence in his nature: nor could he endure either to be the object of arrogance, or to perceive it exercised over others.

---

[a] Robert I (The Bruce), King of Scots, between 1307–09 reversed many of the gains of Edward I and forced the English to retreat to the Forth. He was campaigning for Scotland's complete independence.

Such was Castruccio, when in the beginning of the year 1309 he landed on the English shores.[a] Gavaston had just been expelled by a confederacy of the nobles, who for a while had assumed the royal power into their own hands. But, instead of having been poorly exiled according to the wish of the barons, his royal master had invested him with the Lieutenancy of Ireland, where he signalized himself by his victories over the rebels. Edward however could not be happy in the absence of his favourite, but, melancholy and irresolute, watched / for a fitting opportunity, when the hatred of his nobles should in some degree be softened, to recal him.

Alderigo received his young cousin with the warmest affection, and shewed every disposition to aid by his wealth and influence, in placing him in such a situation as might gratify his ambition. Atawel introduced him at court; and, if the haughty barons of England viewed with a supercilious smile the youthful beauty and accomplishments of the stranger, Edward was pleased to behold one, who by his foreign air, and the refinement of his manners, recalled the memory of his exiled favourite. He distinguished Castruccio among the crowd; and the youth, dazzled perhaps by royal favour, easily altered his prepossessions in favour of the barons, into love and pity for their oppressed sovereign. At balls and tournaments Castruccio shone among the throng. He was yet too youthful to enter into manual contests with the English lords; but the management of his horse, his graceful person, his skill in the dance, and other light games, endeared him to Edward, who was incapable / of sympathizing in the ruder exercises in which his barons were so jealous of their pre-eminence.

Atawel and Alderigo viewed the favour which Castruccio enjoyed with the king, with fearful eyes: they dreaded the jealousy of the nobles; but happily this passion was not excited on the present occasion. On the contrary they were rather pleased, that the king should be amused by the company of one, whose youth and precarious situation withheld him from entering into the lists of rivalry with them. The Italian Castruccio, dependent on the bounty of a merchant of his own country, no conqueror at the tournament, neither thwarting, nor understanding their several plans of aggrandisement, was past over with a scornful smile, which the youth, regarding himself as a sufferer in common with their injured king, did not receive as a degradation. But deeper feelings of sympathy now gave him other sentiments.

Edward's favourite recreation was the game of tennis; in which, it being common in Italy under the name of *la Palla*, Castruccio excelled.[b] / One day after having amused themselves at this exercise in one of the royal gardens, Edward feeling fatigued gave up the game, and leaning on Castruccio's arm,

---

[a] Mary Shelley altered Tegrimi's date (1301). Tegrimi does not deal with English politics, observing merely that Castruccio excited jealousy.

[b] Found only in the Italian of the 1742 edition of Tegrimi (pp. 10–11), where it translates the original Latin 'pilae' (ball games).

35

strolled with him down one of the shady allies. And here for the first time he opened his heart to his new friend: he described Gavaston as the most amiable and the most accomplished knight of the times: he dwelt with touching earnestness on his own attachment to him, and his forced separation; tears started into his eyes as he spoke of the desolate state of his heart, deprived of the company of his first, his only and his dearest friend; and his cheeks glowed with indignation, as he mentioned the arrogance of his nobles, and the state of slavery to which he was reduced.

Castruccio was deeply moved; and the natural feeling of pity, with which he was inspired at the spectacle of the slavery of one, who it was presumed had a divine right to command, was augmented by the idea that he had been found a worthy deposit for the overflowings of the royal sorrows. He offered his services with earnestness, and Edward gladly accepted his / proffers. "Yes, my dear friend," he cried, "the accomplishment of my fondest wishes shall devolve upon you. You shall be my saviour; the saviour of my honour, and the cause of the only happiness I can enjoy on earth, the return of my beloved Piers."

Edward then disclosed to Castruccio the various expedients he had used, to pacify his nobles, and to obtain the re-establishment of his friend. He acknowledged that he had just received from the Pope a dispensation of Gavaston's oath never again to set foot in England; and a faithful messenger was only necessary, to carry this intelligence to his friend, and bid him instantly return; so that the barons, taken unawares, should not have time to plot new disturbances, before the king should be able to defy their worst, secure of the life and the society of his favourite. "That task shall devolve on you, my dear Castruccio," said he; "and I shall be indebted to you for the happiness of again embracing him to whom I have bound myself by the ties of an eternal friendship. Frame a plausible excuse for quitting England, and hasten to Dublin, where / Piers impatiently waits a messenger from me; that you may not be exposed to the slightest risk from the suspicion of the nobles, I will give you no letter: but this ring, as was agreed upon between myself and my friend, will obtain for its bearer his full confidence and friendship."

Castruccio took leave of the monarch, and hastened to the house of Alderigo, full of pride, hope, and joy. He had now indeed entered upon life, and as he hoped, with the best auspices: he had become the chosen confident[a] of a king, and his secret messenger; he readily believed that prudence, and prudence should not fail him, would cause his rise to the highest dignities. His feelings were not entirely selfish; for he deeply pitied Edward, and was sincerely happy in serving him: but to pity and serve a king, was a state of being full of pleasure. In accordance with the prudent plan he had marked out for himself, he remained at the house of his kinsman during several days, secluded from his

---

[a] Obsolete spelling of 'confidant'.

courtly friends, and absenting himself entirely from the palace. On occasion of the arrival of a few letters from / France, he informed Atawel and Alderigo that it was absolutely necessary for him to undertake a journey to that country. As he alleged the most frivolous causes as the motive of this determination, his friends easily perceived that he was endeavouring to mislead them by a false pretext. The Italian, after having in vain endeavoured to win his confidence, contented himself with recommending prudence and caution: Atawel spoke more seriously, and bade the youth beware, before he mixed with the intrigues of a foreign court, in which if he were once detected, he had neither friends nor connections to extricate him from the rage of his powerful adversaries. And then again he intreated Castruccio to consider the justice of the cause in the service of which he enlisted himself, and what would be the probable consequences, if through his means Edward were to establish a correspondence with his favourite. The young man listened with seeming deference, but allowed no word to escape him, that might countenance the idea that his journey was influenced by any except private considerations. /

He departed from London, as if on his way to France; then suddenly changing his route, he traversed the kingdom, and crossing from Bristol to Cork, hastened to Dublin, and carried to Gavaston the welcome command of the king to return immediately to England; the ring that he bore from Edward, was an immediate passport to the friendship of the illustrious exile.

Piers Gavaston was still in the flower of his age. If he were not handsome, yet the expression of his features was manly and interesting; he was graceful in person, and strong of muscle, though agile of limb: he was courteous in general society, though a certain haughtiness was diffused over his whole manner, which forbade any more familiar feeling than that of admiration. Among his friends this air of superiority yielded to the most winning kindness and affability of demeanour, which, being ever a mark of distinguished affection, did not fail to bind them to him by an additional tie of gratitude. He spoke several languages with great fluency; he rivalled the most graceful knights of France, and far surpassed / the English in all chivalrous accomplishments. The consciousness of power with which his dexterity inspired him, generated an independence and frankness of action, which would have rendered him amiable to all, had it not been tainted by vanity and presumption. He was magnificent in his attire, fond of parade, and proud of his dazzling fortunes, all heavy sins among his English enemies. He paid great attention, and made much shew of love to Castruccio, whom if princely affability had before moved, the gracious treatment of Gavaston made a complete conquest of him.

They returned together to England. Edward had arrived at Chester, that he might behold his friend a few days the sooner; and he flew to his arms with the affectionate transports with which a child might welcome the return of its absent mother.

A strict friendship was established between Gavaston and Castruccio. Piers had not learned moderation from adversity; his wealth and luxury were increased, and with these his vanity and insufferable presumption. Atawel in vain endeavoured to win Castruccio from his / society; but, if the deportment of Gavaston was arrogant towards the English lords, it was so much the more affable and insinuating towards Castruccio. The king also loved the Italian; and, not examining the merits of the case, he allowed himself to be entirely led away by the personal attachment that he bore to Edward and Piers.

Gavaston had wealth and rank; and, although he was considered an upstart, yet the possession of these gave him a consequence in the eyes of the nobles, of which Castruccio was wholly divested. They looked on the latter as one may regard a stinging insect, whose insignificance is not to compound for his annoyance.[a] They endured the insolence of Gavaston with the sullenness of men who look into the future for revenge; but they bore the far slighter pain which Castruccio inflicted upon them, with the impatience one feels at an injury, however slight, for which we are by no means prepared. And, if Castruccio himself manifested few symptoms of insolence, yet he was supported by that of Gavaston; and they felt that, though for the present they could / not injure the favourite personally, yet they might wound him through his Italian friend. This latter also was not unfrequently provoked beyond his usual courtesy by the pride and taunts of his enemies; and, if ever he dared reply, or when Gavaston replied for him, the nobles felt a rage they could ill smother at what they deemed so despicable an offender. The indications of mischief which had before slightly manifested themselves, broke out one day with a violence that suddenly terminated Castruccio's visit to England.

He accompanied the king, who went with a train of the first nobility on a hawking party, to Chelsea. The exercise excited Castruccio's blood, and inspired him with an exaltation of spirits which might have exhausted itself in gaiety alone, had not a quarrel, that arose between him and one of the nobles, urged him to a fury he could ill control. The contention began concerning the comparative flight of their birds; and, heated as they were by personal animosity, it became loud and bitter. Edward in vain endeavoured to appease them; but when, seconded by his friends, the English / nobleman established his triumph in the contest, Castruccio replied by a sarcasm which so irritated his antagonist, that, no longer restraining his indignation, he darted forward, and struck Castruccio. The fiery youth, crying in Italian, "By blood, and not by words, are blows to be avenged!" – drew his stiletto, and plunged it into the bosom of his adversary. A hundred swords immediately flashed in the air; Edward threw himself before his friend to protect him: Gavaston, Atawel and others who loved him, hastily withdrew him from the crowd, made him mount his horse, and without a moment's delay they rode to the river's side below the

---

[a] i.e. that the insect is small does not excuse its sting.

Tower, where they fortunately found a vessel on the point of sailing for Holland. Without waiting to see his other friends, without going to the house of Alderigo for money or equipment, they hurried him on board the vessel, which immediately got under weigh, and dropt down with a favourable wind towards the Nore.[a]

The barons, burning with revenge, had sent archers to the house of Alderigo, who, not finding Castruccio, seized upon his kinsman, / and threw him into prison. A law then existed in England, that if a foreigner killed a native and escaped, those with whom he resided became amenable for the murder. Alderigo was therefore in the most imminent peril; but Edward, as the last act of friendship that he could bestow upon Castruccio, saved the life and fortune of his kinsman.[b] And thus, after a year's residence in this island, did the youth bring to a disastrous conclusion all the hopes and expectations which had led him thither. /

Plot — *Castruccio expelled from England for killing an English noble in a quarrel.*

CHAPTER V.

Castruccio in Flanders and France – Alberto Scoto – Benedetto Pepi.

After a favourable navigation of a few hours Castruccio arrived at Ostend. He landed destitute of friends, and even of the equipage of a gentleman. What Castruccio felt during the voyage can hardly be described. Anger, grief and shame kept his spirits in a perpetual fluctuation, which, painful as it was, was far preferable to the extinction of hope, and the sense of utter desertion upon his landing in Flanders. The world was indeed before him:[c] he had been torn with frightful suddenness from the affections he had cultivated for a year, from ease, luxury and the friendship of a powerful monarch, and consigned to utter destitution. He did not even possess the lance and horse, with which knights-errant of old won kingdoms for themselves. Nor did he think with / out remorse of the blood with which his hands were for the first time stained; he had received a blow, and blood alone could expiate this injury: in France or England a duel in regular and courtly form would have terminated the quarrel;

---

[a] The route followed led from west to east along the north bank of the Thames, starting from Chelsea (then a manor to the west of Westminster Abbey). The Nore is an anchorage near the mouth of the river Thames.

[b] The killing, the law and the king's intervention are in Tegrimi (pp. 9–11); twentieth-century research has confirmed that the historical Castruccio was expelled from England after a homicide (Green, p. 43).

[c] cf. *Paradise Lost*, XII. 646.

but in Italy the secret stiletto was the weapon of revenge, and the murder of one was avenged by the assassination of another, until the list of expiatory murders ran high, and were carefully counted by each party, each justifying his own, and blaming those of his adversary. Yet, although the mind of Castruccio was tinctured by the morality of his country, he was too young and too new not to feel a natural horror at having been the cause of the death of a fellow creature. Seated on a rock amidst the wide sands left by the retiring sea, listening to the melancholy roar of the tide, he shed bitter tears of repentance and conscious guilt. One idea alone calmed him, that his adversary might not have died – and then what was he? His rashness and folly had thrown him from a high station of prosperity and happiness, to being the solitary, helpless creature that he then was. /

The sun sunk in a turbid sky. "Ah! how unlike dear Italy," sighed Castruccio; "how different from the clear heavens and orange-tinted sunsets of my native soil!"

He spoke in Italian, and a man who stood near unperceived by him, repeated the word so dear to exiles, the name of the country of his birth: – "*Italia.*" Castruccio looked up, and the man continued: "Italy is also my native country. And who are you, my friend, who, alone and a stranger, mourn for the delights of that paradise of the earth?"

"I am a Lucchese," replied Castruccio; "I am the cousin of Alderigo, the rich merchant in England."

"The name of an Italian," said the other, "is a sufficient passport to my poor hospitality; but, as the relation of my excellent friend, Messer Alderigo, it greatly delights me to offer you all the little service that I am capable of giving. Come with me to my house; you will recal perhaps some not unpleasing associations in the society of an Italian family, who, during a long absence, have never forgotten the olive / groves of Italy, and never ceased to desire to return to them."

Castruccio accepted this friendly invitation with joy. He found his host a rich merchant of Ostend, living in the Italian style, and surrounded by a family, whose language and persons transported him to the plains of Lombardy, or the vallies of his native Tuscany.

During the conversation of the evening his host mentioned the wars that were then carrying on between the French king and the Flemings, and that Alberto Scoto[a] commanded under the banners of the former with a troop of Italians. This account struck Castruccio with a hope, that he should now find some remedy for his misfortunes. Being obliged to enter on a new career, and his inclination leading him to war, he thought that this opportunity of serving

---

[a] Castruccio's service under Alberto Scotto, ousted lord of Piacenza, against the rebellious Flemish subjects of Philippe-le-Bel, is historical, but the dates of the Flemish rebellion are 1302–5 ('Scoto' in Villani, VIII, cap. 7 and Tegrimi, p. 13).

under a fellow-countryman was too favourable a circumstance to be neglected. He made many enquiries concerning this troop and its illustrious chief. Alberto Scoto had once possessed a wide dominion in Lombardy; he had expelled the Visconti from / Milan,[a] and had been constituted tyrant or lord of the most flourishing Lombard states. When by the joint force of revolt and treason he was driven from his power, he had not lost his reputation as a successful general, and Philip le Bel, king of France, eagerly accepted his offered services. In former times he had been considered as belonging to the Guelph faction; but he had changed before he quitted Italy; and, now an exile, the distinction of party was entirely lost to him.

Castruccio had never yet made a campaign; and his eager spirit led him to regard with disdain the sloth in which he had hitherto passed his life. From the moment that he had landed in France he had resolved to commence a military career; and he believed that he should find no better school than that of Alberto Scoto, where he would be disciplined in the modes of his own country, and learn under so experienced a general, the tactics of those armies which he hoped one day to command.

On the following morning he discoursed concerning these ideas with his host, who easily entered into his designs, and promised to / provide him with such an introduction to Scoto as would at least command his attention. His plans were quickly arranged.

The merchant took a kind leave of his young compatriot, and gave him a well filled purse at parting: "You shall repay me," said he smiling, "out of your first spoils: or, if these fall short of my expectations, Messer Alderigo will not suffer a friend of his to lose through his kindness to a kinsman."

Castruccio traversed in safety the plains of Flanders, and arrived at the French camp, which was pitched near Douai. He penetrated with some difficulty into the tent of Scoto: but that experienced general soon perceived in the mien of the youthful stranger a soldier's deportment and air of independence, that prepossessed him at once in his favour. After having read the letter of Castruccio's host, he addressed the youth with kindness. "Our countryman," said he, "informs me that you are the chief of the noble family of the Antelminelli, a name so well known in Italy, as to be itself a sufficient introduction to a native of that country. You desire to serve / under me, and I feel myself honoured by your selection; my troop must be a gainer by the acquisition of so noble a volunteer."

The manners of Scoto were courtly; and in his conversation with the youth his keen judgement quickly discovered the qualifications of Castruccio. They dined together; and afterwards, having equipped him in a becoming dress, he presented him to the French king, from whom he experienced a favourable

---

[a] In 1302. After Scotto's own betrayal by the Guelph cities which had assisted in expelling the Ghibelline Visconti, he vainly offered to help re-instate the latter (Sismondi, ch. xxvi).

reception. Castruccio did not fail speedily to inform Alderigo of his situation, who immediately remitted him a sum of money amply sufficient for his present supply.

Castruccio had now exchanged the idle gaieties of the English court for the active labours of a camp; and on the following day he entered on his military duties. Scoto presented him with a suit of armour, selecting one of the most costly that he possessed. There was a small iron scull cap which fitted the head, and was worn under the helmet. The casque itself was of highly polished iron inlaid with gold in beautiful devices, and the mailed collar for his neck was plated with the same precious / metal. The breast-plate was finely carved, and fastened over the shoulders to the back plate, which was laboured with less delicacy. The greaves which sheathed his legs, were beautifully inlaid, and shone with gold; his sword was of the finest temper, and the scabbard, richly adorned, hung at his side from an embroidered scarf; a shield and a good lance completed his equipment. Arms of less costly manufacture were chosen for his horse, which, selected from the stud of Scoto, was strong, heavy and spirited.

The next day the camp was in motion. It were needless to detail the events of this campaign: several battles were fought, and some towns taken. The French who had hitherto been losers, regained their ground; and in every action the troop of Scoto distinguished itself, and among his troop Castruccio was pre-eminent in bravery, enterprize and success. Scoto perceived, and warmly applauded his courage and conduct: the fame of his actions was spread through the army, and his first campaign crowned him with that reputation to which he had long aspired. King Philip himself / had witnessed his achievements; he beheld him as he led a troop to the onset, and turned in favour of France the dubious fortune of a hard-fought day. The King proved his gratitude by bestowing on him such praises and rewards as filled Castruccio with triumph and delight.

Scoto was quartered during the winter at one of the Flemish towns, and Castruccio was invited to partake of the gaieties of the Parisian court. He obeyed the summons, and spent some weeks in the enjoyment of all those amusements which the palace of Philip afforded. His beauty and grace attracted the notice of the ladies; and his fame in arms caused him to be distinguished by the French nobility.

Towards the close of the winter he returned to the camp of Scoto, in whose esteem he held in a very high place. This general delighted in imparting his experience to so attentive a listener, and in endeavouring to form the genius of one who he foresaw would rise to the highest rank among the lords of Italy. Castruccio was admitted at all hours to his tent; they rode together; and, under the precepts of one / well experienced in the politics of Italy, Castruccio began to understand and meditate the part he should act, when he returned to that country. Yet Scoto's was an evil school; and, if his pupil gained from him a true insight into Italian politics, he at the same time learned the use of those arts which then so much disgraced that people. The *Punica fides*[a] had been transferred across the Mediterranean; and every kind of wile and artifice was practised in the Italian palaces, which ever received from the court of the Popes, as from a well of poison, courtiers and crafty politicians, who never permitted the art to fail for want of instructors. Scoto had been more successful than any other in the exercise of this policy, and he now initiated Castruccio in the secrets of the craft. Hitherto his mind had been innocence, and all his thoughts were honour. Frankness played on his lips; ingenuousness nestled in his heart; shame was ever ready to check him on the brink of folly; and the tenderness of his nature seemed to render it impossible for him to perpetrate a deed of harshness or inhumanity. The court of England / had infused some laxity into his moral creed; but at least he had not learned there hypocrisy, and the wily arts of a hoary politician. Still the strait path of honour and a single mind had ever engaged his choice. But nineteen is a dangerous age; and ill betides the youth who confides himself to a crafty instructor. If Castruccio listened at first with an inattentive ear to the counsels of Scoto, yet their frequent repetition, and the wax-like docility of his mind, quickly gave them power over him.

"You, my dear Castruccio," said Scoto, "will soon return to your native country, where your talents and valour will open for you a brilliant career. A soldier, if he join wisdom of counsel to soldiership, must for a while succeed in Italy; and if he be prudent, he need not fall as I did. A chief in Italy ought to pay strict attention to the discipline and equipment of his followers, and to the spreading the terror of his name among his enemies. This must be his first step; and without that the foundations of his power are as sand; for to have many cities subject to his command is a nothing in the hour of danger, since if he control / them not with iron, gold will ever find its way into the councils of the citizens; and woe and defeat are to that chief, who reigns only by the choice of the people; a choice more fickle and deceitful than the famed faithlessness of woman.

"But, having once formed an army, disciplined it, and shewn its temper by success, then is the time to change the arts of war for those of counsel, and to work your way as the mole, shewing no sign of your path, until your triumphant power comes forth where it is least expected. Nor be lavish of gold; for that is power while you possess it, weakness when surrendered into the hands of another. But alliances, marriages, nominal honours and promises are the fit allurements to be used among our countrymen. By one or other of these means, of such motley materials are Italian confederacies composed, one single chieftain may ever introduce dissention and treason into the enemy's camp. It was thus that I fell; for I did not trust to my own strength, but to that of my allies.[b]

---

[a] Punic (Carthaginian) faith, i.e. pledge-breaking; see Sallust, *Jugurtha*, 108. 3 and Joseph Addison, *Cato* (1713), act II: 'Our Punic faith/ Is infamous, and branded to a proverb'.

[b] One of several passages seemingly anticipatory of Machiavelli's precepts in *The Prince* (written 1513). Mary Shelley, however, regarded Machiavelli himself as a true republican.

"There are two classes of men in Italy, / which indeed often cut like a two-edged sword, and turn upon their master, yet which with proper management are of infinite use in the accomplishment of secret treaties, and the carrying on of correspondence in the very heart of the enemy's councils: these are the priests, and the *Uomini di Corte**. The priests are the least trust-worthy and the most expensive: yet sometimes I have seen them stand by their employer, if he yielded them much respect and apparent submission, and betray him who has paid them well, yet who had neglected the arts of flattery. In their youth men are often led to trust to their actions and their sword; but every day is another page of experience, to shew us that men are governed by words alone, words light as air, yet which have often been found capable of overturning empires: witness / the triumphs of the Popes, who dissipated the armies of their enemies, and despoiled them of rank, possessions and life, by excommunications, and anathemas – words. But, in discovering this infinite power in words, let it make you prudent in their use; be not chary in their quantity, but look well to their quality. But to return to our instruments, – priests, and *Uomini di Corte*.

"These latter are poor dogs, often faithful, easily satisfied, and who can penetrate every where, see every thing, hear every thing, and if you acquire but the art of getting their knowledge from them, they become of infinite utility; this is done by many words, much good humour, and a little gold. When Della Torre and I chased Matteo Visconti from Milan,[a] that chief retired to live on bread and onions in his miserable castle of St. Columban among the Euganean hills. All at once Della Torre began to suspect, that Matteo had received money from Germany, and was secretly collecting arms and men at his castle. So he sent for a *Uomo di Corte*, a famous fellow in those days, one Marco Lombardo, who had in former / times prophesied to count Ugolino his future misfortunes,[b] and said to him; 'Now, my brave Marco, if you would gain a palfrey and a gold-embroidered robe, I have an easy task, which accomplished they shall both be

---

* *Uomini di Corte*, or "men of court:" story-tellers, minstrels, actors, or buffoons, who frequented the feasts and courts held by the Italian noblemen, and contributed no small part to the amusement of those times. They are frequently spoken of by Boccaccio.[c]

[a] The Della Torre contended with the Visconti for the control of Milan between 1262–1310; the expulsion by Guido Della Torre in 1302 of Matteo Visconti (1255–1322) was their last, temporary, triumph (Sismondi, ch. xxvi).

[b] Amended from 'Lombardi', following Mary Shelley's sources and note (Villani, VII, caps 120 and 127; adds. e. 17, p. 227 rev.); Ugolino de la Gherardesca, Guelph tyrant of Pisa; his young sons and grandsons were starved to death with him in 1288/9 in the Tower of Famine (Sismondi, ch. xxiii); Lombardo and Ugolino both appear in Dante, where Lombardo affirms the primacy of human free will (*Purgatorio*, XVI. 25–149); Ugolino tells his story in *Inferno*, XXXIII. 1–90. Palacio (p. 67–8 and n.) proposes Mary Shelley's reading of the *Novellino* on the strength of an anecdote about Lombardo in which he figures as a poor man, as here.

[c] Giovanni Boccaccio (1313–75), Florentine writer and humanist; his collection of prose tales, *The Decameron* (1350), influenced *The Canterbury Tales* of Geoffrey Chaucer (c.1343–1400); Mary Shelley read Boccaccio between May 1819 and October 1820 (*MWSJ*, II, p. 637); *uomini de corte* are also mentioned in Muratori, II, diss. 29, p. 13.

yours. Go, as if on your own pleasure, to the castle where Matteo Visconti now lives; spy well if there be gleam of arms or appearance of soldiers; and, when you take leave of the chief, ask him in a buffoonish manner to answer you two questions: let those questions be, first, how he likes his present state, and if he be not poorly off; and secondly, when he hopes to return to Milan.'

"Marco readily undertook the task, and visited the castle of St. Columban, where he found Visconti ill dressed, ill fed, and worse attended; for there were about him only a few wrinkled and crippled followers, who not being able to gain more in the wars, and too lazy for work, came to starve themselves under his roof. His good lady was worse off, not having a hand-maid to wait upon her, and, as I have heard, there was but one capuchin[a] between her and her husband, which they wore by turns. Marco / made but a short stay in the castle, for he got nothing to eat; but, as he took his leave of Visconti, he intreated the chief to help him to gain a palfrey and a silken robe. 'Willingly,' replied Visconti, 'if I am able; but think not to get them from me, for I have them not.'

"'Noble count,' said Marco, 'answer me two questions, and I shall receive these gifts in pay for your answers.'

"And then he put the two demands, as Della Torre had instructed him. Visconti, who was discerning and cunning, replied: "Truly I find my present situation suited to me, since I suit myself to it; tell this to your master, Messer Guido Della Torre, who sent you; and tell him also, that when his crimes out number mine, then it is God's will that I return to Milan.'

"Della Torre, relieved from his fears, since he undoubtedly feared German gold more than the due punishment for his sins, rewarded Marco as he had promised."[b]

Such were the lessons of Scoto; and the reader will easily forgive me, if I repeat them not so often, or dilate on them so much as the / chief himself did. Castruccio listened with curiosity, half angry, half convinced; and in those days the seeds of craft were sown, that, flourishing afterwards, contributed to his advancement to power and glory. As winter drew to a close, Scoto said to him: "I could have wished, my young friend, that you fought under my banners another campaign, and that I might still enjoy the advantage of your society and valour; but fortune orders it otherwise, and you must away to Italy. Henry of Luxemburgh, now emperor of Germany, has begun to advance towards that country, where he will collect the wrecks of the Ghibeline party, and endeavour to re-establish them.[c]

---

[a] Hooded cloak; in the eighteenth century a female garment, but in medieval Italy universally worn, as Muratori stresses (Muratori, I, diss. 23, p. 266; 25, pp. 322–3; noted in Ab. Dep. e. 274, pp. 56, 57, 58).

[b] The story of the sounding-out of Visconti is told in Villani, VIII, cap. 61 of an unnamed *uomo di corte*; Mary Shelley has altered Villani's 'Guidetto' to 'Guido'.

[c] Henry of Luxembourg (c.1269–1313), Emperor Henry VII, hoped to reunite Germany and Italy. In 1310, having secured the pope's assent, he began his progress, and was initially successful. But his forced levies alienated all parties, and the French-backed Robert, King of Naples exploited the suspicion of the Guelphs. Dante regarded Henry as the potential saviour of Italy (*Paradiso*, XXX. 133–48).

You are a Ghibeline of a high and faithful family, and must not omit this opportunity for your advancement. Return to Italy; join the emperor; and I doubt not that through his means you will be restored to your wealth and rights in Lucca. Go, Castruccio; you are formed for action and command: do not forget my lessons. Here or in England they might be useless, but in Italy they are necessary to your success. I doubt not of the high fortune that awaits / you; and it will warm my old blood, if I think, that I, an exile, and a soldier of fortune, fighting under colours not my own, shall have contributed to the advancement of so lofty a spirit as yours."

Castruccio followed the advice of Scoto; he took an affectionate leave of him, and again received the courteous thanks of the French monarch. He was loaded with many costly presents; and his sword, of the finest temper, the hilt and sheath richly embossed and inlaid with jewels, was presented to him by the hands of the queen. He consigned these gifts, and the spoil by which he was enriched, into the hands of an Italian merchant, to be conveyed by his means into Italy; he travelled himself on horseback, accompanied by a servant, and a mule which bore his armour.

Journeying at this leisurely rate, he arrived after an interval of some weeks, at the south-eastern extremity of France. He approached the beautiful Alps, the boundaries of his native country: their white domes and peaks pierced the serene atmosphere; and silence, the deep silence of an Alpine winter, reigned among their / ravines. As he advanced into their solitudes, he lost all traces of the footsteps of man, and almost of animals: – an eagle would sometimes cross a ravine, or a chamois was seen hanging on the nearly perpendicular rock.[a] The giant pines were weighed down by a huge canopy of snow; and the silent torrents and frozen waterfalls were covered, and almost hid, by the uniform mass. The paths of the vallies, and the ascent of the mountains, ever difficult, were almost impassable; perpetual showers of snow hid every track, and a few straggling poles alone guided the traveller in his dangerous journey. The vulture leaving his nest in the rock, screamed above, seeming to tell the rash adventurer who dared disturb his haunts, that his torn limbs were the tribute due to him, the monarch of that region. Sometimes even, the road was strewed with the members of the venturous chamois, whose sure foot had failed among the snows; and the approach of Castruccio scared the birds of prey from their repast on his half-frozen limbs. One pass was particularly dangerous: the road was cut in the side of a precipitous mountain: below, the stream which had cleared its way in / the very depth of the valley, was hidden by the overhanging of the precipice: above, the mountain side, almost vulture-baffling, black,

---

[a] A possible reminiscence of Virgil, *Eclogues*, I. 76; the phrase 'dumosa pendere procul de rupe' (applied to goats) was translated by William Wordsworth ('Preface to the Edition of 1815') as 'hanging upon the shaggy precipice' and singled out as an example of the poetic imagination at work; in Virgil's eclogue the shepherds lament the state of Italy and their outcast condition.

except where the snow had found a resting-place in its clefts, towered so high that the head became dizzy, when the traveller would have gazed on the walled-in heavens. The path was narrow; and being entirely exposed to the south, the snows that covered it had been slightly melted, and again frozen, so that they had become slippery and dangerous. Castruccio dismounted from his horse; and turning his eyes from the depth below, he led him slowly on, until the widening of the road, and the appearance of a few pines diminished the terror of the surrounding objects.

Then, finding the road less dangerous, he remounted, and was proceeding cautiously along the edge of the precipice, when he heard a voice behind him as calling for help. Hastily dismounting, and tying the animal to a jutting point of the rock, he returned to that chasm, which he had just passed with such tremendous difficulty. There he saw a mule standing quietly by the road side; but, on the steep face / of the precipice a few feet below, he perceived a man clinging to the pointed inequalities of the mountain, with such energy that his whole force and being seemed to live in the grasp, and his voice failed as he again endeavoured to cry for help. Castruccio's servant had lingered far behind, so that he was obliged alone to attempt the fearful task of drawing the sufferer from his appalling situation. He unbound his sash, and, tying one end to the girth of the mule's saddle, and taking the other in his hand, he threw it down to the man below. By these means, with infinite difficulty, he succeeded in hoisting up the poor wretch, who, white and wrinkled with fear, stood almost as entranced, when he found himself safe from the frightful death he had feared. Castruccio soothed him with a gentle voice, and told him that now the worst part of the journey was over, and that they were about to descend by an easier path to the plain of Italy; "where," he said, "you will find a paradise that will cure all your evils."

The man looked at him with a mixture of wonder, and what might have been construed / into contempt, had his muscles, made rigid with cold and fear, yielded to the feeling of his mind. He replied drily, "I am an Italian." And Castruccio smiled to perceive, that these words were considered as a sufficient refutation to his assertion of the boasted charms of Italy.

After resting until the unfortunate traveller had recovered health and life, they proceeded along the mountain, saying little, for the path was too dangerous to admit of conversation. Yet, when Castruccio dared take his eyes from the track of his horse's feet, he could not help examining curiously the companion fortune had given him. He was a man by whose dry and wrinkled face you might guess him to be nearly sixty years of age; and yet, by the agility and more youthful appearance of his person, he could not be more than forty. His eyes were small, black and sparkling; his nose pointed and turned up; his lips were as a line in his face, uncurved and unmarked except by three deep wrinkles at each corner: his eyebrows were elevated as in vanity; and yet a flat high forehead denoted a good understanding. His / figure was tall and lank, yet muscular, and was clothed with a mixture of poverty and rank, which it amused Castruccio to observe. He wore gilt spurs as a knight, and, carefully folded on his saddle before him, was a rich mantle edged with deep gold lace; he was clad in a close, strait dress of threadbare cloth, with a kind of narrow trowsers made of common undressed sheep skin, which fastened with many knots and intersections round his legs; he had a large capuchin cloak wrapped about him, made of coarse flannel, such as was called *sclavina*, because it was manufactured in Sclavonia,[a] and was worn at that time by the poorest class of Italians. On his feet he wore great coarse boots of undressed sheep skin, that furnished a singular contrast to the golden spurs attached to them; his head was covered only by a scull-cap of iron mail sewed to cloth, which was called in those times a *majata*.[b]

The sun descended as they pursued their journey, when, perceiving a house not far distant, Castruccio's companion drew in his mule, and pointing to it, asked if they should not remain there for the night? "Nay," replied / Castruccio, "the moon will be up in half an hour, and being but just past its full, we may, I think, proceed safely."

"Do not trust to the moon," said his companion; "its shadows are deep and fearful, and its light not less dangerous; sometimes a beam cast from among trees across the road, will look like a running stream, and its black shades may conceal the most frightful dangers. I dare not proceed by moonlight, and am unwilling to part company with you on this dreadful road. I beg you to consent to pass the night at that house."

"I readily agree, if that be indeed a house, and not an unroofed sheep-cot; for I hardly expect to find in these regions a bed softer than the rock, or a roof which will shelter me better than the moonlight sky."

The cottage was shut up, and its inhabitants asleep; but, called up by the shrill voice of the elder traveller, a man rolled himself out from his bed of dried leaves and sheep skins, and opened the door. Welcoming the travellers, he quickly blew up the decaying ashes of a fire in the middle of the only room of the cottage, / and it threw a light on the bare walls of this disconsolate apartment; the smoke rose and filled the upper part of the room, while a small portion only escaped through a round hole in the roof. A large bed, or rather dormitory of dried leaves and the stalks of Indian corn, was strewed along one side of the room, on which many both men and women lay, peeping out on the travellers from under their sheep skin coverings: there was no furniture, except a rude bench, and a ruder table; the bare walls were black and falling down, while the sky peeped through many cracks in the roof. The room was so filled with the stench of garlick and smoke, that Castruccio, hastily retreating to the

---

[a] 'The country of the Slavs'; the Slavs were classed with gypsies and Jews as dispersed peoples.
[b] Noted in Ab. Dep. e. 274, pp. 74–5 with *sclavina* (Muratori, I, diss. 23, p. 256 and diss. 24, p. 319).

door, asked his companion, whether he would not prefer proceeding on his journey. The latter appeared better accustomed to the sight and smell of such miserable cabins, and he used his utmost eloquence to persuade Castruccio that the shelter of the cottage was preferable to the pure and keen air of heaven; but finding the latter resolute in his determination not to enter, he told him, that having warmed for a few minutes his half frozen fingers, and / tasted the wine of the cottage, he would proceed with him down the mountain.

The companion of Castruccio had not exaggerated the extreme danger of the road by moonlight. The frightened horses often refused to proceed, or to penetrate the murky depths which the mountain shadows cast around them, even blackening the snow. They rode on slowly and cautiously; and the following morning found themselves little advanced in the descent. It was near noon before they reached Susa,[a] when, having passed the dangers of the journey, the elder traveller, recovering his voice and recollection, rode up to Castruccio, and asked him where he intended to rest after the toil he had undergone. Castruccio replied, that he hoped to find an inn in the town, and, if not, he should apply to some monastery, where he doubted not he should be provided with food and shelter for the following day and night.

"Sir," said his companion, "I am not a stranger in Susa, and have in particular one good old friend, Messer Tadeo della Ventura,[b] well known to the Florentines and other Italians / who pass over this mountain for the purposes of merchandize: this worthy man will receive me as an old friend and guest; and, as you both generously and bravely saved my life, I can do no less than offer to introduce you to the soft couches and good wines of Messer Tadeo."

"Nor will I refuse your offer; for soft couches will be welcome to my aching bones, and good wine a pleasant cordial to my wearied spirits: therefore, sir knight, I thank you heartily for your courtesy." /

---

[a] The first town entered upon crossing into Italy via the Mont Cenis pass; Mary Shelley's impressions may be found in *MWSL*, I, pp. 63–4.
[b] Probably invented, the surname ('fortune' or 'destiny') being chosen for emblematic reasons.

CHAPTER VI.

| *Castruccio in Italy – Susa – Creed of Benedetto.*

Messer Tadeo received his old friend with respect and friendship; and, cour-teously welcoming Castruccio, he led them into a large hall, where the sight of a repast already set out seemed to diffuse joy over the countenances of both travellers. The hall was richly hung with scarlet cloth, and the tables and seats covered with tapestry; at the upper end of the room was a chimney and a fire, near which taking his seat, Messer Tadeo invited the new comers to join several other friends of his, who arranged themselves round the table.

When the long ceremony of dinner was finished, and the servants were busy in removing the tables, Messer Tadeo proposed to the newly arrived guests to conduct them to a bed-chamber, where they might repose after the / fatigues of the journey. They both gladly accepted this offer; and in a deep and refreshing sleep Castruccio forgot his curiosity concerning who or what his companion might be, and the latter recovered from the trembling fear of danger, which had haunted him since his escape of the preceding day.

When Castruccio arose at about six o'clock in the evening, he joined Messer Tadeo, who was sitting with the other traveller in the great hall. The rest of the company had departed; and these two were in earnest conversation, which they changed when Castruccio entered.

After some time, holding up his finger, and drawing down still longer the long wrinkles of his cheeks, the fellow-traveller of Castruccio, in a mysterious manner, pronounced the word which had been given to the soldiers of Alberto Scoto, that they might distinguish one another during the darkness of night, or the confusion of battle; Castruccio, hearing this, easily divined that he had a fellow soldier, and a friend of his chief, in his strange travelling companion; so smiling, he uttered the countersign, / and the other, turning on him, as if the ghost of one whom he had known many years before had risen before him, hastily enquired, "You served then in his troop?"

"Yes," replied Castruccio, "I had the honour of serving under the noble knight, Messer Alberto Scoto; and, in having rendered you a service, I am still more happy to find that I saved one who has fought under the same banners with myself."

"Is your name a secret?"

"I am of a noble Lucchese family, now exiled and wandering; my name is Castruccio Castracani dei Antelminelli."

The elder traveller suddenly arose, and, embracing Castruccio warmly, bestowed on him a brotherly kiss, and then turning to Tadeo, said: "This morning I introduced to you a stranger whose merit with me was that of having saved my life at the imminent risk of his own; now I introduce to you a gallant soldier, whose name has been spread through France, as that of the bravest warrior and the ablest commander that fought in the Low Countries: / the Sieur Castruccio is a name which even the children in France lisp with gratitude, and the Flemings tremble to hear."

Many compliments passed; and then the traveller said: "This pleasant discovery has made friends of three who were before strangers; nor will I conceal from you, Messer Castruccio, that my name is Benedetto Pepi, a Cremonese, now returning to my own country, after having gained laurels and knight-hood under the banners of Messer Scoto. You, my dear companion, say that you are an exile; but great changes are now taking place in Italy, and, knowing who you are, we may well admit you to the confidential conversation that I and Messer Tadeo were holding when you entered, concerning all that has passed since the arrival of the emperor Henry in Italy."

Saying this, Benedetto made a slight sign to his friend, which Castruccio easily guessed to be an admonition to be discreet in his disclosures. Tadeo replied to this sign by a nod, and said:

"Two Florentine usurers who had come through Milan, dined yesterday at my house; / they had witnessed the entrance of the emperor into that city. The lord of Milan, Guido della Torre, was obliged to discharge his soldiers, and unarmed, at the head of an unarmed multitude, went out to meet the emperor, who had the Visconti in his train, and all the Ghibelines, the old enemies of the Torre family. These are now reinstated in their possessions; yet Henry still pretends to impartiality, and in his march has restored all the exiles to their various towns, whether they be Guelphs or Ghibelines."

"I wonder," said Pepi, "how long he will keep on the mask; few men are impartial, an emperor never: to one curious in state affairs it were a fine occasion, to conjecture what will be the issue and crown of these pretensions."

"Why," asked Castruccio, "should not they be as they appear? Cannot the emperor be animated by a generous policy, and wish to reconcile all parties by a just and fair proceeding?"

"Impossible!" cried Pepi with energy; "an emperor just! a prince impartial! Do / not thrones rest upon dissentions and quarrels? And must there not be weakness in the people to create power in the prince? I prophesy; and as a discreet man I prophesy seldom, yet I now securely foretell, that Henry will set all Italy by the ears, to reap the fruits of their dissentions. He procures the recal of all the exiles—— I admire his policy, worthy of being studied and understood by all who would reign. Can Ghibelines and Guelphs live within the walls of the same town? No more than one vessel can contain fire and water. No; the cities of Italy will be filled with brawls, and her rivers run blood, by means of this conjunction. If he had meant to establish peace in Italy, he would have assassinated all of one party, to secure the lives of the other; but to unite them, is to destroy both, and under the mask of friendship to get into his own hands all that each has possessed."

Pepi uttered this harangue with an energy and a vivacity that startled Castruccio; his black eyes sparkled, his brows became elevated, and drawing down the perpendicular wrinkles of his cheeks, and contracting the horizontal / ones of his forehead, he looked round with an air of triumph on his companions.

"You say true, Messer Benedetto," said Tadeo, groaning at the dismal prognostications of his friend; "and I greatly fear lest this pretended justice prove the watchword for war and bloodshed. Yet now all wears the appearance of peace and brotherhood. The lords of Langusco, Pavìa, Vercelli, Novara and Lodi have resigned their tyrannies and given up the keys of their respective towns to Henry, and Imperial Vicars are every where established. Guido della Torre, the proudest and most powerful tyrant of Lombardy, has submitted; and the court of the emperor at Milan is crowded by the lords of the towns in the east of Italy, and the ambassadors of the free states of the south."[a]

"Has Florence submitted?" asked Castruccio.

"No; – that town and its league holds out; Sienna, Lucca and Bologna. Yet, when the emperor marches south, we shall see these proud republicans bow their stiff knees."

"Never!" cried Pepi; "Bologna, Lucca / and Sienna may submit; but Florence never will; they are stiff-kneed, stiff-necked, and hate the name of emperor and master more than Pope Urban hated the house of Suabia.[b] These republicans, whom from my soul I detest, have turned out the Ghibelines, and are now fighting with the nobles, and asserting the superiority of the vulgar, till every petty artizan of its meanest lane fancies himself as great a prince as the emperor Henry himself. Besides, when all else fails, they will buy him off: these Florentines squander their golden florins, and pay thousands to purchase what would be a dear bargain even as a gift. Their watch-word is that echo of fools, and laughing stock of the wise, – Liberty. Surely the father of lies invented that bait, that trap, at which the multitude catch, as a mouse at a bit of cheese: well would it be for the world, if they found the same end; and, as the nibbling mouse pulls down the iron on his head, they, as if they had one neck, were lopped off, as they seized their prize: – but Florence flourishes!"

Pepi ended his speech with a deep groan, and continued lost in thought; while Tadeo / and Castruccio discussed the chances that might arise from the

---

[a] This account of the submission of Lombard cities (September 1310–January 1311) draws on Sismondi, ch. xxvii. By 'free states' Tadeo means non-Guelph cities in Tuscany such as Pisa.

[b] Urban IV, pope from 1261–4, encouraged Charles of Anjou to expel Manfred from the Kingdom of Naples and Sicily.

new order of things established in Italy; and Castruccio owned his intention of joining the train of the emperor, and his hopes of being by his means re-instated in his paternal estates. The evening wore away during these discussions, and they retired early to rest. The next morning Castruccio and Pepi took leave of Tadeo, and departed together on the road to Milan.

For some time they rode along silently. Castruccio was overcome by a variety of feelings on again visiting Italian earth. Although, being winter, the landscape was stript bare, and its vineyards and corn-fields alike appeared waste, yet Castruccio thought that no country could vie with this in beauty, unless it were the plain of Lucca, such as he remembered it, the last time he beheld it, then a child, standing on the summit of his father's palace, – girded by hills, and the many-towered city set as its heart in the midst. He longed for a companion to whom he could pour out his full heart; for his overflowing feelings had for a time swept away the many lessons of Alberto / Scoto. He forgot ambition, and the dreams of princely magnificence which he had cherished for many months. He forgot Milan, the emperor, the Guelphs and Ghibelines, and seemed to bury himself, as a bee in the fragrant circle of a rose, in the softest and most humane emotions; till, half recovering, he blushed to find his eyes dim, and his cheek stained by the pure tears of his deep and unadulterated feeling. Turning hastily round, he was glad to observe his companion somewhat behind him, and he reined in his horse that he might approach. Pepi rode up with his measured pace; and it would have been a curious study to remark the contrasted countenances of the travellers: Castruccio, glorious in beauty; his deep eyes suffused with tears, and his lips breathing passion and delight, was more opposite than light to dark, to the hard lines of Pepi's face, which were unmoved as he glanced his small bright eyes from side to side, while no other sign shewed that he felt or thought; his mouth shut close, his person stiff and strait, his knees pressing his mule's flanks, and his ungainly horsemanship / easily betraying the secret, that his feats in arms must have been performed on foot.

At length tired of silence, and willing to speak although to so unsympathizing a being, Castruccio asked: "Messer Benedetto, you seemed last night to groan under the weight of your hatred of the Florentines. Now I have good reason to hate them, since by their means my party was exiled, and Lucca ranks among the Guelphic cities of Tuscany. But you are of Cremona, a town separated from Florence by many mountains and rivers; whence therefore arises your abhorrence of this republic?"[1]

Pepi fixed his little piercing eyes upon Castruccio, as if to read into his heart, and discover the secret motive of this question; but the frank and noble beauty of his fellow-traveller was such, that it even had an effect on this man's rigid soul; and, as he gazed on him, the hard lines of his face seemed to melt away, and he replied at first with gentleness; until, carried away by his subject, he poured forth the torrent of his hatred with a warmth, strange to observe in one, who in calmer moments appeared / more as a man made of wood or leather, than of flesh and blood:

"My good friend, you say true, I hate the Florentines; yet I may well find it difficult to tell the cause; for neither have they wounded me, nor stolen my purse, nor done me any other great injury of the like nature; but I am a Ghibeline, and therefore I hate them. And who would not hate a people, that despise the emperor, and all lawful authority; that have as it were dug up the buried form of Liberty, which died when Milan fell under the Visconti; who force their very nobles to become vulgar, and counts of the palace, and counts of the empire, to inscribe their names as weavers and furriers;[a] who go about the world enriching themselves by a wicked usury, and return and squander the money in purchasing licence for themselves? Is not their town filled with brawls, and are not their streets strewed with the ruins of the palaces of the noble Ghibelines? Do they not one day undo the acts of the day before, and ever introduce more and more licence? Now create every two months a set of magistrates, who take all power out of / the hands of the rich, and now a captain of the people, who protects and raises the vile multitude, till every lord must cap to his shoemaker? The example is what I abhor; are not Lucca, Bologna and Sienna free? and the contagion spreads over Lombardy. Oh! to every saint in heaven would I put up my prayer, to the devil himself would I give my thanks (but that so good a work could never have been done by his means), if, as was once proposed, the town of Florence had been razed, its streets sown with salt, and its inhabitants scattered like Jews and Sclavonians about the world. Curse thee, curse thee, Farinata, that through thy means this was not done!"[b]

"A disinterested love of the Imperial power causes these emotions? In truth you are the warmest Ghibeline I ever knew."

"My friend, the world, trust me, will never go well, until the rich rule, and the vulgar sink to their right station as slaves of the soil. You will readily allow that war is the scourge of the world; now in free towns war has a better harvest, than where proper and legitimate authority is established. During war neither our / persons, nor our lands, nor our houses are in safety; we may be wounded in brawls, our lands laid waste, our houses and all our possessions despoiled. Now my plan is easy, simple, and practicable: if you are at all read in history, you must know, that the fortunes of the nobles of antient Rome consisted in many hundreds of slaves, whom they brought up to various trades and arts, and then let them out to work, or permitted them to keep shops and make money,

---

[a] The *priori* of Florence, however aristocratic, were required to belong to one of ten major trade-guilds. Dante enrolled in the *speziali*, or dealers in oriental goods.

[b] The Florentine Farinata degli Uberti, who singly and successfully resisted the decision of his fellow Ghibellines to destroy Florence after the battle of Monte Aperto (Arbia) in 1260 (*Inferno*, X. 22–93).

which the masters received, paying them a small sum for their necessary support. Such is the order, which, if I were a prince, I would establish, and every town, such as Florence, where all is noise and talk, should be reduced to silence and peace; about two thousand rich men should possess all the rest of the inhabitants, who, like sheep, would flock to their folds, and receive their pittances with thankfulness and humility."

"But if, instead of sheep, they were to be wolves, and turn rebels to their masters? Methinks their numbers would panic-strike their two thousand drivers."

"Nay, then we would display our whips, / and drive the flock to market. Slaves rebel! we would starve them into decent submission."

Castruccio could not help being amused by the strange policy and earnest manners of the Italian lawgiver, and replied: "But, Messer Benedetto, I dispute your first proposition, and assert that there is as much war and bloodshed under kings, as in republics. You have fought in Flanders, and I who have also visited England, know this to be true; yet in France and England the people do not mingle with the quarrels of the nobles; so I think you must mend your constitution, and reduce your two thousand slave-drivers of Florence to a single one; yet I am afraid that, if there were only one in each town of Italy, or even if there were only two in the whole world, they would contrive to create war and bloodshed."

"That," replied Pepi, with a groan, "is the great fault that I find in the constitution of the world. If the rich would only know their own interests, we might chain the monster and again bury Liberty. But they are all fools; if the rich would agree, if the few / princes that there need exist in the world, would league in amity, instead of quarrelling, such a state as that of Florence would not subsist a year. But, if reason had a trump as loud as that which will awaken us at the last day, the clash of arms of these senseless people would drown it. Now, if instead of quarrelling, the Pope and Frederic Barbarossa had made a league,[a] all Italy would now be on its knees before this Henry of Luxembourgh. And one day this may be; mark my words; tyranny is a healthy tree, it strikes a deep root, and each year its branches grow larger and larger, and its shade spreads wider and wider. While liberty is a word, a breath, an air; it will dissipate, and Florence become as slavish as it is now rebellious; did not Rome fall?"

"I am little acquainted with the history of antient times," said Castruccio gaily; "but, since the world began, I can easily imagine that states have risen and fallen; we are blind with regard to futurity, and methinks it is foolish to

---

[a] Frederick I, nicknamed 'Barbarossa' (b. 1123, Emperor 1155–90), made five attempts to subjugate Italy, provoking the formation of the Lombard League (1167), which included Venice, Verona, Padua, Ferrara, Brescia, Cremona, Milan, Lodi and Bologna. He was in dispute with all the popes during his reign.

build for a longer term than a man's life. Kingdoms are as fragile as a porcelain vessel tossed by the ocean;[a] nay, so very weak are they, / that even the stars, those small, silly points of light, are said to rule them; and often, when they are at their highest glory, God sends his scourges, pest or earthquake, to sink them for ever; let us work for ourselves alone; we may be obscure or famous, grovelling as the worm, or lofty as the kingly eagle, according as our desires sink or mount."

Discoursing thus they arrived at Turin, and were again entertained by a merchant, the friend of Pepi. Here they found a numerous company, who all discoursed with warmth concerning the political state of Italy, and poured forth the most extravagant praises of the emperor Henry. He had passed two months in Piedmont, reconciling factions, hearing complaints, and destroying the vexatious tyrannies of its petty lords. Pepi, not considering this a fit occasion to poison these sanguine hopes by his prophecies, sat in silence with elevated brows and pressed lips, turning his sharp eyes from one speaker to another, as if by their means to drink in all the intelligence the politicians were able to afford.

The next morning Pepi and Castruccio parted; / whether this was caused by the necessities or the prudence of the former cannot be determined. He alleged that his business called him to Alessandria[b] in his way to Cremona, and the road of Castruccio lay directly for Milan. On parting Pepi made a speech, expressive of his gratitude, and the return he was willing to render for the benefit he had received; which was a welcome to his house and board, whenever his preserver should pass through Cremona. "Yet," he added, "if you have any other friends in that town, you may be will prefer them to me. I have, as I related yesterday, suffered many losses, and am endeavouring to repair them by an œconomical mode of life; I have no rich wines or soft couches, and can neither afford to burn wax lights, nor to eat delicate food. I have a good tower in my house; and, now that I am a knight, I shall have a good horse in my stable; and that is all I have to boast. You seem to have no taste for coarse fare or hard beds; and therefore my dwelling would in no manner be agreeable to you." /

Castruccio thanked him, and carelessly replied, that, as a soldier, he had been accustomed to hardship and privation, nor would the poverty of Pepi's dwelling render it less worthy in his eyes; and they coldly took leave of one

---

[a] Loosely referring to Aesop's fable of the vessels (one of which was of china in Godwin's 1805 retelling in *Fables Ancient and Modern*) swept away by the flood.

[b] In Piedmont, reputedly founded in 1168 as a stronghold against Barbarossa and named after their champion, Pope Alexander III, by the Lombard League; this 'free and republican city' was 'destined to immortalise the memory of their resistance and their zeal for the Church and liberty' (Sismondi, ch. x). On 7 March 1821, a Carbonarist insurrection broke out in Alessandria, forcing the king of Piedmont to abdicate in favour of the supposedly liberal Charles Albert of Savoy-Carignan (the rebellion was, however, crushed in the same year by Austrian troops).

another, Pepi trotting gravely on the road towards Alessandria, his head full of plans which he kept carefully locked up in his own brain, and his hard-lined face, faithful to his commands, giving no indications of what was passing in his soul.

Castruccio rode on gaily towards Milan; the cheerless wintry sky and the cold air could not tame his buoyant spirits or his hopes. He panted for action, for distinction, and for power; yet he no longer desired these things as a boy, unknowing of the road which led to them. During the interval which he had spent in England and France, he had studied human nature with the observant eye of genius; and, all careless as he appeared to be, he had learned how to please the multitude, how to flatter the foibles of the noble, and thus to gain the hearts of men and to rule them. Under Alberto Scoto / he had revolved with care the political state of Italy, such as that commander had pictured it to him; his plans of lordship and conquest were already formed; he had only the first step to make, to proceed afterwards with a swift pace to the goal for which he panted. /

CHAPTER VII.

Milan. – Court of the Emperor Henry. – Arrigo Guinigi. – Sack of Cremona. – Benedetto Pepi.

After several days travelling, he arrived at Milan; and his first care was to hasten to the palace of Matteo Visconti.[a] This chief was gone to the meeting of the senate, deliberating with the nobles of Milan on the sum of money which should be voted for the use of the emperor. Castruccio was therefore introduced to his son, Galeazzo, who was then in the hall of the palace, surrounded by all the young Ghibeline nobility of Milan. It was a scene of gaiety and splendour. The young nobles were preparing to attend on the emperor in a royal hunt. They were attired with the utmost magnificence, with full dresses of embroidered silk, cloth, or velvet, and cloaks of precious furs; some were accoutred in short gowns with trowsers tied in the same manner / as that of Pepi, but made of fine linen and embossed silks; their collars were ornamented with strings of pearl. Their hair, parted equally on the forehead, was curled and fell down as far as the shoulders; they wore different kinds of caps, some flat and adorned with plumes of feathers, others high and pointed, and the lower

---

[a] Matteo Visconti, reinstated by Henry VII, was made Imperial Vicar of Lombardy and ruled Milan until 1322, abdicating favour of his son Galeazzo I (1277–1328).

57

part twisted round with pearls fastened with a rich broach; most of them held a falcon on his fist, or caressed a favourite hound, or vaunted the prowess of a noble steed. There were many ladies in company who seemed to vie with their male companions in luxury of dress. Their gowns were made of the same costly stuffs, and ornamented with greater profusion of precious stones; their wide sleeves which fell almost to the ground were edged with pearls, while underneath, a small sleeve of the finest silk fitted tight to the arm; the borders of their dresses were richly embroidered with pearls or golden beads; they wore their veils adorned with the same richness, and small capuchins of oriental fur bordered with fringes of gold and pearls; and their girdles were studded with the most splendid stones.[a] /

Castruccio paused, half dazzled by the scene. In the ruder courts of London or Paris he had never seen so much splendour and luxury: he cast an involuntary glance on his own habiliments, which although rich were soiled by travelling, and in their best days could not have vied with the meanest dress worn by these nobles. He quickly however recovered his self-possession; and his name, whose sound had passed the Alps, and been repeated with enthusiasm by many of the followers of the emperor who had served with him in the Low Countries, caused this brilliant assembly to receive him with flattering distinction. They crowded round him, and courteously invited him to partake of their amusements; while his handsome person won the smiles of the ladies who were present. Galeazzo Visconti received him with that kindness and cordiality which was then in fashion among the Italians; and he, as the most courteous cavalier of the country, was well versed in all the politeness of the age. Castruccio was provided with a beautiful horse, and a mantle of rich fur befitting the cold season, and made one of the gay and splendid / band as they rode towards the palace of the emperor; here they were joined by the sovereign himself, the empress, and the noble Germans of his retinue. Riding through the streets of Milan, they quitted the city at the eastern gate, and dividing into various parties; spread themselves abroad in search of game. The Germans followed the dogs through the open country, chasing down foxes and hares; while the Italians, who were dressed for gala, and would not risk their fine silks among the brambles and impediments of the fields, were content with unmuffling their falcons when they saw game aloft, and making bets on the superior speed of their several birds.

During the first part of the ride Galeazzo observed Castruccio, who appeared to be too much wrapped up in his own thoughts to attend to the discourse of the gay throng around him. He loitered behind, that he might indulge in his reveries; and Galeazzo, who had separated himself from the rest, now rode up to him; and they entered into a conversation together, which at

---

[a] Descriptions of medieval dress and furnishings here and elsewhere derive extensively from Muratori I, diss. 25; noted in Ab. Dep. e. 274, pp. 57–8, 71–5.

length turned into a discussion of the plans and wishes of Castruccio. / They were both men of caution of prudence; yet, being young, they were susceptible of impressions to which men lose their sensibility as they advance in years. They were mutually pleased with each other; and a single glance, a single word, sufficed to make each understand the other, and to unite them in the bonds of friendship.

Castruccio asked what it was believed that the designs of the emperor were; and Galeazzo replied: "You would hardly guess what anxious hearts, throbbing with distrust and fear, are concealed under the apparent gaiety of these hunters. We Milanese are full of dissentions and ambition; and I, as a chief among them, have my head well loaded with care and doubt, while I follow this joyous train with my falcon on my fist. In a few days the game will be up; and we shall see what power the Visconti or the Della Torre will have over Lombardy. At present wait. The emperor is expecting supplies of money, and we are voting them for him with apparent zeal: you, as a politician, must well know that money is the great mover of all change in a state. I prophesy change; / but you as a stranger, must stand aloof, and be guided by circumstances. In the mean time make friends; attach yourself to the emperor and to the lords of Lombardy, many of whom are extremely powerful; and rest assured, that whether he be successful or not, he will not quit Italy without endeavouring to change the politics of the Tuscan republics. Now let us join our friends; tomorrow I will talk further with you; and, if we have recourse to arms, I need not say how proud I should be in having my party distinguished by the acquisition of Castruccio dei Antelminelli."

They then mingled with the rest of the company; and Galeazzo introduced his new friend to the Ghibeline lords of Lombardy. He here saw for the first time the magnificent Cane della Scala, lord of Verona, and the generous Guido della Polenta, lord of Ravenna, and father of the unhappy Francesca of Rimini.[a] These nobles had assembled at Milan, to be present at the coronation of the emperor, which had taken place a few weeks before;[b] all wore the appearance of gaiety and good humour; the empress headed the band, accompanied by / a beautiful youth who bore a bow in his hand; and Cane della Scala was beside her, descanting on the merits of his falcon. Castruccio was struck by the countenance of the youth who rode near the empress. He was dressed with a profusion of magnificence; at his back he wore a gilt quiver studded with gems, and a scarf embroidered with pearls was thrown over one shoulder, and tied under the other arm; in every way he was accoutred as might become the favourite page of an empress. Yet Castruccio thought that he remembered those light blue eyes; and his sweet yet serious smile filled his own with tears of tender recollection. He eagerly asked Galeazzo who and what he was: his

---

[a] The Ghibelline Cane (Can') Grande della Scala (1291–1329) and Guido della Polenta (d. 1323), were both protectors of Dante in exile.
[b] Referring to his Milan coronation, which established him as overlord of Lombardy.

friend replied; "He is the squire of Can' Grande, and he is called Arrigo; I do not know what other name he bears; the empress wishes to attach him to her suite; but the youth would prefer bearing arms under his munificent patron, to the situation of the effeminate page of a queen's anti-chamber."

"That cannot surprize me," said Castruccio; "for his infancy was spent in the labour of the fields, and in listening to the lessons of his / godlike father; he must therefore be ill prepared to enter into the intrigues and follies of a court. If he have not forgotten his childish affection for me, I shall win him from them both; and, if indeed his father be dead, it shall be my pride and boast to be the protector of his Arrigo."

As they re-entered the gates of the town, the trains of the emperor and empress joined; and, Arrigo falling back among the nobles, Castruccio rode up to him. For some time he gazed on him, and heard the gentle tones of his youthful voice; he dared not speak; his heart was full; and to his eyes dimmed by emotion, he fancied that the revered form of Guinigi stood beside his son, smiled on Castruccio, and pointed to the boy. At length, recovering himself, he came abreast with the horse of Arrigo, and whispered, "Does the son of Guinigi forget me? does he forget the farm among the Euganean hills?"

Arrigo started; his countenance became radiant with joy; and he exclaimed, "My own Castruccio!" /

They rode away from the company, and entered the town by more lonely streets. Castruccio saw by the looks of his young friend, that his worst fears were true, and that Guinigi was dead; and Arrigo easily read in Castruccio's face that he was thinking of his father. At length he said: "My brother, if so you will permit me to call you, a year has now passed since I was left an orphan; ten months ago I quitted my happy life among the hills, to dwell with a patron, who is indeed munificent and kind to me; but who is not as my father. It appears to me a vision that such a being ever existed; he was so great, so angelically wise and good; and I now float down the stream with the rest, an esquire, an attendant; I pass my life without enjoyment, and look forward to the future without pleasure; but if, my brother, you would grant me one request, a brighter sun would shine upon me."

"Dearest Arrigo, my dear, dear, brother, I read in your earnest looks all that you would say; be assured we shall never part again! / We will sally forth soldiers of fortune; and the same star shall ascend and descend for both."

"Enough, leave the rest to me; be it my task to contrive my departure from Can' della Scala; inform me of your motions, and fear not but that I shall be at your side."

That same evening a magnificent feast was given at the palace of the emperor; and Castruccio was introduced to this prince by Galeazzo. The lords of Lombardy regarded him with a favourable eye; for they knew that he could not hurt their interests north of the Apennines, and they hoped that by his means the Ghibeline faction might revive and triumph in Tuscany.

Castruccio spent almost the whole evening in conversation with Arrigo. For the youth would not absent himself from him, but recalled with earnest affection all the circumstances of their former intercourse; and related with tears the death of Guinigi; a death, calm as his most innocent life. One afternoon, during the heats of summer, he sat under a cypress with his son, and entered into an / anxious detail of what would be the prospects and probable fate of the young Arrigo, when he, his father and protector, should be no more. The boy, struck with a melancholy foreboding, intreated him not to dwell on a period, which was far distant, and which, when it approached, would bring to him nothing but despair. Guinigi however told him that he would not be overruled in this, and with earnest affection talked for hours on the subject with a wisdom and goodness that appeared more than human. "Alas," said Arrigo, "even as he spoke, I thought I saw his eyes beam with a heavenly light, and the torrent of impressive words that he poured forth, were uttered with a voice deep and tender, filling the air as it were with a harmony sweeter than any earthly music. I listened, till I became almost as a statue with attention; and as he either exhorted to virtue, or described the evils of my country, or marked forth the glorious or peaceful path that I might pursue, I felt my countenance change, as I have seen a cloud vary as it passes before the moon, now, as it advances, beaming in a silver light, and then / again fading into darkness. At length he dismissed me, saying that he wished to sleep, and I saw him stretch himself under the cypress, gazing on the sky, whose dazzling light was softened by the dark foliage through which it passed; and he slept never to wake again.

"Oh! what I then suffered, when our friends crowded round, and the mourning women came,[a] and the mummery of the funeral went on! But all that is passed; and now I should again feel the elasticity of youth, but that I was, until you returned, friendless in the world."

They talked thus, while the company around them were amusing themselves with dances and song; the feast broke up late; and it broke up only to be renewed with greater zeal the following and the following day. Yet, while all appeared so calm, the storm which the politicians prognosticated, broke out, and the quiet of these festive meetings was disturbed by the revolt of Milan against the Germans. And now Castruccio was witness for the first time to the popular commotions of his country: armed knights galloped through the streets crying, "*Libertà!* Death to the Germans!" / And a multitude of the people, who were enraged at the new taxes imposed upon them, joined in the cry. But the revolt thus quickly excited, was as quickly appeased. The Visconti after some hesitation ranged themselves under the emperor; and Della Torre and his partizans were obliged to fly; their houses were razed, their goods confiscated, and themselves declared traitors.

---

[a] In P. B. Shelley's 'Ginevra' (published 1824, composed probably mid-1821), l. 105, inspired by Lastri, I, pp. 119–22, the phrase 'the mourning women came' also occurs.

But the effects of the Milanese revolt were not so easily removed. The various Guelph towns of Lombardy, Crema, Cremona, Brescia, Lodi, and Como, set up the standard of revolt against the emperor; and, spring having now advanced, Henry began his campaign with the attempt to reduce these towns. Castruccio had received from him permission to raise a troop of volunteers, to serve under his command in the Imperial army, and his fame collected a brave band, whose discipline and valour were the admiration of the other generals.

Crema and Lodi submitted to the emperor on his advance, and reaped from their unseasonable resistance an increase of those vexations / which had caused their revolt. Henry marched against Cremona, which at first made shew of resistance; but, when the Guelphs, hopeless of success, escaped from the town, the Ghibelines surrendered to the emperor; who, unmollified by their submission, punished his own innocent partizans, sending them to cruel prisons, razing the walls and fortifications of the town, and delivering over the property and persons of the unprotected citizens into the hands of the brutal Germans who composed the greater part of his army.[a]

Castruccio entered Cremona at the head of his little troop, and beheld with dismay the cruel effects of the conquest of the emperor over this city. Most of the German soldiers were busy in destroying the fortifications, or in compelling the peasants and citizens to raze the walls of their town. Other parties were ranging about the streets, entering the palaces, whose rich furniture they destroyed, by feasting, and tearing down from the walls all that had the appearance of gold or silver. The cellars were broken open; and, after inebriating themselves with the choice wines of Italy, / the unruly, but armed bands were in a better mood for oppressing the defenceless people. Some of these poor wretches fled to the open country; others locked themselves up in their houses, and, throwing what they possessed from the windows, strove to save their persons from the brutality of their conquerors. Many of the noble females took refuge in the meanest cottages, and disguised themselves in poor clothing, till, frightened by the eager glances, or brutal address of the soldiers, they escaped to the country, and remained exposed to hunger and cold among the woods that surrounded the town. Others, with their hair dishevelled, their dresses in disorder, careless of the eyes which gazed on them, followed their husbands and fathers to their frightful prisons, some in mute despair, many wringing their hands, and crying aloud for mercy. As night came on, the soldiery, tired of rapine, went to rest in the beds from which the proprietors were remorselessly banished: silence prevailed; a dreadful silence, broken sometimes by the shriek of an injured female, or the brutal shouts of some of the men, who passed the / night in going from palace to palace, calling up the inhabitants, demanding food and wine, and on the slightest shew of resistance

---

[a] For the revolt of Milan and the sack of Cremona by Henry VII (1311) Mary Shelley drew on Sismondi, ch. xxvii.

hurrying their victims to prison, or binding them in their own houses with every aggravation of insult.

Castruccio divided his little band, and sent his men to the protection of several of the palaces, while he and Arrigo rode all night about the town; and, having the watchword of the emperor, they succeeded in rescuing some poor wretches from the brutality of the insolent soldiers. Several days followed, bringing with them a repetition of the same scenes; and the hardest heart might have been struck with compassion, to see the misery painted on the faces of many, whose former lives had been a continual dream of pleasure; young mothers weeping over their unfortunate offspring, whose fathers lay rotting or starving in prison; children crying for bread, sitting on the steps of their paternal palaces, within which the military rioted in plenty; childless parents, mourning their murdered babes; orphans, helpless, dying, whose parents could no longer soothe or relieve them. Castruccio, though a soldier, / wept; but Arrigo, who had never before witnessed the miseries of war, became almost frenzied with the excess of his compassion and indignation; he poured forth curses loud and bitter, while his eyes streamed tears, and his voice, broken and sharp, was insufficient to convey his passionate abhorrence. Castruccio was at length obliged to use violence to draw him from this scene of misery; and, after soothing him by every argument he could use, and by the most powerful of all, that Henry would be soon obliged to withdraw his soldiers from Cremona to serve him at the siege of Brescia, he dispatched the youth with a letter to Galeazzo Visconti.

Returning to the town, Castruccio saw a figure pass along at the end of the street, which reminded him of one whom he had almost forgotten – Benedetto Pepi. "Alas! poor fellow," said Castruccio to himself, "you will find the pillage of the Germans a tremendous evil. Well; as I restored your life once, I will now try, if I am not too late, to save the remnant of your property."

He enquired of a passenger for the house of / Benedetto Pepi. "If you mean Benedetto the Rich, if any can now be called rich in this miserable city," replied the man, "I will conduct you to his house."

"My Pepi ought rather, I think, to be called the poor; lead me however to Benedetto the Rich; and if he be a tall, gaunt figure with a wrinkled, leathern face, he is the man for whom I enquire."

Castruccio was conducted to a palace in the highest and most commanding part of the town, built of large blocks of stone, and apparently firm and solid enough to bear a siege. The windows were few, small, grated and sunk deep in the wall; it had a high tower, whose port-holes shewed that it was of uncommon strength and thickness; a parapet built with turrets surrounded it at the top, and in every respect the mansion resembled more a castle, than a palace. The entrance was dark; and, by the number of grooves, it appeared as if there had been many doors; but they were all removed, and the entrance free. Castruccio advanced: there were two large halls on the ground-floor, on each

63

side of the entrance-court; / both were filled with German soldiers; they were high, dark, bare rooms, more like the apartments of a prison than a palace. In one of them a number of beds were laid on the paved floor; in the other there was a large fire in the middle, at which various persons were employed in the offices of cookery, and near this, a table was spread out with immense quantities of food, haunches of boiled beef, and black bread; two boys stood at either end of the table, each holding a large flaring torch; and the soldiers with riotous exclamations were choosing their seats on the benches that were placed around. Castruccio paused, unable to discern whether Pepi were among this strange company. At length he observed him standing in one corner filling large jugs from a barrel of wine: he accosted him with a voice of condolence; and Pepi looked up with his little bright eyes, and a face rather expressive of joy than sorrow. After he had recognized his guest, he left his wine barrel, and invited him into another room, for they could hardly distinguish each other's voices amidst the shouts and tumult of the rude feasters. / They ascended the steep narrow stairs; and, Castruccio complaining of want of light, Pepi said: "Let us go to the top of my tower; the sun has been set about ten minutes, and, although dark every where else, it will be light there. If you will wait a short time I will get the key."

Pepi descended the stairs; and from a small port-hole Castruccio saw him cross the court, and then in a few minutes return with cautious and observant steps. When he came near Castruccio, he said: "Those German ruffians are now eating and drinking, and will not mark us; yet let us tread lightly, for I have admitted none of them to my tower, nor is it my intention to do so. It is a place of strength; and the little I have in the world is preserved here, which little in spite of the emperor and his devils I will preserve."

Although the tower had appeared large without, yet its walls were so thick that there was only room left within for a small circular staircase; at the top of this Pepi undrew the bolts, pushed up a trap-door, and they ascended to the platform on the outside. The sky was / darkening; but the west was tinged with a deep orange colour, and the wide and dusky plain of Lombardy lay far extended all around: immediately below was the town of Cremona, which to them appeared as silent and peaceful as if the inhabitants were in the enjoyment of perfect security. They continued some mintues gazing silently, Castruccio on the wide extent of scenery before him, Pepi on the thick walls of his tower. At length the former said; "An evil star pursues you, Messer Benedetto, and I am afraid that you were born in the descent of some evil constellation."

"Doubtless," replied Pepi: yet there was an indescribable expression in his countenance and manner, that startled his companion; his eyes sparkled, and the lines of his face, as plainly as such things could speak, spoke joy and exultation. His voice however was drawn out into accents of grief, and he ended his reply by a groan.

"Your palace is wasted by these ruffians."

"Nay, there is nothing to waste; the walls are too thick to be hurt, and I removed every thing else before they came." /

"They consume your food."

"I have none to consume. I am a poor, lone man, and had no food in the house for them. They bring their rapine here; I send my squire for wood, wherever he can collect it; I make a fire, and they dress their food; and that is all that they get by me."

"Have you lost no friend or relation in the war?"

"There is no one whom I love; I have met with undutifulness and ingratitude, but no kindness or friendship; so I should not have mourned, if my relations had fallen; but they are all safe."

"Then it would appear, that you have lost nothing by the havock of these Germans, and that you are still Benedetto the Rich."

Pepi had answered the previous questions of Castruccio with vivacity, and an expression of triumph and vanity, which he in vain strove to conceal; his brows were elevated, a smile lurked in the corners of his strait lips, and he even rubbed his hands. But, when Castruccio spoke these last words, his face fell, his mouth was drawn down, his arms sunk close / to his sides, and, glancing at his mean clothing, he replied: "I am always poor, always unfortunate; and, Messer Castruccio, you do me great injustice and injury by supposing that I have any wealth. I have a well built palace, and a strong tower; but I can neither eat the stones, nor clothe myself with the plaster; and, God knows, my possessions are now reduced to fifty small acres; how therefore can I be rich?"

"At least, if you are poor," replied Castruccio, "your unfortunate townsmen share your misfortunes. Their habitations are pillaged; those that escape the ravage of the emperor, are driven out, starving and miserable, from the only dwellings, be they palaces or cottages, which they possess."

The countenance of Pepi again lighted up, his eyes sparkled, and he said; "Aye, aye, many are fallen; but not so low – not so low: they have still lands, they are not quite destitute, and the dead have heirs——"

"Yes, indeed, heirs to famine and indignity; unhappy orphans! far more miserable than if they had died with those who gave them birth." /

"Nay, I pity them from my soul; but I also have suffered losses. The first party of Germans that broke into the town, seized upon my horse, and my squire's gelding: I must buy others when our enemies are gone, to keep up the honour of my knighthood. But, enough of this. You, Messer Castruccio, have a troop of Italians, horsemen, I believe, under your command: what do you intend to do with them? Do you stay in Lombardy, or follow the emperor south?"

"Events are now my masters; soon I hope to rule them, but at present I shall be guided by accident, and cannot therefore answer your question."

Pepi paused a few moments, and at length said, half to himself; "No; this is not the time; events are as yet unripe; this siege has done much, but I must still delay;—— well, Messer Castruccio, at present I will not reveal some circumstances, which, when we began this conversation, I had thought to confide to your discretion. Sometime, perhaps when you least expect it, we shall meet again; and if Benedetto of Cremona be not exactly what he seems, / keep the secret until then, and I shall rest your obliged servant. Now, farewel. You came to offer your services to save my palace; I am a prudent man, and ordered my affairs so, that it ran no risk; yet I am indebted to you for this, and for your other generous act in my behalf; a time may come when we shall know one another better. Again farewel."

This speech was delivered with a grave and mysterious mien, and a face that signified careful thought and important expectations. When he had ended, Pepi opened the trap-door, and he and Castruccio descended slowly down the now benighted staircase into the court of the palace: here they again interchanged salutations, and parted. Pepi joined his boisterous guests, and Castruccio rode towards the camp of the emperor. He mused as he went upon what the words of his strange acquaintance might portend; his curiosity was for a time excited by them; but change of place and the bustle of action made him soon forget the existence of Benedetto the Rich, of Cremona. /

CHAPTER VIII.

Death of the Emperor. – Uguccione, tyrant of Pisa, restores Castruccio at Lucca. – Euthanasia.

Quitting Cremona, Henry engaged himself in the siege of Brescia, which made a gallant resistance, and yielded only on honourable conditions, in the month of September. Castruccio served under the emperor during this siege;[a] but his nature was shocked by the want of faith and cruelty of this monarch, who punished his enemies by the most frightful tortures, and treated his friends as if they had been his enemies. Castruccio therefore resolved to separate himself from the Imperial army; and, when Henry quitted Lombardy for Genoa, he remained with his friend Galeazzo Visconti.

The petty wars of Lombardy could only interest those engaged in them; and all eyes were / turned towards the emperor during his journey to Genoa, his unsuccessful negotiations with Florence, his voyage to Pisa, his journey to

---

[a] Castruccio's will, reproduced in Tegrimi, is Mary Shelley's source for his participation, about which otherwise virtually nothing is known, in this campaign. Henry VII went to Genoa in October 1311.

Rome; where, the Vatican being in the hands of the contrary party, he was crowned in the Lateran.[a] And then, his army diminished by sickness, and himself chagrined by the slow progress of his arms, he returned to Tuscany, made an unsuccessful attack upon Florence, and retired to the neighbourhood of Sienna, where he died on the eighteenth of August 1313; leaving Italy nearly in the same situation with regard to the preponderance of the Guelph party, but more heated and violent in their factious sentiments, as when he entered it two years before.

During this long contest Florence was the head and heart of the resistance made against the emperor. Their detestation of the Imperial power, and their fears of the restoration of their banished Ghibelines, excited them to exert their utmost faculties, in gaining allies, and in the defence of their own town. The death of Henry was to them a bloodless victory; and they hoped that a speedy change in / the politics of Italy would establish the universal ascendancy of the Guelphic party.

Pisa had always been constant to the Ghibelines, and friendly to the emperor; by his death they found themselves thrown almost without defence into the hands of the Florentines, their enemies; and they therefore gladly acceded to the moderate terms offered to them by the king of Naples and his ally, Florence, for the establishment of peace in Tuscany.[b] If this treaty had been fulfilled, the hopes of the Ghibelines would have been crushed for ever, nor would Castruccio ever have returned to his country; the scenes of blood and misery which followed would have been spared; and Florence, raising its benign influence over the other Tuscan states, would have been the peace-maker of Italy. Events took a different turn. To understand this it is necessary to look back.

Immediately on the death of Henry, the Pisans, fearful of a sudden incursion of the Florentines, for which they might be unprepared, had engaged in their service a *condottiere*,[c] Uguccione della Faggiuola, who with his / troop of a thousand Germans, took on him the guard of their city. War was the trade of Uguccione; he therefore looked with dismay on the projected peace, and resolved to disturb it. The populace of the Italian towns, ranged under party names, and ever obedient to the watchword and signals of their party, were easily moved to fall on the contrary faction. The Pisan people were Ghibelines; and, while the more moderate among them had advanced far in the negociating of a peace, Uguccione caused live eagles, the ensigns of the Ghibelines, to be carried through the streets: and the cry of, "Treason from the Guelphs!" was

---

[a] i.e the church of St John Lateran. Rome was then in the hands of the papal-backed troops of Robert, King of Naples, who was acknowledged as lord by several cities of northern Italy, including Florence and Lucca. This second coronation established Henry as the Holy Roman Emperor.

[b] Robert, King of Naples stepped into the power vacuum following the death of Henry VII. The main terms offered to the Pisans were that they refuse aid to Robert's enemies and furnish money and ships for three months for his Sicilian campaign.

[c] Leader of a troop of mercenaries. Among the peace terms was the requirement that Uguccione disband his army (Sismondi, ch. xxvii).

the rallying word of fury to the populace. The magistrates in vain endeavoured to assert their authority; their partizans were dispersed, their captains taken prisoners and put to death, and Uguccione declared general of the war against the Florentines. This active chieftain lost no time in his operations; he marched against the Lucchese, the allies of Florence, ravaged their country, brought them to terms, and made peace with them on condition of their recalling their Ghibeline exiles. /

The three years which these events occupied were spent by Castruccio in Lombardy. He made each year a campaign under one or another of the Ghibeline lords of that territory, and passed the winter at Milan. He formed a sincere and lasting friendship with Galeazzo Visconti: but, although this amity contributed to his advancement, his character suffered by the congeniality of sentiment which he acquired with this chief. As they rode, hunted, or fought together, often employed in mutual good-offices one for the other, their affection became stronger; and it was as disinterested and generous as it was firm. Galeazzo sincerely loved Castruccio, and opened to him the dearest secrets of his heart; but these secrets were such as to initiate the latter in the artful policy and unprincipled motives of the Milanese lord, and to make him regard treachery and cruelty as venial faults. He had no saving passion, which by its purity and exalted nature, although it permitted him to forgive, would make him avoid the faults of Galeazzo. Ambition was the ruling feeling of his soul; an ambition for power, conquest and renown, and / not for virtue, and that fame, which as the phœnix, cannot live at the same period as its parent, but springs from his ashes with the strong pinions of immortal being.

It was this aspiring disposition which strongly recommended him to Galeazzo. For it was not with him the wild desire for what he had neither qualities nor capacity to obtain; it was combined with transcendant talents, an energy of action and a clearness of judgement, which greatly surpassed that of his companions. Castruccio was fond of power; yet he was neither arrogant nor tyrannical; words of kindness and winning smiles he bestowed at will on all around. He appeared to fit himself for each scene in which he was to take a part; in the camp he was energetic, valorous, and swift of action; in council he was as prudent and cautious as a grey-haired minister of state: at balls, or during a hunting party, he recommended himself by grace, agility, wit, and a courtesy whose sweetness was untarnished by vanity or presumption. His beauty took a more manly cast; and somewhat of pride, and more of self-confidence, and much of sensibility, / were seen in his upturned lip; his eyes, dark as a raven's wing, were full of fire and imagination; his open forehead was shaded by the hyacinthine[a] curls of his chesnut-coloured hair. His face expressed

---

[a] A classicism, applied in *Paradise Lost*, IV. 301 and Alexander Pope's translation of the *Odyssey*, VI. 274 to the hair of Adam and Odysseus, respectively; variously interpreted as 'blue-black' or 'gleaming'. Castruccio's hair, rich brown at this point, is later described as raven-black.

extreme frankness, a frankness that did not exist in his mind; for his practices among the wily chiefs of Lombardy had robbed him of all ingenuousness of soul, although the traces of that which he once possessed had not faded from his countenance. Amidst all the luxury of Lombardy he was abstemious, nor spent in personal magnificence the money which he rather applied to the equipment of his troop. At length the patient improvement which he had bestowed upon his powers, and his perseverance in preparing for advancement, obtained their due reward; and he among the other Lucchese exiles returned to his native city.

But Castruccio was ill content to return as it were by the endurance of the opposite party; on the contrary he wished to raise his faction to that supremacy which would invest him with dominion as its chief. He therefore carried on a treaty with Uguccione's army, requiring / their assistance for the overthrow of the Guelphs of Lucca, and for placing him in authority over his native town; while the tyrant of Pisa should in return gain a faithful ally, and one more step should be taken towards the final establishment of the Ghibeline ascendancy.

After arranging this scheme, Castruccio and his companions passed the defile of the Serchio;[a] and, advancing towards Lucca, assumed a warlike appearance, and endeavoured to force the gate of San Frediano; the Guelphs opposed him, and a battle ensued. In the mean time Uguccione arrived in another direction, and, not finding free entrance at any of the gates, began to batter the wall. The Guelphs, defeated by the Ghibelines, were in no condition to resist; the Ghibelines, headed by Castruccio, considered Uguccione as their ally, and thought not of impeding his operations; indeed they were fully employed in resisting their adversaries, who, though worsted, would not yield. The breach was effected, Uguccione entered triumphantly, and, treating Lucca as a conquered town, delivered it over to be sacked / by his troops; while he himself made a rich booty of the treasure of the Pope which had been preserved in the church of San Frediano;[b] Lucca having been selected as the safest deposit for such a treasure.

Uguccione thought no more of his promises to Castruccio, and both parties in Lucca were oppressed alike, by one who believed that the best security for a governor was the cutting off the tallest flowers in the field. The prompt exertions of Castruccio alone saved his native city from utter ruin. He collected

---

[a] The treaty (June 1314) was made at Ripafratta (spelled 'Ripafrata' in *Valperga*, *CC Journals* and Villani), the small frontier town on the Pisa-Lucca border near where the Serchio flows through a chasm. Mary Shelley and Claire Clairmont returned through Ripafratta from their August 1820 visit to Lucca (*CC Journals*, p. 169); the defile and Ripafratta are mentioned in P. B. Shelley's 'The Boat on the Serchio' (1824), which he drafted into the second of Mary Shelley's research notebooks, probably during early July 1821.

[b] Visited by Mary Shelley and Claire Clairmont (*CC Journals*, p. 169); Villani (IX, cap. 59) and Sismondi (ch. xxviii) attribute this theft to Uguccioni and the Pisans; other chroniclers, apparently not known to Mary Shelley, implicate Castruccio (Green, pp. 55–6).

his partizans, formed them into a troop, and ranging them under the banners of Uguccione, accepted a command in this chief's army; thus quieting the invaders' fears of a resistance which would have been rash and vain, but having at the same time ready at Castruccio's smallest signal a well armed and disciplined troop, nominally in the service of the tyrant, but really devoted by affection and military oaths to the cause of their immediate commander. Nor did he again betray the confidence of his fellow citizens; but, entering into Uguccione's counsels, and assuming a tone of power which this / chieftain could not resist, Castruccio at the same time opposed a boundary to his arrogance and cruelty.

But, although his first imprudence in inviting Uguccione to the possession of Lucca was pardoned by his countrymen, in consideration of the reparation that he earnestly desired to make, it was looked upon with far different eyes by states who, hating the Pisan Tyrant, and too distant to be acquainted with all the palliating circumstances, regarded Castruccio as a traitor. The news of the entrance of the Ghibeline exiles into Lucca, and the capture of that town by Uguccione, quickly reached his Florentine adversaries, and excited grief and rage in all the hearers. The name of Castruccio as the betrayer of his country was repeated with indignation and hatred.

There was one gentle heart in Florence which felt deep pain, when it heard the name of Antelminelli coupled with an opprobrious epithet. Euthanasia dei Adimari had not forgotten her vow made many years before; she had treasured in her memory the recollection of her young playfellow, and often, when travellers / from Lombardy mentioned the name of Castruccio, her fair cheek was suffused by the eloquent blood.[a]

Euthanasia had long been an orphan; her father had died, and by his death was cut the dearest tie she had to earth. While he lived, she had confined herself almost entirely to his room, and serving as eyes to his blinded sense, she was faithful to his wants as his own orbs had been before their light was quenched. After his death she mingled more with the distinguished youth of Florence, and joined in that society, which, if we may judge from the indications that Dante gives in his prose works,[b] and from the tender and exquisite poetry of Petrarch, was as refined, delicate and cultivated, as the best society amidst the boasted politeness of the present day. Yet among the youth of Florence Euthanasia was as a lily, that overlooks the less illustrious yet beautiful flowers of a garden. Her beauty, her accomplishments, and the gift of flowing yet mild eloquence that she possessed, the glowing brilliancy of her ardent yet

---

[a] Palacio (pp. 486–7) discusses the frequent use of this conceit, ultimately deriving from John Donne's *Second Anniversarie*, in Godwin, P. B. Shelley and Leigh Hunt; see, too, Mary Shelley to Edward Trelawny, 12 October 1835 (*MWSL*, II, p. 256).

[b] The prose sections of the *Convito* and especially of the *Vita Nuova*, the story of his passion for Beatrice Portinari.

tempered imagination, made her the leader of the little band to which / she belonged. It is said, that as Dante sighed for Beatrice, so several of the distinguished youths of Florence fed on the graceful motions and sweet words of this celestial girl, who, walking among them, passionless, yet full of enthusiasm, seemed as a link to bind their earthly thoughts to heaven. Often with her mother's permission Euthanasia retired for months to the castle of Valperga; and alone among the wild Apennines she studied and worshipped nature, while the bright sun warmed the vallies, and threw its beams over the mountains, or when the silver boat of the moon, which displayed in the clear air its heavy lading, sunk swiftly in the west, and numberless stars witnessed her departure. Then again, quitting the eternal, ever-succeeding pages of nature's volume, she pored over the works she had before read with her father, or the later written poetry of Dante, and incorporated the thoughts of the sublimest geniuses with her own, while the creative fire in her heart and brain formed new combinations to delight and occupy her.

Her young friends hailed with heartfelt joy / her return from her seclusion; she joined in all their amusements; who could sing the *canzones*[a] of those times, or relate a pathetic tale, like Euthanasia? Besides she was so prudent, so wise, and so kind, that her assistance was perpetually claimed and afforded in every little misfortune or difficulty of her friends.

But the age of thoughtlessness and fearless enjoyment passed away, and Euthanasia advanced to womanhood. At this period a succession of events deprived her of her mother and her two brothers, so that she remained sole heiress of the possessions of her family. Independent and powerful, she was as a queen in Valperga and the surrounding villages; at Florence she was considered one of its first citizens; and, if power, wealth and respect could have satisfied her, she must have been happy. She had wept bitterly the death of her relations; she grieved for the loss of her brothers, and felt only pain at being advanced to their place. Yet her mind acquired new dignity, and the virtues of her heart new fervour, from the entire independence of her situation, and the opportunities she possessed of / doing good. There was none to gainsay her actions, except the rigid censorship of her own reason, and the opinion of her fellow-citizens, to whose love and esteem she aspired. Most of her time was now spent among her dependents at Valperga; the villages under her jurisdiction became prosperous; and the peasantry were proud that their countess preferred her residence among them to the gaieties of Florence. In the winter she visited her friends of that town; and many a noble, who hoped to rival Dante Alighieri or Guido Cavalcanti,[b] sang of the miraculous change of seasons that had been operated on his city; – that their summers were dreary, bare, and

---

[a] Lyrics resembling the ode.
[b] Guido Cavalcanti (1250–1300), poet and philosopher, Dante's dearest friend, who died of fever contracted during exile in the Maremma; he figures in Boccaccio's *Decameron* (VI. ix).

deserted, while the soul of loveliness dwelt among them during the formerly dull months of winter.

It is said that during this period she had never loved; she admired the illustrious and energetic spirits of Florence, and she bestowed her affections on several whose virtue and talents claimed by right that meed; but she had never loved. It appears wonderful, that one so sensitive of heart and imagination should have attained her twenty-second year without having experienced / the tyranny of that passion; but, if it be true, how tremendous must be the force of that power, which could finally break down the barriers piled by reason and accustomed coldness, and deluge her soul with the sweet waters of earthly love?

She had just entered her twenty-second year, when Castruccio in 1314 returned to Lucca; when under his auspices, the greatest enemy of Florence became master of the neighbour city; when war was declared between the two states, and Castruccio was in arms against the Florentines. The summer was now far advanced; and she hastened to her solitude at Valperga. She was hurt at heart; one of her dearest dreams, the excellence of Castruccio, was over-thrown; and she wished for a while to shut out from her thoughts all memory of the world, which appeared to bring tumult and discord to trouble her tranquillity. She was unable to do this: she was too well known, and too much loved, not to be sought by those with whom she was acquainted; and she was startled to hear from all sides eulogiums of the talents and soldiership of Castruccio, those of the Ghibelines / mingled with hope, those of the Guelphs with fear.

Is there not a principle in the human mind that foresees the change about to occur to it? Is there not a feeling which would warn the soul of peril, were it not at the same time a sure prophecy that that peril is not to be avoided? So felt Euthanasia: and during her evening meditations she often enquired from her own heart, why the name of Castruccio made her cheeks glow; and why praise or dispraise of him seemed to electrify her frame: why a nameless inquietude pervaded her thoughts, before so calm: why, tenderly as she dwelt on the recollection of her infant playmate, she dreaded so much now to see him? And then, strange to say, being thus agitated and fearful, she saw him; and a calm more still than the serene depths of a windless heaven, redescended on her soul, and wrapt it in security and joy.

It was not until October, while Euthanasia still lingered at Valperga, that Castruccio took up his abode in Lucca. He returned thither, covered with glory, but highly discontented / with Uguccione who feared him, and, while he shewed him outward honour, took every occasion to thwart his desires, and to deprive him of all power and voice in his council. But Castruccio was at the head of a large party, who could ill brook the rude arrogance of Uguccione, and the unmasked presumption of his sons. This party augmented every day; it was watched, insulted, and harassed; but all the Ghibeline youth of Lucca made it their boast to attend the person, and partake the counsels of Castruccio.

The winter months were spent in apparent idleness, but in reality in deep plotting on the part of Castruccio. Uguccione was at Pisa, and his son, Francesco, could ill understand the wiles of the pupil of Alberto Scoto. He saw his frank countenance, and watched his gay demeanour; but the conclusion of his observations was, that although Castruccio was careless of danger, and ambitious of glory, he was too fond of pleasure, and of too ingenuous a disposition, to enter into any deep scheme, or to form even the wish of usurping the power of the state. /

Castruccio stood on the tower of the Antelminelli palace; young Arrigo Guinigi was at his side; he was surrounded by half a dozen of his most intimate associates, and after having for a while discussed their plans of political conduct, they remained silent. Castruccio was separated from the rest of the group; the tower of Antelminelli overlooked the town of Lucca, and being raised far above its narrow, dark streets, appeared, together with the numerous towers of the city, as forming a separate and more agreeable town for the nobles over the heads of the meaner inhabitants. The valley was stretched around the city; its fields bare of vegetation, and spotted with black patches of leafless woods; and the view was terminated by the hills, crowned with snow, and their sides clothed with the dark verdure of the ilex, while from among their folds peeped the white walls of villages and castles.

Castruccio fixed his eye on one of these castles. The forgotten scenes of his youth thronged into his memory, and oppressed him with their numbers and life; the low voice of his mother sounded in his ears; the venerable / form of Adimari stood before him, and it seemed to him as if the slender fingers of the infant Euthanasia pressed his hand. He turned suddenly round, and asked: "Does she still live there?" – pointing to the castle.

"Who? The countess of Valperga?"

"Aye, and her daughter Euthanasia?" Many years had elapsed since he had pronounced that name; he felt his whole frame thrill to its musical sound.

"The present countess," replied Vanni Mordecastelli, "is young and unmarried" –

"And her name is Euthanasia," continued count Ludovico de' Fondi;[a] "she is the daughter of Messer Antonio dei Adimari, who while he lived was one of the leaders of the Guelph party at Florence; and through her mother she possesses the castle and villages of Valperga."

"Aye," cried a youth, "and they say that Ranieri della Faggiuola[b] pretends to her hand. It is not well, that the credulity of a woman, who will listen to the first fine speeches that are addressed to her, should cause so strong a / hold as the castle of Valperga to pass into the hands of that insufferable nest of traitors."

---

[a] The Mordecastelli and the Fondi were among the families exiled with the Antelminelli (Villani, VIII, cap. 45; Tegrimi, p. 9; noted in adds. e. 17, p. 234 rev.).
[b] Uguccione's second son, called Neri in Tegrimi and Sismondi.

"You are ignorant of whom you talk," said the aged Fondi, "when you speak thus lightly of the young countess of Valperga. She is a lady of great prudence, beauty, and learning; and, although for years she has been sought by the first nobles of Italy, she glories in her independence and solitude. She mingles little with the citizens of this town; her friends reside at Florence, where she often passes many months, associating with its first families."

"Is she as beautiful, as she is said to be?" asked young Arrigo Guinigi.

"Indeed she is lovely to a miracle; but her manners almost make you forget her beauty; they are so winning and graceful. Unfortunately she does not belong to our party, but is as strongly attached to the Pope's as the countess Matilda of old."[a]

"Aye, these women are so easily cajoled by priests."

"Nay, Moncello, you will still be in the wrong, if you apply common rules to the conduct / of the countess Euthanasia. She is attached to the cause of the freedom of Florence, and not to the power of her Popes. When I visited her on her return to her castle, I found her full of grief at the renewal of war between these states. She earnestly asked me whether I saw any prospect of peace; 'For,' said she, 'I am more attached to concord and the alliance of parties, than to any of the factions which distract our poor Italy.'"——

The conversation then turned on other subjects. Castruccio had listened silently to the praise which the old count Fondi had bestowed on the friend of his childhood; and presently after, taking Arrigo aside, he said: "My young friend, you must go on an embassy for me."

"To the end of the world, if you desire it, my dear lord" –

"Nay, this is a shorter journey. You must ride tomorrow morning to the castle of Valperga, and ask permission of the countess that I may visit her. Our families, though of opposite interests, were much allied; and I ought to have sought this interview before."

On the following day Castruccio waited / anxiously for the return of Arrigo. He arrived a little before noon. "I have seen her," he cried; "and, after having seen her, I wonder at the torpor of these Lucchese that they do not all emigrate from their town, to go and surround her castle, and gaze on her all day long. I seem only to live since I have seen her; she is so lovely, so enchantingly kind and gentle. I have heard you say, my good brother, that you never met with a

---

[a] Matilda, 'Great Countess' of Tuscany (1046–1115), contended all her life with the emperor, who levelled her fortresses and attempted to annex her vast estates; recovering them eventually, she willed them to the Church, thus alienating what the emperor maintained was an imperial fiefdom. In the wrangles between pope and emperor over her bequest, her former subjects seized the opportunity to establish themselves as independent city-states. At her castle of Canossa in 1077 the emperor Henry IV reputedly abased himself to the pope by standing for three days in the snow. She has been identified with the Lady of the Earthly Paradise in Dante's *Purgatorio* (XXVIII. 37–148, XXIX. 1–16); she is called 'valente Contessa Matelda' and 'valorosa Donna Matilde' (Villani, IV, caps 29, 30; Tegrimi, p. 51). Muratori mentions her frequently; Sismondi (ch. iii) presents her as ambitious and fanatical.

woman whom you could enshrine in your inmost heart, and thus pay worship to the exalted spirit of loveliness, which you had vainly sought, and never found. Go to Valperga, and, gazing on Euthanasia, you will tremblingly unread your heresy."

"To horse then, my dear Arrigo. Does she consent to receive me?"

"Yes, she desires to see you; and with the most ingenuous sweetness, she bade me tell you the pleasure it would give her, to renew her acquaintance with one whom she has not forgotten during a long separation." /

CHAPTER IX.

Castle of Valperga described – Friendship and Love.

"This is a well known road to me," thought Castruccio, as he rode across the plain of Lucca towards the hills of the Baths;[a] "there is still that mountain, that as a craggy and mighty wall surmounts and bounds the other Apennines; the lower peaks are still congregated round it, attracting and arresting the clouds that pause on their summits, and then slowly roll off. What a splendid garb of snow these old mountains have thrown over themselves, to shield them from the *tramontano**, that buffets them all the winter long, while their black sides appear almost as the shadows of a marble statue. Looking at these hills, it / seems to me as if I had suddenly a recollection of a previous existence, such a crowd of ideas rush upon me, the birth of my early years, long dead, now revived. There on that hill stands the old sheep-cot, in which I once took refuge during a storm; there is the castle of the Fondi, near which grow the largest ilexes of these hills; and in that recess of the mountain is the holy spring, near which on summer mornings Euthanasia and I have often gathered flowers, and placed leaves for boats, seeing them swallowed up and again cast forth in the whirl of that strange pool; I wonder if that tall cypress still throws its shade upon the water; methinks it would well please me, to sit as of yore, Euthanasia by my side, on its moss-covered roots."

Castruccio's heart was much softened, as he successively recognized objects, which he had forgotten for so many years, and with which he had been most intimately acquainted. The peculiar form of the branches of a tree, the winding of an often-trod mountain-path, the murmurs of small streams, their banks

*The *Tramontano* is the north wind; the *Scirocco* the south-west; and the *Libeccio* the south-east.

[a] The Bagni a Corsena, known later as the Bagni di Lucca, surrounded by wooded hills. The Shelleys resided there (11 June-30 August 1818); described in *MWSL*, I, pp. 73–4.

bedecked with dwarf shrubs; things which would / have appeared uncharacterized to one who viewed them for the first time; bore for him some distinguishing mark, some peculiar shape, which awoke within him memories that had been long laid asleep.

The road that led from Lucca to Valperga struck directly across the plain to the foot of the rock on which the castle was built. This rock overhung the road, casting a deep shade; and projected, forming a precipice on three sides; the northern side, at the foot of which the Serchio flowed, was disjoined from the mountain by a ravine, and a torrent struggled in the depth, among loose stones, and the gnarled and naked roots of trees that shaded the side of the cleft. Castruccio began to ascend the path which led to the portal of the castle, that was cut in the precipitous side of this recess, and was bordered by hedges of stunted myrtles overtopped by chesnut trees; the foliage of these had fallen; and their spoils, yellow, and brown, and red, were strewed on the shining leaves of the myrtle underwood. The path was steep, serpentine and narrow; so that Castruccio, who now looked on nature / with a soldier's eye, remarked what an excellent defence Valperga might make, if that were the only access to it: the torrent roared below, keeping the air for ever awake; for that commoner babbles more and louder among huge mountains, and solitudes which may never be still, than among the haunts of men; but all sounds are melodious there; none harsh and obtrusive.

At the summit of the path was a drawbridge that connected it with the almost isolated platform of rock on which the castle stood: – the building nearly covered this space, leaving room only for a small plot of ground, which overlooked the plain, and was guarded by a barbican; and on which a few trees, dark ilexes, and light acacias,[a] mingled their contrasted foliage. Behind the castle the mountain rose, barren and nearly perpendicular; and, when you looked up, the dark and weather-stained precipice towered above, while the blue sky seemed to rest upon it. The castle itself was a large and picturesque building, turreted, and gracefully shaded by trees. Castruccio entered the gate on the side of the drawbridge, / and passed between the main building and the barbican which guarded the pass; so coming round to the front of the castle, which opened on the grassy plot; here he was met by several servants, and conducted to the apartment of Euthanasia. The counts of Valperga had been rich; and the castle was more magnificent than those rocky strong holds usually were. The great banqueting hall was painted with various figures, which, though rude, and defective in shade and perspective, were regarded with admiration in those days. A large fireplace, now illumined by a blazing fire,

---

[a] Associated, through Gibbon, with meditation. It was in his acacia walk that he mused upon finishing the *Decline and Fall of the Roman Empire*, as recounted in his *Memoirs of My Life and Writings* [etc.] (1796), read by Mary Shelley in 1815 (*MWSJ*, I, p. 88; see also pp. 62–3). The acacia's pinnate leaves are among the first to fall in autumn; the ilex is an evergreen.

gave an air of cheerfulness to the hall; several serving-men, and two large and beautiful dogs, were cowering round the fire, as a cold January blast rushed through the opposite door, through which Castruccio passed into an inner, open court of the castle.

This court was surrounded by gothic cloisters on all sides except one, where the huge mountain formed the barrier: high, near the summit of the rock, grew a few cypresses; and, as you gazed upwards at them, they seemed to pierce the sky with their dark and motionless / spires. On one side of this court was a handsome staircase built of the marble of Carrara, and by this he ascended into the audience chamber. It was then, being winter, hung with scarlet cloth; the ceiling was painted; and the bright marble pavement reflected in dim colours the Venus and her Cupids depicted above. A small tripod of white marble curiously carved, stood in the middle of the room, supporting a bronze censer in which incense was burning; several antique vases and tripods adorned the room; the tables were of the finest stones, or of glass mosaic; and the seats or couches were covered with scarlet cloth inwoven with gold. Within this was Euthanasia's own apartment; it was hung with blue silk, and the pavement was of mosaic; the couches were richly embroidered, and a small table of *verde antique*[a] stood in the middle of the room. In the recesses were several stands for books, writing materials, &c.; and in the embrasures of the windows were bronze stands, on which were placed finely embossed gold vases, filled with such flowers as the season afforded. But, amidst all this / luxury, the richest ornament of the room was the lovely possessor herself.

Castruccio and Euthanasia met; after many years of absence, they gazed on each other with curiosity and interest. Euthanasia had awaited his arrival with unwonted anxiety: she could not explain to herself the agitation that she felt at the idea of meeting him; but, when she saw him, beautiful as a god, power and love dwelling on every feature of his countenance, and in every motion of his graceful form, the unquiet beatings of her heart ceased, and she became calm and happy. And was she not also beautiful? Her form was light, and every limb was shaped according to those rules by which the exquisite statues of the antients have been modelled. A quantity of golden hair fell round her neck, and, unless it had been confined by a veil that was wreathed round her head, it would almost have touched the ground; her eyes were blue; a blue that seemed to have drunk-in the depths of an Italian sky, and to reflect from their orbs the pure and unfathomable brilliance, which strikes the sight as darkness, of a Roman heaven; but these / beauteous eyes were fringed by long, pointed lashes, which softened their fire, and added to their sweetness: the very soul of open-hearted Charity dwelt on her brow, and her lips expressed the softest sensibility; there was in her countenance, beyond all of kind and good that you could

---

[a] Usually *verd-antique* or *verde antico*, green serpentine marble.

there discover, an expression that seemed to require ages to read and understand; a wisdom exalted by enthusiasm, a wildness tempered by self-command, that filled every look and every motion with eternal change. She was dressed according to the custom of the times, yet her dress was rather plain, being neither ornamented with gold nor jewels; a silk vest of blue reached from her neck to her feet, girded at the waist by a small embroidered band; the wide and hanging sleeves were embroidered at the edge, and fell far over her hands, except when, thrown back, they discovered her rosy-tipt fingers and taper wrist.

They met then and often again; and the difference of their political parties only drew them closer. Euthanasia perceived that Castruccio intended to work some change in the state of her country; and she earnestly wished, – / not to draw him over to her party, – but to shew how futile that distinction and enmity were, if one love of peace and good animated all hearts. She wished also to read his mind, to know if the love of liberty lived there. Euthanasia had this foible, if indeed it might be called one in her, to love the very shadow of freedom with unbounded enthusiasm. She was bred a Guelph among the leaders of that party at Florence, a party whose watchword was liberty; her rank itself would have forced her to take part in the contentions of the times; but she was no narrow partizan; her father, and the studies she had followed under him, had taught her higher lessons; and the history of the Roman republic had increased her love of freedom, while it had annihilated in her mind all interest in petty intrigue. Castruccio was a staunch Ghibeline, and his soul was set on the advancement of that party; he did not sympathize with Euthanasia, but he appeared to do so, for he loved her, and listened, his eyes shining with pleasure, while she spoke in silver tones, and all appeared wise and good that came from her lips. Often her gentle eloquence / would for a while carry him along with it, and he would talk of republics, and the energy and virtue that every citizen acquires, when each acting under the censure of each, yet possesses power; and men, not as children obedient to the mere word of command, discuss and regulate their own interests. Her admiration for the character of several of the Florentine chiefs gave interest to her details respecting the changes that had occurred there during the last years, and to the many anecdotes that she dwelt upon as demonstrating the power and grandeur of her beloved Florence.

Nor were their conversations only political. Euthanasia's mind was stored with sweet lore; she loved poetry, and sang or repeated the verses of Guido or Dante; and, as she made excursions among the woods, or joined in hunting-parties with Castruccio and her other friends, her conversation appeared one strain of poetry. Castruccio related his adventures, and Euthanasia was never weary of listening to the details of the English and French courts and manners; two systems of society, so widely opposite to each other, and both so different / from the scenes to which she had been accustomed. Their love for one another, and their confidence increased: the winter months passed on, and the first days of spring, bringing with them green leaves and soft air, found them vowed friends, each believing[a] to be knit to the other for life with the strongest ties of enduring love.

Euthanasia said that she loved for the first time, and a falsehood had never stained her purest soul; a well of intensest and overflowing passion was opened in her heart; every feeling was softened, every emotion modulated by this change: she was penetrated with love; and, admiration and esteem forming but a part of this, she made a god of him she loved, believing every virtue and every talent to live in his soul. Thus, unrestrained by any latent fear or ungenerous suspicion, she gave up her heart to him, and was for a while happy. They passed much time together; and every day each made a discovery of some new excellence, some till then unobserved accomplishment.

Her feelings were indeed entirely changed by the birth of this new and powerful sentiment. / Hitherto she had been in a great degree alone in the world; finding none who entirely sympathized with her, she had poured out the treasure of her heart to the ear of silence alone. She was happy among the gaieties of Florence; the wit and imagination of the people formed an agreeable variety to her life; but there was a mutable and changeful spirit among them, that did not invite her confidence. Her eyes had often been lighted up, and her spirit awakened in conversation, where wit sharpens wit, and the ideas of one mind seem to cause the birth of the children of another. But, when tenderness softened her heart, and the sublime feeling of universal love penetrated her, she found no voice that replied so well to hers as the gentle singing of the pines under the air of noon, and the soft murmurs of the breeze that scattered her hair and freshened her cheek, and the dashing of the waters that has no beginning or end.

It was not thus now; the words and looks of Castruccio replied to her, and she felt happier than she had ever been. There was no doubt, no sorrow; all was security and calm; / and her heart softened, until tears sprang forth under the weight of unmitigated pleasure. She was frank, generous and fearless; therefore she instantly believed and trusted; while the master-passions which ever ruled her life were not forgotten, but, mingling with and heightened by love, glowed with greater energy. They passed several months in the enjoyment of this intercourse; they hoped, they felt, that their destinies were intertwined never to be separated; and their union was only deferred until Castruccio should free his country. The summer advancing would soon give the signal for separation. On one of these days, one of the last before their parting, Euthanasia related to Castruccio the few events of her peaceful life which had occurred since their separation ten years before. The tale was short, but it was one that deeply interested the listener. /

---

[a] i.e. trusting (obsolete; see 'believe', *OED*).

79

CHAPTER X.

Euthanasia's Narrative.

"It is strange for one to speak, who never before has uttered the sentiments of her heart. With my eyes I have spoken to the starry skies and the green earth; and with smiles that could not express my emotion I have conversed with the soft airs of summer, the murmur of streams, and the chequered shades of our divine woods: but never before have I awakened sympathy in a human countenance with words that unlock the treasure of my heart.

"I have lived a solitary hermitess, and have become an enthusiast for all beauty. Being alone, I have not feared to give the reins to my feelings; I have lived happily within the universe of my own mind, and have often given reality to that which others call a dream. I have had few hopes, and few fears; but every passing sentiment has been an event; and I have marked the birth of a new idea with the / joy that others derive from what they call change and fortune. What is the world, except that which we feel? Love, and hope, and delight, or sorrow and tears; these are our lives, our realities, to which we give the names of power, possession, misfortune, and death.

"You smile at my strange words. I now feel livelier emotions arise; and, as is my custom, I try to define and understand them. Love, when nurtured by sympathy, is a stronger feeling, than those breathless emotions which arise from the contemplation of what is commonly called inanimate nature, and of the wondrous and eternal changes of the universe; and, feeling as I do, that if I give it place in my heart, it must bear my whole being away with it, as the tempest bears the rack along the sky, wonder not, dear friend, that I have paused, and even shuddered, when I thought that an unknown power was about to dwell in my soul, which might make it blind to its former delights, and deaf to the deep voice of that nature, whose child and nursling I call myself. But now I doubt no more; I am yours, Castruccio; be my fortune tearful or smiling, it / shall be one that will bring with it human sympathy, and I resign that savage liberty of which I was ere while jealous.

"You have asked me to relate the events of my life; I may say that it is a blank, if you would not hear the history of many a strange idea, many an exalted feeling, and reverie of wondrous change. You left me at Florence the favourite daughter of a father I adored: I was ever near him reading and conversing with him; and if I have put order in my day dreams, and culled the fruit of virtue and some slight wisdom from my meditations, it is to his lessons

80

that I owe this good. It is he who taught me to fathom my sensations, and discipline my mind; to understand what my feelings were, and whether they arose from a good or evil source. He taught me to look on my own faults fearlessly; humbly as a weak being – yet not with mock humility, but with a modest, yet firm courage, that led me to know what indeed I might become. He explained to me the lessons of our divine master; which our priests corrupt to satisfy the most groveling desires; and he taught me to seek / in self-approbation, and in a repentance, which was that of virtuous action, and not of weeping, for the absolution of which they make a revenue.

"Do I speak with vanity? I hope that you do not so far mistake me. I have been a solitary being; and, conversing with my own heart, I have been so accustomed to use the frank language of a knowledge drawn from fixed principles, and to weigh my actions and thoughts in those scales which my reason and my religion afforded me, that my words may sound vain, when they are only true. I do not think then that I could speak with vanity; for I was enumerating the benefits that I received from my father. I read with him the literature of ancient Rome; and my whole soul was filled with the beauty of action, and the poetic sentiment of these writers. At first I complained that no men lived now, who bore affinity to these far shining beacons of the earth: but my father convinced me, that the world was shaking off her barbaric lethargy, and that Florence, in her struggle for freedom, had awakened the noblest energies of the human mind. / Once, when we attended a court in Lombardy, a minstrel sang some of the Cantos of Dante's *Divina Comedia*, and I can never forget the enthusiastic joy I experienced, in finding that I was the contemporary of its illustrious author.

I endeavour to mark in this little history of myself the use of the various feelings that rule all my actions; and I must date my enthusiasm for the liberties of my country, and the political welfare of Italy, from the repetition of these Cantos of Dante's poem.[a] The Romans, whose writings I adored, were free; a Greek who once visited us, had related to us what treasures of poetry and wisdom existed in his language, and these were the productions of freemen: the mental history of the rest of the world who are slaves, was a blank, and thus I was irresistibly forced to connect wisdom and liberty together; and, as I worshipped wisdom as the pure emanation of the Deity, the divine light of the world, so did I adore liberty as its parent, its sister, the half of its being. Florence was free, and Dante was a Florentine; none but a freeman could have poured forth the / poetry and eloquence to which I listened: what though he were banished from his native city, and had espoused a party that seemed to

---

[a] For instance, Canto VI of the *Purgatorio*, here imagined as in circulation before publication; cf. the praise of Dante by P. B. Shelley in *A Defence of Poetry* (written early 1821 and fair-copied by Mary Shelley). Dante, Guelph by birth, was a Ghibelline by persuasion and a White; in 'Giovanni Villani' (*MWS Matilda etc*, p. 138) his politics are discussed.

support tyranny; the essence of freedom is that clash and struggle which awaken the energies of our nature, and that operation of the elements of our mind, which as it were gives us the force and power that hinder us from degenerating, as they say all things earthly do when not regenerated by change.

"What is man without wisdom? And what would not this world become, if every man might learn from its institutions the true principles of life, and become as the few which have as yet shone as stars amidst the night of ages? If time had not shaken the light of poetry and of genius from his wings, all the past would be dark and trackless: now we have a track – the glorious foot-marks of the children of liberty; let us imitate them, and like them we may serve as marks in the desart, to attract future passengers to the fountains of life. Already we have begun to do so; and Dante is the pledge of a glorious race, which tells us that, in clinging to the freedom which gave / birth to his genius, we may awake the fallen hopes of the world. These sentiments, nurtured and directed by my father, have caused the growth of an enthusiasm in my soul, which can only die when I die.

"I was at this time but sixteen; and at that age, unless I had been guided by the lessons of my father, my meditations would have been sufficiently fruitless. But he, whether he taught me to consider the world and the community of man, or to study the little universe of my own mind, was wisdom's self, pouring out accents that commanded attention and obedience. At first I believed, that my heart was good, and that by following its dictates I should not do wrong; I was proud, and loved not to constrain my will, though I myself were the mistress; but he told me, that either my judgement or passions must rule me, and that my future happiness and usefulness depended on the choice I made between these two laws. I learned from him to look upon events as being of consequence only through the feelings which they excited, and to believe that content of mind, love, and benevolent feeling ought to / be the elements of our existence; while those accidents of fortune or fame, which to the majority make up the sum of their existence, were as the dust of the balance.

"Well; these were the lessons of my father, a honey of wisdom on which I fed until I attained my eighteenth year; and then he died. What I felt, my grief and despair, I will not relate; few sorrows surpass that of a child, who loses a beloved parent before she has formed new ties which have weakened the first and the most religious.

"Do you remember my mother? She was a lady with a kind heart, and a humanity and equanimity of temper few could surpass. She was a Guelph, a violent partizan, and, heart and soul, was taken up with treaties of peace, acquisitions in war, the conduct of allies, and the fortune of her enemies: while she talked to you, you would have thought that the whole globe of the earth was merely an appendage to the county of Valperga. She was acquainted with all the magistrates of Florence, the probabilities of elections, the state of the troops, the receipt of imposts, and every circumstance / of the republic. She was interested in the most lively manner in the fall of Corso Donati*, the war with Pistoia, the taking of that town, and the deaths and elections of the various Popes.[a] She was present at every court held by the Guelph lords of Lombardy;[b] and her poor subjects were sometimes rather hardly taxed, that we might appear with suitable dignity on these occasions. The marriage of her children was her next care; but she could never come to a decisive resolve as to which alliance would be the most advantageous to her family, and at the same time most promote the cause of the Guelphs in Italy.

"When my father died, she sent for my eldest brother from Naples; and for several months her mind was occupied by his accession, and the dignity that the houses of Adimari and Valperga would acquire by having a young warrior at their head, instead of a woman and a blind philosopher. My brother was a soldier, a brave man, full of ambition and party spirit; and a new field was opened / to my mother's politics by him, when he detailed the intrigues of the Neapolitan court; she was for ever occupied in sending messengers, receiving dispatches, calculating imposts, and all the pygmy acts of a petty state.

"When I was nineteen years of age, we heard that my younger brother had fallen ill at Rome, and desired to see some one of his family. My uncle, the abbot of St. Maurice, was on the point of going to Rome; and I obtained my mother's leave to accompany him. Oh, what long draughts of joy I drank in on that journey! I did not think that my brother's illness was dangerous, and indeed considered that circumstance more as the pretext, than the object of my journey; so I fearlessly gave myself up to the enthusiasm that deluged my soul. Expression lags, as then my own spirit flagged, beneath the influence of these thoughts: it was to Rome I journied, to see the vestiges of the mistress of the world, within whose walls all I could conceive of great, and good, and wise, had breathed and acted: I should draw in the sacred air which had vivified the heroes of Rome; their shades would surround me; and / the very stones that I

---

* Dante: *Purgatorio*, Canto xxiv. [82–90][c]

---

[a] Referring to the war of 1305–6; the Whites were expelled from Pistoia by the victorious Florentines; the elections and deaths of the relevant popes were irregular: Boniface VIII (1294–1303), accused by Dante (*Inferno*, XIX. 52–7) of becoming pope by guile, implacable enemy of Philippe-le-Bel, was imprisoned by Philippe's allies, ill-treated and died mad; Benedict XI (1303–4) excommunicated Florence for disobeying his order to bring back the White leaders; this revealed him as a potential threat to Philippe, who had him fed poisoned figs; Clement V (1305–14), the Gascon pope, 'the shepherd without law' (Dante, *Inferno*, XIX. 83), defected to Philippe's side in return for his election, and thenceforward became his tool; their stories are vividly told in Sismondi, ch. xxiv and xxvi.
[b] i.e. *placiti*, occasions for ceremony, display and entertainment (Muratori, II, diss. 31, p. 47; noted in Ab. Dep. e. 274, p. 82).
[c] Corso Donati (d. 1308), head of the Florentine Blacks and thus of the Guelph faction to which the Adimari belonged, invited Philippe-le-Bel's brother, Charles of Valois (1302) to Florence; this resulted in Dante's expulsion. He was later condemned to death for plotting with his father-in-law Uguccione della Faggiuola to seize power in Florence; attempting to escape, he fell from his horse and was mangled to death.

should tread were marked by their footsteps. Can you conceive what I felt? You have not studied the histories of ancient times, and perhaps know not the life that breathes in them; a soul of beauty and wisdom which had penetrated my heart of hearts. When I descended the hills of the Abruzzi, and first saw the Tiber rolling its tranquil waters glistening under the morning sun; I wept; – why did not Cato live?[a] – why was I not going to see her consuls, her heroes, and her poets? Alas! I was about to approach the shadow of Rome, the inanimate corse, the broken image of what was once great beyond all power of speech to express. My enthusiasm again changed; and I felt a kind of sacred horror run through my veins. Thou, oh! Tiber, ever rollest, ever and for ever the same! yet are not thy waters those which flowed here when the Scipios and the Fabii[b] lived on thy shores; the grass and the herbage which adorn thy banks have many thousand times been renewed since it was pressed on by their feet; all is changed, even thou art not the same! /

"It was night when we entered Rome; I dared hardly breathe; the stars shone bright in the deep azure of heaven, and with their twinkling beams illuminated the dark towers which were black and silent, seeming like animated beings asleep. A procession of monks passed by chaunting in a sweet and solemn tone, in that language which once awoke the pauses of this Roman air with words of fire. Methought they sang their city's *requiem*; methought I was following to their last narrow home all that had existed of great and good in this god-inhabited city.[c]

"I remained in Rome three months; when I arrived, my brother was considerably better, and we entertained every hope of his recovery. I spent my life among the ruins of Rome; and I felt, as I was told that I appeared to be, rather a wandering shade of the ancient times, than a modern Italian. In my wild enthusiasm I called on the shadows of the departed to converse with me, and to prophesy the fortunes of awakening Italy. I can never forget one evening that I visited the Pantheon by moonlight:[d] the soft beams of the planet streamed / through its open roof, and its tall pillars glimmered around. It seemed as if the spirit of beauty descended on my soul, as I sat there in mute extacy; never had I before so felt the universal graspings of my own mind, or the sure tokens of

---

[a] Both Catos exemplified Roman virtue; the younger Cato is the one to whom Mary Shelley and Godwin habitually allude. A statesman and Stoic, Marcus Porcius Cato wore mourning for republican liberty and committed suicide rather yield to the conquering Julius Caesar after the defeat of Pharsalia in 48 BC.

[b] The Scipios and the Fabii were among the noblest and most patriotic families of republican Rome; their members included Quintus Fabius Maximus Cunctator ('The Delayer') and Scipio Africanus, both heroes of the second Punic War (218–202 BC) and renowned for their upright lives.

[c] cf. 'It was at Rome, on the fifteenth of October, 1764, as I sat musing amidst the ruins of the Capitol, while the barefooted fryars were singing Vespers in the temple of Jupiter, that the idea of writing the decline and fall of the City first started to my mind' (Edward Gibbon, *Memoirs*, 1796 version).

[d] Visited by Mary Shelley on 9 March 1819 (*MWSJ*, I, p. 251 and *MWSL*, I, p. 89).

other spiritual existences, as at that moment. Oh! could I even now pour forth in words the sentiments of love, and virtue, and divinest wisdom, that then burst in upon my soul, in a rich torrent—— such as was the light of the moon to the dark temple in which I stood – the whole world would stand and listen: but fainter than the moon-beams and more evanescent are those deep thoughts; my eyes glisten, my cheeks glow, but words are denied me. I feel as it were my own soul at work within me, and surely, if I could disclose its secret operations, and lay bare the vitals of my being, in that moment, which would be one of overwhelming extacy – in that moment I should die.

"Well; to return to the events that sealed my residence in Rome, and by shedding the softness of affectionate sorrow over my feelings, added to their deep holiness. The last month of / my residence there, I was a constant attendant on the sick bed of my dying brother: he did not suffer pain; his illness was lethargic; and I watched with breathless anxiety the change from life to death. Sometimes, when the *Ave Maria* had sounded, and the heats of the day had subsided, I stole out into the air to refresh my wearied spirits. There is no sky so blue as that of Rome; it is deep, penetrating, and dazzling: but at this hour it had faded, and its soft airs, that made wild and thrilling music among the solitudes of its hills and ruins, cooled my fevered cheeks, and soothed me in spite of sorrow. I then enjoyed grief; I may now say so, although I then felt anguish alone; truly I wept, and bitterly over the illness of my brother: but, when the soul is active, it brings a certain consolation along with it: I was never so much alive as then, when my wanderings, which seldom exceeded one or at most two hours, seemed to be lengthened into days and weeks. I loved to wander by the banks of the Tiber, which were solitary, and, if the scirocco blew, to mark the clouds as they sped over St. Peter's and the many towers of Rome: / sometimes I walked on the Quirinal or Pincian mounts which overlook the city, and gazed, until my soul was elevated by poetic transport. Beautiful city, thy towers were illuminated by the orange tints of the fast-departing sunset, and the ghosts of lovely memories floated with the night breeze, among thy ruins; I became calm; amidst a dead race, and an extinguished empire, what individual sorrow would dare raise its voice? subdued, trembling, and over-come, I crept back to the sick bed of my brother.[a]

"He died; and I left this city of my soul. I know not whether I shall ever again breathe its air; but its memory is a burning cloud of sunset in the deep azure of the sky: it is that passage in my life since my father's death, on which my intellectual eye rests with emotion, pleasurable now, although I then endured poignant sorrow.

"The passenger that carried the intelligence of my younger brother's death to my mother was crossed on the road by one who came to inform me that the

---

[a] Here, as in *Matilda* and *The Last Man*, the description of a death-bed vigil draws on memories surrounding William Shelley's death in Rome, 7 June, 1819.

eldest also was no more. He was killed in an assault on Pistoia. Thus / death quickly mowed down the ranks of our family; and at last I have become a solitary scion of the stock.

"I returned home by very slow journies, and in my way was detained a fortnight at Perugia. When I arrived, I was met by my mother at our palace in Florence; she burst into tears as she folded me in her arms, and wept for some time, lamenting with bitter grief her sad losses. I mingled my tears with hers, and alas! I soon shed them alone; doubly an orphan through her death, I mourned over the last of my family. So many losses, following swift one upon the other, astounded me; and I passed many months, as one who had wandered from the true path, and had no guide to set her right. I retreated to my castle, and the solitude frightened me; I returned to Florence; but the gaieties of that city only told me more plainly that I was alone, since I sympathized with none there. But time has healed these wounds, leaving only a tinge of melancholy in my character which had not belonged to it till now." /

CHAPTER XI.

Capture of Monte Catini. – Castruccio treacherously made prisoner by Ranieri, Governor of Lucca. – Delivered, and proclaimed Consul.

The winter passed away, and with the summer the toils of the soldier began. Castruccio left Lucca, and joined the army of Uguccione against the Florentines. He took leave of his lady; yet she neither tied the scarf around him, nor bade him go and prosper. Florence was her native town; and love of their country was a characteristic of all Florentines. There was in that city an energy of spirit, which panting to expand itself, sought for new emotions, or exalted those that were before felt, until each sentiment became a passion. The Florentines were patriots; there was not one among them, who would not have sacrificed wealth, life, and happiness, to the prosperity of his native city. Euthanasia was / brought up the the midst of public discussions and of expressions of public feeling; the army of the Florentines contained her best friends, the companions of her youth, all among men whom she had esteemed and loved; how then could she bid her lover, go, and prosper, when he went to destroy them? She would have been still more unhappy, could she have anticipated the event of the campaign.

Uguccione engaged himself in the siege of the castle of Monte Catini; and the Florentines, after having made every exertion to assemble and discipline their troops, advanced against him with a larger army than they had ever before brought into the field. Nor were the preparations of Uguccione inferior in vigour; he assembled all his allies, and awaited with confidence the arrival of the enemy. During this interval however, the chief fell ill, and was obliged to retire from the camp: the nominal command of the army devolved on his eldest son Francesco; but all looked up to Castruccio as their real leader. The Florentines advanced full of hope; and the Lucchese awaited them with steady courage. The battle / was long and bloody; in the beginning of the combat Francesco was killed, and Castruccio perceived the soldiers make a sudden halt, when they saw their general fall: instantly feeling that the command devolved upon him, he galloped to the front of the lines, he threw off his casque that he might be distinguished, and, bidding the trumpets sound, he led his troops to a fresh assault. His army was drawn out on the plain, and every eye was turned upwards towards the castle, which, situated on the height of a steep hill, was the goal they must win. Castruccio had seen service in France; but with far different feelings did he now engage in battle. He was surrounded by his friends; he saw those he loved advance with a steady eye to the danger towards which he led them; he looked up, and saw above the high seated castle that he must storm; he saw the closely set ranks of the enemy; he beheld all this with one glance, one feeling quicker than a look, and the trumpets sounded while he waved his sword; his spirits were exhilarated, his heart swelled, – tears – tears of high and uncontrolable emotion, filled his eyes, / as he dashed through the ranks of the enemy, and cried, "Victory, or death!" None dared disobey his voice. His dark brown hair, on which the sun shone, might be distinguished amidst a forest of hostile javelins. He was wounded; but he refused to retire; and fixing his eye on the castle walls – he cried, "There is our home!" All gave way before his fury; that part of the Florentine army which had been drawn out on the plain, was dispersed and fled – the rest retreated towards the castle; when he saw them retreat, when he first perceived that they gave ground before him, his triumph and extacy rose almost to frenzy; the mountain was steep, he threw himself from his horse, his troop followed his example; he called on them by the names of father and brother to follow his steps. "Go on!" they cried, "go on!" And they broke through all the impediments placed to impede their ascent, and were seen in close array, winding up the steep path towards the castle.

The victory was due to him alone; he, ever foremost, scaled the height, and first displayed the Ghibeline banner from the walls of the / castle of Monte Catini; while, his cheek pale with pain, and his limbs trembling from loss of blood, it seemed almost as if his own death would seal the bloody conquest. The Florentines sustained irreparable loss; their general, the son of the king of Naples, several of his relations, and many members of the noblest families in Florence, fell. The loss is compared by the Florentine historians to the defeat of

Cannæ; and many years elapsed before Florence could fill up the gap among her citizens made by the havoc of that day.[a]

Such was the news that blanched poor Euthanasia's cheek. She had spent the period that had elapsed since the departure of Castruccio, in utter solitude. Her anxiety, and the combat of feelings which she experienced, destroyed all her peace: she dared not give her prayers to either side; or if, following the accustomed bent of her inclinations, she wished success to her townsmen, the idea of Castruccio defeated, perhaps killed, turned all her thoughts to double bitterness. Yet, when the Florentines were indeed defeated, when messenger after messenger brought intelligence / from her terror-stricken friends of the sad losses they had sustained, when the name of Castruccio as the slayer was repeated with fear and curses by those whom she tenderly loved; then indeed the current of her feelings returned with violence to its accustomed channel, and, bitterly reproaching herself for having dared to hesitate in a cause where her country was concerned, she knelt down, and solemnly and deliberately made a vow, sanctifying it by an appeal to all that she held sacred in heaven and upon earth, – she made a deep and tremendous vow, never to ally herself to the enemy of Florence: and then, somewhat calmed in soul, though ever sorrowing, she waited for the return of Castruccio to Lucca, so to learn if he could clear himself, or if indeed he were that enemy to Florence against whom her vow was made.

If the overthrow and massacre of the Florentines had moved her soul to its very depths, her horror was tempered with tenderness, when she heard that Castruccio had been brought back wounded to Lucca. The glory of this victory was attributed to him alone; and this / glory, which appeared a shame to Euthanasia, excited in her feelings of confusion and sorrow. Now for the first time she felt the struggle in her soul, of inclination warring with duty; for the first time she feared that she ought not to love Castruccio; she thought of retreating to Florence, and of shutting him out from her sight, if possible from her thoughts; yet as she meditated this, she thought she heard the soft tones of his melodious voice sounding in her ears, and she sank into grief and tears.

This painful struggle ceased not, until she saw him again; and then, as before, all pain and doubt vanished. His cheek was pale from the consequences of his wound, and his person, having thus lost its usual decision of mien, was more

---

[a] Montecatini (29 August, 1315) is described by Villani (IX, caps 69–70), Tegrimi (p. 21), Sismondi (ch. xxviii), and Machiavelli. Mary Shelley here follows Tegrimi and Machiavelli, who incorrectly list the general, Philip of Tarento, among the slain and equally incorrectly call him the son of Robert, King of Naples. (It was his son who was slain; he himself was Robert's brother, as Villani and Sismondi correctly stated.) The comparison to Hannibal's devastating victory of 216 BC over the Romans at Cannae in Apulia (Livy, XXII. xliv-l) is found in Tegrimi (p. 21); according to Livy, 40,000 were killed at Cannae; 10,000 were estimatedly killed at Montecatini (Green, p. 68). Only Machiavelli presents the victory as due to Castruccio; Tegrimi (1742 Chronology) and Sismondi attribute to him merely a large part in it.

interesting; but his eyes shone, and they beamed unutterable love upon her. Truly did he look a hero; for power sat on his brow, and victory seemed to have made itself a home among the smiles of his lips. "Triumph, my sweet girl," he said; "all my laurels are spoils for you. Nay, turn not away as if you disdained them; they are the assurances of the peace that you desire. Do not / doubt me; do not for a moment suffer a cloud of suspicion to darken your animated countenance. This sword has made me master of peace and war; and need I say, that my wise and gentle Euthanasia shall direct my counsels, her love and honour being the aim and purpose of my life?"

Upon such words could aught but pardon and reconciliation attend?

Castruccio's wound was slight, and soon healed. But he was now more than ever immersed in his political plans: throwing off the mask, he appeared openly as the leader of a party against Uguccione; his palace was for ever open, and crowded with friends and followers; and, when he rode through the streets, he was attended by a band of the first nobles in Lucca. To his other talents Castruccio joined a vein of raillery and bitter irony, which, when he chose to exert it, seemed to enter into and wither the soul of its object. His scoffs and mockery of the Faggiuola family were repeated through Lucca;[a] and the person against whom they were particularly directed, the governor whom Uguccione had appointed, / was a man formed to feel in every nerve the agony of derision.

Francesco having been killed at the battle of Monte Catini, Uguccione had set his son Ranieri over the Lucchese. Ranieri was only two-and-twenty years of age; but his straight black hair fell over a forehead prematurely wrinkled; without the courage of his father, he possessed all his cunning and ambition, as much cruelty, and even more deceit. He had long been a pretender to the hand of the countess of Valperga, – with no hope except that with which his own vanity inspired him: yet, when he perceived that Castruccio was his favoured rival, he felt as if he had been robbed of his inheritance; and the beauty, talents, and glory of his adversary made him taste to the dregs the cup of envy. The consciousness of power alone for a while restrained the manifestation of his feelings. He soothed himself with the idea that Castruccio's life was in his hands; yet a lurking doubt prevented him from putting forth his strength; he glared on his enemy, as a tiger who crouches within reach of his prey; but he dared not spring. He would gladly / have got rid of his rival by private assassination; but Castruccio was too cautious, and ever went too well attended, to afford an opportunity for such a measure. Rivalry in love was however but a small part of the cause of the hate with which Ranieri was filled; for Castruccio no longer disguised his abhorrence of the cruelty of Uguccione, or his contempt for the cowardly and artful policy of his son; and a man far less

---

[a] Machiavelli is the chief source for the image of Castruccio as a master of biting repartee.

cunning than Ranieri might easily perceive that he laboured day and night for the overthrow of the Faggiuola family.

An accidental scuffle brought these feelings into action; it were idle to attempt to discover the cause of a quarrel, at a period when civil broils were so common, not only among the Italians; but when the capitals of the French and English monarchs were often stained with blood on the most trivial occasions.[a] This affray arose between the dependents of Ranieri and of count Fondi; Castruccio and his companions joined in it; and it ended in the rout and flight of Faggiuola's men, one of whom was killed. Ranieri seized this opportunity to send to his father with greater effect an account / of the haughty conduct and machinations of Castruccio. The truth had been sufficient to awaken the suspicions of a man, whose rule it was never to permit an enemy to live; but the colouring that Ranieri gave to the affair, made it appear as if open war had been declared between the parties at Lucca. Uguccione had bathed his hands that very winter in the best blood of Pisa; and he considered one life more as a small sacrifice towards the completion of his security. His advice therefore was to act cautiously, but swiftly, and that the next messenger might bring intelligence of the death of his adversary.

This direction filled Ranieri with unwonted joy; it smoothed the wrinkles of his brow, and lighted up his eyes with ferocity: he would willingly have led forth his troops, and seized Castruccio in the midst of his partizans; but his deceitful disposition suggested to him a quieter, and as he imagined, a surer mode of proceeding. The enemies met at church; they disposed themselves on opposite sides of the aisle, – the followers of Castruccio viewed their opponents with a careless smile of contempt, / which was returned by a sullen scowl; while Ranieri manifested an alternation of gaiety and uneasiness, which his art could not entirely conceal. High mass being over, Castruccio was about to retire, when Ranieri, quitting his attendants, walked across the aisle; seeing his movement, the followers of Antelminelli crowded about him; but he bade them fall back, and with a haughty step, and a smile of conscious superiority, he also advanced towards his enemy; they met midway, and the two parties, their hands on their swords, watched every motion of their respective chiefs during this unexpected parley. Had not Ranieri's character for artifice been impressed on every mind, his appearance might now have lulled suspicion; – he smiled, and spoke with a loud, careless voice; and what was hidden under this friendly outside seemed rather timidity, than enmity: Castruccio fixed his eagle-eye upon him; but fear appeared to be the only feeling which lurked behind the frankness that Ranieri wished to assume: nor did he shrink from the examination; he spoke:

---

[a] Mary Shelley's sources diverged here. According to Machiavelli, Castruccio harboured the murderer of a Lucchese gentleman; Sismondi cites Machiavelli, saying also that Castruccio had slaughtered villagers of Camaiore who had threatened his life. Tegrimi (p. 23) says merely that he was accused of the latter.

"Messer Castruccio, methinks you are much / a stranger to my councils and board. Do you suppose that my father forgets your services in his cause, or that he does not pray for an opportunity of shewing his gratitude? Evil reports, I own, have gone abroad to your disadvantage, and your absence from my palace might give some colour to these; but I am not a suspicious man, and trust the actions of my friends which speak in their favour, more readily than the hearsay which traduces them. If any ill blood exists between us, and I am the cause of it, I freely ask your pardon for any offence I may have given you, and request, as the seal of our reconciliation, that you would honour with your presence a poor banquet I am to give to-night to the nobility of Lucca."[a]

Castruccio was somewhat astounded by this speech, which was concluded by the offer of his hand from the speaker. Castruccio drew back, and replied; "My poor services, my lord, were offered to my country; from her I hope for gratitude, from your father I neither deserve nor expect this meed. It were as well perhaps not to attempt to mix jarring elements; but, since you offer hospitality, I will freely accept / it; for, whatever cause of alienation may exist between us, you are a knight and a soldier, and I do not fear deceit."

Castruccio withdrew; and the certainty of revenge alone could have quelled the deadly anger of Ranieri at the haughty and supercilious treatment that he had received.

Before the hour for the banquet had arrived, Castruccio rode to the castle of Valperga, and related the occurrence to Euthanasia. She listened attentively, and then said: "There is some deep plot in this; I know Neri della Faggiuola; he is at once cowardly, artful, and cruel. Be on your guard; I would intreat you not to go to this feast, but that, going with your followers, I do not see what danger you can incur; but doubt not, that this, or any other friendly overture that may follow, is only a snare in which it is expected that you will entangle yourself."

"Fear not, dear girl; I am open-hearted with my friends; – but I have been a soldier of fortune; and at such a school I may well have learned to detect wiles more deep, and politicians more cunning then Ranieri. Let him / beware; this moon which has just bent her bow among the clouds of sunset, will not be two weeks old, when you may see this deep schemer take his solitary way to Pisa, glad to escape from the vengeance that he so well merits."

Castruccio attended the feast of Ranieri, accompanied by count Fondi and Arrigo Guinigi. He had expected to find the rest of his friends and partizans assembled there, since they had all received invitations: but Ranieri had acted with the utmost caution; and, a very short time before the hour fixed for the banquet, he had sent messages to the friends of Castruccio, and under various pretexts, had, unknown one to the other, employed them on different affairs

---

[a] Tegrimi (p. 23) and Machiavelli mention the banquet; both give the date as 1 April, 1316. The church-scene is Mary Shelley's invention.

which he pretended to be of the greatest urgency. When therefore Castruccio entered the banquetting hall, he found only the officers of the German troop attached to the Faggiuola faction, some old men who had retired from public affairs, and a few Guelph families who Ranieri supposed would remain neuter on the present occasion. Castruccio observed this, and felt that all was not / right; yet not for a moment did the expression of his physiognomy change, or his frank demeanour betray any sign of suspicion. It was not then the custom, as in the more barbarous society of France and England, to attend peaceful meetings as if armed for mortal combat; and Castruccio was unarmed, except with a small dagger, which as a matter of caution he concealed about his person.

The repast was sumptuous; course succeeded course; and the most delicate sweetmeats and richest wines invited the guests to a prolongation of their pleasures. Castruccio was both from habit and principle abstemious, and the quiet of the banquet was first interrupted by a sarcasm of Ranieri, as he pointed to the quantity of water which his guest mingled with his wine. The latter replied; and his irony was the more keen from the reputation of cowardice and luxury which his enemy bore. Ranieri grew pale; and, filling his own cup with pure wine, he presented it to Castruccio, saying; "Nay, Messere, before you depart, dishonour not my pledge, but drink this / cup of generous Cyprus, to the overthrow of the enemies of Faggiuola."

These words were the signal agreed upon with his soldiers; they suddenly entered, surrounded the other guests, and throwing themselves upon Castruccio, endeavoured to secure him. Twice he threw them off: and once he had nearly drawn his stiletto from his bosom; but he was overpowered and manacled with heavy chains – yet, standing thus impotent, his eagle-glance seemed to wither the soul of Ranieri, who, unable to give voice to the irony with which he had intended to load his victim, gave orders that he should be carried to prison.

Ranieri then addressed his guests, telling them, that the riotous behaviour of Castruccio the preceding week, and the murder of one of his servants, were the just causes of his imprisonment. He bade them not fear any danger to their own persons, unless they should rashly attempt to disturb the due course of justice. Arrigo, with all the warmth of youth, would have replied with bitter reproaches; but count Fondi, making him a signal of silence, and / deigning only to cast on Ranieri a smile of contempt, retreated with the youth from the violated board. Ranieri invited his guests to continue their festivity, but in vain: they were silent and confounded; one by one the Italians withdrew, and Ranieri was left only with his officers who were chiefly Germans, and the remainder of the evening was spent in that intemperate enjoyment of the bottle, which the Italians held in wonder and contempt. Ranieri did not wish to drown the voice of his conscience, for that was his servant, and not his monitor; but his coward spirit failed, when he reflected on his critical situation, and the number and resoluteness of Castruccio's friends: wine inspired him with boldness; and a riotous night succeeded and crowned a misspent day.

No feelings could be in more perfect contrast one to the other, than those with which the jailer and his prisoner hailed the morning of the ensuing day. Castruccio had slept soundly on the pavement of his dungeon; and, though his limbs were weighed down by chains, his spirit was light and tranquil; he trusted to his friends, and he trusted to the intimate persuasion / he felt, that his star was not to stoop before that of the cowardly and treacherous Ranieri. Looking at the clouds as they passed swiftly across the sun borne along by an irresistible wind, he chaunted a troubadour song of victory.

Ranieri awoke with those feelings of listless depression that succeed to drunkenness; the idea that Castruccio was his prisoner struck him with affright; and now, repenting that he had taken so decided a measure, he sent for his favourite attendant, and bade him go and reconnoitre the town, and endeavour to discover the opinions and temper of the citizens. During the absence of this man he was several times on the point of sending an order for the instantaneous death of his prisoner; but his heart failed him: he felt that he might be disobeyed, and that the mandate of death might be the signal for the deliverance of Castruccio. Thus he waited, irresolutely, but impatiently, till circumstances should decide the course he was to pursue.

The report of his messenger was ill calculated to allay his apprehensions. Knots of citizens / stood in the streets and market-place, who, with serious mien and angry fervour, talked over the occurrence of the preceding evening. Some friend of Castruccio was at the head of each of these, who incited the people to action, and, ridiculing the cowardice, and reprobating the treachery and cruelty of Ranieri, awakened in every heart love and reverence for Castruccio, by the well deserved praises that he bestowed upon him. The word Liberty seemed to be creeping among them and warming every soul, while it struck a blight upon the sensations of Ranieri: he dared not act, but sent a messenger to his father at Pisa, recounting what he had done, and desiring his assistance in the accomplishment of his revenge.

A few weeks before, Uguccione had caused Bonconti and his son, two Pisan nobles, much loved and esteemed in that town, to be put to death:[a] he had before committed flagrant injustices and legal murders in that city, and to these the people had submitted: but Bonconti was a man of understanding and courage; the Pisans had looked up to him as the instrument / of their deliverance from the tyrant; by his death this task seemed to devolve into their own hands, and their sullen looks and whispered discontents shewed plainly that

---

[a] The beheading of the Bonconti ('Buonconti' in Sismondi) had actually taken place in 1314, at the time of Uguccione's refusal to accept the terms of Robert, King of Naples, which the elder Bonconti had been involved in negotiating on behalf of Pisa (Villani, IX, cap. 73; Tegrimi, p. 23; Sismondi, ch. xxvii).

they were about to right themselves. Uguccione sat unsteadily on his seat of power; and his uneasiness, as is often the case in minds untamed by humanity, begot in him a hasty courage, and fierce rashness, that resolved not to yield to any obstacle; he was a stag at bay, and the Pisans stood about him watching some weak side on which they might commence their attack.

At this moment the messenger of Ranieri arrived, relating the seizure of Castruccio, and the fears of the governor. "Fool!" cried Uguccione, "does he not know that the members walk not without the head?"

So, without giving one moment to reflection, he hastily called his faithful troop together, consisting of about four hundred men, and, leaving Pisa, hastened at full gallop towards Lucca. The Pisans dared not trust their good fortune, when they saw their enemy and his adherents voluntarily desert their post, and deliver / a bloodless victory into their hands; before Uguccione had reached the summit of Monte San Giuliano, which is, as Dante says, the

Perchè i Pisan veder Lucca non ponno,[a]

the cry of liberty, and death to the tyrant, arose in the town; the multitude assailed the house of Uguccione; some of his household fell; the rest fled; and the crowd, now somewhat appeased, assembled to constitute as their chief, a man of understanding and valour, who might bring under discipline the furious passions of the injured Pisans.

Uguccione found Lucca in open revolt: he entered the town, and at the head of his troop endeavoured to charge the mutinous multitude. It was vain; firm barriers thrown across the streets impeded the horses, and the tyrant was obliged to parley with the heads of the revolters. They demanded Castruccio; and he was brought forth chained, and delivered to them; his fetters were knocked off, and, mounting a charger brought by one of his friends, his manacles carried as a trophy before him, he was led in triumph to his palace. The people almost / worshipped him as he passed, and the air rang with acclamations in his favour; a crowd of his adherents, well armed, clustered about him, proud of their victory, and proud of the chief whom they had delivered. His chains were affixed to the tower of his palace, in commemoration of this sudden change of fortune. Uguccione fled: – he did not wait to be expelled by the furious populace; the news reached him of the revolt of Pisa, and it struck him with a panic; he was accompanied by Ranieri; and, quitting Lucca by the northern gate, they hastened across the mountains to Lombardy, and in one day fell from the rank of powerful chieftains, to be soldiers of fortune at the hire of the first prince who might require their services.

Castruccio and his adherents assembled in his palace to deliberate on the government they should choose; the multitude assembled round, and demanded

---

[a] 'reason why the Pisan cannot see Lucca' (Dante, *Inferno*, XXXIII. 30, editor's translation). The Bagni di Pisa lie at the foot of this hill on the Pisan side.

to behold their beloved chief. – Castruccio shewed himself at the balcony, and was saluted with one cry, as Lord of Lucca, and captain[a] of the war against the Florentines: his friends joined in the acclamation; but Castruccio, / who never allowed a momentary enthusiasm to obliterate the plan of conduct that he had marked out for himself, made a sign for silence, which was obeyed. He then addressed the people, and, thanking them for their love and services, declared that he could not alone support the government of his town, and, after many modest observations, requested a companion in the weighty task. The people acceded to his wishes, and the Cavaliere Pagano Quartezzano was named as the sharer of his dignities and power under the appellation of consul.[b] /

CHAPTER XII.

Peace between Lucca and Florence. – Bindo.

The ill news had travelled fast; and Euthanasia knew of the imprisonment of Castruccio the same evening that it had taken place. Well acquainted with the cruel policy of the Faggiuola family and in particular with the dastard ferocity of Ranieri, her fears were wound up to an agonizing height: more unhappy than the prisoner himself, she slept not, nor did she seek sleep; but her thoughts were bent on the consideration of whether she were able in any manner to assist her friend. She resolved at least to employ all the influence her possessions and connexions gave her, to arrest the hand of the murderer.

Early in the morning young Guinigi arrived at the castle. If Arrigo admired Castruccio, he adored Euthanasia; her sex and beauty might well have a powerful effect on his youthful / heart, and her simplicity and purity were more calculated to influence his inexperienced but active understanding, than the more studied courtesies of Castruccio. Her pale cheek and heavy eyes indicated the anxious thoughts that beset her; and Arrigo hastened to tranquillize them. "Fear not," he said, "he shall not, he cannot die. His friends watch over him; and Ranieri has by this time learned, that he is more a prisoner among the guards in his palace, than Castruccio chained in his dungeon."

He then detailed the plans of the Ghibeline party for the deliverance of their

---

[a] He was given the title *dux*. (This elevation, and the expulsion of the della Faggiuola which preceded it, took place in April 1316; Villani, IX. cap. 78; Tegrimi, 1742 chronology; Sismondi, ch. xxviii).

[b] Thus in Tegrimi's 1742 Chronology. Napoleon was awarded the title of consul (1799), one of the parallels between him and Castruccio ('a little Napoleon' according to P. B. Shelley in a letter to Charles Ollier, 25 September, 1821; *PBSL*, II, p. 353); the office originated in republican Rome, and was an elective one with a fixed term.

95

chief; and, having somewhat calmed the uneasiness of the countess, he returned with haste to his post at Lucca.

Euthanasia passed an anxious day. She was alone; if one may be called alone, whose thoughts descended not to the calm of solitary meditation, but were actively engaged in the imagination of events passing but a few miles distant. It was a warm April day, but sunless: for the Libeccio had veiled the blue heavens with clouds which seemed to press / down the atmosphere, that unmoved by any breeze appeared even by its weight to encumber the flowers, and to destroy all elasticity either in vegetable or animal life. Poor Euthanasia walked restlessly on the plot of ground before the gate of her castle; and her languid eyes, bent towards Lucca, were able to discern objects afar off, sharpened as their sight was by love and fear. In the afternoon she saw a band of soldiers ride along the road beneath the rock on which her castle was built, directing their course towards the northern mountains. She thought that she could distinguish the uncouth figure of Uguccione in the tallest among the horsemen who led the troop; while in the rear she felt sure that she beheld the form of Ranieri.

Her heart was now relieved from many of its fears; and she watched with greater calmness the fading hues of sunset, and the moon, now but a day older than when Castruccio had foretold the overthrow of the tyrant. She had a favourite retreat near a spring that issued from the rock behind her castle. The mountain was almost perpendicular from which it / gushed; but a rude flight of steps had been cut, by which she ascended to it through a postern. The spring rose from a rift above, and fell first on a narrow rocky platform about seventy steps above the castle. Euthanasia had caused a basin to be scooped here for the reception of the water, and had covered it with a light portico, supported by fluted columns of the Etruscan order[a] made of the finest marble; a few mossy seats surrounded the fountain. The rock shaded her as she sat, on whose stony face grew nothing but heath, and such shrubs as seem to find nutriment and growth in stone itself; but the top was crowned by ilex trees and stunted myrtle underwood.[b] Thither she now retired, and watched the coming night; when suddenly she thought she heard a rustling above her, and a small bunch of myrtle fell on her lap; she looked up; and, gazing earnestly, perceived Castruccio, with one hand grasping a myrtle shrub, leaning from the summit of the precipice.

"Euthanasia! – Victory!" he cried.

"Victory and security!" she repeated with a deep sigh of joy. /

"And glory, and all the blessings of heaven!" he replied. She answered, but he was far above, and could scarcely hear the words she spoke; he threw another sprig of myrtle, and said, "To-morrow!" and retreated. She continued

---

[a] The Tuscan (or Etruscan) was the simplest of all the five orders of architecture.

[b] The myrtle is the emblem of Venus. The sentence exemplifies Mary Shelley's occasional use of Latinate word order.

to look upwards to the spot where he had leaned; the rustling of the leaves was still – the myrtles that had bent as he leaned upon them, slowly upraised themselves – yet still she thought that she heard his voice, until the murmuring of the near stream recalled her to herself, and told her how moveless every thing else was.

And now Euthanasia was happy – too happy; and fast-falling and many tears alone relieved her full heart. She was happy in the assurance of the safety and triumph of her friend; but it was his love that touched her heart, and made her thrill with delight. What sweeter meed is there in life, than the approbation and sincere friendship of those whom we approve and admire? But to be loved by such a one; to feel the deep sympathy of united affections, the delicious consciousness of being loved by one whom all the world approves, by / one who fully justifies his claim to the world's esteem by an oblivion of self, and heroic sacrifice of personal felicity for the public cause, touches a chord – opens a spring of feeling which those have never known, whose hearts have not been warmed by public feeling, or who have not entered with interest into the hopes and fears of a band struggling for liberty. The human soul disdains all restraint, and ever seeks to mingle with nature itself, or with kindred minds; to hope and fear for oneself alone often narrows the heart and understanding; but if we are animated by these feelings in unison with a multitude, bound by the same desires and the same perils, such participation of triumph or sorrow exalts and beautifies every emotion.

Yet triumph is a feeling which oppresses the human heart; and that strangely fashioned instrument seems more adapted for suffering than enjoyment; it is rather a passive, than an active principle; abundant joy fills it with melancholy, but it can extract pleasure from the depths of despair. Euthanasia was over-powered; and she felt, in that moment of satisfaction / to her hopes, an agitation and unquiet repining, which, though it were indeed only the rebellion of the heart against peace, seemed to her in after times as the foreboding of the unlooked for catastrophe to so much happiness.

The following evening Castruccio again visited her, and restored her to calm. He sat at her feet, and fixing on her his dark eyes, related the circumstances of his imprisonment and liberation. "Did you not wonder," said he, "at your eagle's visit yesternight? I would indeed that I had been one, so that I could have cast myself at your feet, instead of the silly myrtle that I threw! Yester evening, after the business of the day, I went to the castle of Mordecastelli, which is on this same mountain, not far from the Fairy's Fountain and the cypress, under which as children we often sat – which we visited a few weeks ago, clambering to it from the valley. When I left his castle, I passed by that spot; and, pausing there, I thought that perhaps I could not only attain the summit of the rock that overlooks your fountain, but in some way get down to the alcove itself, and thus surprize your retreat. I / was disappointed; the precipice is too high above; – but as I looked down, I caught a glance of your robe, and was repaid for my toil, in being able to communicate to you the news of my success. And now, dearest girl, be happy, and smile contentedly on me; for now that I have overcome my domestic enemies, and have supreme power in this hive of ours, you shall direct me, and there shall be the peace that you love, and the concord you so much desire between us and the proud republicans, your friends."

Euthanasia smiled, and said, "Well may it please one so nearly useless as I am, that I can save the lives of some of my fellow-citizens. Do you not know, dearest Castruccio, that when you draw your sword against the Florentines, it is always wetted with the blood of my best friends? Love you indeed I always must; but I know, for I have studied my own heart, that it would not unite itself to yours, if, instead of these thoughts of peace and concord, you were to scheme war and conquest."

"You measure your love in nice scales," replied Castruccio, reproachfully; "surely, if / it were as deep as mine, it would be ruled alone by its own laws, and not by outward circumstances."

Euthanasia answered earnestly, "So can it not be with me; I have been bred in a city distracted by domestic faction, and which, when it obtains a moment of peace in its own bosom, loses the flower of its children in petty wars. A hatred and fear of war is therefore a strong and ruling passion in my heart; but other feelings mingle with these in my zeal for your concord with my fellow-townsmen. Florence is my native city; its citizens are bound to me by the ties of consanguinity and friendship: the families of the Pazzi, the Donati, the Spini, and other noble or plebeian Florentines, against whom you fight when you war with them, each contains individuals whom I love and honour. I should be a traitor to the best feelings of human nature, and a rebel to my country, if I allied myself to its enemy: think you that I who have joined in the social meetings of the Florentines, who as a child was caressed by them, and as a woman loved, who have been present at their marriages, and have / mourned among them at their funerals, – when my own beloved father was attended to his grave by these men whom you call your enemies, and my own bitter sorrows assuaged by the sympathy of their daughters, – think you, that thus linked by every social tie, having prayed, and rejoiced, and wept with them, that I could say to you, 'Go, prosper!' when you should go to destroy them? Dearest Castruccio, if, united to you, such an event were to ensue, in that moment I must die, or live a death in life."

Castruccio replied only by fresh assurances of his earnest desire for peace, and kissed from the brow of Euthanasia the cloud that for a moment had gathered there.

It had been a strange task to unveil the heart of Antelminelli, and to disentangle the contradictory feelings that influenced him at that moment. There can be no doubt that he never forgot his designs for the aggrandizement of his native city; and he had seen too much of courts, and felt too strongly his own superiority to the men about him, to allow us to suppose that he entertained the idea of establishing a free republic / there, and submitting his actions and intentions to be controled by the people. It had long been his earnest desire to raise and reinstate the fallen Ghibeline party in Tuscany; and this was not to be accomplished except by the humiliation of the Florentines: yet at this time his whole policy was employed in concluding a peace with them, – a peace, which was ratified the following April, and preserved for three years.[a] These three years it is true were not spent in inactivity, but in the reduction of the surrounding country,[b] and, latterly, in preparation for the successful war he afterwards carried on against Florence. Are therefore his protestations to Euthanasia to be considered as wholly deceitful? His frank countenance and unembarrassed voice forbade that idea for a moment to cross her imagination: we may perhaps form this conclusion; – that he now found it for his interest to conclude a peace with Florence; and he made the sincerity of his present purpose lend its colour to his assurances for the future.

A whole year was spent in the arrangement of the treaty. Euthanasia passed all / that time at her castle; and her content was again disturbed by the successes of Castruccio; who in treating for peace did not fail to make it more desirable to his enemies, by seizing every opportunity to defeat their forces, and lay waste their country; nor did the knowledge of the pain which these operations caused his friend, in any degree check his activity. Euthanasia loved Castruccio; but her judgement was penetrating, and she was so accustomed to meditate on the events and feelings of each day, that, during this time, she in part penetrated the character of her lover. He was formed for victory and daring, rather than for magnanimity: he was swift of design and steady in execution; bold, valiant, yet gentle of manner; his wit was keen; his penetration into the dispositions of men instantaneous; and he possessed also, as by instinct, the faculty of adapting himself to every character, and of acquiring the love of all around him: men always love those who lead them successfully through danger. He was temperate in his habits; and in his mien, though the exterior were ardent and even rash, there might be perceived / underneath a reserve of caution, a presence of mind, which never permitted him to be carried beyond the dictates of prudence, and an eagle-eye which caused him swiftly to distinguish danger from impracticability. He trod the most perilous acclivities, but his foot was sure like that of the chamois; and he could discern from afar where the path was broken, and would check himself in the most headlong course. All this was well; but, underneath a frankness of behaviour, and an

---

[a] This peace of 1317 was general between the Guelphs and Ghibellines of Tuscany and ended the phase of conflict initiated by Henry VII; Castruccio was not the leading initiator (Sismondi, ch. xxviii).

[b] The historical Castruccio spent the period (1317–19) extending the territory of Lucca as far as the present Genoese Riviera.

apparent nobleness of nature, there was the craft of a grey-haired courtier, and even at times the cruelty of a falling tyrant. Euthanasia saw not all this; but at times a glance, a tone seemed to open a mine of undiscovered evil in his character, that made her shudder in the very depths of her nature: yet this sensation would pass away, and she, prompt to forget evil in others, thought no more of it.

This year might be called the happiest of her life; yet it was that which first schooled her to the pain and anguish which were afterwards her portion. The flower of love can never exist without its thorns. She loved, and / was beloved: – her eyes beamed with a quicker fire; and her whole soul, perfectly alive, seemed to feel with a vividness and truth she had never before experienced. Nature was invested for her with new appearances; and there was a beauty, a soul, in the breeze of evening, the starry sky, and uprising sun, which filled her with emotions she had never before so vividly felt. Love seemed to have made her heart its chosen temple; and he linked all its beatings to that universal beauty which is his mother and his nurse.

There are feelings, which overpower the human soul, and often render it morbid and weak, if virtuous action does not give dignity to reverie. Euthanasia had many occupations, and among them the glorious and delightful one of rendering her numerous dependents happy. The cottages and villages over which she presided, were filled by a contented peasantry, who adored their countess, and knew her power only by the benefits she conferred on them. Castruccio often accompanied her in her visits to these; and he, accustomed as he was to count men as the numerals of a military / arithmetic, even he was touched by her care for the sick, her many ways of displaying her judgement and abounding benevolence towards her people. Yet sometimes he laughed at the difference between her practice and her theory, and asked the youthful sovereign, why she did not erect her states into a republic?

She smiled; but then, collecting herself, answered seriously; "When I first inherited my mother's power, I gave much consideration to this very question; not of forming a separate republic of my poor villages, but of incorporating them, as many nobles have done, and as doubtless the lords of Valperga will one day be obliged to do, with some neighbouring and more powerful republic. My inclinations led me to join myself to Florence; but the distance of that city, and the immediate vicinity of Lucca, shewed me the impracticability of that project. Valperga must one day fall into the hands of the Lucchese; but, if I had at any time made an alliance with them, I should have destroyed the present happiness of my people; there would have been war instead of peace, instead of concord and plenty, party / agitations and heavy taxes. This, my friend, must be my excuse for my tyranny; but, when the alliance between you and the Florentines can be sure, when Lucca is as peaceful and happy as Valperga, believe me, I will no longer arrogate a power to which I ought not to have a pretension."

Castruccio smiled; he hardly believed the simple sincerity of Euthanasia; he understood well and judged with sagacity the balancing objections in a

question of interest; but the principle of decision was always with him, that
which would most conduce to the fulfilment of his projects, seldom that of the
good or evil which affected others. Yet this was veiled even to his own mind, by
a habit of gentleness and forbearance, which even in this age of the world, often
fills the place, and assumes the form of virtue.

And now Euthanasia was busy in preparing for a court, which she had
determined to hold, when peace should be ratified between the contending
powers of Tuscany; and Castruccio found her employed in the, for her,
unwonted toils, of the arrangement of silks, jewels, / and tapestry. She said:
"You know that the dependents of Valperga are lightly taxed; and the little
money that enters my coffers is chiefly expended in the succour of their own
necessities: yet of that little I have reserved a sum for periods of sickness,
scarcity, or any more agreeable occasion that may call for it. A part of this will
be expended on the present solemnity. Nor do I think that I hurt my good
people by such an extravagance: their joy on this occasion will be far greater
than mine; their pride and love of pleasure will be gratified; for in arranging the
amusements of my court the country people will have a full share; and, if *we*
engage the attention of Borsiere, Guarino[a] and other distinguished *Uomini di
Corte*, the buffoons, jugglers, and dancers, will spread glee among the villagers."

The castle was fuller than usual of dependents and workmen, and its cloister-
like silence was exchanged for the noise of the hammer, and the voices of
Italians, ever louder than need is. Euthanasia witnessed their eagerness with
pleasure; and her undisguised sympathy in their feelings made her adored by
her servants / and dependents. She had now about her several of the daughters
of her richer subjects, who assisted in the arrangement of her castle: and there
were gathered in the hall men who had grown grey on her estate, who
remembered the dreadful battle of Monte Aperto, the fall of Manfred, and the
death of the last unfortunate descendant of Frederic Barbarossa.[b] These

---

[a] Not found as a historical personage; perhaps to be thought of as a forbear of a distinguished
literary family, whose members included Guarino of Verona (1370–1460), like Petrarch a collector
of Greek manuscripts, and Baptiste Guarini (1537–1612), author of *Il Pastor Fido* (1585). A
'Guarnerio or Irnerio' was an interpreter of the law under the countess Matilda, according to
Muratori. 'Guarino' appears on a list of names, ruled off from other entries on p. 95 of Ab. Dep.
e. 274, apparently derived from several sources. Some have been seemingly picked at random from
the index to Muratori; others appear to have been found incidentally through searching for
information relating to the countess Matilda in Muratori, others are untraced. The list is as follows:
Leodino, Guido, Radolfo, Marcello, Alfano, Ildone, Guarino, Ivone, Abselmo, Arrigo, Irnerio,
Casaregi, Malvezzi, Pagi. For Borsiere see p. 105.

[b] Alluding to Manfred's victory over the Florentine Guelphs (1260), which, but for Farinata,
would have resulted in the destruction of Florence; his fall at Benevento (1266); the execution of
his half-nephew Conradin (1252–68), last of the Hohenstaufen kings. Conradin inherited the
throne of Naples and Sicily at the age of two, but was displaced by Manfred (1258) and by Charles
of Anjou, victor of Benevento. In 1268, Charles's rebellious Ghibelline subjects petitioned Conradin to claim his inheritance and liberate Italy, but his initial victories were followed by defeat. He
was handed over to Charles, tried, and beheaded at Naples (Sismondi, chs xviii, xix, xxi).

recounted the feats and dangers of their youth to their descendants, until, so strange are the feelings of our nature, war, peril and ruin seemed joys to be coveted, not perils to be eschewed.

Among the attendants who most constantly waited on her person, was a man who, from his diminutive stature, and strange dress, might have been taken for the buffoon or dwarf so common at the courts of princes in those days, had not the melancholy of his looks forbidden that supposition. Yet he had some of the privileges of the licensed fool; for he mingled in the conversation of his superiors, and his remarks, generally pithy, were sometimes bitter and satirical: yet indeed they were more commonly / characterized by a wild and imaginative originality, than by wit; and, if they sometimes made others laugh, he never smiled. The playful and witty disposition of Castruccio would often make him enter into conversation with, and reply to, and try to draw out this strange being, who was no less uncommon in his person than in his mind. He was of that race of which there are a few native specimens in Italy, generally called Albinois;[a] his complexion was of a milky fairness, his hair white, and his long white eyelashes hardly shaded his light red eyes: he was brief of stature, and as slender as he was short; the softness of his features, and the roundness and flexibility of his limbs, manifested his want of strength; his mild, but almost meaningless physiognomy betrayed the want of judgment, courage, and all the more manly virtues. His mind seemed to approach the feebler spark of animal life, had it not been redeemed by an imagination of which he hardly appeared conscious himself, but which raised him above many of the brutal and rough peasants who despised him. Sometimes Castruccio / laughed at Euthanasia for keeping this strange creature about her, but she defended herself, saying:

"Indeed, my lord, you must shew no disrespect towards this servant of mine, and truly you will be little inclined to do so, when I have summed up all his good qualities. First, he has by heart, ready to quote on any suitable occasion, every prophecy that has been made since the time of Adam, and knows all the vulgar expositions of the sacred texts. Then he is an adept in the knowledge of sacred trees, fountains, and stones, the flight of birds, lucky and unlucky days; he has an extensive acquaintance with witches, astrologers, sorcerers, and *tempestarii**; he knows every peculiar ceremony for remarkable days, how to celebrate the calends of January, those of August, and the *Vindemie Nolane*; none of our cattle are blest by St. Anthony until he has bound on their crowns; the ceremonies attendant on the Nativity, Easter, and other feasts, are / all conducted under his guidance.[b] He interprets all the dreams of the castle, and

---

* Persons supposed to have the power of commanding the elements.

---

[a] This spelling of 'Albino' has not been found in Italian, but 'Albinos' is found as a French singular form. cf. Fantoni ('Labindo'), court poet and patriot (fl. 1770–90).

[b] Details of folk-belief derive from Muratori, III, diss. 59, pp. 235–6 (noted in Ab. Dep. e. 274, p. 95), except for St Anthony's cattle. The *Vindemie Nolane* are festivities connected with the vintage, presumably at Nola.

foretells the point of time when to begin any enterprize: he has a wonderful assortment of holy legends and strange relics; such as a lock of Adam's hair, a little of the sawdust from Noah's saw-pit when he clove the planks for the ark, a brick of the tower of Babel, and a tooth of St. Theresa; he has presented many of these to the priest of San Martino, and the people go and adore these shreds and patches of religion with the veneration that its divine morality alone demands.[a] Although of a feminine and un-muscular form, he is healthy; he is silent to a miracle; and among my noisy household he alone flits about unheard, so much so that I have been assured that grass yields not beneath his feet, and that he has no shadow; but you can yourself ascertain that fact. I believe him to be faithful, yet I think him to be attached to none, except the wild beings whom his imagination invests with supernatural powers. But he is an excellent guide for me in my various wanderings, since, as if he had a clue of thread, he can find his unerring way amid the most / pathless desarts and forests. With all these wonderful acquirements he is generally disliked; he is said to be the son of a witch, and to have a natural propensity to evil; yet I have never heard of any ill act of his doing; although in truth some strange events have taken place with regard to him, that look as if he had communion with the spirits of air.

"I have said that he is attached to no one among us, yet I may be wrong. If he is always near my person, it is because he seizes every moment, when he is permitted to enter, to creep near me. Once, when I left him here during a visit to Florence, he pined for some time, till every one believed that he was about to die; and then taking a sudden resolution, like a dog following the scent of his master, he departed on foot, and in less than twenty-four hours, arrived half dead with fatigue at my palace at Florence.

"I have another motive for being attached to him: he was a favourite of my father. He found him when a child, in a village not far from Florence, half starved, and ill treated by the country people; for he could not work, / and, being an orphan, was destitute of every resource; the idea of his unholy parentage and his strange appearance, rendering the country-people even malignantly inclined towards him. He loved my father, and almost sunk to the grave with sorrow when he died; nor at that time would he leave the room where I was, or if obliged to go, he crept near the door crouching like a dog for the moment of admittance."

This being was now very busy amidst the preparations for the court; preparations which engaged all the hands and all the heads of Valperga. While the countess made provision for the entertainment of her guests, her dependents practised the games and exercises with which they should amuse the nobles: all

---

[a] Saint Martin is the dedicatee of the cathedral church of Lucca. There was no saint of the church named Theresa at this period; while this could be the point, another possibility is that Mary Shelley's manuscript read 'Thekla'. Like St Walburga, St Thekla (died c.790) was an English missionary nun enlisted by St Boniface of Crediton to work in Germany.

was bustle and animation, but all was joy and good humour. Castruccio and Euthanasia became dearer to each other, as he perceived the pleasure he was able to bestow upon her by a compliance with her wishes; and she felt gratitude for the delight she enjoyed, towards him whom she fondly looked upon as its cause. /

CHAPTER XIII.

Euthanasia holds a Court.

As the day approached on which Euthanasia was to hold her court, her castle became thronged with the nobility, wealth, and beauty of Tuscany and Lombardy. She had wished indeed to make this a public union of the two parties which distracted Italy; but she was so noted a Guelph that few Ghibelines appeared, although some were attracted by the name of Castruccio, to come under his escort, and in his company. First arrived her uncle, the lord Radolfo di Casaregi;[a] he was an old man, but he loved to encircle his bare temples with an iron helmet, and to try his well used sword against the unfleshed blades of the sons of his companions in arms in days gone by. Then came the marquess Marcello Malespino of Valdimagra,[b] his wife, and three lovely daughters; / they were accompanied by three brothers of the Bondelmonti family of Florence: these claimed affinity to the house of Adimari, and when by the laws of her country Euthanasia was obliged to choose a guardian for her maiden state, she had selected the eldest, count Bondelmonte de' Bondelmonti to be her *Mondualdo*;[c] this relationship had given rise to a sincere friendship, which, although the difference of age was inconsiderable, and the same reverence and obedience could never be felt or exercised, yet in some sort was to Euthanasia in the stead of her dead parents. There arrived soon after the chief members of the Pazzi, Donati, Visdomini, Gianfigliazi, and other Guelph families of Florence; there was Alberti count of Capraia, and all the numerous troop that claimed

---

[a] See the note on Guarino (p. 101).

[b] Perhaps suggested by Moroello Malespina di Valdimagra (died c.1315), the probable addressee and recipient of of Dante's Canzone XI, and his host in 1306. The Malespini were a Ghibelline family, except for Moroello, and owned large estates around the river Magra.

[c] The name 'Bondelmonte' indicates that he was the clan leader; in 1215 his ancestor broke his engagement with a Ghibelline maiden and was assassinated; as a result, open warfare broke out between Florentine Guelphs and Ghibellines. The Mondualdo ('Monualdo' in Villani, II, cap. 9) was a Lombardy institution (Muratori, I, diss. 20, p. 196; noted in Ab. Dep. e. 274, p. 49).

relationship to him; and many others, both Bianchi and Neri, both Guelph and Ghibeline, whose names it would be needless to detail.[a]

Then arrived a multitude of *Uomini di Corte*; story-tellers, *improvisatori*,[b] musicians, singers, actors, rope-dancers, jugglers and buffoons. The most distinguished among the first class / was William Borsiere*; a man of courteous yet frank manners, nice wit and keen penetration: he was about forty years of age; but he had lost none of the jovial temper of youth, and his generous and even noble disposition made him more respected than men of his class usually were. There was Bergamino,[c] a man more caustic than Borsiere, but whose insinuating address obtained pardon for his biting words; no one knew better than Bergamino to cure the wounds his tongue had made. There was Andreuccio,[d] whose satirical mood and rough manners frequently drew upon him the anger of the nobles on whose favour he depended; and he was so often dismissed, disgraced and unrewarded, from the courts, where his companions were loaded with presents, that, from his mean and sometimes ragged appearance, and his snarling habits, he went by the name of the *Cane Mendicante*.[e] He wished to rival Borsiere and Bergamino who were staunch friends, and endeavoured to make up for his lack of the more delicate kind of wit by / caustic sayings and contemptuous remarks. There was Ildone,[f] a foolish, smiling fellow, but who sang sorrowful airs with so sweet and touching a voice, that, if you shut your eyes, you might have imagined that St. Cecilia[g] herself had descended to entrance the world with heavenly melody.

Guarino, the *Improvisatore*, closed the list of the distinguished *Uomini di Corte*. He was sought in every court in Lombardy for his entertaining qualities: his tales displayed the fire of genius, and the delicate observations of a lover of nature. But he was eaten up by vanity and envy; he hated all those who were admired, from the princely beauty who attracted all regards, down to the lowest buffoon at court. If he were sought by the great, so much the more was he avoided by his equals and inferiors; to the first he tricked himself out with a flattering tongue, a mean and servile address, and gross adulation; for the second he expressed hatred and contempt; and he tyrannized over the last with

---

* See Boccaccio: *Giornata* I. *Novella* 8.[h]

---

[a] Names found together in Villani, V, caps 38 and 40; details of the Alberti of Capraia are taken also from Targioni, I, pp. 20–24; 61–70.

[b] Extempore poets, for which Tuscany was famous.

[c] Bergamino plays a similar part to Borsiere in the *Decameron* (I. vii). Both *uomini di corte* give witty rebukes to stingy patrons.

[d] The main character in *Decameron*, II. v, but he is a horse-dealer, not an *uomo di corte*.

[e] 'Begging dog'; the nick-name probably contrasts with Cane Grande (The Great Dog), Bergamino's patron in the *Decameron*.

[f] See note on Guarino (p. 101).

[g] The patron saint of music.

[h] In Dante (*Inferno*, XVI. 70–2), newly arrived in the seventh circle of Hell, he reports the wretched state of the city and adds to the torments of patriotic Florentines among the damned.

a hand of iron. But all three classes might equally dread his malignant calumnies, and hatred of all that was good. / He spared no art, no wit, no falsehood, to detract from merit, however exalted or lowly; and so full was he of wiles, that he was seldom detected in his serpent craft. He had been a Ghibeline, and at one time was imprisoned by the Dominican inquisitors[a] as a heretic; but now he surpassed all the Italians in superstition and credulity; his friends said that he was truly pious, his enemies that he was the most deceitful of hypocrites: but the trait that sealed his character, was his intolerance and violent persecution of his former heretical associates. Those who were most indulgent said, that he had been first actuated by fear, and was now a sincere convert; he himself pretended to attribute his conversion to a miracle, and of such consequence was he in his own eyes, that he almost affirmed that a saint from heaven had informed him, that the redemption of mankind had been undertaken by the Almighty Saviour for his benefit alone.

Many others followed and joined these; but they were a nameless multitude, distinguished only for vulgar talents; some trying to raise a laugh by folly, others by pert wit; many by / manual jests upon each other, in which innumerable were the blows given and received: they were a strange set, and whether they were handsome or ugly, old or young, agile or slow, expert or awkward, they turned even their defects to account, and with a never-ceasing grin, thronged around the nobles, forming a contrast to the dignified deportment and rich dresses of the latter, by their supple and serpentine motions, strange gait, and motley habiliments; some being ragged from lack of wit, others from detected roguery, all regarding with the eagerness of starved curs the riches of the castle, and the generosity of its mistress.

The court opened on the first of May; it was to last four days; and, on the evening before, surrounded by her guests, Euthanasia issued forth the laws for their amusements on the occasion: "The first day," said she, "we will give to hunting and hawking; the country is well stocked with game, and each guest has surely his falcon on his fist. I will instal Antelminelli, the *liberatore* of Lucca, king for that day; for he has been in foreign countries, and has studied these amusements under the best / masters of the age; and I doubt not is well able to direct our exertions, and secure us plentiful sport.

"The second day we will give up to our friends, the *Uomini di Corte*: they shall do their best to please us, and to deserve the rewards in store for them; certainly none will censure my choice, when I name William Borsiere king of that day. Let him direct the exertions of the rest, so that their tales, their songs, and their feats may succeed one another in agreeable variety.

"On the third day the lists shall be set, and the knights will tilt for the honour

---

[a] The Inquisition, the ecclesiastical court founded in 1232 to combat heresy in the Holy Roman Empire by the Emperor Frederick II, rapidly became a papal prerogative. Inquisitors were largely appointed from among the Dominican friars (established 1215).

of their ladies' beauty; the conqueror shall receive as the reward of his prowess the liberty of choosing the queen for the following day, who will direct the sports of the ladies, and close with their games the gaieties of my court."

A shout of applause followed the enunciation of these laws; and it was declared by all, that no better could be devised for the promotion of amusement among their joyful assembly.

On the first of May the sun arose in cloudless / splendour. The steeds richly caparisoned were led from the stable, the ladies were mounted on gentle palfreys, and were followed by the esquires, holding the hawks, or with the dogs in leash; others sounding the awakening horn, while the air resounded with voices which called the idlers from their rooms, and said that the hunter deserved no game, who was not with the first a-field to brush the morning dew from the grass. Euthanasia headed a chosen band supreme in beauty; her soft and enthusiastic eyes now sparkled with joy, which the fair expanse of her smooth brow shewed to be yet uninvaded by the fang of a bitter sorrow; a smile hovered on her beautiful lips, like Love playing among the leaves of a rose; her golden hair shone under the sunbeams, and clustered round her neck white as marble, and, like that enriched by many a wandering vein, eclipsing the jewels of her dress; her motions, free as the winds, and graceful as an antelope of the south, appeared more than human in their loveliness; and, when she awoke the air with her silver voice, silence seemed on the watch to drink in the sound. /

And now away!—— They rode down the steep on which the castle stood, to a chesnut wood, and thence along a plain covered with brushwood: all was alive and gay; the huntsmen called to their dogs; – the knights reined in their restless steeds; – and the ladies with animated gestures, laughing looks, and upturned eyes, watched the flight of their birds, and betted upon their speed.

When noon approached, they became heated and tired, and looked around for a shady spot where they might repose. Castruccio rode forward, and said: – "I should ill deserve the honour of being king of this day, if I suffered my fair subjects to wander as in a desart without refreshment or repose – follow me!"

They entered a chesnut wood; and, after riding about half a mile, they came to a small plot of ground, encircled by trees, and protected from the heat by canopies which were fastened to the boughs: a magnificent repast was prepared in this retreat; a profusion of wines glittered in glass vessels; the tables were piled with every delicate sweetmeat, as well as with the more substantial fare of flesh and fowl. / The esquires having fastened their falcons to the branches of the trees, and covered their eyes with the hood, seized the large carving knives, and began their ministry; while the joyous band seated themselves on the cushions that had been provided for their accommodation.

After the repast was ended, they reposed under this delicious shade, watching the changeful shadows of the trees, and listening to the songs of the birds – "How delightful it would be," cried Calista di Malespino, "if Ildone or Guarino were here, whose songs rival the sweetest birds!"

"To-morrow these men will display their talents," said Castruccio; "to-day we must amuse ourselves." Then clapping his hands, several servants brought forward musical instruments, such as were then in fashion, unlike in form those now used, but which in sound and construction might be compared to the lute, the harp, the guitar, and the flute. Many of the company had sweet voices; some who came from Genoa, sang the romances of the Provençal minstrels; the Florentines sang the / canzones of Dante, or chosen passages from the Tesoretto of his master, Ser Brunetto Latini,[a] or indeed stanzas of their own composing, for the Florentines were an ingenious race, and few among the nobles had passed the boundary between youth and age, without having indited more than one sonnet to his mistress's eyebrow: the inhabitants of each separate town had a favourite poet, whose verses they now rehearsed.

Thus the time passed, till the sun descended, and the lengthening shadows told them that the heat was gone, and the light of day well nigh spent; when they mounted their horses, and rode towards the castle along the skirts of the chestnut wood. The high Apennines were still white with snow; and, as evening came on, a refreshing breeze blew across the plain, and sang among the branches of the trees, – at a distance was heard the murmuring of the Serchio, as it travelled along in its unwearied course; the air was perfumed by a thousand scents, for the grass was mowing, and bathed the element in sweetness. From out one copse a nightingale poured forth its melodious notes, / singing as it were to one lone star that peered through the glowing sunset; Arrigo taking his flute drew a responsive strain which the sweet bird strove to imitate, while the cavalcade passed silently along. Darkness closed around, and the first fire-flies of summer issued from their deep green bowers among the bushes, and darted forth their gentle, ineffectual flame, skimming over the fields, which, as a phosphoric sea, or as a green heaven of evershifting planets, now was dark, and again thickly studded by these stars. The glow-worm on the ground slowly trailed his steady light; a few bats flew from the rocks; and the regular moan of the Aziolo[b] wheeled about the trees, and spoke of fine days to come. As the home-ward hunters ascended the mountain, the breeze died away, and a breathless stillness pervaded the atmosphere; Euthanasia rode near Castruccio; her sweet countenance bespoke a deeper joy than mere gaiety, and her wild eyes shone with her emotion. She had thrown her capuchin over her head; and her face, fair as the moon encircled by the night, shone from beneath the sable cowl, while her golden locks twined themselves / round her neck:

---

[a] Brunetto Latini (c.1210–94), a Florentine Guelph, greeted by Dante as 'Ser Brunetto' in the *Inferno* (XV. 16–124). Cary has an extensive note on the allegorical *Tesoretto*, which he calls 'perhaps but little known'; his summary mentions the encounter with the ladies 'Love, Hope, Fear and Desire'.

[b] The 'little downy owl' of P. B. Shelley's 'The Aziola' (1829); corrected from 'Agiolo', probably stemming from a misreading of Mary Shelley's long-tailed 'z'. The setting recalls P. B. Shelley, 'Letter to Maria Gisborne' (1824), ll. 274–91, written in 1820.

Castruccio gazed on her, and would have given worlds to have embraced her, and to print on her glowing cheek a kiss of love; he dared not, – but his heart swelled with joy, when she turned to him with an affectionate smile, and he whispered his heart – "She is mine."

The second day William Borsiere was prepared to amuse the guest by his own and his companions' talents. His task was more difficult to perform than that of Castruccio, for his materials were not so easy to be controled as hawks and hounds. Guarino was mortally offended by the choice of Euthanasia with regard to the king of the day, and declared that he had a cold, and could not sing. Nothing but his intolerable vanity vanquished his sullenness; for, when he found that, upon his refusal, Borsiere passed him by, and that his ill humour would only punish himself by consigning him to obscurity, he consented to be numbered among the recruits of the day. Andreuccio was less tractable, for he was less vain; and it was sheer avarice that caused his anger, when he imagined that Borsiere would be the / best paid of the company; he absolutely refused to perform his part in story-telling, but reserved his wit for endeavours to turn to ridicule the amusements and exertions of his favoured rival.

In the morning at break of day, each fair lady was awakened by a song, bidding her arise and eclipse the sun; and, as he awoke, and gave life to the flowers and fruits of the earth, so must she spread her benign influence over the hearts of men. The guests assembled in the hall of the castle, which was hung with festoons of evergreens and flowers; and, as they sat, an invisible concert was played, and, between the pauses of the music, a strain of rich melody broke upon the air, that by its unrivalled sweetness betrayed that the singer was Ildone, who, thus concealed, could wrap the soul in Elysium, while his presence must have destroyed the enchantment.

After the music, they were conducted to a small amphitheatre, constructed on the little green platform before the castle, where they were amused by the tricks of the jugglers, sleight of hand, fire-eating, rope-dancing, and / every prank that has been known from the shores of the Ganges to those of the Thames, from the most distant periods, even down to our own times. After these had displayed their arts, a number of the peasantry of Valperga presented themselves to run at the ring. Three pieces of cloth, and two of silk, the prizes for the various games, streamed from the props that supported the amphitheatre. Two poles were erected, and a string was attached to these, on which were strung three rings. A peasant on horseback, with his lance in rest, galloped past in a line parallel to the string, endeavouring to catch the three rings on the point of his lance; the first, second and third failed, – the fourth was more successful; he caught the three rings, and bore off the piece of scarlet-cloth as his prize. A wrestling match succeeded, a foot-race, and then a horse-race; the prizes were distributed by Borsiere; and then, it being noon, the company adjourned to their mid-day meal.

It were needless to enumerate the dainties that made their appearance;

Borsiere resolved that the feast neither of the preceding, nor of / the two following days, should exceed his; and, having been often regaled at the tables of the most luxurious princes of Europe, he now displayed the skill that he had there acquired, in the directions he gave to the ruder cooks of Euthanasia. When every one had satisfied his appetite, the conversation flagged, and the eyes of the ladies wandered round in search of new amusement. Borsiere appeared at the head of his party; Bergamino, Guarino, Ildone and a score others of less fame came forward; while Andreuccio edged in sideways, neither choosing to join, nor be left out of the company. Advancing in a courteous manner, Borsiere intreated the company to follow him: they all rose, each lady attended by her cavalier. Borsiere had been bred at courts, and knew how to marshal them with the science of a seneshal; as they quitted the hall, they, as by magic, fell each into his proper place, and every noble dame felt that neither could she have preceded the person before her, nor would she have gone behind the one who followed her. Thus, in courtly guise, they proceeded through several passages of the castle, till they quitted / it by a small postern; the rocky face of the mountain rose, as I have already said, immediately behind the castle, and almost overhung the battlements; but this postern opened on the little winding staircase I have before mentioned, that, cut in the rock, enabled them to scale the precipice; they ascended therefore, and before they could feel fatigued, they came to a small platform of turf-covered rock, which Borsiere had prepared for their accommodation. The fountain, that gushed from a cleft, trickled down with a gentle murmur, and filled the basin prepared to receive it with its clear and sparkling liquid. This fountain had, like many other springs of those mountains, peculiar qualities: in summer it was icy cold, and in winter it became warmer and warmer as the temperature of the air decreased, until on the frosty mornings of December it smoked in its passage down the rock. To preserve the waters of this basin from the rains, Euthanasia had, as already mentioned, built an alcove over it, supported by small columns; this was a favourite retreat of our young mountain-nymph; and Borsiere had adorned it for the occasion / with a master's hand. The boughs of the trees were bent down, and fastened to the rock, or to the roof of the alcove, and then, being interlaced with other boughs, formed a web on which he wove a sky of flowers, which shut out the sun's rays, and, agitated by the gentlest airs, cast forth the most delicate scents: the artificer of the bower had despoiled an hundred gardens to decorate only the floor of the platform, forming a thousand antic devices with the petals of various flowers. Anemones, narcissi, daffodils, hyacinths, lilies of the valley, and the earliest roses, had all lent their hues, making a brief mosaic of these lovely and fragile materials; and the white columns of the alcove shone in the midst of this splendid shew in elegant simplicity. Seats were placed round in a semicircle for the company; from hence they could behold the whole country; the platform was so high, that it surmounted the battlements of the castle, and they viewed the entire plain of

Lucca, its defiles and woody hills, and the clear Serchio that loitered on its way across it. An exclamation of delight burst from all lips, as they entered this flowery paradise, / where every gay colour of nature was heaped about in rich and lovely profusion, while the deep green of the ilex trees, the soft and fan-like foliage of the acacia, mingled with the shining foliage of the laurel, bay and myrtle, relieved the eye from any glare of colours. The joyous company sat down; and Borsiere, coming forward, announced, that he and his companions were ready to present the assembly with their songs and tales; Euthanasia accepted the offer in the name of her guests; and Guarino first shewed himself: that he should be the first to attract the attention of the noble guests had been the bribe which won him to forget his hoarseness, and, having entered upon his task, there was no doubt that his vanity would induce him to exert his utmost powers to surpass his companions.

He sang extempore verses on the event of the late war with Florence, changing his notes, from the hurry of battle, to the wailing for the dead, and then to the song of triumph, whose thrilling melody transported the hearers with admiration. Then, leaving this high theme, he described himself as Dante descending to / hell; but, as he had ventured thither without a guide, rude Charon had refused him a passage, and he only saw the wandering ghosts of those recently dead, and some few who bewailed their unburied bones, as they flitted about the dreary coast. Here he found Manfred, who, addressing him, told him that he was now paying, and hereafter would more painfully pay, the deadly penalty for his many crimes – "Well did they for me, and benignly," he cried, "who cast my bones from their unhallowed sepulchre; for now I wander here untormented; but, when the cycle of an hundred years is fulfilled, and I pass that dark river, fire and torture await me, dire punishment for my resistance to the Holy Father." And then continuing, he sent a message to his friends on earth, bidding them repent; and Guarino introduced into this the bitter gall of his sharp and cruel satire against his enemies. He ended; and small applause followed for he had offended many who were present by his strictures, and few could sympathize in the deep malignity of his anathemas.[a]

He was followed by the story-tellers, who / repeated various anecdotes and tales which they had collected in their rambles; they seldom invented a new story; but an old one well told, or some real occurrence dressed up with romantic ornaments, formed the subjects of their narratives. /

---

[a] Dante, by contrast with the zealous ex-Ghibelline Guarino, places Manfred in Purgatory, still unsubmissive to the pope. Clement IV, succeeding Urban IV, had had Manfred's body exhumed and reinterred in unconsecrated ground (*Purgatorio*, III. 103–45, unpublished in 1317).

CHAPTER XIV.

Euthanasia's Court continued. – Pepi arrives.

Castruccio had not joined the amusements of the day; for he had returned to Lucca, and assembled his council to deliberate on some knotty question in the Lucchese policy. Having dispatched this weighty affair, he mounted his horse, and turned his head the accustomed road to the castle of Valperga. As he quitted the gate of the town, he heard a voice behind calling him; and, reining in his horse, he saw approach at a tremendously high trot, Benedetto the Rich of Cremona. Although at some distance he instantly recognized his old fellow-traveller, by his uncouth dress which was still unchanged, his high shoulders, strait back and bent in knees. Pepi, approaching with a humble salutation, said that he had affairs of importance to communicate to the noble consul of Lucca, and intreated him to give him audience. /

"Willingly," said Castruccio: "I am going to ride to yonder castle; do you accompany me; we will discourse on the way; and when there you will find hospitality as well as I."

"You must check your steed then," said Pepi, "for mine will hardly gallop after the hard day's journey he has had."

They rode on together, and Pepi seemed oppressed by a weighty secret, which he longed, yet did not know how, to disclose. He praised the fortifications of Lucca, the fertility of its plain, and its mountains, those inexpensive barriers against the incursions of enemies; and then he paused, – coughed, – scolded his horse, – and sunk into silence.

"And now," asked Castruccio, "what is this affair of importance concerning which you would speak to me?"

"Ah! *Messer lo Console*, it is a matter of such consequence that I hardly know how to disclose it; and methinks you are in too merry a mood to listen with requisite attention, so for the present I will waive the subject."

"As you please; but, when we arrive at / yonder castle, we shall find little opportunity to talk of business; for amusement and gaiety are there the order of the day."

"Gaiety! – Well; it perhaps will do my heart good to see merry faces once again; I have seen few of them since you were on the donjon[a] of my palace.

---

[a] 'Dongione – the highest point of a castle built on a hill' (Mary Shelley's note in Ab. Dep. e. 274, p. 79; taken from Muratori, I, diss. 26, p. 367).

112

Cremona has not yet recovered[a] its cruel siege and storm; many of its palaces still lie in their ashes; and many good and fertile acres have been sold at a low rate, to trim the despoiled apartments in the guise they once were. Yet the Guelphs have again attained the upper hand there; my townsmen are proud and rebellious, and have not acquired through their misfortunes the humility of poverty, which sits better on a subject than the insolence of prosperity. Were I a prince, all my subjects should be poor; it makes them obedient towards their master, and daring towards their foes, on whose spoils they depend for riches. Yet, alas! so obstinate is man in his wickedness, that, as we see in Cremona, famine, fire and slaughter[b] cannot tame their factious spirits."

"Ah! Messer Benedetto, you are ever the / same; you have neither changed your dress nor opinions since I saw you last; ever immersed in politics."

"Indeed, my good lord, I am fuller of those than ever, and that of necessity; as, when you hear what I have to say, you will perceive. Ah! the Cremonese are still proud, though they ought to be humble; yet a small power might now easily overcome them, for they are thinking more how to replant their burnt vineyards, than to resist their lawful prince. Sovereigns make war in a strangely expensive way, when they collect armies and man fleets against a country: a dozen bold fellows with fire-brands, when all the town is asleep in their beds, will do as well to the full, as an hundred thousand armed men by broad day-light: a well timed burning of harvests is a better chastiser of rebels, than an army headed by all the sovereigns of Europe. I was ever an admirer of the Hebrew warrior who sent foxes with torches to their tails among the enemy's corn;[c] these are sleights of war that are much neglected, but which are of inestimable benefit." /

"Messer Benedetto, I listen with admiration to your wisdom; but trust the word of a friend, and do not talk thus openly in yonder castle; or if you cannot rein your tongue now, turn your horse's head towards Lucca. They are Guelphs up here."

"Strange company for me to enter; for in Cremona I never cap to a Guelph, whoever he may be; but if you, my lord, are safe, surely so am I, and trust Benedetto Pepi for discretion. You are I believe my friend, and a Ghibeline; and, being now lord of this noble country, you can well judge of the truth of my remarks. As it is I am glad to enter the company of Guelphs, and glad to find that you are well with them; for it is always expedient to have a spy in the enemy's camp."

If Castruccio had not fully understood the eccentric mood of his companion,

---

[a] i.e. recovered from (recover s.v. 13 OED).
[b] cf. 'Fire, Famine and Slaughter: A War Eclogue' by Coleridge, recited by Mary Shelley at the Villa Diodati 1 June 1816 (The Diary of Doctor John William Polidori, ed. William Michael Rossetti (London: Elkin Mathews, 1911), p. 113).
[c] Samson (Judges 15: 4–5).

he might have been offended at this speech; and even now he felt his cheek flush at the name of spy being thus as it were applied to him; but he replied laughing; "Aye, Messer Benedetto, there will be fine sport for you; the lady of / the castle is holding a court, and tomorrow we have a tournament; will you not enter the lists against these priest-ridden knights?"

"Not the less powerful for being priest-ridden; not the less powerful if they were priests themselves; as I well know to my misfortune, having been beaten almost to death by a young canon who was my enemy; and that took place many years ago, when I was younger, and more active than I am now. But I was revenged; aye, Benedetto Pepi was never yet injured in a hair of his head, but the heart's anguish of his enemy paid for it."

Pepi looked at his companion with the elevated brows of triumph and vanity, while his sharp eyes spoke, not ferocity, but successful cunning. Castruccio regarded him with a glance of distrust, which he did not observe, but continued: – "This young rascal had been forced into the priestly dress, but had not yet made vows, when he resolved to supplant me with a rich, young heiress whom I intended to marry. I was well off in the world, with a good estate, and a noble palace, so the father gave his consent, and all went on prosperously; / till this roguish priest laid a plot for my destruction. He waylaid me on the wedding day, as I was conducting the bride to my own house; she loved him, and left me; aye, at the first whistle of this brave dame-hunter I felt her snatch her hand from mine, and saw her throw herself into his arms. I resisted, more as an angry, than a wise man, for they were armed, and I defenceless: so, as I told you, the villain beat me, till I was carried home nearly dead from the blows I received. During my recovery, as I lay there in my bed, my bones aching with the bruises I had received, I formed my plan of revenge, which I carried on, till he and she, and his kin and her kin, knelt to me for mercy; but I did not bend, and was most gloriously revenged. And now where is he? a grey-haired wretch; old before his time, rotting in the dungeons of the Inquisition. She has long been dead; of grief, they say, – at least she never enjoyed a moment with her paramour."

Castruccio started, as he heard the devilish confession of his companion. He did not reply; but he no longer felt that careless amusement / which he had formerly done, in his conversation and uncouth manners; but watched him warily as if he had been an old and wrinkled serpent, whose fangs had fallen to decay, but whose venom still lurked in his toothless gums.[a]

Pepi rode on, unconscious of the emotions he had excited; he imagined that he had just recited the finest passage of his life. For this old craftsman was fully impregnated with the Italian policy, which has stained the history of her lords

---

[a] cf. 'Vipers kill, though dead' (P. B. Shelley, Dedication to 'The Witch of Atlas' (1824), l. 2, addressed to Mary Shelley and composed shortly after his visit to Monte San Pellegrino in August 1820).

and princes with the foul blots of fraud and cruelty: he did not admire the conqueror of a nation (although that were almost an object of adoration to him), so much as he worshipped the contriver of frauds, the base intriguer, who, not by the open combat of power and passion, but by dastardly and underhand means, brings his enemy on his knees before him.

When they arrived at the castle, they were conducted to the fountain of the rock, and Castruccio introduced Pepi to the company. The Cremonese bowed to the fair countess; and then darted his quick glances around, to / discover if he knew any of the company; many he had seen before, and he could not help muttering as he seated himself – "Guelphs to the core! a pretty nest of hornets this!"

The company in the mean time were examining with curious eyes the garb and manners of their visitor. His dress was more shabby than that of the poorest of the jugglers; for he had not brought his gold-fringed cloak with him on this occasion; and, but for the introduction of Castruccio, and the gold spurs which he wore, he would have hazarded the disgrace of being dismissed to the company of the valets of the castle. Pepi observed their contempt, and addressed them as follows.

"For you, noble lords and ladies, who with upturned lips sneer at my homely garb, listen to my story, and do not despise my words, because they are those of a Ghibeline. You shine in silk, and jewels, and costly furs; I am clothed in sheep-skin and sclavina, and perhaps my capuchin may have a hole in its well worn texture; but look at my golden spurs; I am a knight, and have a palace, and a tower, and a good horse, as an Italian nobleman / should have. Now listen, and then tell me whether I am right or wrong, in not throwing away the prudence of my friends in trinkets and trumpery.

"I dare say that you all know, that there was once an emperor of the West, called Charlemagne.[a] He was a great conqueror, and during his life lorded it nobly over all Europe, even from the tepid waters of the Mediterranean to the frozen Baltic sea; Italy did not murmur against his sway, and Germany was obliged to submit to the force of his arms. It was a glorious thing to see this great prince ride out among his followers, clothed, as I may be, in common skins, and greater than the meanest soldier in his camp only through his superior prowess and wisdom. But the nobles of his court were such as the nobles have continued to be to this day; and the money they should have kept for the maintenance of their followers, and the furniture and works of war, they expended upon dress and foppery.

"One day Charlemagne was at the town of Fugolano,[b] clothed as I have said

---

[a] Charlemagne (c.742–814) crowned 'Emperor of the West' by the pope in 800. It was out of the break-up of his empire in 843 that the Holy Roman Empire eventually emerged. The following anecdote was taken from Muratori, I, diss. 25, p. 310; noted in Ab. Dep. e. 274, p. 70.
[b] 'Fujolanum' in Muratori, and explained as 'Friuli'.

in a well worn vest of fox's fur, and his only jewel the / well-tempered blade of his trusty sword. The courtiers gathered round this royal eagle, and he was indignant at heart to view their tawdry attire: they had just come from Pavia, which place, then as now, the Venetians made the mart for all the rich merchandize they brought from the East. They were dressed with every extravagance of luxury; they wore tippets of the feathers of Phœnician birds, lined with silk; robes of rich brocade, trimmed with the feathers of the back and neck of peacocks. Their flowing cloaks of fur were made of the skins of a thousand minute animals, brought from the wilds of Tartary, and in their caps they had jewels and feathers of extraordinary price. Thus they jutted[a] up and down before their master, fancying that he would admire them, he who loved a well hacked helmet, boots bespattered with riding after fugitive enemies, a blood-stained sword, and a spirited war horse, more than ten armies of such fair-weather birds. 'Come, my brave comrades,' cried the emperor, 'we have no battle and no siege to amuse us; and the gloomy day with its drizzling rain makes the quiet of my palace irksome / to me; mount your steeds, and let us away to the chase.'

"It had been a fine sight, to see the courtiers, as they gave a last pitying glance to their gay dresses, and bestrode their horses to follow their master. He led the way; no ditch or hedge or thick cover of copse-wood, could obstruct his path; his noble steed surmounted all, and every bramble had rich spoils from his companions: silk, fur, and feathers strewed the ground, and hung on the thorns by the road-side; what escaped the dangers of land, was shipwrecked by water, for the rain wetted them to the skin, and the materials of their clothes, in losing their gloss, had lost all their value.

"When they returned, they bitterly complained among themselves for the losses they had sustained: the emperor was advised of their murmurs, and sent to command their attendance. They obeyed, and approached his throne in a guise much unlike the gay figure they had exhibited in the morning; their feathers broken, their jewels lost, their silk torn, and their furs, which had been wet, and afterwards dried by the fire, were shrunk, disfigured / and spoiled. 'Oh, most foolish mortals!' cried Charlemagne, 'how are these furs precious or useful? Mine cost only a few pence; yours cost not only silver, but many pounds of gold!'"

Pepi ended his most apposite tale by a laugh of triumph; and it might easily be perceived that some of the young nobles were by no means pleased with the uncouth manners of their teacher. But the sun had now set, and the bell of the *Ave Maria* rung from the chapel of Valperga; so the company descended the rock, and joined in the devotions of the priest, who celebrated vespers, attended by all the more humble guests of the castle.

In the evening several mimes were represented under the direction of Borsiere. No nation can excel the Italians in the expression of passion by the

---

[a] Variant of 'jetted', i.e. swaggered; this instance in *Valperga* is cited in the *OED*.

language of gesture alone, or in the talent of extemporarily giving words to a series of action which they intend to represent; even in those ruder times they were able to draw tears from the audience, or shake them with convulsions of laughter. The actors now at the castle, first performed the touching story / of Palamon and Arcite, and afterwards the favourite tale of the loves of Troilus and Cressida,[a] and told with animated action the story of the ill repaid constancy of the worthy knight of Troy, and the black treachery of the faithless Cressida; so that few eyes were undimmed with tears, when this unhappy knight, who had sought death in vain, but who survived his country and his friends, was supposed to stand beside the half choked cistern of a once often visited fountain among the ruins and burnt palaces of Troy, and to behold Cressida, in a mean garb, and deformed by disease, bearing a heavy pitcher on her head, come to draw water from the spring; and every bosom thrilled at the bitter grief of Troilus, and the humble repentance and heart-felt self-reproaches of his once wanton mistress, as, calling for pardon, she died.[b] To relieve the company from their painful sympathy, the mimes came forward to act the antic pantomimes of the day: these were neither very decent nor very clever; a miller and a priest were over-reached in their love, and were left shivering in the snow during a winter-night, while two young students / of Bologna, whom the other worthies had combined to trick, enjoyed that for which in their dreary condition they ardently pined.[c] Night had now run half its course; and the company retired, after bestowing the praises well due to Borsiere's successful exertions.

The next morning before daylight Castruccio heard some one enter his apartment. It was Pepi, who approached his bed, and said: "My lord, I come to take my leave of you. After what passed last night, you may well believe that the young countess would rather not count me among her guests. I am about to return to Cremona, but would first ask you, whether you would not prefer that a staunch friend of yours should be lord of that town, than that it should remain in the hands of the people, who have become Guelphs and traitors, body and soul?"

---

[a] Borsiere, a character in Boccaccio's *Decameron*, is here imagined as staging versions of two stories which are in the future to become Boccaccio's *Teseida* and *Il Filostrato*, which, in turn, Chaucer will rewrite as *The Knight's Tale* and *Troilus and Criseyde* (c.1385) respectively. In both works of Chaucer, though not in Boccaccio's versions, 3 May figures as a portentous turning point, as at this moment in the narrative of *Valperga* and also in 'The Mourner' (*MWST*, p. 90). Mary Shelley read *Troilus and Criseyde* 24–26 September, 1820.

[b] Cressida's beggary and disease (leprosy) are not in Boccaccio or Chaucer, but derive from Robert Henryson (?1424–?1506), whose *Testament of Cresseid* was included as a continuation of the *Troilus* in editions of Chaucer up to and including Chalmers's *The Works of the English Poets* (1810). They are considered to have been Henryson's invention, but Mary Shelley imagines a pre-existent dramatic version, a supposed fragment of a lost *Troilus and Criseyde* corpus.

[c] Probably no particular stories are intended; rather, they are invented examples of an oral tradition from which the comic tales of cuckoldry in Boccaccio and Chaucer's tales of the Miller and the Reeve may be supposed to derive. In Boccaccio, *Decameron*, VIII. vii, a lady torments her student lover by making him stand all night in the snow. A story involving a student of Bologna, but not cuckoldry, appears in the *Novellino* (no. LVI).

Castruccio's thoughts instantly fixed on Galeazzo Visconti, or Cane della Scala, as the promised lord of Cremona; and he replied eagerly: "Messer Benedetto, you would do me an inestimable benefit, if by any means, either in your power, or with which you are / acquainted, you could place the government of your town in the hands of one of my friends."

"And are you prepared to assist in such an undertaking?"

"Now I cannot; but I have promised to be in Lombardy at the end of the month of July. In August I will visit you at Cremona; and, if you will disclose to me the contrivers and instruments of this change, – "

"Now I can tell you nothing. Come to me on the fifteenth of August, alone, or with but one attendant; but come not with the shew of a prince; on that day, at five o'clock in the evening, you will meet a person on the bridge of the rivulet you cross about half a mile from Cremona; say to him the word, Lucca, and he will conduct you to my palace by an obscure way, and then I will disclose every thing to you. As you may not be able to command your time to a day, I will wait for you one month, until the fifteenth of September; then if you do not appear, the enterprize must proceed by other means. During this interval promise me inviolable secrecy."

"What, may I not tell——?" /

"No living soul must hear of this – If you impart that with which I have intrusted you, my plan must instantly fail. I trust to your discretion."

"It is well, Messer Benedetto," replied Castruccio, recalling to mind the impressions of the preceding evening, and gazing on his companion with distrust: "I do not clearly understand your plans, and cannot promise to assist in them; but I assure you of my secrecy, and that you shall see me before the fifteenth of September."

"I am satisfied; farewel. The stars are disappearing, and I would reach your town before sunrise."

Pepi departed with a brow of care; while every heart in the castle of Valperga was light, and every countenance expressed gaiety. This was the third day of the court, the day for which a tournament had been proclaimed. But it would be tedious to dilate on the remainder of these ceremonies, and from what has been related a judgement may be formed of those which were yet to come.

The summer months passed on, and the / time approached when Castruccio had promised Galeazzo Visconti to meet him at Rovigo.[a] Euthanasia desired during the autumn to revisit her native city, from which she had been long absent. They agreed to journey thither together; and on Castruccio's return from Lombardy their long delayed marriage was to take place.

END OF VOLUME I. /

---

[a] In the province of Venezia, among the cities possessed by the House of Este.

VALPERGA:

OR, THE

LIFE AND ADVENTURES

OF

CASTRUCCIO,

PRINCE OF LUCCA.

BY THE AUTHOR OF "FRANKENSTEIN."

IN THREE VOLUMES.

VOL. II.

LONDON:

PRINTED FOR G. AND W. B. WHITTAKER,
AVE-MARIA-LANE.

1823.

VALPERGA.

CHAPTER I.

Conference of Castruccio and Galeazzo Visconti – of Castruccio and the Bishop of Ferrara.

When Castruccio and Euthanasia arrived at Florence, they found the citizens celebrating a festival: the bells were ringing; the country people were flocking into the town; and the youths of both sexes, of the highest rank, and richly dressed, were parading the streets, covered with wreaths of flowers, and singing the poems of Dante, or his friend Guido, to the accompaniment of many instruments. Castruccio said: "I must ask you, fair Euthanasia, who are so learned in Florentine customs, to inform me of the meaning of this gaiety."

"Indeed, I am entirely ignorant. I know that during peace joyful meetings take place / every May, among the young nobility; but this seems a general festivity. Let us ask that grave gentleman in the black capuchin, if he knows the reason of a merriment, which at least has not communicated itself to his face."

The man, on being asked, replied: "You must be but lately arrived, not to have heard of the cause of our rejoicings; the Florentines, Madonna, are celebrating the occurrence of a most favourable omen with which God and St. John have blest our city. Yesterday one of the lionesses kept at the expence of the republic, brought forth five whelps."

"And is this the momentous occasion of so much serious amusement?" asked Castruccio, laughing.

"My lord," said the man, "you are a stranger in this town; or you would not find cause for laughter in this event. The Florentines keep a number of lions, as the signs and symbols of their strength; and God and St. John have plainly manifested on many occasions, that the prosperity of Florence, and the welfare of the lions are bound together. Three of the finest and largest died on the eve of the fatal battle of Monte Catini."[a] /

"So these wise republicans, whom you, dear Euthanasia, so much vaunt,

---

[a] Information about the symbolic importance of lions to the Florentines derives from Lastri, II, pp. 129–6 (read in April 1821; noted in adds. e. 17, p. 222 rev.). Specific details are invented; the greatest wonder recorded by Villani was the birth of twin lions in 1331 (X, cap. 185).

believe in these childish omens. I would wager my best charger, that their records are full of the influence of stars, and the appearance of comets!"

"And I do not at all know that you would lose: indeed their noblest citizens have a great faith in astrology and portents. If you speak of a scarcity, they will tell of a meteor; if you say that the king of France has lost a battle, they will assure you that the whole kingdom has become, by the will of God and St. John, weaker and more miserable, ever since Philippe le Bel seized upon the Florentine usurers.[a] We love to find a cause for every event, believing that, if we can fit but one link to another, we are on the high road for discovering the last secrets of nature. You smile at the celebration of the birth of these lion's whelps; yet I own that it pleases me; how innocent, yet how active, must the imagination of that people be, who can find cause for universal joy in such an event!

"It is this same imagination more usefully / and capaciously employed, that makes them decree the building of the most extensive and beautiful building of modern times. The men who have conceived the idea, and contributed their money towards the erection of the Duomo, will never see its completion;[b] but their posterity will, and, if they be not degenerate, will glory in the noble spirit of their ancestors. Many years ago, when the Florentines warred with the Siennese, they took by storm a tower of great strength, which commanded a most important pass. They destroyed the tower; and, when half demolished, they filled it up with earth, and planted there an olive tree, which still flourishes, an emblem of the peace which would follow their conquests."[c]

Castruccio staid only a few days at Florence; and, recommending himself to the constancy and love of Euthanasia, he took an affectionate leave of her, and hastened on his journey to Rovigo, where he had promised to join Galeazzo Visconti.

Galeazzo, having now succeeded to his father in the tyranny of Milan, was the most powerful chief of Lombardy. He was about / thirty-five years of age:[d] he had all the characteristics of an Italian face, arched brows, black eyes, an aquiline nose, and a figure where there was some strength and little grace. He had a great portion of talent, quickness in the combination of plans, yet not sufficient patience to watch their progress, or perseverance to carry them through. He was crafty, ambitious, and vain; yet, where his own interests were not concerned, he was good-natured, and on all occasions exceeded even the Italians in the courtesy of his demeanour. He had seen much of the world, and suffered many misfortunes; this gave him a pliancy of disposition, as well as of

---

[a] In 1291; Villani (VII, cap. 146) says merely that the king imprisoned all Italians in France on the pretext that they were usurers.

[b] Begun in 1294; completed 160 years later (Lastri, pp. 1–4; noted in adds. e. 17 p. 226 rev.); the façade was not finally finished until 1888.

[c] From Villani, VI, cap. 77; noted in adds. e. 17, on both p. 228 rev. and p. 230 rev.

[d] The historical Galeazzo was just over forty years old.

manner, which made him appear more kind-hearted than he really was; for in truth he never for a moment lost sight of his own interest; and, if he sometimes wandered from the path which led to its attainment, want of judgement, and not of inclination, caused the error.

He wished to attach Castruccio to his party and designs. He saw in him the head of the Ghibeline faction in Tuscany, and the tamer of his Florentine enemies. He felt that his own situation was precarious; but, if he could gain / Castruccio for his ally, he hoped to awe his enemies. More than all, he desired the destruction of the Guelph strong-hold, Florence; and Castruccio was to become its destroyer. He heard of his peace with that city with dismay; he trusted it could not last; but the very name of it blasted his hopes. He wished to see the consul, and to win him to the plan which he had conceived would conduct to the full ascendancy of the Ghibelines; and, circumstances leading him to Rovigo, he had intreated Castruccio to visit him there, making the intended restoration of Ferrara to the marquess of Este the pretence of this request.[a]

The friends met with every demonstration of regard. Galeazzo watched with care every word, by which Castruccio might reveal his intentions, before he would venture to communicate his own wishes. Their first topic of conversation was the immediate business before them, the restoration of the marquess Obizzo to the sovereignty of Ferrara. "This town," said Galeazzo, "which so long obeyed the Este family, is now in the hands of the Guelphs, and the vicar of the Pope, with a / couple of hundred Gascon soldiers for a garrison, keeps possession of it. The people, fleeced by the excellent policy of the Roman court, whose first, second, and third maxim is to fill its own coffers, eagerly desire the restoration of their rightful prince. We have often thought of besieging the town; but that would be a long and expensive business, and even its success would be doubtful; for, if the Ghibelines raised their war-cry, all the Guelph foxes would unearth themselves and have at them, and you know that our lands are much overstocked by this vermin. Stratagem is a surer and a far easier mode of warfare, and not half so bloody as the regular way; we have so many friends within the walls, that I doubt not we should succeed, if a proper communication were established between us. The bishop, who, though a churchman, is our sure friend, sent us a message some days ago, which, although mystically worded, seemed to say that he would betray the town into our hands, if we would commission one of our chiefs to treat with him; for he refused to disclose his project to an underling. / Now, you, my good friend, must undertake this

---

[a] Ferrara was a Marquisate of the House of Este, formerly staunchly Guelph, but dissensions within the family had allowed the Gascon Pope Clement V to become in 1308 the *de facto* power. In 1314, Clement appointed Philippe-le-Bel's cousin, Robert, King of Naples, as Imperial Vicar of all Italy. Robert expelled Obizzo, Marquis of Ferrara, with Gascon troops. Obizzo took refuge in Rovigo and went over to the Ghibellines (Sismondi, chs xii, xxviii and xxvix).

task; we are all of us too well known to get admission into the city; but a slight disguise will take you safely past their guards, and I doubt neither of the bishop Marsilio's[a] power or inclination."

Castruccio acceded to his friend's request; and in the evening he was introduced to the marquess of Este, who received him with deference and distinction.

The next morning, when he and Galeazzo rode out together, Galeazzo said: "I am sure, my dear Castruccio, I can never shew myself sufficiently grateful for your kindness in quitting Lucca at my request, and wandering away from your government, which I ardently hope will not suffer from your absence. But I feel less remorse, since the truce you have concluded with Florence must afford you some leisure."

"Not a truce, but a better thing; I have concluded a peace."

"Aye, a truce, or a peace; it is the same thing; either will be sufficiently short-lived." /

"Are you then so deep-read in the counsels of the enemy, that you know how and when this peace will change to war?"

"I am deep-read in nothing, my friend, but the politics and changes of Italy; and I have suffered by them enough, and mixed with them sufficiently, to foresee their issue a long way off. Fire and water will make as kindly coalition as Guelph and Ghibeline, Bianchi and Neri. Their interests are at war, and therefore so must they be. But why do I say this to you, who have every prospect of being Imperial Vicar in Tuscany;[b] and think you that peace is the pilot to that haven?"

"My dear Galeazzo, let us understand one another; I am a Ghibeline, faithful to my party and the emperor; and, if I thought there were a fair chance of suppressing the Neri, by the Holy Face of Lucca*, I would make a crusade against them, such as has not been seen in the world since the days of Saladin.[c] Let the emperor come to Italy, and something may be / done; but why carry on a petty warfare, which destroys the country, and starves the peasant, while it hardly takes a florin from the coffers of the Florentine merchants, or advances us one inch nearer the goal we desire to reach?"

* A portrait of Christ, said to have been painted by Nicodemus.[d]

---

[a] The name was possibly suggested by Marsilio of Padua (d. 1328), not a bishop but a doctor of medicine and theologian who questioned the authority of the pope (Sismondi, ch. xxxi). He belonged to the 'Spiritual' wing of the Franciscans which asserted Christ's poverty. He was later to support Louis of Bavaria.

[b] By the emperor, as a reward for his support for the imperial cause. Emperor and pope frequently contended for the right to appoint Imperial Vicars.

[c] Saladin (Salah-ed-Din) (c.1138–93), leader of the Saracens, and captor of Jerusalem; by the Third Crusade (1192), led by Richard Coeur de Lion, Saladin was forced to render up some of his conquests. He is placed by Dante in the Limbo of Heroes (*Inferno*, IV. 129), and figures in two of Boccaccio's tales.

[d] The infrequently shown 'volto santo' in the cathedral of San Martino, actually the face of the crucified Christ carved in wood; said to have been used in oaths by William Rufus (Muratori, I, diss. 28 p. 410; noted in Ab. Dep. e. 274, p. 80). It is mentioned in Dante, *Inferno*, XXI. 48.

"And is this the end of our dreams of triumph and dominion with which you entered Lucca three years ago? And now that you have the government of that town of oranges and lemons, the mighty aim of your life is accomplished, and you are ready to sleep upon your acquisition, calling yourself a great man?"

"In truth there is little time or place to sleep at Lucca. Do you think that I shall be idle, while a dozen rebel castles hold out against me which must be subdued? Let me conquer them first; let me see no enemy for many miles round; and then we will talk of Florence."

"Nay, my friend, you must leave nothing to the decision of circumstances; a wise man foresees and provides for all. Florence must one day be yours; and you, prince of Tuscany, of Italy, if you will, will give laws to us all. Do not start; among so many prophecies as we have of Merlin[a] and the rest, I venture to / make one more; and, like most others, let its announcement contribute to its completion. My dear Castruccio, this is no child's play; for men are both our die and our stake: put forth your hand, and you must win. In Lombardy the Ghibelines flourish; but, except Pisa, and your Lucca, the Guelphs domineer throughout Tuscany. But this must not continue; the Popes are out of Italy,[b] and Rome, become a mere resort of robbers, is a blank in our account. Naples and Florence are our only enemies; the emperor must conquer one, and you the other. Let all your efforts tend to that; you talk of rebel castles near Lucca, – aye, subdue those first, that without dread you may hunt down the Florentines; let your will be as a wind to drive all before it: at first, it will pause, collecting its force in the horizon; and then it breaks forth sweeping every thing along with it: Florence must fall before it – I swear it shall; but give me your hand, your faith, Castruccio, and swear that you also will have it so."

"Nay, by the Virgin! I will not be backward in doing my part to tame the cubs of this / wild lioness: if Florence ever can be mine, she shall, and may God's will and your prophecy be fulfilled."

"That is well. – At present you are at peace with them; but it must be a peace to crush, and not to invigorate them. You are freshly entered into your lordship, your authority is new, perhaps unstable; but form your troops, be a prince among your own people, and then fall upon these enemies of all princes. Oh! believe me, give up this old fashioned name of consul;[c] it is tainted by the idea of that which I abhor – a commonwealth: make yourself a prince, and then so pure and ardent a hatred of Florence will arise in your mind, that you will not need my spurring to ride them to their destruction. The contagion of liberty

---

[a] The Arthurian Merlin, known in medieval Italy as a magician (Muratori, III, diss. 44, p. 36; noted in Ab. Dep. e. 274, p. 89).

[b] Since 1309, the papal residence had been in Avignon in Provence, under the influence of Philippe-le-Bel and his cousin Robert, King of Naples, who was Duke of both Provence and Anjou. Clement V was succeeded by John XXII (reigned 1316–34).

[c] As Napoleon did in 1804 for the title of emperor, thus abandoning pretensions to embodying the ideals of republican Rome.

is dangerous; – the Ghibelines must fall in Lucca, if the Guelphs be not destroyed in Florence. Think you, if your people are allowed free intercourse with this republic, that the plague of liberty will not spread to your state? For no quarantine will eradicate that spot, if once it has entered the soul: plots, rebellions will be formed against you; Florence, the watchword, / the rallying point for all. Choose; for that choice alone is left you, to quell that city, or depart once more to exile."

These were the lessons with which Galeazzo awakened the latent flame in the soul of Castruccio; a flame, covered, but not extinguished, and which now burned more fiercely than ever. He swore the destruction of the Guelphs, and interminable war to Florence; and his blood flowed more freely, his eyes shone brighter, his soul was elevated to joy, when he thought that one day he might be the master of that proud city.

In the mean time the marquess of Este occupied their attention; and Castruccio prepared for this embassy to the bishop of Ferrara. He took no papers with him that might be dangerous, if discovered; but, habiting himself like a merchant from Ancona, and taking such documents as might enable him to support this character, he left Rovigo for Ferrara, which was about twenty miles distant, and entering that town at ten o'clock in the morning he hastened, unquestioned by any, to the episcopal palace. The bishop was an old man of / the most benign physiognomy, and a sweet, mild tone of voice; he was tall, and upright in figure, with an air of dignity and benevolence, that won, yet awed every one; his temples were slightly shaded by his silver locks, and his white beard, reaching to his girdle, increased the dignity of his appearance. Castruccio, who by his intercourse with the world had learned always to honour age, approached him with respect, and disclosed to him his rank and mission. The bishop replied:

"My noble lord, the marquess has done that which I have long desired, in sending to me one to whom I may intrust the important secret, which I do not doubt will be the means of his re-establishment in his government. This evening my friends will assemble at my palace; with their counsel all shall be arranged, the means disclosed to you by which I propose to deliver Ferrara into the hands of its rightful prince, and the day fixed for the commencement of the enterprize."

The bishop and Castruccio continued together the whole day, both mutually delighted with each other; and, as is often the case / where sympathy of opinion and feeling exists, they became as intimate in a few hours, as in other circumstances an intercourse of years would have effected. Castruccio had a great taste for theological knowledge, and the bishop, as a man of the world, was delighted with the conversation and remarks of one who had passed through so many scenes, and visited so many nations. Confidence quickly arose between them; so well did each seem to understand the feelings and character of the other. The bishop was a Ghibeline; but his motives were pure: his indignation at the corruptions of the Papal court, and his disapprobation of the faction and brawls which appeared to him inseparable from a republic, attached him strongly to the Imperial party, and to those lords who, reigning peacefully over a people who loved them, seemed to him to ensure the quiet of Italy.

In the evening the partizans of the marquess of Este assembled at the episcopal palace to deliberate on their projects. Castruccio[2] was introduced among them, and received with cordiality and respect by all. The assembly / consisted of nearly the whole nobility of Ferrara, chiefly indeed Ghibelines, but there were even some Guelphs, disgusted by the introduction of foreign troops, and the haughtiness and tyranny of their governors. The government however was formidable; they possessed the gates, and the fortress; their armed guard was numerous and faithful; and the restoration of Obizzo could be achieved by stratagem alone.

In one corner of the vast apartment in which the assembly sat, were two women. One was old, and dressed in the fashion of an age gone by: she was in black as a widow; her vest was close and strait, trimmed with beads, and made of black cloth; a black veil covered her head, and her capuchin thrown aside discovered the years and wrinkles of the venerable wearer. It was impossible to judge of the age, and hardly of the sex, of the figure that sat beside her; for her capuchin was wrapped closely round her form, and the hood drawn over her face, as she sat silently, turned away from the company, in the darkest part of the room.

The bishop at length addressed Castruccio: / "My lord," said he, "you now possess the details of our plan, and may perceive the sincerity of our intention, and the eagerness of our desire to receive again our rightful prince: it alone remains to shew you the secret entrance of which I spoke, and to fix the day for our attempt."

The old lady, who had been hitherto silent, now turned quickly round, and said: "My brother, Beatrice ought to name the fortunate day on which we may undertake this work. Speak, my child, and may the holy Virgin inspire your words!"

As she spoke, she threw back the hood of her young companion; and Castruccio gazed on her exquisite and almost divine beauty. Her deep black eyes, half concealed by their heavy lids, her curved lips, and face formed in a perfect oval, the rising colour that glowed in her cheeks which, though her complexion was pure and delicate, were tinged by the suns of Italy, formed a picture such as Guido has since imagined, when he painted a Virgin or an Ariadne, or which he copied from the life when he painted the unfortunate Beatrice / Cenci.[a] Her jet hair fell in waving luxuriance on her neck and

---

[a] One of Mary Shelley's frequent expressions of admiration for Guido Reni (1575–1642). The Shelleys saw the *Madonna Lattante*, and other genuine and supposed Guidos, at Bologna in November 1818. At the Colonna Palace, Rome, they saw Guido's *Ariadne* and the so-called *Beatrice Cenci*, at that time thought to be by Guido (*PBSL*, II, pp. 49–53; *MWSJ*, I, pp. 235–6). Beatrice Cenci was executed in Rome in 1599 for parricide. The incestuous rape which provoked her crime, and her trial, supplied the plot of P. B. Shelley's drama *The Cenci* (1819).

shoulders below her waist; and a small silver plate was bound by a white riband on her forehead.[a] Castruccio could only gaze for a moment on this lovely being; for, turning a supplicating look on her aged friend, she again drew the hood over her face, speaking in so low a tone, that he could not distinguish the words she uttered; the elder lady acted as interpreter, and said: "Beatrice intreats you not to fix the day until to-morrow, and then she hopes, by the grace of God and the Virgin, to name such a one as will bring your enterprize to an happy issue."

Castruccio turned quickly round to see what effect these words would produce upon the bishop; he thought that he saw a slight smile of derision hover on the old man's lip; but he replied: "Be it so; my lord Castruccio, you will accompany my sister, Madonna Marchesana, to her palace; she will disclose to you the secret entrance, and acquaint you with the means by which you may find it, when you return with the marquess Obizzo and his troops." /

The assembly broke up; and Castruccio followed Madonna Marchesana and her beautiful companion. His horse was brought to the door; they mounted their white palfreys, and attended by several esquires and pages carrying torches, arrived at a magnificent palace close to the eastern gate of Ferrara. When they had entered, Madonna Marchesana dismissed her servants, and led Castruccio into a room, hung with tapestry, and furnished with the rich and heavy furniture of the age. She lifted up the hangings; and, while Castruccio supported them, she pushed back a pannel in the wainscot, and discovered a long, dark gallery; then, taking up a torch that lay within, and lighting it at a lamp which hung from the ceiling of the room, she presented it to Beatrice, saying: "Do you, my child, light us, and lead us the way, that success may attend our steps."

A small snow white hand and taper wrist were put out from beneath the capuchin; and Beatrice silently took the torch, and led the way, along the gallery, down several flights of stairs, and then along numerous vaults / and corridors, until they arrived at what appeared the end of these subterraneous passages. "You, my lord," said the lady Marchesana, "must help me." She pointed to a large stone, which Castruccio rolled away, and discovered behind it a small, low door. The lady drew back the bolts, and bade Beatrice hide the light, which she did, placing it within a kind of recess in the passage that seemed formed for the purpose of receiving it; the lady then opened the door; and Castruccio, creeping out, found himself in an open country, covered with bushes, and surrounded by marshy land, at some distance from the strong fortifications of the town. Castruccio smiled: "Ferrara is ours!" he cried; and the old lady with a countenance expressive of the greatest delight, said: "I intreat you, my lord, to lay my respectful submission and zealous fidelity at the

---

[a] i.e. a disc; a fashion possibly belonging to a later period. In Leonardo da Vinci's so-called *La Belle Ferronière* (c.1490) the subject has a round jewel bound to her forehead.

feet of the marquess Obizzo; tell him the joy and triumph that I feel, in being the humble instrument of restoring him to his sovereignty and inheritance. When you mention the name of the viscountess di Malvezzi[a] he may distrust my professions; since the viscount, my late / husband, was his bitter and determined enemy. But he is no more; and I have been brought to a true knowledge of the will of God by this divine girl, this *Ancilla Dei*,[b] as she is truly called, who is sent upon earth for the instruction and example of suffering humanity."

Castruccio listened with astonishment; while the gifted damsel stood, her face covered by her cowl, and her arms crossed over her breast: the eyes of the old lady beamed with joy and pride. "I do not entirely fulfil my commission," she continued, "until I have taught you how you may again discover this place. Do you see those straggling sallows that skirt that stagnant drain, and which, although they appear to be without order, are the clue by which you will be guided thither? Four miles distant from Ferrara, on the right-hand side of the road, you will find a mulberry tree, a poplar, and a cypress, growing close together; strike from the road at that point, and follow the line of sallows, however they may lead, until you come to that where the line ends. You / must then mark the drains of the marsh, remembering to follow only those which are bordered by dwarf myrtles, and which at every turn have a cross carved in a low stone on their banks; that line will lead you hither; and you will stop at that cross of wood which you see half buried in the tall grass and bulrushes, until this door is opened for your entrance."

The viscountess di Malvezzi repeated her instructions a second time in the same distinct manner; and, finding that Castruccio fully apprehended them, she led the way back to her subterranean passages; and with quick steps they regained the tapestried apartment. Beatrice remained a moment behind to extinguish the torch; and, when she re-appeared, she had thrown off her capuchin, and shone in the light of her divine beauty. Her dress was of the finest white woollen; and in fashion it partook of the usual dress of the age, and of the drapery of the antient statues: it was confined at her waist by a silken girdle, and fell about her figure in thick and rich folds; a golden / cross glittered upon her bosom, on which lay also the glossy ringlets of her hair; on the silver plate bound to her forehead Castruccio could distinguish the words, *Ancilla Dei*. Her black eyes beamed as with inspiration, and the wide sleeves of her vest discovered her white and veined arm, which she threw up in eager gesticulation as she spoke:

"Mother, I promised that tomorrow I would name the day for my sovereign's enterprize; I feel the spirit coming fast upon me; let this noble gentleman inform your revered brother, that tomorrow in the church of St. Anna I shall

---

[a] See note on Guarino (p. 101).

[b] Mary's words to the Angel in the Vulgate, 'the handmaid of the Lord', a title usually given to nuns.

speak to my countrymen, and in the midst of the people of Ferrara tell in veiled words the moment of their deliverance."

With a light step Beatrice glided out of the room, and the viscountess, not regarding the surprize of Castruccio, said to him: "Fail not, my lord, to convey the message of my Beatrice to the bishop. God has been gracious to us, in bestowing on us his visible assistance through this sacred maiden, who by her more than human beauty, the excellence / of her dispositions, and, above all, by her wisdom beyond that of woman, and her prophecies which have ever been fulfilled, demonstrates, even to the unbeliever and the Gentile, that she is inspired by the grace and favour of the blessed Virgin." /

CHAPTER II.

Parentage of Beatrice. – She is arrested by the Inquisition.

Thus dismissed, Castruccio returned, burning with curiosity and admiration, to the bishop. He delivered the message with which he had been intrusted, and then eagerly asked who this enchanting Beatrice really was, and if it were true that she was an angel descended upon earth for the benefit and salvation of man. The bishop smiled.

"My lord," he replied, "so much have you won my confidence and esteem, that I am willing to satisfy your curiosity on this subject also. But you must recollect, that neither my sister, nor even the lovely girl herself, knows what I shall now reveal, and I shall tell it you under the most solemn vow of secrecy."

Castruccio readily promised discretion and silence, and the bishop then related the following particulars. /

"Have you never heard of a heretic and most dangerous impostor, of the name of Wilhelmina of Bohemia*? This woman appeared first in Italy in the year 1289: she took up her residence at Milan, with a female companion called Magfreda.[a] Outwardly professing the Catholic religion, and conforming in the strictest manner to its rules, she secretly formed a sect, founded on the absurd and damnable belief, that she was the Holy Ghost incarnate upon earth for the

---

* See Muratori, *Antichità Italiane*, No. 60.[b]

[a] 'Mayfreda' in Muratori, III, diss. 60, p. 257; probably a misreading of Mary Shelley's 'y' as 'g'; cf. 'Agiolo' (p. 108).
[b] More fully, volume III, diss. 58 and 60, pp. 208, 255–8 (noted in Ab. Dep. e. 274, p. 96). 'Antichità' is corrected here from 'Antichristà', which, in its seeming pertinency, suggests a misreading of Mary Shelley's hand rather than a straightforward typesetting failure.

salvation of the female sex. She gave out that she was the daughter of Constance, queen of Bohemia; that, as the angel Gabriel had descended to announce the divine conception to the blessed Virgin, so the angel Raphael announced to her mother the incarnation of the Holy Spirit in favour of the female sex; and that she was born twelve months after this heavenly annunciation. Her tenets were intended entirely to supersede those of our beloved Lord Jesus, and her friend Magfreda was to be papess, and to succeed to all the power and privileges of the Roman pontiff. / Wilhelmina died in the year 1302[a] in the odour of sanctity, and was buried in the church of St. Peter at Milan: she had led so holy a life, and kept her heresy so profound a secret, except from her own sect, that she was followed as a saint, and even priests and dignitaries wrote homilies in praise of her piety, her abstinence, and modesty.

"I was at Milan two years after, when the Dominican inquisitors first discovered this lurking pestilence; and the terror and abomination of the discovery filled the town with horror. Magfreda, and her principal follower, Andrea Saramita,[b] were led to prison; the other disciples who threw themselves on the mercy of the priests, being commanded to perform several pilgrimages, and give large alms to the church, were absolved. I had just then become a *Padre*, and filled the confessor's chair: I was young, full of zeal, eloquent in the cause of truth, and tainted by an enthusiastic bigotry against heretics and schismatics. I preached with animation against this new heresy; it appeared to me so impious, so absurd, so terrifically wicked, that I was touched / by an holy impulse as I declaimed against its followers. Having thus distinguished myself, the father inquisitors intreated me to use my fervid arguments to persuade the obstinate Magfreda to recant. They had exhausted every reason, and had had recourse even to torture, to convert this woman from her damnable impieties; but she with haughty insolence declared that she was in readiness to perish in the flames, but that her last breath should be spent in the praise of her divine mistress, and an exhortation to her tormentors to repent and believe.

"I was filled with worldly vanity, and fancied that my learned sentences, my anathemas, and eloquent exorcisms could not fail of their desired effect, and that by the aid of God and truth I should be covered with the glory of success in this holy warfare. Thus secure, I entered the dungeon of the heretic: it was a low, damp vault, where she had been confined for several weeks without even straw for her bed. She was kneeling in one corner, praying fervently, and for a moment, I stopped to contemplate a heretic, a monster I had never before / seen. She was an aged, respectable woman, in the dress of a nun, and with an appearance of sanctity and modesty that astounded me. When she perceived me, she rose, and said with a faint smile: 'Is my condemnation passed? or is a new scene of torture prepared?'

---

[a] 1281, according to Muratori.
[b] An associate of Mayfreda (Muratori, III, diss. 60, pp. 257–8) who shared her fate.

"'Daughter,' I replied, 'I come indeed to torture, not your body, but your mind; to torture it with a knowledge of itself; to hold a mirror before it, wherein you will contemplate its blots and deformities, of which by the grace of the Virgin you may repent and be purified.'

"'Father, you are the master, I a slave, and I am willing to listen. But your benevolent countenance, so different from those to which I have been long accustomed, fills me with such confidence, that I dare hope for your indulgence, when I intreat you to spare yourself a useless labour, and to leave in peace the last hours of my life. I know that I must die; and God and She know how willing I am to expire for Her justification, even in pain and burning: but my spirit is worn, my patience, which I have cherished with determined zeal, / as the sacred flame of my religion and the life of my heart, now begins to wane; do not bring on my soul the sins of anger and intolerance; – leave me to prayer, to repentance, and to my hopes of again seeing my beloved mistress, there where there is no sorrow.'

"She spoke with dignity and mildness, so that I felt my spirit subdued; and, although almost angry at the stubbornness of her impiety, I followed her example in speaking with gentleness. Our conversation was long; and the more it continued, the more my animation in the cause of truth, and zeal for the conversion of the heretic, increased. For her manner was so sweet and winning, her words so soft yet firm, that it lay like a sin on my heart that I could not save her from eternal condemnation.

"'You did not know Her,' she cried, 'you never saw my Wilhelmina. Ask those who have seen her, even the vulgar, whose eyes are horn, and whose hearts are stone, whether they were not moved to love and charity, when she passed like an angel among them. She was more beautiful than aught human could / be; more gentle, modest and pious than any woman ever was, though she were a saint. Then her words possessed a persuasion that could not be resisted, and her eyes a fire, that betrayed even to the unknowing that the Holy Spirit lived within her.

"'Father, you know not what you ask, when you desire me to leave my faith in her Divinity. I have felt my soul prostrate itself before her; the very blood that vivifies my heart has cried to me, so that, if I had been deaf, I must have heard, that she was more than human. In my dreams I have seen her arrayed in divine light; and even now the sacred radiance that announces her presence fills my dungeon, and bids me for her sake submit with patience to all that ye, her enemies, can inflict.'

"I repeat to you the mad words of Magfreda, that you may judge of the excess of insanity that possessed this unfortunate woman. I combated with the evil spirit within her for eight hours, but in vain; at length I was retiring in despair, when she called me back. I returned with a look of hope, and saw that / she was weeping violently and bitterly. As I approached, she seized my hand, and kissed it, and pressed it to her heart, and continued pouring forth, as it

were, a fountain of tears. I believed that she was now touched by true repentance, and began to thank divine mercy, when she waved her hand impatiently,
beckoning me to be silent. By degrees she calmed her tears; but she was still
agitated by passion, as she said: "Kneel, father, kneel, I intreat you, and by the
cross you wear swear secrecy. Alas! if I die, another must perish with me, one
whom I have vowed to protect, one whom I love far, – far beyond my own life.'

She paused, endeavouring to overcome the tears, that, in spite of herself, she
shed: I comforted her, and pronounced the desired oath, when she became
calmer. 'Father, you are good, benign and charitable; and I do believe that She
has manifested Her will in sending you to me in my distress; you, who are so
unlike the wolves and harpies that have of late beset me. There is a child – Her
child: / – but, father, before I reveal further, promise me, swear to me, that she
shall be educated in my faith and not in yours.'

"I was indignant at this proposal, and said angrily: 'Woman, think you that I
will sacrifice the soul of an infant to your monstrous unbelief and vicious
obstinacy? I am a servant of the Lord Jesus, and, believe me, I will never
discredit my holy calling.'

"'Must it be so?' she cried; 'yet grant me a few moments to resolve.'

She knelt down, and prayed fervently for a long time; and then arose with a
smiling aspect, saying: 'Father, you wish to convert me; methinks at this
moment I could convert you, if indeed faith did not come from God, and not
from the human will. She has revealed Her will to me, and by Her command I
now confide to you the treasure of my soul.

"'Two years before the death of Wilhelmina, she had a child. I cannot tell
you who was the father of this child; for, although I believed that her conception partook of the divinity, she never confirmed my faith, or said aught against
it: but with her heavenly smile / bade me wait until the hour of knowledge
should arrive. I alone knew of the birth of this infant; and it has ever been
under my care: it was brought up in a cottage five miles hence by a good
woman, who knew not to whom it belonged; and I visited it daily, gazing with
wonder on its beauty and intelligence.

"'After its birth Wilhelmina never saw it. She always refused to visit the
cottage, or to have it brought to her, but would sit for hours, and listen to my
descriptions and praises. I have ever believed that this separation, whatever was
its cause, shortened the life of my divine mistress; for she pined, and wept, and
faded like a flower unwatered by the dews of heaven. The last words she
uttered, were to recommend her infant to my care. I have fulfilled my task, and
now, by her command, deliver up my charge to you.

"'A year ago the nurse of the child died; and I took her secretly to my own
home, and tended her, and preserved her as her mother had commanded. No
love can equal mine for the divinity, her mother: it is a burning / affection, an
adoration, which no words can express: – I shall never see her more, until we
meet in heaven, but I submit with patience to the will of God.

133

"'When I heard that Andrea Saramita and our other disciples were taken, I was transported with terror for the fate of this infant. I expected every moment to hear the steps of the blood-hounds on the stairs, to seize me, and discover this flower of paradise, which I cherished thus secretly. When suddenly a thought, an inspiration, came over me, and I cried aloud, Better are the wild beast of the forest, and the tempests of heaven, even when they shake us most; better are plague and famine, than man hunting after prey! So I took the infant in my arms, a small purse of gold, and a bag of such provisions as I had in the house; and, it being already dark, I hastened from Milan to the forest that skirts the road to Como: I walked fast, and in two hours arrived at my goal. I knew that one afflicted with leprosy* / lived in the depth of the forest, a miserable wretch, who with his wooden spoon and platter, collected alms at the road side. Thither I went fearlessly; – mistake me not; this man is not my disciple, he had never seen me before; but I knew not whether the blood-hunters were acquainted with the existence of the divine child, this I knew, that they would not dare seek her in a leper's dwelling. I dreaded not the contagion; *for is not her mother above all the saints in heaven?*

"'I wandered long among the tangled paths of the wood, ere I could discover his hut; the babe slept, cherished near my heart, which bled with anguish. To me in all the world there existed but this little creature; the earth seemed to reel under me; yet still I felt her warm breath upon my bosom, and heard the regular heaving of her gentle breast. At length / I found the cavern of the leper: it was half-built in the earthy hill against which it rested, and half of the boughs of trees plastered with mud, which was hardened in the sun; black, dilapidated, and filthy, it was worse than a manger for the reception of my poor innocent.

"'The wretched possessor of this sty slept on his miserable straw as I entered. I roused him, put gold in his hand, and, placing food before him, I said—— Protect this child, and God will reward you. Feed it, wash it, and above all keep if from the sight of man: deliver it not except to one who may come to ask for it in the name of the Holy Wilhelmina. In one month I hope to return for it, and will reward you as you have obeyed my charge. – I then, with a heart bursting with agony, embraced the daughter of my Wilhelmina for the last time: I blest her, and tore myself away.

"'I have now been five weeks imprisoned, and I dread lest the leper should have thrust her from his abode. Will you not, father, preserve and love this child?'

"The discourse of Magfreda moved me strangely. I felt a wonder, a pity, an

---

* This disease was then common in Italy. The person affected with it, was accustomed to retire and dwell in a cave in a forest, from whence he resorted to the road-side, and with beating a wooden spoon upon a platter, demanded alms of travellers, which, when they were retired to a convenient distance, he came and took from a stone upon which it was to be deposited.[a]

[a] Taken from Muratori, I, diss. 16, pp. 157–8; noted in Ab. Dep. e. 274, p. 51.

excess / of commiseration, I could not express: but kissing the cross I wore, I said: 'Listen to me, unhappy woman, while I swear never to desert this innocent; and may God so help me, as I keep my faith!'

"Magfreda poured forth warm and joyful thanks; then, with a heavy heart, I recommended her to the mercy of God, and left her dungeon.

"As soon as I could tear myself from the questions and childish curiosity of the inquisitors, I hastened to the place that Magfreda had indicated. In the tumult of my soul, I only thought of the danger of the lovely babe in the hands of this outcast of man and nature. I was possessed with a passionate sense of pity, which I cannot now explain, but for which I do not reproach myself; at length, about four miles from the town, I heard the sound of the beggar as he struck his platter with his spoon in token of his wants, and I turned aside from the road to seek him. At that moment the spirit of God almost deserted me, and I was overcome by fear——the fear of disease, and a nameless horror at the expectation of meeting / one whom all wholesome life had deserted: but I made the sign of the cross, and approached. The wretch was seated under a tree eating some crusts of bread; miserable, filthy, deformed, his matted hair hung over his eyes and his ragged beard half concealed the lower part of his visage; yet there was to be seen a savage eye, and an appearance of brutal ferocity, that almost staggered me. I made a sign that he should not approach, and he dropped on his knees, and began to gabble *pater-nosters*, so that the word that God himself had spoken seemed the jargon of the devil. I stopt at some distance from him: 'Bring me,' I cried, 'to the child who was confided to you in the name of Wilhelmina of Bohemia.'

"The wretch, who had almost forgotten human speech, jumped up, and led the way among the tangled underwood, along savage paths, overgrown with rank herbage, and bestrewn with stones, till we came to his miserable hut, – a low, dark, squalid den, which I dared not enter; 'Bring me the child,' – I cried.

"Oh; it was a woful sight, and one which / to death I shall remember, to see this child, this morning star of beauty and exceeding brightness, with eyes shining with joy, rosy lips melted into the softest smiles, her glossy hair strewn upon her lovely neck, her whole form glowing with the roseate hues of life, led by the leper from his hut; his body wrapt in a ragged blanket, his grizzly hair stretched stiffly out, and his person and face loathsome beyond words to describe. The lovely angel took her hand from his, and coming up to me, said : 'Take me to mamma; lead me from this ugly place to mother.'

"This was Beatrice; and need I say how much I have ever loved this hapless girl, and cherished her, and tried to save her from the fate to which her destiny has hurried her?

"I returned to Milan, and found that in the morning, while I had been absent, Magfreda had been burnt, and her ashes scattered to the winds, so that I had become this poor babe's only guardian. I placed her under the care of a pensioner of the church in the neighbourhood of Milan; and when I was promoted to the see of Ferrara, I brought her with me, and / intreated my sister

135

to receive her, and cherish her as her own. The lovely little being won all hearts, and Marchesana soon became attached to her with maternal fondness. She was educated in the Holy Catholic faith; and I hoped that, untainted by her mother's errors, she would lead an unblamed and peaceful life, unmarked and unknown; God has ordered it otherwise.

"Beatrice was always an extraordinary child. When only six and seven years of age, she would sit alone for hours, silently contemplating; and, when I asked her of what she thought, she would weep, and passionately desire me not to ask her. As she grew older, her imagination developed; she would sing extempore hymns with wild, sweet melody, and she seemed to dwell with all her soul on the mysteries of our religion; she then became communicative, and told me how for hours she meditated upon the works of nature, and the goodness of God, till she was filled with a sentiment that overwhelmed and oppressed her, so that she could only weep and sigh. She intreated me to unfold to her all I knew, and / to teach her to read in the sacred book of our religion.

"I was fearful that her ignorance and enthusiasm might lead her astray, since, in her accounts of her meditations, she often said things of God and the angels that were heretical; and I hoped that a knowledge of the truth would calm her mind, and lead her to a saner devotion. But my labours had a contrary effect; the more she heard, and the more she read, the more she gave herself up to contemplation and solitude, and to what I cannot help considering the wild dreams of her imagination. It seemed to me as if her mother's soul had descended into her; but that, regulated by the true faith, she had escaped the damnable heresies of that unhappy woman. She delighted to read, and pretended to explain the prophecies of the sacred writings, and the modern ones of Merlin, the abbot Joachim and Methodius:[a] beside these studies, she grew wonderfully familiar with all vulgar superstitions, holy trees and fountains, lucky and unlucky days, and all the silly beliefs that jugglers and impostors encourage for their own profit. / At length she began to prophesy; some of her prophecies were interpreted as true, and since that time her fame has been spread through Ferrara. Her followers are numerous; and my poor sister is the first of her disciples: Beatrice herself is wrapt up in the belief of her own exalted nature, and really thinks herself the *Ancilla Dei*, the chosen vessel into which God has poured a portion of his spirit: she preaches, she prophesies, she sings extempore hymns, and entirely fulfilling the part of *Donna Estatica**, she

---

* These inspired women first appeared in Italy after the twelfth century, and have continued even until our own days. After giving an account of their pretensions, Muratori gravely observes, "We may piously believe that some were distinguished by supernatural gifts, and admitted to the secrets of heaven; but we may justly suspect that the source of many of their revelations, was their ardent imagination, filled with ideas of religion and piety."[b]

[a] All three are mentioned together in Muratori, III, diss. 44, p. 36; noted in Ab. Dep. e. 274, p. 89; both have the spelling 'Methordius'.

[b] Mary Shelley's translation of Muratori, III, diss. 56, p. 182; the original is copied into Ab. Dep.

passes many hours of each day in solitary meditation, or rather in dreams, to which her active imagination gives a reality and life which confirm her in her mistakes.

"Thus, my lord, I have revealed the birth / of this extraordinary girl, which is unknown to every one else. Why I have done this I can hardly tell; for I have done it without premeditation or foresight. But I am glad that you know the truth; for you seem humane and generous; and I wish to secure another protector for my poor Beatrice, if I were to die, and she fell into any misfortune or disgrace."

Castruccio and the good bishop passed almost the whole night in conversation concerning this wonderful creature; and, when the consul retired to rest, he could not sleep, while the beauty of Beatrice was present to his eyes, and her strange birth and fortunes to his memory. In the morning he went to the church of St. Anna: mass was performed, but he looked in vain for the prophetess; – yet, when the service was finished, and the people assembled in the porch of the church, she appeared among them with her aged protectress at her side. She wore her capuchin of light blue silk, but her cowl was thrown back, and her eyes, black as the darkness which succeeds a midnight flash of lightning, full and soft as the shy antelope's, gleamed with prophetic fire. /

She spoke; her words flowed with rich and persuasive eloquence, and her energetic but graceful action added force to her expressions. She reproached the people for lukewarm faith, careless selfishness, and a want of fervour in the just cause, that stamped them as the slaves of foreigners and tyrants. Her discourse was long and continued, with the same flow of words and unabated fervour: her musical voice filled the air; and the deep silence and attention of her numerous auditors added to the solemnity of the scene. Every eye was fixed on her, – every countenance changed as hers changed; they wept, they smiled, and at last became transported by her promises of the good that was suddenly to arise, and of the joy that would then await the constant of heart; – when, as this enthusiasm was at its height, some Dominican inquisitors came forward, surrounded her, and declared her their prisoner. Until that moment Castruccio had observed her only, – her flashing eyes and animated manner; the smiles and then the tears, that, as the sunshine and clouds of an April day, succeeded each other on the heaven of her countenance. / But, when the inquisitors surrounded her, her voice was silent, and the mute deference of the multitude was no more. All became clamour and confusion; screams, vociferation, ejaculations and curses burst from every tongue; – they declared that the prophetess, the *Ancilla Dei* should not be torn from them, – she was no heretic, – of what

e. 274, p. 94. The inspired women of 'our own days' include the millenarian prophetess Joanna Southcott (1750–1814) who believed herself pregnant with a Messiah, female improvisators such as La Fantastici and La Bandinetti, described by Forsyth (p. 51), read by Mary Shelley in April 1819 (*MWSJ*, pp. 256–7) and de Staël's fictitious Corinne.

137

crime had she been guilty? – The inquisitors had with them a guard of Gascon soldiers, and this inflamed the multitude still more; it was plain that her adherence to the party of the marquess Obizzo, and the prophecy of his restoration were her only crimes. The noise of her arrest spread through the town, and all Ferrara flocked to the church of St. Anna; the crowd, transported with rage, seemed prepared to rescue the prisoner, who, silent and resigned, stood as one unconcerned in the animated scene. The people armed themselves with stones, sticks, knives, and axes; the inquisitors sent for a reinforcement of Gascon troops, and every thing appeared to menace violence, and bloodshed, when one of the priests attempted to take the hand of Beatrice as if to lead her / away; she looked at him with a steady glance, and he drew back, while she made a sign as if about to speak, and the multitude hushed themselves to silence, and were as still, as when a busy swarm of bees, buzzing and flying about, all at once drop to silence, clinging round their queen, who is the mistress of their motions.

She said, "I appeal to the bishop."

"Yes, to the bishop, – to the good bishop; he is just, – take her to him, – he shall decide the cause."

The inquisitors were prepared to resist this appeal: but the will of the people became a torrent not to be stemmed by them, and it hurried them away. They led the prophetess to the episcopal palace, surrounded by the Gascon soldiery, and followed by an immense multitude, which rent the sky with the cries of their anger and despair.

The bishop received the appeal with deep sorrow. Beatrice stood before him, her arms crossed on her breast, her eyes cast down; but on her face, although the gentlest modesty was depicted, there was no trace of fear; she / looked intrepid, yet as if she relied not on her own strength, but on that of another. The inquisitors accused her of being an impostor, a misleader of the people, a dangerous and wicked enthusiast, whom the penitence and solitude of a cloister must cure of her extravagant dreams. They talked long and loud, uninterrupted either by the judge or the prisoner, although the lady Marchesana who stood near could not always restrain her indignation.

At length they were silent; and Beatrice spoke: "You call me an impostor, – prove it! I shrink from no trial, I fear no danger or torture, – I appeal to the *Judgement of God*, – on that I rest the truth or falsehood of my mission."[a]

She looked around her with her flashing eyes and glowing cheeks; she was all loveliness, all softness; yet there was a spirit within her, which elevated her above, although it mingled with the feminine delicacy of her mind and manners,

---

[a] The *Judicium Dei*, a direct appeal to God to make manifest the guilt or innocence of an accused, often through the test of an ordeal by fire (Muratori, II, diss. 38, pp. 395–6; noted in Ab. Dep. e. 274, p. 86); the 'false ordeal' by burning ploughshares is alluded to in Byron, 'Ode on Venice', ll. 71–5.

and which inspired all who saw her with reverence and tenderness. But a small part of the multitude had found their way into the hall of the bishop's palace; but these could / no longer contain themselves; the *Judgement of God* was a thing suited to their vulgar imaginations, as a strange and tremendous mystery, that excited their awe, their pity, and their admiration: they cried, "God can alone judge of this! let the trial be made!" and their screams overpowered every other sound. The inquisitors joined in the clamour, whether to consent or dissent it was impossible to distinguish; at length the scene became calmer, and the bishop interposed his mild voice, but vainly, – the inquisitors repeated the words, impostor! heretic! madwoman! and Beatrice disdainfully refused all composition.[a] It was finally agreed, that she should be confined for that night in the convent of St. Anna, and on the following morning, under the auspices of the monks of the adjoining monastery, should undergo the *Judgement of God*, to be pronounced guilty or innocent as that should declare.

Both the inquisitors and Beatrice retired in security and triumph, followed by the multitude, who were careless of the dismay but too plainly painted on the faces of the prophetess's / friends. The lady Marchesana was in dreadful agitation, fluctuating between her faith in the supernatural powers of Beatrice, and her dread lest the trial should bring ruin upon her: she wept, she laughed, she was in a state approaching to madness; until her brother, bidding her confide in God, soothed her to resignation and some degree of confidence. She then retired to pray, leaving the bishop and Castruccio overwhelmed with pity, horror, and indignation.

Then the old man for the first time gave vent to his sorrow: – "Ill-fated victim! headstrong, foolish girl! what are thy prophecies now? thy inspirations and divine aid? alas! alas! the hand of God is upon thee, born in an evil day of a guilty and impious mother! His wrath wraps thee as a cloud, and thou art consumed beneath it; – my love is as bitter ashes, – my hopes are extinct; – oh, that I had died before this day!"

Castruccio was at first too much confounded to offer consolation; but, when he spoke, and bade his friend not despair, the bishop replied: "My lord, she has won my whole soul, and / all my affections; why this is, I know not; – is she not beautiful? and she is as good as she is beautiful. She calls me father, and loves me with the tenderness of a child; day and night I have offered up my prayers to God, not to visit on her the sins of her mother; – for her sake I have fasted and prayed, – but all is vain, and she must perish."

"Not so, father; say not that so lovely a being shall perish under the fangs of these cruel hell-hounds. Do not, I earnestly intreat you, despair: flight! flight is her only safety; father, you have authority, and must save her. I will take charge of her, when she has quitted the walls of the convent, and I will place her in safe

---

[a] Terms.

and honourable guardianship. Let her fly, – by the sun in heaven she shall escape!"

This bishop remained silent for some time; the same ardent blood did not warm his veins, which boiled in those of Castruccio: he saw all the difficulties; he feared for the success of their scheme; but he resolved to make the attempt. "You are right," said he; "flight is her only safety: yet it will be rather a rape, than a flight; for willingly she will never consent / to desert the high character she has chosen to assume. Did you not mark her triumph, when the Judgement of God was agreed upon? Mad, wild girl! – Let me consider our plan, and weigh our powers. The abbess is a Guelph; but the abbot of the visiting monastery is a Ghibeline; besides the edicts of the church pronounce against these temptations of God's justice. I will exert myself; and she may be saved."

When night closed in, these two anxious friends, alone and wrapt up from observation, hastened to the monastery. Castruccio remained in the parlour; and the prelate entered the interior of the convent. He remained two hours; while Castruccio, full of anxiety, continued alone in the parlour, which looked on an interior court with no object to call off his attention, in silent and anxious expectation. He thought of the beauty of the prophetess, her animation and numberless graces, until he almost believed in the divinity of her mission: but he shuddered with horror, when he reflected upon her danger, that her ivory feet should press the burning iron, that, if she fell, she / would fall on the hot metal, and expire in misery, while the priests, the accursed, self-constituted distributors of God's justice, would sing hymns of triumph over her untimely and miserable fate; – he felt tears gather in his eyes, and he would have devoted himself for her safety. At length the bishop reappeared, and they silently returned to the palace.

"Well! where is she?" were the first words of Castruccio.

"Safe I hope; I trust that I shall not be deceived. I endeavoured to move the abbot to let her escape; I would have gone to the abbess, whose consent I must have obtained, and have used all the influence my station would have given me with her; but the abbot stopped me; – he assured me that he would take care that no harm befel the devoted victim; he begged me not to ask an explanation; – that he and his monks had the charge of the preparation for the Judgement, and that much was in their power; again and again he assured me that she should receive no injury."

"I do not like this: – she must be protected by falsehood and perjury, a lying and blasphemous / mockery of the name of God. The abbot, who was a servant of the Popes at Avignon, laughs at my scruples; and I am obliged to yield. She will be saved, and God, I hope, will pardon our human weaknesses. Let the sin lie on the souls of those blood-hounds, who would pursue to destruction the loveliest creature that breathes upon earth." /

CHAPTER III.

Judgement of God. – Revolution of Ferrara.

The old man was gloomy and depressed; he retired early to prayer. Castruccio had not slept the preceding night, and he felt his eyes weighed down, although in mind he was agitated and restless; he slept some hours, starting from feverish dreams, in which Euthanasia and poor Beatrice, alike in danger, alike weeping and imploring his aid, filled him with agony. He was awaked before day-break by the bishop's servant; he repaired to the bed-chamber of the prelate, who was sitting on a couch, with haggard looks, and eyes red and inflamed with watching.

"My dear lord," cried the bishop, "I pray you pardon me that I disturb your rest; I cannot sleep. In two hours this ceremony – this mockery begins. I shall not be there; it / becomes not my character to be present at such temptations of God's justice: this is my excuse. But I could not go; I should die if I were to behold Beatrice bound and suffering. Yet, do you go, and come quickly back to tell me of her success; – go, and see, if the abbot keeps his word, and if ever I shall behold my child again."

Castruccio endeavoured to console his unhappy friend; but the strong affection and fears of the good man would listen to no comfort. "Let her be saved," he said, "and I am content; but this doubt, this pause of horrid expectation, is more than I can bear; I love her more than father ever loved a child, and she was mine by every tie; – I feel my very life-strings crack, sometimes I am apprehensive I shall die in the agony of doubt; go, go, my dearest lord, go and return quickly, if you love me!"

The bell of the church now began to toll, and announced that the monks were occupied in the prayers that were to precede the ceremony; Castruccio hurried to the scene. It was to take place in a large square of Ferrara, under / the walls of the garden of the convent of St. Anna, and before the gates of the monastery to the care of whose monks the Judgement was intrusted. As Castruccio approached, he found every avenue choked up by the multitude, and the house-tops covered with people, – even on towers, whence the square could only appear a confused speck, the people crowded in eager expectation. He joined a few nobles who were admitted through the garden of the monastery; as he passed the sacred precincts, he saw the chapel filled with the brothers, who were praying, while high mass was performed to sanctify their proceedings, and the eucharist was distributed as a pledge of their truth.

141

The square presented a busy, but awful scene; the houses, the windows of the monastery, the walls of the convent, were covered by people; some clinging to the posts, and to the walls; fixing their feet upon small protuberances of stone, they hung there, as if they stood on air. A large part of the square had been railed off in a semicircle round the door of the monastery, and outside this the people were admitted, while it was guarded on the / inside by Gascon soldiers, that with drawn swords kept in awe the eager spectators, whose fury of hope and fear approached madness: their voices it is true were still, for the solemn tolling of the bell struck them with awe, and hushed them, as the roar of the lion in the forest silences the timid herd; but their bodies and muscles were in perpetual motion; some foamed at the mouth, and others gazed with outstretched necks, and eyes starting from their sockets.

Within this inclosure one part was assigned for the Dominican brothers, who, in their black habits and red crosses, at an early hour occupied their seats, which were raised one above the other in the form of a small amphitheatre; another part was assigned to some of the nobles of both sexes, the spectators of this piteous scene. Within this inclosure was another small one, close to the gate of the monastery; it had two corresponding entrances, near one of which a large cross was erected, and near the other a white standard with the words *Agnus Dei* embroidered on it. This inclosure was at first empty, except that in one corner a pile of wood was heaped. /

Half an hour passed in tremendous expectation: Castruccio felt sick with dread; the heavy and monotonous tolling of the bell struck on his soul, his head ached, his heart sunk within him. At length the gates of the monastery were thrown open, and a number of monks came forward in procession, carrying lights, and chaunting hymns. They saluted the cross, and then ranged themselves round the outside of the inner inclosure; after a pause of few moments, another party came out with Beatrice in the midst of them; she was wrapt in her capuchin, the cowl drawn over her face; the crowd spoke not as she appeared, but a sound, as of the hollow north-wind among the mighty trees of a sea-like forest, rose from among them; an awful, deep and nameless breath, a sigh of many hearts; she was led to the cross, and knelt down silently before it, while the brothers continued to chaunt alternately the staves of a melancholy hymn.

Then came forth a third party of monks; they bore ploughshares and torches, mattocks and other instruments, that again spread a / groan of horror through the multitude. The pyre was lighted; the shares thrown in among the blazing wood; while other monks threw up the soil of the inclosure with their mattocks, forming six furrows, two feet distant one from the other. At length the bell, which had been silent for a few minutes, began again to toll, in signal for the ceremony to begin. At the command of the monks Beatrice arose, and threw off her capuchin; she was drest in a short vest of black stuff, fastened at the waist with a girdle of rope; it was without sleeves, and her fairest arms were crossed on her breast; her black and silken hair was scattered on her shoulders; her feet, whiter than monumental marble, were bare. She did not notice the crowd about her, but prayed fervently: her cheek was pale, but her eyes beamed; and in her face and person there was an indescribable mixture of timidity, with a firm reliance on the aid of a superior power. One of the monks bound her arms, and tied a scarf over her eyes: the shares, white with their excessive heat, were drawn from the fire with large / tongs, and the monks crowded round, and fixed them in the furrows; the earth seemed to smoke with the heat as they were laid down.

Then the barrier of the entrance to the inclosure was thrown down; the monks quitted it at the opposite end, and one of them with a loud voice, recommending Beatrice to the justice of God, bade her advance. Every heart beat fast; Castruccio overcome by uncontrolable pity, would have darted forward to save her, but some one held him back; and in a moment, before the second beating of his heart, before he again drew breath, horror was converted to joy and wonder. Beatrice, her eyes covered, her arms bound, her feet bare, passed over the burning shares with a quick light step, and reaching the opposite barrier, fell on her knees, uttering an exclamation of thanksgiving to God. These were the first words she had spoken: they were followed by a long and deafening shout of triumph from the multitude, which now manifested its joy as wildly, as before they had painfully restrained their pity and indignation. They were no longer to be contained by the palings of the inclosures; all / was broken through and destroyed; the inquisitors had slunk away; and the Gascon troops galloped off from the ground.

Immediately on the completion of her task, Beatrice had been unbound, and her capuchin was thrown over her; the noble ladies who were present crowded round her; she was silent and collected; her colour indeed was heightened by her internal agitation, and her limbs trembled with the exertion of her fortitude; but she commanded her countenance and spirits, and at least wore the appearance of serenity. She received the congratulations and respectful salutation of her friends with affectionate cordiality; while the air resounded with the triumphant *Te Deum* of the monks, and the people pressed around, awed, but joyful. They endeavoured to touch the garment of the newly declared saint; mothers brought her their sick children; the unhappy intreated for her prayers; and, however bashful and unwilling, she was obliged to bestow her blessing on all around. Suddenly a procession of nuns came forth from the garden-gate of the convent; covered with their long veils, and singing / their hymns, they surrounded Beatrice, and led her, attended by the other ladies in company, to their cloisters, where her maternal friend the viscountess Marchesana waited to clasp her in her arms.

Castruccio had already returned to the bishop; yet he came not so quickly, but that the news of the success of his Beatrice, passing from mouth to mouth, had reached him. His first emotions were joy, gratitude, and wonder; but these subsided; and the good old man kneeling humiliated, trembling and penitent, when he considered that God's name had been called on in vain, that his consecrated servants were perjured, and that falsehood was firmly established, on foundations where truth alone ought to rest. He listened to the account of Castruccio with interrupted exclamations and tears; and when it was ended he exclaimed, "This is the most miserable – the happiest day of my life!"

In the evening the palace of the prelate was crowded by his friends, who, knowing the interest he took in Beatrice, came to congratulate him on her victory, and to express their / delight that God had thought their town worthy of this manifestation of his grace. The bishop, joyful, but full of shame, listened in silence to their conjectures, exclamations, and long relations of the morning's scene; his heart was glad, but he was angry with himself for feeling pleasure at the triumph of falsehood; and, although a smile played on his lips, a blush spread itself over his aged cheeks.

The viscountess Malvezzi, radiant with delight, and the lovely Beatrice blushing under her newly acquired honours, now entered; the nobles pressed round the prophetess, kissing her hand, and the hem of her garment; while she, modest, half abashed, yet believing in her right to the reverence of her friends, smiled upon all. Castruccio was not among the last[a] of her worshippers; she had never appeared so beautiful; her eyes, sparkling with the light of triumph, were yet half hid by their heavy lids, her cheeks glowing, her graceful person, clothed in her modest garb of white woollen, moved with gestures ever new and beautiful: – she seemed another being from her he had before seen, as inspired, as ethereal, but more lovely. /

After the crowd of visitors had retired, a few of the intimate friends who formed the council of the bishop remained; the lady Marchesana invited them immediately to adopt some plan for the entrance of their prince into the city; she continued: "I speak but the words of my child, when I say this; pardon me, saintly Beatrice, that I call you thus. It is sweet to me to fancy that you are my daughter, although I am much unworthy of such a child, and you are the offspring of heaven alone."

Beatrice kissed the hand of her excellent friend with respect and gratitude; the bishop was much troubled at his sister's expression; the remembrance of her heretic mother, and his prison-scene with Magfreda, was full in his recollection, and he looked up to heaven, as if to ask God to pardon him, and to avert the punishment of deceit from the guileless Beatrice.

One of the nobles present asked the sacred maiden, to name the day when the prince should enter the town. She said in a gentle voice: "My lords, the hour of victory is at hand: the Popes, in despite of their duty, have / deserted their sacred city, have relinquished their lawful rule, and would now establish tyranny among us, – it will not be. Four days hence, on the evening of Monday,

---

[a] i.e. he was one of those 'pressing' round her; possibly, however, 'least' was intended.

we shall receive our sovereign, and on the following morning his banner will be unfurled on the battlements of this city."

"On Monday," cried a noble, "my heart misgives me; methinks it is an Ægyptian day;[a] has no one a calendar?"

"It is an Ægyptian day," exclaimed Beatrice, with vivacity; "but the adverse aspect of the stars falls on our adversaries; for us there is joy and victory."

"Monday is an early day," said Castruccio; "but as the holy Beatrice commands, so shall it be. And, my honoured lord, I shall leave you at day-break to-morrow. I shall not see you again, divine prophetess, until I come with your prince, to assert his right. I pray you therefore to bless my arms, and cause, that I may be doubly valiant, approved by one whom heaven has sent us."

Castruccio kneeled to the beautiful girl; he looked up at her with his ardent eyes, his passion-formed / lips, and countenance of frank and noble beauty; she blushing placed her hand on his raven hair, and said, "May God bless and prosper thee and thy cause!"——— Then, beckoning her aged friend, she silently saluted the company, and withdrew, abashed, confused, but her heart beating with a new and strange sense of pleasure.

The plan for the entrance of the marquess was now arranged. On the night of the fourth of August he was to pass Lago Scuro,[b] and halt with his troops, at the path which led to the secret entrance to the Malvezzi palace. The marquess, Castruccio, and a small party were to enter the house of the viscountess; and Galeazzo to lead the greater part of the remainder to the gates of the town by day-break the following morning; a part was to remain as a *corps de reserve*, if the small escort of the marquess should prove insufficient to force the opening of the gates, and the entrance of Galeazzo. In that case this more numerous troop was to enter the city through the house of the viscountess, and bring the necessary succour to their prince. /

The assembly then broke up; and Castruccio, wearied by the events of the day, fatigued with want of rest, his spirits sinking after their relaxation from the powerful excitements they had sustained, retired early to repose. He took an affectionate leave of the good old prelate, who charged him with many messages of fidelity and attachment to his prince.

The dawn of day beheld Castruccio on the road to Rovigo. The wide plain of Lombardy awoke to life under the rising sun. It was a serene morning; the cloudy mists that settled on the horizon, received the roseate glories of the rising sun, and the soft clouds of gold and pink that awaited his appearance in the east, would have pictured forth to a Grecian eye the chariot of Aurora, or

---

[a] Unlucky day, so called after Egyptian fortune-tellers (Muratori, III, diss. 59, p. 240; noted in Ab. Dep. e. 274, p. 95).

[b] On the Po, a few miles north of Ferrara; details of the Ghibelline repossession of Este in 1317, including the date, were taken from Sismondi, ch. xxix.

the golden gates which the Hours threw back as Phœbus entered upon his diurnal path.[a]

And does the beauteous prophetess seek her tower to behold the glories of the morn? Beatrice is on the *donjon* of the palace; and it is true that her eyes are directed towards the rising sun; but there is a casque which flashes under its first beams, a horseman who / gallops away from Ferrara, whose form her eyes strain to behold, even when he appears only as a black spot in the distance. She leans her cheek upon her hand, and, lost in meditation, she, most unfortunate, mistakes for the inspirations of Heaven the wild reveries of youth and love: but still her heart was hidden even from herself by a veil she did not even wish to throw aside. She felt gently agitated, but happy; a kind of Elysian happiness, that trembled at change, and wished only for a secure eternity of what it was.

Castruccio was hailed with joy by his friends at Rovigo; and, when the intelligence he brought was heard, every voice was busy in congratulation, every hand in preparation. The knights assisted the squires in furbishing their arms, and securing the various joints and fastenings of their heavy armour, in looking that the trusty blade of the sword was well fixed in the pummel, in selecting the stoutest lances, and in attending to all the other equipments of war; while the fair hands of the ladies prepared the scarfs, which, tied over the hearts of their knights, would preserve them from every / wound. No thought of danger and death, – this was to be rather a tournament, wherein with blunted lances they tilted for a sovereignty; and the idea of the Pope, and of their priest-ridden opponents and their foreign guards excited derision alone.

The sun set on the fourth day, and the troops of the marquess Obizzo to the number of four hundred were drawn out before the gates of Rovigo. The expedition was ordered as it had been arranged; and in the depth of night the viscountess, opening the low door of her secret entrance, found the marquess, Castruccio, and their followers, waiting in silence round the short half-buried cross on the marshy moor. A few whispered words of recognition having been spoken, she led them along her galleries, and up the staircase to the inhabited rooms of the palace, lifting up the tapestry of the first apartment; Castruccio did not again know the old, neglected chamber with its decaying furniture. It was hung with silk, festooned with flowers, and lighted by a hundred wax lights; a table was spread with wines, and fruits, and sweetmeats, and other more substantial refreshments; / several couches also were placed round the room for the convenience of those who wished to repose.

The viscountess with courtly grace welcomed the marquess to her palace. "My lord," she said, "for a few hours you must be imprisoned in this

---

[a] The goddess of dawn and the sun god.

apartment; I have endeavoured to decorate your poor dungeon to the best of my power, and indeed shall ever hold this room honoured, since it affords refuge and protection to my sovereign."

The old lady received the marquess's heartfelt thanks, and then retired satisfied, to recount to Beatrice the arrival of her guests, and the whispered enquiry of Castruccio concerning the health of the prophetess. But, although she had gilt their cage, the hours passed heavily to the imprisoned chiefs; they watched the stars as they still burned brightly in the sky, and almost uttered a cry of joy when they first perceived them, one by one, fading in the morning light. At length the steps of men were heard about the streets; and the horses which the bishop had provided for the troop came to the door of the palace. The trampling of these / horses as they were led to their destination, attracted a small crowd along with them; and, when the strange knights mounted them, and advanced in slow procession along the streets, the crowd increased, and the name of the marquess was whispered, while every one gazed in wonder. At length, when the troop had reached the principal street of Ferrara, they put their horses to the gallop, and raising the Ghibeline war-cry, rode through the town calling on the people to join them, and invoking downfal to the foreign tyrants: a band of citizens, who had been already prepared, obeyed the summons, and they were followed by others, who espoused the party of the prince in their hearts, and joyfully aided his restoration.

The trampling of the steeds, the clash of arms, as the knights struck their shields with their spears, the war-cry of the troops, and the *vivas* of the crowd, awoke the papal governor, who called out the Gascon soldiery. But it was too late; the marquess reached the gate of the town, put the sentinels to flight, and admitted Galeazzo into the city: then, joined by / all the nobility of Ferrara, he rode towards the palace of the governor. The Gascons were drawn up in the great square of the town, but they were unable to withstand the first onset of Obizzo's party; they fled, and shut themselves up in Castel Tealdo, the fortress of the town, where they were at least safe from sudden attack. The marquess drew his troops around, and threw up his works to prevent their egress; and, leaving to his principal captain the care of the siege, returned to his palace to receive the congratulations of his delighted subjects.

Now joy was the order of the day; the Italians, who had been intrusted with the charge of some of the gates of the town, brought the keys to the feet of their sovereign; the others were broken open; every magistrate brought in his resignation, and many of them petitions for mercy; and lying traitors, who assured him that their faith had never been broken, crowded to the presence-chamber. His throne was erected in the great square, covered with the richest cloth, and surmounted by a magnificent canopy; the troops were marshalled before / him, the standards brought and lowered to his feet. A deputation of the noblest counts and knights of Ferrara were sent to convey

147

the caroccio* to the throne of the prince. They went to the cathedral; and the monks led it forth, adorned with its splendid trappings and standards, the gold cross and white flag of the Popes waving above all. They yoked to it four beautiful dove coloured oxen, on whom they cast rich trappings of scarlet cloth; and then, to the sound of trumpets, surrounded by the knights, and followed by a procession of priests singing *Te Deum*, it was drawn to the square before the throne of Obizzo; then with a triumphant flourish, the standard of the Pope was lowered, and that of the house of Este raised to its ancient eminence. Festivities / of every kind followed this joyful event, triumphant festivities, untarnished with blood; for few of the subjects of the marquess were hostile to his return, and these either went into voluntary exile, or joined the refugees in Castel Tealdo. /

CHAPTER IV.

Fall of Beatrice.

Castruccio was no inactive partaker in this busy scene. But, after the combat was finished, and he perceived that Obizzo was engaged in acts of peaceful sovereignty alone, he hastened to the palace of the bishop; for he was painfully surprised in not seeing him among the nobles who waited on the prince. The old man was ill: he had been dreadfully agitated by the scenes of the preceding days, and his health for a while sunk under it. Castruccio was introduced into his chamber, where he lay peacefully sleeping on a magnificent couch, his adopted child, the lovely Beatrice, watching before him, who, when she beheld Castruccio, blushed deeply, while, in spite of every effort, a smile of delight spread itself over her expressive countenance.

"He is not very ill," she said in a low voice, / in answer to Castruccio's enquiries; "the fever has left him entirely; he is weak, but recovering. He sleeps sweetly now: look at him; at his reverend grey hairs strewn over his naked temples; look at his eyes, sunken with age, yet, when open, beaming with benevolence and affection: look what a gentle smile there is upon his pale lips; there he sleeps, affection, benevolence, matchless virtue, and excelling wisdom,

---

* The Caroccio was introduced after the tenth century. It was a large car, painted red, adorned with numerous standards, the spoils of vanquished enemies, and surmounted by the banner of the *commune* to which it belonged. It made a considerable figure in the wars of Frederic Barbarossa. Its loss was an indelible disgrace, and its capture the greatest of triumphs.[a]

[a] Derived from Villani, VI, cap. 77 and Muratori, I, diss. 26, p. 362; noted in Ab. Dep. e. p. 274, p. 77–8.

all cradled by the baby Sleep; I have been contemplating him for more than an hour; he draws his breath as regularly as a sleeping infant who has sucked its fill, and his heart heaves slowly, but calmly. It is a heavenly sight to look on the repose of this good old man; it calms wild passion, and sheds the fresh dew of healthful meditation over the strange reveries of youth."

She spoke in a whisper; but her countenance was all animation. The old man moved; and, pressing her finger on her lips, she paused. "Beatrice, my child," he said, "I have slept long and soundly, and feel quite well. Who is that stranger? does he bring news from the marquess? Aye, I remember / this is the day, – I am strangely confused; I recollect now that I heard of his success before I slept."

"Father, it is my lord Castruccio, who, after having reinstated our prince in his sovereignty, visits your sick chamber."

Castruccio remained several hours conversing with the bishop; he gave him an account of the action of the morning, and Beatrice listened with her whole soul in her eyes; yet, attentive as she was to the narration, she watched with sweet earnestness her sick friend, turning her looks from him to the animated face of Castruccio; and again, as she crept near her adoptive father, she adjusted some pillow, or performed some little office that marked her earnest observation.

"How beautiful she is!" thought Castruccio, "and what will become of her?" He fixed his eyes on the silver plate on her forehead, "Yes, she is the *Ancilla Dei*, a maiden vowed to God and chastity; yet her eyes seem penetrated with love; the changeful and blooming colours of her face, her form, which is all that imagination can conceive of perfect, appear / not like those of a cloistered nun. Ah! Beatrice, if you would be sacred to your God, you ought to hide your surpassing loveliness with thick veils, behind treble grates. But she is a prophetess; something more than human; – a character unapproachable even in thought."

Thus Castruccio tried to disentangle his perplexed thoughts, still looking on the maiden, who, suddenly raising her eyes, and meeting his which were fixed on her silver plate, blushed even till the tips of her fingers became a rosy red; and then, complaining in an hesitating voice, that the plate hurt her brow, she untied it; while her silken hair, no longer confined, fell on her neck.

Thus many hours passed, and when at length the prophetess retired, it was to feverish meditation, and thoughts burning with passion, rendered still more dangerous from her belief in the divine nature of all that suggested itself to her mind. She prayed to the Virgin to inspire her; and, again giving herself up to reverie, she wove a subtle web, whose materials she believed heavenly, but which were indeed stolen from the glowing wings of love. Kneeling, / her eyes raised to heaven, she felt the same commotion in her soul, which she had felt before, and had recognised as divine inspiration; she felt the same uncontrollable transport and burst of imaginative vision, which she believed to flow

149

immediately from the invisible ray of heaven-derived prophecy. She felt her soul, as it were, fade away, and incorporate itself with another and a diviner spirit, which whispered truth and knowledge to her mind, and then slowly receding, left her human nature, agitated, joyful, and exhausted;—— these were her dreams, – alas! to her they were realities.

The following morning she again met Castruccio in the chamber of the bishop. She now looked upon him fearlessly; and, if the virgin modesty of her nature had not withheld her, her words would have been as frank as she innocently believed them to be inspired. But, although she was silent, her looks told that she was changed. Her manner the day before had been soft, concentrated, and retiring; now she was unconstrained; her eyes sparkled, and a joyous expression dwelt in / every feature. Her manner towards her guardian was endearing, nor was the affectionate modulation of her voice different when she addressed his guest: Castruccio started to hear it. It reminded him of the accents of Euthanasia, whom for a while he had forgotten; and, looking at Beatrice, he thought, "How lovely she is, and yet how unlike!"

Several days passed thus; Beatrice became embarrassed; it seemed as if she wished to speak to Castruccio, and yet dared not: when she approached, she blushed, and again drew back, and would again seek him, but again vainly. She had framed the mode of her address, conned and reconned the words she should say; but, when an opportunity occurred to utter them, her voice failed her, the memory of what she was about to utter deserted her, and it was not until the approach of a third person took from her the possibility of speaking, that speech again returned, and the lost occasion was uselessly lamented. At night she sought the counsels of heaven, and gave herself up to her accustomed extasies; they always told her the same things, until to / her bewildered and untamed mind it seemed as if the spirit that had power over her, reprimanded her hesitation, her little trust in the promises of heaven, and her reluctance to follow the path it pointed out.

"Surely, oh! most certainly," she thought, "thus I am commanded by the Power who has so often revealed his will to me. Can I penetrate his hidden designs? can I do more than execute his decrees? did I not feel thus, when with prophetic transport I foretold distant events that surely came to pass? when I foresaw yet afar off the death of Lorenzo, that lovely child blooming in health, when every one called me a false prophet? And yet he died. And now, the marquess's return? nay, am I not approved by heaven? did I not escape from the malice of my enemies through its miraculous interposition? Oh! I will no longer scan with presumptuous argument, purposes that are ruled by mightier hands than mine; I will resign myself to the guidance of what has ever conducted me aright, and which now points out the path to happiness."

The next morning, her cheeks flushed, her / eyes weighed down, trembling and abashed, she sought Castruccio. It is impossible that there should not have been much tenderness in his manner towards this lovely girl; her history, her strange and romantic contemplations and impulses, and the great intimacy which had arisen between them, were sufficient for this. He regarded her also as a nun; and this made him feel less restraint in the manner of his address, since he feared not to be misconstrued; while at the same time it gave an elevation and unusual tone to his ideas concerning her, that made him watch her every motion with interest. She now approached; and he said playfully; "Where is thy mark, prophetess? art thou no longer the *Maiden of God*? For some days thou hast cast aside the hallowed diadem."

"I still have it," she replied; "but I have dismissed it from my brow; I will give it you; come, my lord, this evening at midnight to the secret entrance of the viscountess's palace." Saying these words, she fled to hide her burning blushes in solitude, and again to feel the / intoxicating delusions that led her on to destruction.

Castruccio came. If it were in human virtue to resist the invitation of this angelic girl, his was not the mind, strictly disciplined to right, self-examining and jealous of its own integrity that should thus weigh its actions, and move only as approved by conscience. He was frank and noble in his manner; his nature was generous; and, though there lurked in his heart the germ of an evil-bearing tree, it was as yet undeveloped and inanimated;[a] and, in obeying the summons of Beatrice, he passively gave himself up to the strong excitements of curiosity and wonder.

He went again and again. When the silent night was spread over every thing, and the walls of the town stood black and confused amidst the overshadowing trees, whose waving foliage was diversified by no gleam of light, but all was formless as the undistinguishable air; or if a star were dimly seen, it just glistened on the waters of the marsh, and then swiftly the heavy web of clouds hid both star and water; / when the watch dogs were mute, unawakened by the moon, and the wind that blew across the plain alone told to the ear the place of the trees; when the bats and the owls were lulled by the exceeding darkness; it was on such nights as these, that Castruccio sought the secret entrance of the viscountess's palace, and was received by the beautiful Beatrice, enshrined in an atmosphere of love and joy.

She was a strange riddle to him. Without vow, without even that slight shew of distrust which is the child of confidence itself; without seeking the responsive professions of eternal love, she surrendered herself to his arms. And, when the first maiden bashfulness had passed away, all was deep tenderness and ardent love. Yet there was a dignity and a trusting affection in her most unguarded moments, that staggered him: a broken expression would sometimes fall from her lips, that seemed to say that she believed him indissolubly hers, which made him start, as if he feared that he had acted with perfidy; yet

---

[a] Unendowed with life.

151

he had never solicited, never promised, – what could she mean? What was she? He loved her as / he would have loved any thing that was surpassingly beautiful; and, when these expressions, that intimated somewhat of enduring and unchangeable in their intercourse, intruded themselves, they pained and irritated him: he turned to the recollection of Euthanasia, his pure, his high-minded, and troth-plight bride; – she seemed as if wronged by such an idea; and yet he hardly dared think her purer than poor Beatrice, whose soul, though given up to love, was imbued in its very grain and texture with delicate affections and honourable feelings; all that makes the soul and living spark of virtue. If she had not resisted the impulses of her soul, it was not that she wanted the power; but that, deluded by the web of deceit that had so long wound itself about her, she believed them, not only lawful, but inspired by the special interposition of heaven.

Poor Beatrice! She had inherited from her mother the most ardent imagination that ever animated a human soul. Its images were as vivid as reality, and were so overpowering, that they appeared to her, when she compared them to the calm sensations of others, as something / superhuman; and she followed that as a guide, which she ought to have bound with fetters, and to have curbed and crushed by every effort of reason. Unhappy prophetess! the superstitions of her times had obtained credit for, and indeed given birth to her pretensions, and the compassion and humanity of her fellow creatures had stamped them with the truth-attesting seal of a miracle. There is so much life in love! Beatrice was hardly seventeen, and she loved for the first time; and all the exquisite pleasures of that passion were consecrated to her, by a mysteriousness and delusive sanctity that gave them tenfold zest. It is said, that in love we idolize the object; and, placing him apart and selecting him from his fellows, look on him as superior in nature to all others. We do so; but, even as we idolize the object of our affections, do we idolize ourselves: if we separate him from his fellow mortals, so do we separate ourselves, and, glorying in belonging to him alone, feel lifted above all other sensations, all other joys and griefs, to one hallowed circle from which all but his idea is banished; we walk as if a mist or some / more potent charm divided us from all but him; a sanctified victim which none but the priest set apart for that office could touch and not pollute, enshrined in a cloud of glory, made glorious through beauties not our own. Thus we all feel during the entrancing dream of love; and Beatrice, the ardent, affectionate Beatrice, felt this with multiplied power: and, believing that none had ever felt so before, she thought that heaven itself had interfered to produce so true a paradise. If her childish dreams had been full of fire, how much more vivid and overpowering was the awakening of her soul when she first loved! It seemed as if some new and wondrous spirit had descended, alive, breathing and panting, into her colder heart, and gave it a new impulse, a new existence. Ever the dupe of her undisciplined thoughts, she cherished her reveries, believing that heavenly and intellectual, which was indebted for its force to earthly mixtures; and she resigned herself entire to her visionary joys, until she finally awoke to truth, fallen, and for ever lost.

In the mean time peace was entirely restored to Ferrara: on the fifteenth of August Castel / Tealdo surrendered, and the Pope's governor, with his foreign guard, quitted the territories of the marquess of Este.[a] Galeazzo Visconti returned to Milan, but still Castruccio lingered: he wished to go; he found himself out of place as a dangling courtier in the train of Obizzo; but how could he leave Beatrice? What did she expect or wish? The passionate tenderness that she evinced, could not be an ephemeral spark of worthless love; and how often did the *We*, she used in talking of futurity, make him pause when he wished to speak of their separation! She seemed happy; her words flowed in rich abundance, and were adorned with various imagery and with delicate thoughts, shewing that her soul, at rest from fear, wandered as it was wont amidst the wilds of her imagination. He found her untaught, undisciplined, but so sincere, so utterly forgetful of self, so trusting, that he dared not speak that, which each day shewed more clearly would be as a dagger to her heart. A thousand times he cursed himself for having mistaken her, and imagining, inspired as she believed herself to be, that her actions and feelings / had not been dictated by the loftiest impulses. But the time arrived, when he was obliged to undeceive her; and the hand, that tore away the ties her trusting heart had bound round itself, at the same time tore away the veil which had for her invested all nature, and shewed her life as it was – naked and appalling.

They sat in her apartment at the Malvezzi palace; she radiant, beautiful, and happy; and, twining her lovely arms around Castruccio, she said: "The moon will set late to-morrow night, and you must not venture here; and indeed for several nights it will spread too glaring a beam. But tell me, are you become a citizen of Ferrara? They averred that you were the head of a noble city; but I see they must have been mistaken, or the poor city must totter strangely, so headless as your absence must make it. How is this, my only friend? Are you not Antelminelli? Are we not to go to Lucca?"

Castruccio could not stand the questioning of her soft yet earnest eyes; he withdrew himself from her arms, and taking her hands in his, / kissed them silently. "How is my noble lord?" she repeated, "have you had ill news? are you again banished? that cannot be, or methinks my heart would have told me the secret. Yet, if you are, be not unhappy: – your own Beatrice, with prophetic words, and signs from heaven that lead the multitude, will conduct you to greater glory and greater power than you before possessed. My gentle love, you have talked less about yourself, and about your hopes and desires, than I should have wished: – Do not think me a foolish woman, tied to an embroidery frame, or that my heart would not beat high at the news of your success, or that

---

[a] Derived from Sismondi, ch. xxix.

with my whole soul I should not enter into your plans, and tell you how the stars looked upon your intents. In truth my mind pants for fitting exertion; and, in being joined to thee, dearest love, I thought that I had found the goal for which heaven had destined me. Nay, look not away from me; I do not reproach thee; I know that, in finding thee, in being bound to thy fate, mine is fulfilled; and I am happy. Now speak – tell me what has disturbed thy thoughts."

"Sweetest Beatrice, I have nothing to tell; / yet I have for many days wished to speak; for in truth I must return to Lucca."

The quick sensations of Beatrice could not be deceived. The words of Castruccio were too plain; she looked at him, as if she would read the secret in his soul, – she did read it: – his downcast eyes, confused air, and the words he stammered out in explanation, told her every thing. The blood rushed to her face, her neck, her hands; and then as suddenly receding, left even her lips pale. She withdrew her arms from the soft caress she had bestowed; playfully she had bound his head with her own hair and the silken strings entangled with his; she tore her tresses impatiently to disengage herself from him; then, trembling, white, and chilled, she sat down, and said not a word. Castruccio looked on with fear; he attempted consolation.

"I shall visit thee again, my own Beatrice; for a time we must part; – the viscountess – the good bishop – you cannot leave them, – fear not but that we shall meet again."

"We shall meet again!" she exlaimed with a passionate voice; "Never!"

Her tone, full of agitation and grief, sunk / into the soul of Castruccio. He took her hand; it was lifeless; he would have kissed her; but she drew back coldly and sadly. His words had not been those of the heart; he had hesitated and paused: but now compassion, and the memory of what she had been, awoke his powers, and he said warmly, and with a voice whose modulations seemed tuned by love: "You mistake me, Beatrice; indeed you do. I love you; – who could help loving one so true, so gentle, and so trusting? – we part for a while; – this is necessary. Does not your character require it? the part you act in the world? every consideration of honour and delicacy? – Do you think that I can ever forget you? does not your own heart tell you, that your love, your caresses, your sweet eyes, and gentle words, have woven a net which must keep me for ever? You will remain here, and I shall go; but a few suns, a few moons, and we shall meet again, and the joy of that moment will make you forget our transient separation."

How cold were these words to the burning heart of the prophetess; she, who thought that / Heaven had singled out Castruccio to unite him to her, who thought that the Holy Spirit had revealed himself to bless their union, that, by the mingled strength of his manly qualities, and her divine attributes, some great work might be fulfilled on earth; who saw all as God's command, and done by his special interposition; to find this heavenly tissue swept away, beaten down, and destroyed! It was to his fortunes, good or bad, that she had bound herself, to share his glory or soothe his griefs; and not to be the mistress of the passing hour, the distaff of the spinning Hercules.[a] It was her heart, her whole soul she had given; her understanding, her prophetic powers, all the little universe that with her ardent spirit she grasped and possessed, she had surrendered, fully, and without reserve; but alas! the most worthless part alone had been accepted, and the rest cast as dust upon the winds. How in this moment did she long to be a winged soul, that her person heedlessly given, given only as a part of that to the whole of which he had an indefeasible right, and which was now despised, might / melt away from the view of the despiser, and be seen no more! The words of her lover brought despair, not comfort; she shook her head in silence; Castruccio spoke again and again; but many words are dangerous where there is much to conceal, and every syllable he uttered laid bare some new forgery of her imagination, and shewed her more and more clearly the harsh reality. She was astounded, and drank in his words eagerly, though she answered not; she was impatient when he was silent, for she longed to know the worst; yet she dared not direct the course of his explanations by a single enquiry: she was as a mother, who reads the death-warrant of her child on the physician's brow, yet blindly trusting that she decyphers ill, will not destroy the last hope by a question. Even so she listened to the assurances of Castruccio, each word being a fresh assurance of her misery, yet not stamping the last damning seal on her despair.

At length grey dawn appeared; she was silent, motionless and wan; she marked it not; but he did; and rising hastily he cried, "I must go, or you are lost; farewel, Beatrice!" /

Now she awoke, her eyes glared, her lovely features became even distorted by the strength of her agony, – she started up – "Not yet, not yet – one word more! Do you – love another?"

Her tone was that of command; – her flashing eyes demanded the truth, and seemed as if they would by their excessive force strike the falsehood dead, if he dared utter it: he was subdued, impelled to reply: –

"I do."

"Her name?"

"Euthanasia."

"Enough, I will remember that name in my prayers. Now, go! seek not to come again; the entrance will be closed; do not endeavour to see me at the house of the bishop; I shall fly you as a basilisk, and, if I see you, your eyes will kill me. Remember these are my words; they are as true, as that I am all a lie. It will kill me; but I swear by all my hopes never to see you more. Oh, never, never!"

---

[a] According to Lemprière, Hercules, made slave to Queen Omphale, proved so enamoured of her that he took to spinning; he became the lover of both the queen and one of her maids. When the period of his slavery ended, he reverted to lion-skin and club, and left her in order to re-instate the expelled King of Sparta.

She again sank down pale and lifeless, pressing her hands upon her eyes, as if the more speedily to fulfil her vow. Castruccio dared / stay no longer, he fled as the dæmon might have fled from the bitter sorrows of despoiled Paradise;[a] he left her aghast, overthrown, annihilated.

He quitted Ferrara that day. He was miserable: careless of the road, he sought solitude alone. Before night he was among the wild forests of the Apennines, – and there he paused; he was surrounded by the dark pine-forests that sung above him, covered by a night which was cloudy and unquiet, for the swift wind drove the rack along the sky, and moaned, and howled; while the lightnings of a distant storm, faint, but frequent, displayed the savage spot on which he rested. He threw himself from his horse, and abandoned himself to sorrow: it stung him to reflect, that he was the cause of sharpest pain to one who loved him; and the excuses he fondly leaned upon before his explanation, broke as a reed under the wild force of Beatrice's despair. He had heard her story, he knew her delusions, and ought not to have acted towards her, as to a fellow-being who walked in the same light as himself, and saw objects dressed in the same / colours: a false sun made every thing deceptive for her eyes, – and he knew it.

Yet what could he now do? Go again to Beatrice? Wherefore? What could he say? but one word – "forget me!" And that was already said. His early vows, his deepest and his lasting hopes, were bound up in Euthanasia: she depended on him alone; she had no father, no relation, none to love but him. She had told him that she gave up her soul to him, and had intreated him not to cast aside the gift. Beatrice had never demanded his faith, his promise, his full and entire heart; but she believed that she had them, and the loss sustained by her was irretrievable.

Yet she would soon forget him: thus he reasoned; hers was one of those minds ever tossed like the ocean by the tempest of passion; yet, like the ocean, let the winds abate, and it subsides, and quickly again becomes smiling. She had many friends; she was loved, nay, adored, by all who surrounded her: utter hopelessness of ever seeing him again would cause her to forget him; her old ideas, her old habits would return, and she would be happy. / His interference alone could harm her; but she, the spoiled child of the world, would weep out her grief on some fond and friendly bosom, and then again laugh and play as she was wont.

He spent the following day and night among these forests; until the tempest of his soul was calmed, and his thoughts, before entangled and matted by vanity and error, now flowed loose, borne on by repentance, as the clinging weeds of a dried-up brook are spread free and distinct by the re-appearance of the clear stream. He no longer felt the withering look of Beatrice haunt even his dreams; it appeared to him that he had paid the mulct of remorse and error; the

---

[a] i.e. not as Milton's Satan in *Paradise Lost*, X. 332–46, who exults.

impression of her enchantments and of her sorrows wore off; and he returned with renewed tenderness to Euthanasia, whom he had wronged; and, in the knowledge that he had shamed her pure lessons, he felt a true and wholesome sorrow, which was itself virtue. Yet he dared not go back to her; he dared not meet her clear, calm eye; and he felt that his cheek would burn with shame under her innocent gaze. He suddenly / remembered his engagement to visit Pepi, the old Ghibeline politician, who, without honesty or humanity, snuffed up the air of self-conceit, and who, thus inflated, believed himself entitled to cover others with the venom of sarcasm and contempt.

"Yes, old fox!" he cried, "I will unearth you, and see if there is aught in your kennel worth the labour. Methinks you would give out as if gold were under the dirt, or that power and wisdom lurked beneath your sheepskin and wrinkles; but believe me, my good friend, we Italians, however base our politics may be, are not yet low enough to feed from a trough with you for the driver."

The recollection of something so low and contemptible as Benedetto of Cremona, relieved Castruccio from a load of dissatisfaction and remorse. Comparing Pepi with himself, not directly, but by inference of infinite contempt, he felt that he could again unabashed raise his eyes. This was not well; far better was the blush of humiliation which covered him in comparing his soiled purposes and strayed heart to something high and pure, / than the ignoble heavings of self-consequence in matching himself with such a blotted specimen of humanity as Pepi. So, as we are wont, when we return from solitude of self-examination to the company of fellow-sinners, he twisted up again the disentangled tresses of his frank and sincere thoughts into the million-knotted ties of the world's customs and saintly-looking falsehoods; and, leaving the woods of the Apennines, something wiser in self-knowledge, and but little improved in generous virtue, and the government of his passions, he put spurs to his horse, and turned his steps towards Cremona. /

CHAPTER V.

Visit to Pepi at Cremona.

It was on the evening of the tenth of September[a] that Castruccio arrived at the bridge which Pepi had indicated. No one was there, except an old woman spinning with a distaff, who from her age and wrinkles might have served for a model of the eternal Fates; for her leathern and dry, brown skin, did not seem

---

[a] For the possible significance of this day see p. 325n. The 10 September is a day of crisis in *Frankenstein* (p. 165).

formed of the same frail materials as the lily cheek of a high-bred dame. She looked full at Castruccio; so that he laughing asked her, whether she would tell him his fortune.

"Aye," replied the beldame, "though no witch, it is easy for me to tell you what you are about to find. Say the word you were bid repeat here, and I will conduct you where you desire to go."

"Lucca." /

"Enough; follow me. He of whom you wot, will be glad that you come alone."

She led him out of the high road, by numberless lanes through which his horse could hardly break his way, among the entangled bushes of the hedges. The woman trudged on before, spinning as she went, and screaming out a few notes of a song, returning to them again and again with a monotonous kind of yell, as loud as it was discordant. At length they arrived at a mean suburb of Cremona; and, traversing a number of dirty alleys and dark streets, they came to one bounded on one side by the high, black, stone wall of a palace. The old woman knocked at a small, low door in this wall, made strong with iron clamps, and which, when cautiously opened, appeared not less in thickness than the wall of the palace itself. It was Pepi's muscular, but withered hand, that turned the massy key, and forced back the bolts of three successive doors that guarded this entrance. After having admitted Castruccio (the old woman being left behind with the horse, to lead him to the front gate of the palace), he closed the doors / with care; and then, it being quite dark within the passage, he un-covered a small lamp, and led the way through the gallery, up a narrow staircase, which opened by a secret door on the great and dreary hall of the palace. This vast apartment was hardly light, although at the further end a torch, stuck against the wall, flared with a black and smoky flame.

"Welcome again, noble Castruccio, to my palace," said Pepi: "I have waited anxiously for your arrival, for all my hopes appear now to depend upon you. At present, since you appear wet and cold, come to the further hall, where we shall find fire and food: and pardon, I intreat you, my homely fare, for it is by œconomy and privation that I have become that which I am."

The manners of Pepi were unusually inflated and triumphant; and Castruc-cio wondered what new scene a being, whom he considered as half a buffoon, and half a madman, intended to act. A large fire blazed in the middle of the second hall, and a pot hung over it containing the supper of the family: Pepi took Castruccio's cloak, and spread it / carefully on the high back of a chair; and then he pushed a low bench close to the fire, and the two friends (if so they might be called) sat down. There was no torch or lamp in the room; but the flame of the burning wood cast a broad glare on Benedetto's face, which Castruccio observed with curiosity; his brows were elevated, his sharp eyes almost emitted sparks of fire, his mouth was drawn down and compressed with a mixed expression of cunning and pride; he threw another log on the blazing hearth, and then began to speak: –

"My lord Castruccio, I think it were well that we should instantly enter on our business, since, when we have agreed upon our terms, no time must be lost in our proceeding. My proposition last May, was, as you may remember, to restore this town to the Ghibelines; and this is in my power. Cane, the lord of Verona, is I know about to approach with an army to besiege it, and it rests with me whether he shall succeed or not. If he do not agree to my terms, he must fail, as I may well say that the keys of this town rest with me. It is true, that when I spoke to you in May, I / did not know that Can' Grande would attempt the town, and in that case I should have needed no more aid from you than your mere interposition: but in affairs of importance a mediator's is not a humble task; and I hope that you will not disdain to act a friendly part towards me."

Pepi paused with an inquisitive look; and Castruccio, assuring him of his amicable dispositions, intreated him to continue his explanation, and to name what he called his terms. Benedetto continued: "My terms are these, and truly they may easily be fulfilled; of course Cane only wishes to take the town out of the hands of the Guelphs, and to place it in trust with some sure Ghibeline; now let him make me lord of Cremona, and I will engage, first to put the town into his hands, and afterwards on receiving the investiture, to aid him with men during war, and pay him a tribute in time of peace. If he agree to this, let him only lead his troops to the gate of the town, and it shall be his without costing him one drop of blood."

Castruccio listened with uncontrolable astonishment. He looked at the wrinkled and hardly human face of the speaker, his uncouth / gait and manners, and could scarcely restrain his contempt; he remembered Pepi's want of every principle and his boasted cruelty; and disgust overcame every other feeling; but, considering that it was as well to understand the whole of the man's drift, after a moment's pause he replied: "And where are the keys of the town which you say are in your possession?"

"Would you see them?" cried Pepi, starting up with a grin of triumph; "follow me, and you shall behold them."

He called his old woman, and, taking the lamp from her hand, he bade her prepare the supper; and then with quick steps he conducted Castruccio from the apartment: they crossed the court into the second hall, and he opened the door of the secret staircase. After Pepi had again carefully closed it, he opened another door on the staircase, which Castruccio had not before observed, and which was indeed entirely concealed in the dirty plaster of the wall. "Even she," said Pepi, pointing towards the hall, "even my old witch, does not know of this opening."

After closing it, he led the way through a / dark gallery, to another long and narrow flight of stairs, which seemed to lead to the vaults underneath the castle. Castruccio paused before he began to descend, so deeply was he impressed with the villainy of his companion; but, remembering that they were man to man, and that he was young and strong, and his companion old and weak, and that he was armed with a sword, while Pepi had not even a knife at his girdle, he followed his conductor down the stairs. Flight after flight succeeded, until he thought they would never end; at length they came to another long gallery, windowless and damp, which by its close air indicated that it was below the surface of the ground, and then to various dreary and mildewed vaults in one of which stood two large chests.

"There," cried Pepi, "are the keys of the town."

"Where?" asked Castruccio, impatiently, "I see them not."

Pepi turned to him with a grin of joy; and, taking two keys from his bosom, he knelt down, and exerting his strength, turned them in their / locks, and threw back the lids of the chests, first one, and then the other: they were filled with parchments.

"I do not understand this mummery; how can these musty parchments be the keys of your town?"

Pepi rubbed his hands with triumphant glee; he almost capered with delight; unable to stand still, he walked up and down the vault, crying, "They are not musty! they are parchments of this age! they are signed, they are sealed; – read them! read them!"

Castruccio took up one, and found it to be a bond obliging the signer to pay the sum of twenty thousand crowns on a certain day, in return for certain monies lent, or to forfeit the sum of thirty thousand, secured on the lands of a noble count of Cremona.

"They are usurious bonds," said Castruccio, throwing it down angrily.

"They are," replied Pepi, picking up the deed, and folding it carefully; "said I not well that I had the keys of the town? Every noble owes me a part, many the best part, of his estate. Many bonds are forfeited; and the / mulet hangs over the signer by a single thread. There is count Grimaldi,[a] whose bond was due the very day after his castle was plundered and burned, and his lands laid waste by the Germans; he owes me more than he can ever pay, though his last acre with his patent of nobility went with it, and he after with his brats, to beg at the doors of the Guelphs, his friends. There is the marquess Malvoglio[b] who bought the life of his only son, a rank traitor, from the emperor by the sums which I lent him, which have never been repaid. This box is full of the bonds made before the siege of Cremona; it was concealed above in my tower when you last visited me; and this is full of those made since that time; you see the harvest the good emperor brought me. When the Germans quitted the town, my halls were filled with the beggarly Guelph nobility—— 'Messer Benedetto, my wife has not a garment to cover her!' 'Messer Benedetto, my palace is in

---

[a] A leading Guelph family (Sismondi, ch. xxix), but of Genoa, rather than Cremona; a Grimaldi is the stingy patron in Boccaccio's story of William Borsiere.
[b] Not further identified.

ruins!' 'Messer Benedetto, my beds are destroyed, my walls are bare of furniture!' – 'Oh! Messer Benedetto, without your aid my children must starve!' /

"'Aye, my friends,' said I, 'I will help you most willingly; here are parchments
to sign, and gold to spend!' – For in the interim I had called in my debts from
various other towns, and had two chests of gold ready for the gaping hounds;
some read the bonds, and complained of the conditions; the greater number
signed without reading them; none have been paid; now they are all mine, body
and soul; aye, with these bonds, the devil himself might buy them."

"And this is the trade by which you have become rich, and to support which
you have sold your paternal estate?"

"Ah! Messer Castruccio," replied Pepi, his countenance falling; "not only
have I sold every acre, but I have starved myself, exposed myself by my
beggarly garb to the jeers and mocks of every buffoon and idiot, who had been
weaned but a year from his mother's milk: a knight in sheep-skin was an
irresistible subject for ridicule; I have been patient and humble, and by my
submissive mien have lulled my debtors into security, till the day of payment
passed; then I have come upon them, / received no payment, but got fresh
bonds, and then with renewed hypocrisy, blinded them again till I have drawn
their very souls from their bodies; – and they and theirs are mine. Why, Cane
is himself my debtor, here is his bond for ten thousand florins of gold, which I
will burn with my own hands, when by his exertions I am made lord of
Cremona."

Castruccio, who had steadily curbed his contempt, now, overcome by indignation, burst forth like thunder on his host: "Thou vile Jew," he exclaimed,
"utter not those words again! Thou, lord of Cremona! A usurer, a blood-
sucker! – Why all the moisture squeezed from thy miserable carcase would not
buy one drop of the noble heart's tide of your debtors. – And these parchments! Thinkest thou men are formed of straw to be bound with paper chains?
Have they not arms? have they not swords? Tremble, foolish wretch! Be what
thou art, – a sycophant. – No, thou art not human; but in these filthy vaults
thou hast swollen, as a vile toad or rank mushroom; and then, because thou
canst poison men, thou wouldst lord it over them! Now, thou base-minded /
fellow, be advised to cast off these presumptuous thoughts, or with my armed
heel I will crush thee in the dust!"

Pepi was pale with rage; and, with a malignant, distorted smile, which his
quivering lips could hardly frame, he said, "Fair words, my lord of Lucca;
remember this is my palace, these vaults are mine, and of these passages, I alone
have the key, know alone of their existence."

"Slave! do you threaten?"

Castruccio had scarcely uttered these words, when he perceived Pepi gliding
behind him; with eyes that flashed fire, he darted round, and transfixed by their
gaze the wretched traitor; as he cast up his arm with the passionate gesture of
indignation and command, Pepi grew pale with terror; it seemed to him, as if

he already felt the menaced vengeance of his youthful enemy; his sharp eyes became glazed, his knees trembled, his joints relaxed, and the dagger that he had already drawn from his bosom fell from his nerveless hand. All had passed so silently, that the fall of the weapon seemed to strike like thunder on the pavement, / and it re-echoed along the vaults. Castruccio smiled with a feeling too lofty even to admit contempt; it was the smile of power alone. – Pepi fell upon his knees; when, suddenly perceiving that Castruccio glanced his eye from the lamp to the parchments, and then to the lamp again, the fear of losing his precious documents overcame every other feeling, and he tried, prostrate as he was, to dart past his foe, and blow out the light; Castruccio waved his hand to keep him off, and the miserable traitor again shrunk back, and fell upon the ground in an agony of impotent rage and terror.

Castruccio now spoke in a restrained and firm tone: "Fear not; I came hither as a friend; and, though you have broken your faith with me, yet will I not mine with you: – I promised not to betray your secret, and I will not. But remember; if by these or any other means you attempt to oppress your townsmen, I will raise such a nest of hornets about you, that then, as now, you may intreat my mercy. Now give me the keys of your vaults and passages; and then up, and shew me the way from this infernal den." /

Trembling and aghast, his strait lips white with fear, Pepi gathered himself from the pavement; with unwilling hand he gave up the keys of his vault, cast one lingering glance on his treasure, and then, followed by Castruccio, who held the lamp, he quitted his den with a hesitating and unequal gait; for his late terror made him halt, and even his coward fear lest Castruccio should yet stab him in the back as they ascended the stairs. The doors were unlocked and thrown open; for no time was allowed, as in descending, for the careful drawing of bolts and turning of locks in their progress. Castruccio was eager to leave the pestilential air of the place, and to bid farewell to his treacherous and loathsome host. They at length arrived at the head of the staircase; and Pepi would have opened the door that led to the hall.

"Down, villain!" cried Castruccio, "let me go the shortest way from your devilish abode."

"But your cloak; you left your cloak in the further hall."

"It is my legacy to thee, old fox; – it will / serve to wrap your crazed limbs, and to remind you of my promises when you descend again to your tomb."

Pepi went down stairs, and opened the several doors of his palace; and Castruccio hastened past him, feeling new life as he breathed the fresh air of the open street. His enemy, now seeing him on the other side of the gates, threw off his terrors, and collecting all his malice from his heart to his miserable physiognomy, he said: "My lord Castruccio, might I say one word to you?"

"No, not one syllable: remember this night, and so farewell."

"Yet not farewel without my curse; and that I will spit after thee, if thou hadst the speed of an eagle."

The impotent wretch grinned and stamped with rage, when he saw his enemy pass on unheeding, and quickly disappear. Yet anger was not a passion that could long hold the possession of the heart of Benedetto; he remembered that his dear chests were safe; and, although he still shuddered at their imminent peril, yet he / satisfied himself with the deep contempt he felt towards his foe, who had allowed him, while thus in his power, to escape unhurt.

As he ascended the stairs he gazed on the lamp, and with a ghastly smile, said: "Thou wert the instrument he purposed to use, and I will tread thee to dust. His time will come, and his heart's blood and his soul's agony shall repay me for my wrongs; and so will I wind my snares, that he himself shall proclaim me lord of Cremona."

In a journey that Castruccio made to Lombardy some years after, he enquired concerning his old enemy; and, hearing that he was dead, he listened with curiosity to the relation of the last scenes of Benedetto's life. Ten days after their interview (in the September of the year 1317), Cane della Scala approached Cremona to besiege it; but, after passing some weeks before the walls, the rains, and the ravages which had been effected in the territory of his allies, the Modenese, obliged him to withdraw. Whether Pepi were terrified by the warning of Castruccio, or feared a similar reception to his propositions from Can' Grande, cannot be / known: but it is certain that he made no effort to enter into a treaty with him at that time.

In the month of March of the following year Cane received a visit from the ambitious usurer at his palace in Verona. Pepi had grown wise by experience, and in this interview managed his treaty with great skill. He bought for the occasion a vest of scarlet silk and boots of Tartarian fur; fastening on his gilt spurs, throwing his gold fringed cloak over his shoulders, and putting on his head a conical cap of the newest fashion, encircled with a golden band, he mounted a good horse; and, thus caparisoned, he appeared, in his own and in his old woman's eyes, as accomplished and noble a knight as by the stroke of a sword it were possible to dub; nor did he, in his conference with Cane, mention what his means were by which he intended to betray the city, but merely boasted of his power of admitting the army of the lord of Verona, if it should appear before the gates, and named, as the condition of this service, his being instituted its lord in vassalage to Cane, if his Ghibeline townsmen should / agree to receive him as their chief. The veteran commander easily acceded to these stipulations; and, the time and other circumstances being agreed upon, Pepi returned to Cremona to prepare for his future government.

His great art consisted in attacking all the nobles for their debts at the same time; and these were so numerous, and of so considerable an amount, that it created much confusion in a town which had been enfeebled by perpetual wars. The nobles, as Castruccio had predicted, reflected that they had arms in their hands, and that their debts being all due to one man, they could by his death easily free their shoulders from a heavy burthen. It was then that Pepi began to disclose to each separately his readiness to destroy their bonds, if through their means he was admitted to be lord of Cremona. The Ghibelines objected the strong opposition they should meet with from the Guelphs; to these he confided the hopes he entertained of aid from Cane della Scala. The Guelphs, now much enfeebled, appeared more tractable, since he endeavoured to persuade them that it would be wholly in his power to / prevent the Ghibelines from exiling them; and he promised to act as a moderator between the parties. He was listened to, and many promised him their assistance, each in his heart despising the usurer, but believing that each by his single vote would be of no service to raise him to the sovereignty, and that by fair words they should discharge their heavy debts.

Pepi had so managed, that he had got the keys of one of the gates into possession; he admitted the troops of the lord of Verona; but he found that after all he did not possess the influence he had hoped over the minds of his townsmen. When the Ghibeline war-cry was raised, all the Guelphs of the city, distrusting either the promises or the power of their creditor, assembled in arms; and a tumult ensued, which ended in the defeat of the popular party, and the triumphant entrance of Cane into the town.[a]

Pepi fell in that tumult: whether by a chance-blow, or by the resolved dagger of one of his debtors, cannot be ascertained. But his dead body was discovered among the slain; and, so great was the enmity of his townsmen against him, / that, although Cane and his troops had already entered the city, the whole population rushed in fury towards his palace, and in a few hours the massy walls, the high tower, and all the boasted possessions of Pepi were, as himself, a loathsome and useless ruin. The hidden and unknown vaults were undisturbed; and the paper wealth of the usurer lay buried there, to rot in peace among the mildews and damps of those miserable dungeons. /

CHAPTER VI.

Galeazzo Visconti at Florence. – Castruccio and Euthanasia meet at Valperga: Doubts and Reserve.

Immediately after the restoration of the marquess of Este to the government of Ferrara, Galeazzo Visconti returned to Milan; and thence, after a short delay, he made a journey to Florence. The apparent motive of this visit was to

---

[a] Can' Grande della Scala's taking of Cremona in March 1318 is apparently Mary Shelley's invention; Villani and Sismondi say merely that he besieged it in 1315; it was Galeazzo Visconti who eventually possessed it (in 1322).

accompany a younger brother, who had been long betrothed to a Florentine lady; and the period had now arrived for the celebration of their marriage. But he had other secret views: he had heard of the engagement of Castruccio to the countess of Valperga; and, this name being famous as belonging to a Guelph family, he thought that he had now discovered the cause of the peace concluded by Castruccio with Florence, and he resolved to ascertain the motives and plans of his friend; / and if the countess were really the jealous[a] Guelph fame gave her out to be, he determined to spare neither artifice nor falsehood to disturb their union.

The destined bride of young Azzo Visconti was a near relation of Euthanasia. The family of Adimari to which she belonged, although originally Guelphs, had been united to the party of the *Bianchi*, and had been expelled with them; with the exception of that branch which adhered to the *Neri*, of which the father of Euthanasia was the chief. But the children of several of these exiles continued with those of their relations who remained in Florence; and Fiammetta dei Adimari, although the daughter of an exile of the faction of the *Bianchi*, had continued to reside in Florence under the protection of an aunt. Her father had made himself famous in the wars of Lombardy; and it was there that the union between her and Azzo Visconti had been projected.[b]

When the youth came with Galeazzo to celebrate the marriage, Fiammetta removed to the palace of Euthanasia, it being from her / abode, as the head of the family, that the bride ought to be taken, when her husband should come to demand her. Galeazzo calculated on the frequent occasions of meeting that this circumstance would afford, to commence the plot he had formed on the mind of Euthanasia.

These illustrious visitors were received with honours by the magistrates of Florence: a palace was assigned for their abode, and several nobles were commissioned to shew them all that was curious in the city. Florence was then one of the finest towns in Italy; yet certainly its beauty must have been far inferior to that which it boasts at present. Its chief ornaments were palaces of massy stone, surmounted by high towers, each able to sustain a siege: some specimens of this architecture, the Palazzo Strozzi, and the Palazzo Pitti, now a ducal residence, exist to this day. They are grand and imposing; but the sombre air which they give to the streets, was better suited to those warlike and manly times, than to the taste of the present age, when the Italian heaven shines on few who would defend their own home, though its strength were that of an impregnable / fortress.[c] The Cathedral, or Duomo, afterwards the pride of

---

[a] Fierce.

[b] Azzo Visconti (1302–39) was Galeazzo's son, aged fifteen in 1317; Fiammetta is also the name under which Boccaccio addressed his lady.

[c] cf. Forsyth on the Strozzi and the Pitti: their 'harsh and exaggerated strength' is owing to 'a construction which fortified the whole basement of the palace with large, rude, rugged bossages, and thus gave always an imposing aspect, and sometimes a necessary defence to the nobility of a town for ever subject to insurrection' (p. 57); see also Sismondi (ch. xiii).

Florence, was then just commenced; but the extent of its area, and the solidity of its foundations, justified the high tone of the public decree for its erection, which declared that it should surpass in beauty every other building then existing in Italy, and be the wonder of the modern world. Among other curiosities, Galeazzo was conducted to the dens of the numerous lions and lionesses kept at the expence of the republic: there were nearly an hundred of these animals, that lived sumptuously, maintained by the superstition of the Florentines, who believed their welfare to be symbolical of that of the state.[a]

In their visits to these wonders of Florence the Visconti were accompanied by many of the young nobles of both sexes, and Euthanasia and Fiammetta were among the number. Galeazzo, from the moment of his arriaval, had directed his entire attention to the unravelling the character of Euthanasia, and from all that he heard and saw, became convinced that she was the cause of the fluctuations of Castruccio's mind, and that their union must be prevented; / otherwise he would never proceed against the Guelphs with the vigorous hostility which was necessary to their suppression. At first Galeazzo kept apart from Euthanasia; he was unwilling to enter into conversation with her, until, finding out the secret chords of her mind, he might play upon them with a master's hand.

They visited among the other curiosities of Florence the tomb of the family of the Soldanieri. This vast receptacle for the dead was built under ground, and received but small light from a grated window which opened into one of the cloisters of the church: it was the custom of this family to coffin their dead in brazen statues, apparently armed *cap-à-pié;*[b] and these statues were mounted on brazen figures of horses, so that the population of the cemetery resembled a party of armed knights ready for action.[c] The tomb was viewed by the light of innumerable torches; and there was a grim solemnity in the appearance of this troop of bronze horses, each carrying the brazen statue which imitated the living form and mien of the corpse therein coffined, that might well strike / the spectator with awe; each voice was hushed as they gazed, and the younger part of the assembly hastened to quit a place which damped all their hilarity. The lights disappeared with them; and for a while Euthanasia lingered behind almost in the dark; for the solitary torch that remained, could hardly do more than make darkness visible; and the sunbeam which had strayed from its right path[d] into the abode of the dead, tinged with its light a few of the casques of the knights, who, though their eyes and brain were within the case, neither saw nor felt the ray. Such a sight must have impressed any one with melancholy; all was still;——— Euthanasia, apparently surrounded by an armed band on horseback, for the twilight gave life to the figures, yet felt about her the silence

---

[a] Repeating material on p. 121 derived from Lastri.
[b] 'From head to foot', normally spelled cap-à-pie or cap-à-pé.
[c] Developed from Lastri, II, pp. 126; noted in adds. e. 17, p. 223 rev.
[d] An echo of Byron, 'The Prisoner of Chillon', l. 31.

of death; her own step, her own breath, were noisy intruders in the cavern: –
nor did her mute companions rest in an enchanted sleep – they were dead, –
decay was at work among their frames, and the chill of mortality exhaling from
the brass, made the vault as cold as it was silent.

She left the tomb with slow steps; and, at / the foot of the stairs by which she
would mount to daylight, Galeazzo was waiting to conduct her. Her companions were already far distant; their voices even had died away; and, as she
traversed the cloisters, she appeared little inclined to break the silence between
herself and her companion. At length Galeazzo spoke; and, after a few trivial
remarks on the scene which they had visited, he said:

"I have long sought the opportunity now afforded me, Madonna Euthanasia,
to introduce myself more particularly to your notice. As the friend of Castruccio, I hope to find myself already recommended to some portion of your
kindness and regard."

Euthanasia replied with courtesy to this speech; and Galeazzo continued:
"Being at the head of the Ghibelines of Lombardy, it is not wonderful that an
intimacy should subsist between Castruccio and myself; – for our interests are
the same; and, if by his alliance I hope to extend my dominion in the north of
Italy, I trust that my name as his friend and ally, will aid him in his future
designs even on this town itself." /

"His designs on this town!" repeated Euthanasia.

"Aye; for in truth he encourages the hope, whether it be wild or practicable
I hardly know, of overthrowing this nest of republicans, and making himself
prince or imperial vicar of Tuscany. But why should I talk of his plans to you,
Madonna, who must know them far better than I? Besides, it may be dangerous
to speak here, even in whispers, of such things; who knows if some Guelph may
not overhear me?"

"Indeed, my lord," replied Euthanasia, with a faint smile, "you divine like an
astrologer; for truly I overhear you, and I am Guelph."

"A Guelph!" repeated Galeazzo, with well feigned astonishment; – "Are you
not an Adimari? Madonna Euthanasia dei Adimari?"

"I am also countess of Valperga; and that name will perhaps unravel the enigma.
Yes, my lord, I am a Guelph and a Florentine; it cannot therefore be pleasing to
me, to hear that Castruccio has formed such designs upon my native town. Yet I
thought that I knew him well; and, if you had not seen him since our / separation,
I should believe that your information was founded on some mistake. As it is –
tell me, if you be not bound to secrecy, what you know of his plans."

"Madonna, Castruccio honours me with the title of his friend, and secrecy
and faith are the bonds of friendship. When I spoke so unguardedly of his
designs, I thought I spoke to one who knew them far better than myself: if I
have unawares betrayed the concealed counsels of Antelminelli, I do most
bitterly repent me; and do you graciously remit to me my fault, by laying no
stress on my foolish words."

Euthanasia was silent; her mind was too much disturbed to know immediately what part to take. She had believed in Castruccio's promises of peace; and the foundations of her very life seemed to give way, when his faith appeared tainted with falsehood. She knew him to be ambitious; and suddenly the thought struck her, that Galeazzo alluded only to his romantic conception of future union among the Italian states, into which she also had entered, and which might easily be mistaken for schemes of war and conquest. Upon this belief / she renewed the conversation, and told her companion that he must have mistaken the meaning of Castruccio; that it was that chief's wish, as it was of all patriotic Italians, to unite the factions that caused so much bloodshed and misery to their country; but that war was not the measure he intended to adopt to bring about a pacific termination.

It was now Galeazzo's turn to be silent; he looked down, and answered in monosyllables, and seemed to wish to make Euthanasia believe, that she might have divined well the plans of Castruccio, though he could not himself believe they were of so peaceful a nature. Euthanasia continued to talk; for she seemed to gather faith in what she desired from her own words. Galeazzo remained silent, and replied with downcast eyes to her appealing words and looks; – at length, after a pause, he appeared to make a struggle to throw off the embarassment of his demeanour; and looking up, "Madonna," said he, "let me intreat you to mention this subject no more. If I thought that your conjectures were right, I would frankly say so; but I do not: – each word / that you utter makes me believe that Antelminelli conceals his true designs from you; and, since he has chosen me as the depositary of his secret, I should be a traitor to friendship and honour, if I disclosed it. You will see him soon, and then you can unravel the mystery; in the mean time, I pray you rest content with my assurance, that Castruccio meditates nothing unworthy his name and glory."

These few words destroyed the peace of Euthanasia. She became sorrowful and disturbed; her countenance, betraying the secret of her heart, no longer displayed that calm and softness which were before its characteristics; the brightness of her eyes, if it was not quenched, only shone forth at intervals, and she mingled most unwillingly in the festivities of the nuptial ceremony. Galeazzo watched her carefully; he perceived the effect his words had had on her; and he determined to follow them up by a system of conduct, which should leave no doubt in her mind as to the truth of his assertions. Instead of avoiding Euthanasia, he now sought her society on all occasions, and often talked to her of Castruccio, whom / he always mentioned in a style of excessive praise; yet with this he contrived to mix words, hints, or looks, which seemed to say that he followed other counsels, and devised other schemes than those of which she was aware; meanwhile all this was done in so light a manner, touched on so cursorily, and then dismissed, that, as she listened, the clue of truth slipt from her, and she felt as if lost in a pathless wilderness.

The preparations for the marriage were sumptuous. Every day large parties assembled at the palace of Euthanasia; and, when the day declined, song and dance passed away the hours of darkness. The day at length arrived, when Fiammetta should first be led to church, and thence to the palace where her husband resided. Early in the morning she and her noble friends of her own sex prepared for the ceremony, by attiring themselves in the most magnificent manner. Gold and jewels sparkled on their robes, and their dark hair twisted with pearls, hung in tresses on their shoulders; married ladies only were admitted to the nuptial procession and feasts; and Euthanasia / alone, as an independent chieftainess and sovereign, claimed an exemption from this rule.

This day, so gay in appearance, and full of joyous demonstrations, Euthanasia had passed more sadly, than if she had spent it in silence and solitude, where she would not have been obliged to hide the sorrow she felt at her heart. In the evening Galeazzo informed her, that a courier, coming from Ferrara, had brought a letter to him from Castruccio; and he appeared with difficulty to yield to her intreaties to shew it to her. It contained merely excuses for his delay at Ferrara, and mentioned his speedy return: – "Yet," added he, "I shall not meet you in the cave of the Lioness*, for you will surely be gone before my return. Were it not for a pearl which the wild animal guards for me, I would never enter her den but as her enchainer. But no more of this; you know my plans; and, if the viper and the eagle unite in firm accord, surely both her heel and her head may receive a deadly wound." /

The meaning of these words was too plain; the viper was the crest of the Visconti, the eagle of the Antelminelli, and union between them was to destroy fair Florence, her native city. Euthanasia felt sick at heart; she gave back the letter in silence, and looked as a lily bent by the wind, which bows itself in patience and suffering to the storm. She remembered her vow not to unite herself to the enemy of Florence; and she resolved to abide by it. Her residence of these few weeks in her native town had endeared its inhabitants to her; she had renewed her early friendships; she was again among them, one of them; – and could she unite herself to a man who would bring havoc upon her best friends? She dreaded the reproachful voice of her conscience; and, in her well regulated mind, the fear of self-condemnation would have been sufficient to deter her from incurring such a penalty: but all the feelings of her heart here interposed; her youthful friendships; her daily habits of intercourse and mutual kindness. The favourite companion of her younger days was now married to the chief of one of the citizen-bands of Florence, who / would be exposed foremost to the swords of Castruccio's soldiers; the dearest friend of her father would lead his troop also against them. Her marriage with him, on condition of being a party in his victories over the Florentines, and rejoicing in the death of those she loved, would be as if she united herself to the rack, and bound herself for life, body and soul, to the every renewing pangs of some tyrant-invented

* Florence.

torture. It could not be: her resolution was made; and the energy of her soul qualified her to complete the sacrifice.[3]

The following day Galeazzo and his brother returned with Fiammetta to Milan. They took a kind leave of Euthanasia; and the last words of Galeazzo were, "Forget, Madonna, all that I may have said to pain you; let not Castruccio find that I have done him an ill office in your favour; and be assured that my sorrow will be most poignant, if you find that I have infused *erroneous* ideas into your mind as to his plans and wishes."

Shortly after their departure, news arrived that Castruccio would return to Florence in two days. Euthanasia heard this with trembling; – / but a short time before she had earnestly desired to see him, that she might clear up all her suspicions, and that certainty of good or evil might decide her fate; – now she feared the death that might suddenly come to all her hopes; and she felt as if but to gain a day, or a few hours, of doubt and expectation, were to gain so much of life: to insure this she took the hasty resolution of quitting Florence, and returning to her castle before the arrival of her suitor. Accordingly, attended by her domestics alone, after having taken a sudden leave of her friends, she departed.

How different was her present journey from that undertaken with Castruccio but a few months before! She was then happy and confiding; but now anxious doubt pervaded her, and fears that would not sleep. She had resolved, if the ambition of Castruccio could not content itself except with the destruction of the liberties of Florence, that she would never be his; but this resolution gave her no calm; the seal neither of life nor death was placed on her hopes: and she strove to expect good; while the fear of evil flushed her cheek, and / filled her eyes with unshed tears. The year was on its decline; the myrtle flowers had faded from the mountains, and the chesnut-woods were tinged with brown and yellow; the peasants were busy among the vines; and the trellised arbours they had formed, and the sweet shades of green among which the purple grapes hung, were now pulled down, defaced and trodden upon: the swallows were collecting for their flight, and the chill mornings and evenings announced the near approach of hoary winter. The sluggish scirocco blotted the sky with clouds, and weighed upon the spirits, making them dull and heavy as itself.

Euthanasia saw all this with the observant eye of grief, which refers all things to itself, and forms omens for its own immortality from combinations more unsubstantial than the Sybilline leaves.[a] The autumnal rains threatened nigh at hand; and the year had been much curtailed of those sweet days which follow the hot Italian summer, when the hunter feels his bow injured by the heavy

---

[a] The Sibyl of Cumae wrote her prophecies on leaves. Those consulting her were required 'to take up those leaves before they were dispersed by the wind, as their meaning then became incomprehensible.' (Lemprière, 'Sibyllae', summarising Virgil, *Aeneid*, III. 441–51; see also the opening of *The Last Man*).

dews of night, but when the noonday sun shines with tempered heat, and sets leaving the downcast eyelids of / night heavy with tears for his departure; when we feel that summer is gone, and winter is coming, but the fresh-looking evergreens, the stately cypress, the fruit-burthened olive, and the dark ilex, tell us that nature is not merely a fair-weather friend. Our sorrowing traveller compared the quick advance of winter that she now witnessed, with its long delay of the preceding year, and sighed.

She arrived at her castle on the first of October; and the moment she had arrived, the storm, which for many days had been collecting from the south the force of autumnal rains and thunders, broke over her head. The white lightning sped in forked chains around the sky, and without pause or interval, deluged the midnight heaven with light, which shewed to her, as she stood at the window of her apartment, the colours of the trees, and even of the few flowers which had survived to witness the advent of the storm. The thunder broke in tremendous and continued peals, and the rain awoke in a moment the dried up sources of the mountain torrents; yet their liquid career was not heard amidst the tumult: for, if the thunder / paused, the echoes prolonged the sound, and all nature seemed labouring with the commotion. Euthanasia watched the progress of the tempest; and her ear, filled with its almost deafening noise, could not distinguish the sounds, which at other times would have been audible, of horses' hoofs as they ascended the rock of Valperga, or the clang at the castle-gate, or the letting down of the draw-bridge; the first sound alien to the storm that visited her sense, was her own name pronounced in a well known and soft voice:

"Euthanasia!"

"Castruccio! you here?"

"Yes, it is I, – Castruccio; – yet I will instantly depart, if you command. I have followed fast upon your steps; – but why are you here? Why did you not remain at Florence?"

For nearly two years Euthanasia had cherished, unblamed by herself, the most fervent love for Castruccio. The union had been delayed; but the sentiment continued as a deep and clear stream, or rather like a pure lake, which in its calmness reflects more vividly and enduringly the rock that hangs eternally / above it, than does the tempest-shaken water. They had been separated nearly three months; and, now that she saw and heard him again, her first impulse was, clasped in his arms, to seal with one caress a joyous forgiveness; but she checked herself. Confounded by his sudden appearance, and distracted by the many feelings that pressed upon her, she wept: – she wept long and silently; while her lover stood near her without speaking, looking at her by the glare of the continued lightnings, as they flashed in fast succession, and made day in the chamber.

After a long pause, he spoke with less impetuosity: "Why did you not remain at Florence?"

She looked up at him, and her voice quivered, as she replied: "I cannot tell you now; I am confused, and words refuse themselves to me: my heart is full, and I am most unhappy, – to-morrow I will explain all."

"Now or never; – Euthanasia, you must not trifle with me, – are you mine?"

"If you are your own."

"What does this mean?" cried Castruccio, / starting. "Of what then do you accuse me? You speak in riddles: understand, I intreat you, a plain speech, and answer me with frankness. I love you; I have long loved you; and you alone have so long delayed the union which God knows how much I desire. Now you have brought it to a crisis: – Will you be mine?"

It is difficult to answer the language of passion with that of reason: besides Euthanasia was not herself passionless, and there was a feeling in her heart that pleaded more strongly in Castruccio's favour than all his arguments. She felt subdued; yet she was angry with herself for this, and remained a long time silent, endeavouring to collect herself. At length she replied:

"Why do you press me to answer you now? or rather, consult your own heart, and that will answer for me. You have known mine long. – I love you; – but I have other duties besides those which I owe to you, and those shall be fulfilled. My father's lessons must not be forgotten, when the first occasion arrives for putting them in practice; nor must I / be wanting to that sense of duty, which until now has been the rule of my life. I am a Florentine; Florence is my native country; nor will I be a traitor to it."

"Well, – and what do you conclude from this?"

"Are you not the enemy of Florence? Are you not contriving war and chains for its happy and free state? You turn away impatiently; to-morrow I will see you again, and you will then have reflected on my words: my fate depends on your true and frank reply to my question. Now leave me; I am worn out and fatigued, and to-night I cannot support the struggle into which you would lead me. To-morrow I shall see you; farewel; the storm has now passed, and the rain has quite ceased. Good night!"

"You leave me thus; and thus you reward me for suspense, jealousy and despair. Good night, Euthanasia. You sacrifice me to a bubble, to the shadow of a bubble, – be it so! Great God! that you should be influenced by such a chimæra! Well, you decide; and I shall expect your award with what patience I may. Again, good night." /

He left her to doubt, suspense and grief. But her high mind bore her through all; and, having marked for herself the line of duty which she believed she ought to pursue, the natural enthusiasm of her character aided her to struggle with the misery which her sensibility inflicted upon her. Castruccio himself came to her aid; and the events which followed fast on the scene of this night, served to strengthen her resolution, and, if they did not make the sacrifice more easy, they rendered its necessity more palpable. /

CHAPTER VII.

Castruccio exiles three hundred Families from Lucca – Visits at Valperga – His Character further developed.

During his absence Castruccio had reduced in his own mind his various political plans to a system. He no longer varied either in the end which he desired to attain, or the means by which he resolved to accomplish it. He thought coolly on the obstacles in his way; and he resolved to remove them. His end was the conquest of Tuscany; his means, the enslaving of his native town; and, with the true disposition of a conqueror and an usurper, he began to count heads to be removed, and hands to be used, in the furtherance of his designs. He had no sooner returned to Florence, than messengers brought him intelligence of a plot, which would speedily break out in Lucca to deprive him of his government; / and this information, joined to the departure of Euthanasia, determined him instantly to return to the Lucchese territory.

He was no longer the same as when he had quitted it; he returned full of thought, – with a bent brow, a cruel eye, and a heart not to be moved from its purpose by weakness or humanity. The change might appear sudden, yet it had been slow; – it is the last drop that overflows the brimming cup, – and so with him the ambition, light-heartedness, and pride which he had long been nourishing, now having made for itself a form, "a habitation and a name,"[a] first manifested itself in its true colours to the eyes of man. Ambition, and the fixed desire to rule, smothered in his mind the voice of his better reason; and the path of tyranny was smoothed, by his steady resolve to obtain the power, which under one form or other it had been the object of his life to seek.

The morning after his return to Lucca he reviewed his troops: they were devoted to him, and by their means he intended to secure his power. He assembled the senate, and surrounded the palace of government with his / soldiers; he took his seat at its head, with the countenance of one who knows, and can punish his enemies. He addressed the assembly in few words, saying, that it was by their power he had been raised to the government, and that it now behoved them to support him in its exercise. "I know," he cried, "I have many enemies here, – but let any one of them step forth, and say the ill that I have done to the republic; – I who have fought its battles, secured its prosperity,

---

[a] *A Midsummer Night's Dream*, V. i. 17 (with 'local' omitted).

173

and raised it from the being the servant of proud Florence to be its rival. What, will none of you come forward to denounce me, now that I appear, face to face, to answer your accusations? Randolfo Obizzi,[a] I call upon you, who would despoil me of the power this senate conferred upon me; – and you, Aldino, who have plotted even my death; – can ye whisper as traitors, and cannot ye speak as men? Away! – the moment of mercy is short: – three hours hence the gates of Lucca will be shut, and whoever among you or your partizans are found within its walls, will pay the forfeit of his life for his temerity." /

The senate would now have broken up; but, when Castruccio saw that his enemies had all departed, he called on the rest to stay, and aid him on this momentous occasion. The decree for banishing the conspirators was then formally passed, and another for demolishing three hundred towers of so many palaces, which were as strong holds and fortresses within the town. The senate was then dismissed, – the troops paraded the streets, and before night-fall three hundred families, despoiled of their possessions, and banished their native town, passed through its gates in mournful procession. The soldiers were employed in demolishing the towers; and the ruins were carried to the eastern quarter of the city, to be used in the erection of a new wall.[b] Castruccio, now master of Lucca, and triumphant over his enemies, felt that he had taken the first step in the accomplishment of his plans.

Euthanasia had remained in her castle in anxious expectation of a visit or a message from Castruccio; – neither came: but late in the afternoon Teresa Obizzi, one of her dearest friends, was announced to her. /

"Why so mournful, dear Teresa?" asked her friend. "What has happened? Are you also unfortunate?"

"I hardly know what has happened, or where I am," replied Teresa. "Methinks the thunder of heaven has fallen among us; all the Obizzi family is banished Lucca, and not these alone, but the Bernardi, the Filippini, the Alviani, and many more, are exiled, and their possessions confiscated."[c]

"Why, how is this? What new change has occurred in Lucca?"

---

[a] Not to be confused with Obizzo, Marquess of Ferrara. The Obizzi (or Obizi), a leading and many-branched Lucchese family allied to the Blacks and the Guelphs, were long-standing enemies of the Antelminelli; Tegrimi's Chronology (1742) records them as having been expelled by Uguccione and Castruccio in 1314. 'Randolfo' and 'Aldino' appear not to be historical names.

[b] The expulsions and demolitions are a conflation of Tegrimi (pp. 36–7) and Muratori, I, diss. 26, p. 366; noted in Ab. Dep. e. 274, p. 79.

[c] Mary Shelley here diverges from her sources by making the Obizzi the chief family accused of plotting in 1317; according to Tegrimi (1742 Chronology) and others it was the Avogadi. However, Sismondi (ch. xxx) dated the expulsion of the Avogadi (Avvocati) from Lucca as 1320; though incorrect, this may have licensed her to reject Tegrimi's record in part and invent freely. She locates this plot at the end of 1317 (in the absence of a stated month in Tegrimi) and introduces the Avogadi later as abettors of the Quartezzani plot. Bernardini and Filipini were senators during Castruccio's consulship (Tegrimi, p. 29); their expulsion appears to be her addition too. 'Alviani' has not been found.

"Nothing new, dear countess. In truth I believe there was a plot against Antelminelli, and that some of the Obizzi were concerned in it. But Castruccio examines nothing; and, including us all in one general sentence, has wrapt us like a whirlwind, and carries us, God alone know whither. And my poor father! I threw myself at the consul's feet; yes, I, the wife of the proud Galeotto Obizzi, and prayed that my poor father might be allowed to remain."

"And he refused?"

"He said, 'You have heard the sentence; he / best knows whether he be implicated in it; I have sworn by God and St. Martin that this nest of Guelphs and *Neri* shall be rooted out of Lucca, and that the will of the senate shall be obeyed. Let him look to it; for after three hours the life of a partizan of the Obizzi will be held no dearer than the earth on which I tread.'"

"Castruccio said this? Did he answer you thus, Teresa?"

"He did, dear Euthanasia; but I must away; I came to bid you farewel, – a long farewel; my father and my husband wait for me; pray God to pity us; – farewel!"

"Not so, Teresa. This castle is not his, and may afford an asylum to his victims. Come here; repose here awhile at least. Bring your father, your babes; come and teach me what sorrow is, and learn from me to bear it with fortitude."

As the evening advanced, others of her friends arrived, and confirmed all that Euthanasia had before heard. She was confounded, and unable to believe that it was indeed Castruccio who had caused these evils. / Whence arose this sudden change in his character? Yet, was it sudden? or, was there indeed any change? She remembered words and looks, before forgotten, which told her that what now took place was the offspring of deep thought and a prepared scheme. Yet again, unable to believe the full extent of the evil that she heard, she sent to Lucca to intreat Arrigo Guinigi to hasten to her. Arrigo was with Castruccio when the message came.

"Go, my dear boy," said the latter; "her woman's heart trembles perhaps at this day's work. Shew her the necessity of it; and make her think as little unkindly of me as you can. Notwithstanding her coldness and perplexing ideas about duty, I love her, and must not have her be my enemy. If she would be content with any thing except the peace with Florence for her *morgincap*, all my power and possessions were at her feet*." /

Arrigo went to Valperga: Euthanasia saw him alone; and, pale and almost

---

* *The morgincap* was a boon granted by the husband to the wife the morning after the nuptials. It consisted generally of a gift of part of his possessions, sometimes of the half, often of a quarter of his property. Laws were made in some states to restrain this excessive generosity, but the custom of the *morgincap* continued a long time in Florence.[a]

---

[a] Conflating information from Muratori, I, diss. 20, pp. 196–8, and Lastri, I, p. 103; noted in Ab. Dep. e. 274, p. 49 and adds. e. 17, p. 224 rev.

breathless, she asked what had caused this change, and whether he knew what the schemes of Castruccio were?

"Indeed, Madonna," replied Arrigo, "I do not; I believe that he aims only at the security of his own state; and many of those he has exiled had plotted against his government."

"It is possible; tyrants ever have enemies; but it were as well to raze the city, as to banish all her citizens. There cannot be less than a thousand souls included in his edict; women and infants, torn from all the comforts, all the necessaries of daily life, cast upon the world to weep and call down curses on him. What does he mean?"

"He suspects all whom he has banished, and has strong secret reasons for his conduct; of that, Euthanasia, you may be sure. When I asked him why he banished so many of his / fellow-citizens, he replied laughing, 'Because this city is not big enough for them and me.' And then he told me seriously, that his life was alone preserved by the vigorous measures of ths morning."

"Be it so; I wish I could believe him; I do indeed trust that there is nothing wanton in his severity; yet methinks he had better have banished himself, than so many families, who now go as beggars through the world. He also was banished once; they say that princes learn from adversity; I believe it; they learn a cunning in cruelty the prosperous can never know."

"Nay, dear countess, speak not so hardly of him. Castruccio was born to rule; he is noble-minded, but firm of resolution; and can you blame him for securing a life on which the welfare of Lucca, perhaps of Italy, depends?"

Euthanasia did not reply; she knew, although from the gentleness of her nature she had never participated in it, that there was then in Italy a spirit of cruelty, a carelessness for the life and pain of others, which rendered it less wonderful that Castruccio should have / adopted a mode of conduct similar to that of most of his contemporaries. It is strange, that man, born to suffering, and often writhing beneath it, should wantonly inflict pain on his fellows; but however cruel an individual may be, no one is so remorseless as a ruler; for he loses even within himself the idea of his own individuality, and fancies that, in pampering his inclinations, and revenging his injuries, he is supporting the state; the state, a fiction, which sacrifices that which constitutes it, to the support of its mere name. Euthanasia knew that she ought not to apply the same rule of conduct to a prince, as to a private individual; yet that Castruccio should have tainted himself with the common vices of his tribe, was a shock, that unsettled the whole frame of her mind; it unveiled at once the idol that had dwelt in the shrine of her heart, shewed the falseness of his apotheosis, and forced her to use her faculties to dislodge him from the seat he had usurped.

A few days after, Castruccio came himself to the castle of Valperga. He came at a time when many other visitors were there, and / among them several whom he knew to be his secret enemies. He took no notice of this; but, with the frankness of manner for which he was remarkable, he entered into conversation with them, and treating them as on a perfect equality with himself, he soon softened the angry mood with which they had at first regarded him. All political discussion was avoided; and the conversation turned on one of those domestic tragedies which were then too common among the petty courts of Italy, where each little lord possessing supreme power, and unrestrained by principle, was ever ready to wash supposed dishonour from his name in the blood of those who had caused the stigma. The one at present under discussion was of peculiar horror, and was the more singular, since nature had vindicated her violated laws on their infringer, and he who boasted of his morality in indulging his passionate revenge, was now pursued by remorse and madness, and the ghosts of his victims hunting him through the world, gave him no rest or hope. One of the company, a Milanese, said, that it was impossible that remorse / could have caused the madness of Messer Francesco; since in revenging the injury his wife had done him, he only followed the example set him by hundreds of his countrymen; and if he had gone beyond them in cruelty, it merely proved that his love, and his sense of honour transcended theirs."

Castruccio replied; "Far be it from me to plead for those childish notions, which would take the sword out of the hand of princes, and make them bind men of iron with chains of straw. But it does surprize me, that any man should dare so to idolize himself, as to sacrifice human victims at the shrine of his pride, jealousy or revenge. Francesco was a monster, when he tortured and murdered his wife; he is now a man, and feels the fitting remorse for so foul a deed. Man may force his nature, and commit deeds of horror; but we are all human beings, all the children of one common mother, who will not suffer that one should agonize the other, without suffering in his turn a part of the anguish he has inflicted*." /

After a time the other visitors departed; and Euthanasia was left alone with Castruccio. For a while they were silent; the changeful colours of her cheek might shew, that love had not forgotten its accustomed course, but rushed in a warm flood to her heart, and then ebbed, commanded by a power hardly less strong than that which bids the ocean pause; the power of virtue in a well formed human heart. Castruccio watched her; but, in the returning calmness of her eye, and in her unhesitating voice when she did speak, he read all of female softness, but none of female weakness.

"Will you pardon me," she said, at length, "if I speak frankly to you;and not take in ill part the expression of those reflections to which your late words have given rise?"

---

* The story here alluded to, is told by Bandello, and is related with that air of truth which this writer delights to give to his narrations.[a]

---

[a] Identified by Palacio (pp. 67–8 and n.) as not by Matteo Bandello (1480–1561), but by Ser Giovanni Fiorentino (flourished c.1400) in his *Pecorone*, VII. i, 'Crudelità orribile di Francesco Orsino contro Lisabetta sua moglie'; Palacio conjectures confusion with a similar tale (Bandello, *Novelle*, II. xii) and infers that Mary Shelley had read both works.

177

Castruccio smiled, and replied, "Madonna, I know already what you are about to say; but you are mistaken in your conclusions. I said that no man could with impunity sacrifice the lives of his fellow-creatures to his own / private passions; but you must not torture my meaning; the head of a state is no longer a private man, and he would act with shameful imbecility, if he submitted to his enemies because he dared not punish them."

Euthanasia replied to this, and drew a lively picture of the sufferings of the exiles; but Castruccio answered laughing, "You speak to one wiser on that subject than yourself. Have not I been an exile? and do you think that I forget our mournful procession, when we poor Ghibelines left Lucca nearly twenty years ago? And do you think that the *Neri* would have reigned, if they had not turned us out; and how should I reign, if I permitted this horde of Guelphs to sit here, and plot in my citadel? Their very number is an argument against them instead of being one in their favour. But let us leave this discussion, my too compassionate Euthanasia, and for a moment cast our thoughts on our own situation. There must be some end put to the riddle, some crown to a work, which seems as if it were to have no conclusion. I will be frank with you; I am neither going to turn hermit, and, laying down / my sceptre, to take up with a crucifix: nor like your friends, the holy fathers of the church, am I going to war with money and falsehood, instead of with my sword. I am lord of Lucca, and shall continue so as long as God permits me. I am at the head of the Ghibelines in Tuscany, and my design is that the Ghibelines should put down their old enemies; and, seeing a fair prospect of success, I shall neither spare words nor blows against those who would oppose me in this undertaking. You are a Guelph; but surely, my dear girl, you will not sacrifice your happiness to a name, or allow party-spirit to get the better of all the more noble feelings of your nature."

Euthanasia listened with attention, and answered in mild sadness; "It does not appear to me, Castruccio, that I sacrifice any thing noble in my nature, when I refuse to unite myself to the enemy of my country. As a Ghibeline you know that I loved you; and it is not words alone that cause my change; fight the Florentines with words only, and I am still yours. But more than I love Florence, or myself, / or you, Castruccio, do I love peace; and my heart bleeds to think that the cessation of bloodshed and devastation which our poor distracted country now enjoys, is to be of short duration. Have you not lived in a country suffering from war? Have you not seen the peasants driven from their happy cottages, their vines torn up, their crops destroyed, often a poor child lost, or haplessly wounded, whose every drop of blood is of more worth than the power of the Cæsars? And then to behold the tears and despair of these poor creatures, and to find men who would still inflict them, – and for what? The bubble is yours, Castruccio. – What would you have? Honour, fame, dominion? What are these if peace do not purchase them, but contempt, infamy and despotism! Oh! rule your own heart; enthrone reason there, make virtue the high priest of your divinity; let the love of your fellow-creatures be your palace to dwell in, and their praises your delicate food and costly raiment; and, as all sovereigns have dungeons, so do you have them, in which your pride, ambition, and, forgive / the word, your cruelty, may be enchained; and then the purple-clad emperors of Constantinople may envy your state and power.[a]

"Why do you cause this cruel combat? or, why would you increase the struggle in my heart? As the enemy of Florence I will never be yours; as the deliberate murderer of the playmates of my infancy, of the friends of my youth, of those to whom I am allied by every tie of relationship and hospitality that binds mankind, as such, I will never be yours. Here then is the crown of the work; the sea in which the deep and constant stream of my affections loses itself, – your ambition. Let these be the last words of contest between us: but if, instead of all that I honour and love in the world, you choose a mean desire of power and selfish aggrandizement, still listen to me. You are about to enter on a new track, yet one on which the course of thousands of those that have gone before you is to be seen: do not follow these; do not be sanguinary like them; – the Italians of the present day have all a remorseless cruelty in them, which will stain / the pages of their history with the foulest blots; let yours be free from these!

"Pardon me that I speak to you in this strain. From this moment we are disjoined; whatever our portions may be, we take them separately. Such is the sentence you pronounce upon us."

Castruccio was moved by the fervour of Euthanasia; he tried to alter her determination, to argue her from the point of difference between them, but in vain; he moved her to tears. She wept, but did not reply: her purpose was fixed, but her heart was weak; she loved for the first and only time; and she knew that she sacrificed every hope and joy in life, if she sacrificed Castruccio. But she was firm, and they parted; a parting that caused every nerve in Euthanasia's frame to thrill with agony.

She tried to still these feelings, to forget that she loved; but tears, abundant tears, alone eased the agony of her heart, when she thought, that the soft dreams she had nourished for two years were vain, gossamer that the sun of reality / dissipated. Sometimes she schooled herself as being too precise and over-wise, to sacrifice all her hopes to the principles she had set up. But then the remembrance of the grief she had endured during the last war with Florence, and the worse struggles she would feel, if she dared unite herself to an enemy, if, by binding her fate to his, she might neither pray for the cause of her husband, nor for that of her beloved country; when to wish well to Castruccio would be to desire the success of tyranny and usurpation; and to have given her vows to the Florentines in their necessary defence, was to wish

---

[a] Emperors of Constantinople (i.e. of the Eastern Roman empire, which endured until 1453) were known as the Porphyrogenites ('born to the purple').

the overthrow of the companion of her life – the idea of these struggles gave her courage to persevere; and she hoped, that the approbation of her own heart, and that of her dearest and most valued friends, would in some degree repay her for her sufferings. She thought of her father and his lessons; and her heart again swelled with the desire of the approbation of the good, with the warm and ardent love of right which ever burned within her soul. Hers had been a natural and a lawful passion; she could not live, / believing that she did wrong; and the high independence and graceful pride of her nature would never permit her, to stoop beneath the mark she had assigned as the object of her emulation.

Yet when, in the silence of night and of solitude, she consulted her own heart, she found that love had quenched there every other feeling, and not to love was to her to die. She looked on the quiet earth, where the trees slept in the windless air, and the only sound was the voice of an owl, whose shriek now and then with monotonous and unpleasing sound awoke the silence, and gave a melancholy life to what else were dead; she looked up to the sky where the eternal lamps of heaven were burning; all was unchanged there; but for her all was different. It was on a night, in an Italian autumn, that she sat under her acacia tree by the basin of the fountain of the rock. To look on the hues of sunset, to see the softened tints of the olive woods, the purple tinge of the distant mountains, whose outline was softly, yet distinctly marked in the orange sky; to feel the western breeze steal across her cheek, like / words of love from one most dear; to see the first star of evening penetrate from out the glowing western firmament, and whisper the secret of distant worlds to us in our narrow prison; to behold the heaven-pointing cypress with unbent spire sleep in the stirless air; these were sights and feelings which softened and exalted her thoughts; she felt as if she were a part of the great whole; she felt bound in amity to all; doubly, immeasurably loving those dear to her, feeling an humanizing charity even to the evil. A sweet scent coming from the lemon-flowers, which mingled with the gummy odour of the cypress trees, added to the enchantment. Suddenly, – list! what is that? Music was heard, and sweeter than all other instruments, the human voice in chorus singing a national song, half hymn, half warlike; Euthanasia wept; like a child she wept, – but there was none near to whom she could tell the complicated sensations that overpowered her: to speak to those we love in such moments, exhilarates the spirits; else the deep feeling preys on the heart itself. She became sad, and looked up to the many-starred / sky; her soul uttered silently the bitter complaint of its own misery.[a]

---

[a] A possible draft of the foregoing passage (from 'To look on the hues of sunset') is pencilled in Mary Shelley's hand in adds. e. 17, pp. 25–6 (incorrectly ascribed by Richard Garnett to P. B. Shelley in 1862 and printed as the third of three 'Fragments on Beauty'; reproduced in the *'Charles the First'* Notebook, pp. 58–61).

"Must I then forget to love? Oh! sooner shall that restless lamp, which walketh up the heavens, and then descendeth, and abideth no where, Oh! sooner shall that forget its path which it hath ever traced, since God first marked it out, than I forget to love! The air still surrounds the earth, filling the recesses of the mountains, and even penetrating into their caverns; the sun shines through the day, and the cloudless heavens of night are starred with the air's fire-bearing children; and am not I as unchanged and unchangeable as nature's own, everlasting works? What is it then that startles every nerve, not as the sound of thunder or of whirlwind, but as the still, small voice, that clings to me, and will not be made silent, telling me that all is changed from that which it once was?

"I loved! God and my own heart know how truly, how tenderly! How I dwelt on his idea, his image, his virtues, with unblamed affection: how it was my glory, my silent boast, when in solitude my eyes swam in tears, and / my cheek glowed, to reflect that I loved him, who transcended his kind in wisdom and excellence! Is this a dream? Oh! then all is a dream; and the earth, and the fabric of the adamantine sky are as the gossamer that may not endure! Yet, oh, ye stars, ye shine! And I live. Pulse, and breath, and thought, and all is changed; I must no longer love, – so let me suffer the living death of forgetfulness.

"Surely my heart is not cold, for I feel deep agony; and yet I live. I have read of those who have pined and died, when the sweet food of love was denied to them; were their sensations quicker, deeper, more all-penetrating than mine? Their anguish greater? I know not; nor do I know, if God hath given this frame a greater capacity for endurance than I could desire. Yet, methinks, I still love, and that is why I live. A dark, blank, rayless, motionless night is before me, a heavy, overwhelming annihilation is above me, when for a moment I imagine that hope is not for me. But for an instant does that idea live within me, yet does it come oftener and stay longer than it was wont. The knowledge that I have / nought to expect but death, must become a part of my mind. When a dear friend dies, what painful throes does one undergo, before we are persuaded to know that he is no more! So now that hope dies; it is a lesson hard for my heart to learn; but it will learn it; and that which is now reality, will be as a dream; what is now a part of me will be but a recollection, a shadow thrown upon life, from which I at length shall emerge. And what is the state of being that shall follow?

"Yet will I arouse all the pride and all the nobility of my nature; I will not sink beneath this trial; the great and good of past ages have left their lessons for me to meditate, and I will be no indocile pupil; the honey of the cup is exhausted, but all is not gall that remains."

The winter passed on thus: Euthanasia feared Castruccio as the enemy of *Florence*; but she avoided Florence as *his* enemy. Disappointed in her dearest hopes, her very heart destroyed, she hated society, and felt solace in the contemplation of nature alone; that solace which the mind gathers, in communing with its sorrows, and, having lost every other resource, / clings as to a friend, to the feelings of woe with which it is penetrated.

The winter was chill; the mountains were covered with snow; yet, when the sun gleamed on them, the Serchio, taking life from his smiles, sped down in his course, roaring and howling, as if, pursued by innumerable and overflowing streams, he hurried to find repose in his home among the waters of the boundless ocean. The air was filled with his turmoil; and winter, asleep among the icy crags of the mountains, feared a sound, which he had not power to silence, and which was the dirge that tolled out his passing hour: the cold northern wind swept along the plain of Lucca, and moaned as a repulsed beggar about the walls of Euthanasia's castle. Within those walls, late the scene of content and joy, sat the disconsolate mistress, a prey to all those sad, and sometimes wild reveries, which utter hopelessness had made her companions. Duty, and the associations of her early youth, had breathed in her ear the terrible command to love no more; but her soul rebelled, and often she thought that, in so mad a world, duty was but / a watch-word for fools, and that she might unblamed taste of the only happiness she should ever enjoy.

But, in one who had so long submitted her very thoughts to the control of conscience, such ideas found brief habitation; and her accustomed feelings returned to press her into the narrow circle, whence for her all peace was excluded. Duty, patriotism, and high religious morality, were the watch-dogs which drove her scattered thoughts, like wandering sheep, into their fold: alas! the wolf nestled in the pen itself. If for a moment her will paused, and love, breaking every bank she had carefully built up to regulate her mind's course, burst in at once, and carried away in its untameable course reason, conscience, and even memory, Castruccio himself came to repair the breach, and to restrain the current; some castle burnt, some town taken by assault, some friend or enemy remorselessly banished, filled her with shame and anger, that she should love a tyrant; a slave to his own passions, the avenger of those of others. Castruccio was ever at war; peace subsisted between him and Florence; / but the siege of Genoa by the Ghibelines of Lombardy, gave him occasion to turn his arms on that side; and, his march extending from Lucca to beyond the Magra, he deluged the country in blood, and obtained that which he desired, dominion and fame.[a]

It were curious to mark the changes that now operated in his character. Every success made him extend his views to something beyond; and every obstacle surmounted, made him still more impatient of those that presented themselves in succession. He became all in all to himself; his creed seemed to contain no article but the end and aim of his ambition; and that he swore

---

[a] Refers to Castruccio's campaign in the Lunigiana in 1318–19 (see p. 99); this siege of Genoa began in March 1318 (Tegrimi 1742 chronology; Sismondi, chs xxix and xxx). The Magra flows into the Gulf of Spezia.

before heaven to attain. Accustomed to see men die in battle for his cause, he became callous to blood, and felt no more whether it flowed for his security on a scaffold, or in the field of honour; and every new act of cruelty hardened his heart for those to come.

And yet all good feelings were not dead within him. An increased ardour in friendship seemed to have taken the place of innocence and general benevolence: virtue, as it were seeking to build her nest in his heart, and / thrust out of her ancient one, taking up with the resting-place whose entrance still was free. Bravery and fortitude were to him habitual feelings: but, although he were kind and bounteous to his friends, so that he was loved with ardour, and served with fidelity, there was no magnanimity, and little generosity in his character. His moderate habits, abstemiousness, and contempt of luxury, often gave him the appearance of self-sacrifice; for he bestowed on others what they greatly valued, but what he himself contemned. But, when it came to the sacrifice of his own inclinations, his boundless ambition, and love of sway, then no obstacle either of nature or art could stop him; neither compassion which makes angels of men, nor love which softens the hearts of the gods themselves, had over him the slightest power, – he fixed his whole soul on the point he would attain, and he never either lost sight of it, or paused in his efforts to arrive there.

It were difficult to tell what his sensations were with regard to Euthanasia; he had loved her, tenderly, passionately; and he considered her refusal of his offers as a caprice to be surmounted. / Sometimes he was deeply grieved, sometimes angry; yet he ever loved her, and believed that she would relent. Sometimes he thought of poor Beatrice, her form, beaming with beauty, and alive with the spirit of the sybil; or again, pale, struck to the heart as a poor deer in the forest, and sinking beneath the wound: – he then felt that he would give the world to assuage her sorrows. On returning through Bologna, he had sent to Ferrara, and heard that she was alive, that no change in her situation had taken place; and, satisfied with this, he sought no further. Ambition had become the ruling passion of his soul, and all bent beneath its sway, as a field of reeds before the wind: love himself had brief power in his mind; and, although this passion sometimes caused him pain, and the sickness of disappointed hope, yet this was short, and yielded to the first impulse that occurred, which hurried him along to new designs and new conquests.

Once indeed he had loved, and he had drank life and joy from the eyes of Euthanasia. His journey to Lombardy, his connexion with Beatrice, although indeed he loved her little, / yet was sufficient to weaken the bonds that confined him; and love was with him, ever after, the second feeling in his heart, the servant and thrall of his ambition.

His military exploits were now bounded[a] to the entire reduction of the

---

[a] i.e. directed, a rare sense found in Edmund Spenser and Joanna Baillie (*OED*).

territory around Lucca; Sarzana, Pontremoli, Fucecchio, Fosedenovo, – castles
even beyond the Magra, Valdinera, Aquabuona, La Valle, fortified villages
among the Apennines, which had hitherto been under the jurisdiction of the
lords of Lombardy, now submitted to the Lucchese consul.[a] During the winter
he was for some time confined by the floods to the town of Lucca itself, where
he employed himself in establishing a vigorous system of police, in discovering
and punishing his enemies, and in the design and foundation of public edifices.
He was beloved by the nobles of his own party, and by the common people,
whose taxes he lightened, and whom he relieved in a great measure from the
tyranny of their superiors; he was beloved even by the clergy, for, although an
enemy to the temporal usurpations of the Popes, he valued the learning, and
respected the persons of the priests. / He was hated by all the rich not
immediately connected with his person and faction, for they were deprived of
power; despised by his followers, and watched by himself, they could find no
asylum from the suspicion and severity of a tyrant who felt himself insecure on
his seat of power. /

CHAPTER VIII.

Beatrice, disguised as a Pilgrim, visits Valperga. – Castruccio relates her Story.

Spring advanced, and the mountains looked forth from beneath the snow: the
chesnuts began to assume their light and fanlike foliage; the dark ilex and cork
trees which crowned the hills, threw off their burthen of snow; and the olives
now in flower starred the mountain paths with their small fallen blossoms; the
heath perfumed the air; the melancholy voice of the cuckoo issued from the
depths of the forests; the swallows returned from their pilgrimage; and in soft
moonlight evenings the nightingales answered one another from the copses; the
vines with freshest green hung over the springing corn; and various flowers
adorned the banks of each running stream. Euthanasia beheld the advance of
summer with careless eyes: her heart was full of one thought, of / one image;
and all she saw, whether it were the snow-clad mountains of winter, or the
green and flowery fields of spring, was referred by her to one feeling, one only
remembrance. She determined to think no more of Castruccio; but every day,
every moment of the day, was as a broken mirror, a multiplied reflection of his
form alone.

---

[a] The names are all taken from Tegrimi. Their submission occurred mostly in 1319.

They had often met during the winter in the palaces of the Lucchese nobles, and sometimes at her own castle; he was ever gentle and deferential to her, and sometimes endeavoured to renew the courtship that had formerly subsisted between them. Euthanasia had not strength of purpose sufficient to avoid these meetings; but each of them was as the life-blood taken from her heart, and left her in a state of despair and grief that preyed like fever upon her vitals. To see him, to hear him, and yet not to be his, was as if to make her food of poison; it might assuage the pangs of hunger, but it destroyed the principle of life. She became pale, sleepless, the shadow of what she had been; her friends perceived the change, and knew the cause; and they endeavoured to persuade / her to go to Florence, or to take some journey, which might occupy her mind, and break the chain that now bound her to sorrow. She felt that she ought to comply with their suggestions; but even *her* spirit, strong and self-sustaining as it had been, sank beneath the influence of love, and she had no power to fly, though to remain were death. Tears and grief were her daily portion; yet she took it patiently, as that to which she was doomed, and hardly prayed to have the bitter cup removed.

A circumstance that occurred just at this crisis, when she seemed to stand on the sharp edge which divides life from death, saved her from destruction, and led her back to taste for a few more years the food of sorrow and disappointment which was doled out to her.

The summer solstice had passed, and Castruccio had been absent during several months, carrying his conquests along the shore beyond the Magra, while every day brought the news of some fresh success he had obtained. This was the season of pilgrimages to Monte San Pelegrino, a wild and high Apennine in the / neighbourhood of Valperga.[a] It is said that a king of Scotland, resigning his crown to his son, and exiling himself from his country, finished his days in penitence and prayer on this mountain. In Italy every unknown pilgrim was a king or prince: but this was a strange tradition; and it would seem as if the royal penitent, disdaining the gladsome plains of Italy, sought for the image of his native country on this naked peak among the heaped masses of the Apennines.[b]

His memory was there canonized, and many indulgences were the reward of three successive visits to his rocky tomb; every year numberless pilgrims

---

[a] About twenty miles north of the Bagni di Lucca, in what had formerly been part of Countess Matilda's lands, in Modenese territory; it was visited by P. B. Shelley on 12 August 1820, while Mary Shelley and Claire Clairmont continued to explore Lucca (*MWSJ*, I, p. 328; see also ibid., p. 74 and *MWS Matilda etc*, 'Note on the Poems written in 1820', p. 316); 'neighbourhood' is to be loosely interpreted, as 'within thirty miles', a rough estimate based on the supposed location of Valperga, six 'long' miles from Lucca on the road to the Bagni (pp. 75, 187).

[b] The legend was attached to Alexander III (Muratori, III, diss. 58, p. 210). Mary Shelley took notes from Muratori on pilgrimages to San Pellegrino and the difficulties experienced by female pilgrims (Ab. Dep. e. 274, p. 95).

flocked, and still continue to flock thither. Straining up the rugged paths of the mountain, careless of the burning sun, they walk on, shadowed by their broad pilgrim's hats, repeating their *pater-nosters*, and thus, by the toil of the body, buy indulgence for the soul's idleness. Many on their return visited the castle of Valperga, and partook its hospitality. One party had just withdrawn, as the *Ave Maria* sounded from the vale below; and they chaunted the evening hymn, as they / wound down the steep. Euthanasia listened from her tower, and heard the last song of the sleepy cicala among the olive woods, and the buz of the numerous night insects, that filled the air with their slight but continual noise. It was the evening of a burning day; and the breeze that slightly waved the grass, and bended the ripe corn with its quick steps, was as a refreshing bath to the animals who panted under the stagnant air of the day. Amid the buzzing of the crickets and dragon flies, the aziolo's monotonous and regular cry told of clear skies and sunny weather; the flowers were bending beneath the dew, and her acacia, now in bloom, crowning its fan-like foliage with a roseate crest, sent forth a sweet scent. A few of the latest fire-flies darted here and there, with bright green light; but it was July, and their season was well nigh past. Towards the sea, on the horizon, a faint lightning shewed the over-heated state of the atmosphere, and killed by its brightness the last glories of the orange sunset; the mountains were losing their various tints in darkness; and their vast amphitheatre looked like a ponderous unformed / wall, closing in Lucca, whose lights glimmered afar off.

Euthanasia was awaked from the reverie, half painful, half pleasing, that engaged her as she sat at her window; for she was too true a child of nature, not to feel her sorrows alleviated by the sight of what is beautiful in the visible world; – she was roused, I say, by her servant who told her that a female pilgrim was at the gate, and desired to see the lady of the castle. "Receive her," said Euthanasia, "and let her be led to the bath; I will see her when she is refreshed."

"She will not enter," replied the servant, "but desires earnestly, she says, to see you: she absolutely refuses to enter the castle."

Euthanasia descended to the gate; her quick light steps trod the pavement of the hall, her long golden tresses waved upon the wind, and her blue eyes seemed to have drunk in the azure of departed day, they were in colour so deep, so clear. The pilgrim stood at the door leaning on her staff, a large hat covered her head, and was pulled down over her brows, and her coarse cloak fell in undistinguishing / folds round her slim form; but Euthanasia, accustomed to see the peasantry alone resort to this mountain, was struck by the small white hand that held the staff, and the delicately moulded and snowy feet which, shod in the rudest sandals, seemed little used to labour or fatigue.

"I intreat you," she said, "to come into the castle to rest yourself; the *Ave Maria* is passed, and your toils for the day are ended; you will find a bath, food and rest; will you not enter?" Euthanasia held forth her hand.

"Lady, I must not. I intreat you only to bestow your alms on a pilgrim going to Rome, but who has turned aside to perform a vow among these mountains."

"Most willingly; but I also have made a vow, which is, not to suffer a tired pilgrim to pass my gates without rest and food. Where can you go to-night? Lucca is six long miles off; you are weak and very weary: come; I ask you for alms; they are your prayers which must be told on the soft cushions of a pleasant bed amid your dreams this night. Come in; the heavy dews that fall from the clear sky / after this burning day may hurt you: this is a dangerous hour in the plain; can you not be persuaded?"

Euthanasia saw quick drops fall from the flashing and black eyes of the poor pilgrim: she raised them to heaven, saying, "Thy will be done! I am now all humbleness."

As she threw up her head Euthanasia looked on her countenance; it was beautiful, but sunburnt and wild; her finely carved eyes, her lips curved in the line of beauty,[a] her pointed and dimpled chin still beamed loveliness, and her voice was low and silver-toned. She entered the castle, but would go no further than the outer hall. The eloquence of Euthanasia was wasted; and she was obliged to order cushions and food to be brought to the hall: they then sat down; the pilgrim took off her hat, and her black and silken ringlets fell around her face; she parted them with her small fingers, and then sat downcast and silent.

Euthanasia placed fruit, sweetmeats and wine before her; "Eat," she said, "you are greatly fatigued."

The poor pilgrim tried; but her lips refused / the fruit she would have tasted. She felt that she should weep; and, angry at her own weakness, she drank a little wine, which somewhat revived her; and then, sitting thus, overcome, bent and sorrowing, beside the clear loveliness of Euthanasia, these two ladies entered into conversation, soft and consoling on one part, on the other hesitating and interrupted. At first the pilgrim gazed for a moment on the golden hair and bluest eyes of Euthanasia, her heavenly smile, and clear brow; and then she said: "You are the lady of this castle? You are named Euthanasia?"

"Most true: and might I in return ask you who you are, who wander alone and unhappy? Believe me I should think myself very fortunate, if you would permit me to know your grief, and to undertake the task of consoling you. If you mourn for your faults, does not a moment of real repentance annihilate them all? Come, I will be your confessor; and impose on you the light penances of cheerfulness and hope. Do you mourn your friends? poor girl! weep not; that is a sorrow time alone can cure: but time can cure it, if with a patient heart you yield / yourself to new affections and feelings of kindness. Sweet, hush the

---

[a] The 'serpentine line', which William Hogarth (1697–1764) in *The Analysis of Beauty* (1753) argued was the most aesthetically pleasing; its application to facial expression (including the mouth) is found in the fifteenth chapter and the plates. The aesthetics of this 'line' rejected the mathematical basis of beauty, and sought to locate it in fitness for purpose and organic nature.

187

storm that agitates you: if you pray, let not your words be drops of agony, but as the morning dew of faith and hope. You are silent; you are angry that I speak; so truly do I prize the soft peace that was for years the inmate of my own heart, that I would bestow it on others with as earnest a labour, as for myself I would try to recal it to the nest from which it has fled."

"How! and are you not happy?" The eyes of the pilgrim glanced a sudden fire, that was again quenched by her downcast lids.

"I have had my share of tranquillity. For five-and-twenty years few sorrows, and those appeaseable by natural and quickly dried tears, visited me; now my cares rise thick, while, trust me, with eager endeavour, I try to dissipate them. But you are young, very young; you have quaffed the gall, and will now come to the honey of your cup. Wherefore are you bound for Rome?"

"It were a long tale to tell, lady, and one I would not willingly disclose. Yet, methinks, you should be happy; your eyes are mild, and / made for peace. I thought, – I heard, – that a thousand blessed circumstances conduced to render you fortunate beyond all others."

"Circumstances change as fast as the fleeting clouds of an autumnal sky. If happiness depends upon occasion, how unstable is it! We can alone call that ours which lives in our own bosoms. Yet those feelings also are bound to mutability; and, as the priests have doubtless long since taught you, there is no joy that endures upon earth."

"How is this! He is not dead!" – he must be———" The pilgrim suddenly stopped, her cheek burning with blushes.

"Who dead? What do you mean?"

"Your father, your brother, any one you love. But, lady, I will intrude no longer; the dews are fallen, and I find the air of the castle close and suffocating. I long for the free air."

"You will not sleep here?"

"I must not; do not ask me again; you pain me much; I must pursue my journey!"

The pilgrim gathered up her raven locks, and put on her hat; then, leaning on her staff, she held forth her little hand, and said in a smothered / voice, so low that the tone hardly struck the air, "Your alms, lady."

Euthanasia took out gold; the pilgrim smiled sadly, saying, "My vow prevents my receiving more than three soldi; let that sum be the limit of your generous aid."

Euthanasia found something so inexplicable, reserved, and almost haughty, in the manner of her guest, that she felt checked, and ill disposed to press her often rejected services; she gave the small sum asked, saying, "You are penurious in your courtesies; this will hardly buy for me one *pater-noster*."

"It will buy the treasure of my heart in prayers for your welfare; prayers, which I once thought all powerful, may be as well worth perhaps as those of the beggar whom we fee on the road-side. Farewell!"

The pilgrim spoke earnestly and sweetly; and then drawing her cloak about her, she left the castle, winding slowly down the steep. After she had awhile departed, Euthanasia sent a servant to the nunnery of St. Ursula,[a] which was on the road the pilgrim was to follow, with a loaded basket of fruits, wine and other food, / and a message to the nuns to watch for and receive the unhappy stranger. All passed as she desired. The pilgrim entered the convent; and, after praying in the chapel, and silently partaking a frugal meal of fruit and bread, she went to rest in her lowly cell. The next morning the abbess had intended to question her, and to win her to some comfort; but, before the dawn of day, the pilgrim had left the convent; and, with slow steps and a sorrowing heart, pursued her way towards Rome.

This occurrence had greatly struck Euthanasia. She felt, that there was something uncommon in the visit of the stranger, and that, although unknown to her, there must be some link between them, which she vainly strove to discover. It happened, that, about a fortnight after, she was at the Fondi palace in Lucca,[b] where Castruccio was in company; and she related this incident, dwelling on the beauty of the pilgrim, her graceful manners, and deep sorrow. When she described her form and countenance, Castruccio, struck by some sudden recollection, advanced towards Euthanasia, and began to question her earnestly as to the / very words and looks of the stranger; then, checking himself, he drew back, and entered into conversation with another person. When however Euthanasia rose to depart, he approached, and said in a low tone: "I am afraid that I can solve the riddle of this unfortunate girl; permit me to see you alone tomorrow; I must know every thing that passed."

Euthanasia assented, and waited with impatience for the visit.

He came; and at his request she related minutely all that had happened. Castruccio listened earnestly; and, when he heard what had been her last words, he cried, "It must be she! It is the poor Beatrice!"

"Beatrice! – Who is Beatrice?"

Castruccio endeavoured to evade the question, and afterwards to answer it by the relation of a few slight circumstances; but Euthanasia, struck by his manner, questioned him so seriously, that he ended by relating the whole story. Euthanasia was deeply moved; and earnest pity succeeded to her first astonishment; astonishment for her powers and strange errors, and then compassion for her sorrows and / mighty fall. Castruccio, led on by the memory of her enchantments, spoke with ardour, scarcely knowing to whom he spoke; and, when he ended, Euthanasia cried, "She must be followed, brought back, consoled; her misery is great; but there is a cure for it."

She then concerted with Castruccio the plan for tracing her steps, and inducing her to return. Messengers were sent on the road to Rome, who were

---

[a] A legendary British princess who, with 11,000 virgins, was martyred by the Huns while on a pilgrimage near Cologne; the nunnery appears to be Mary Shelley's invention.
[b] Not the same as the Fondi castle, which Castruccio saw on the road to Valperga (p. 75).

189

promised high rewards if they succeeded in finding her; others were sent to Ferrara to learn if her friends there had any knowledge of her course. These researches occupied several weeks; but they were fruitless: the messengers from Ferrara brought word, that she had left that city early in the preceding spring in a pilgrimage to Rome, and that she had never since been heard of. The lady Marchesana, inconsolable for her departure, had since died; and the good bishop Marsilio, who had not returned from France, where he had been made a cardinal, was at too great a distance to understand the circumstances of her departure, or to act upon them. Nor were the tidings brought from Rome more satisfactory; / she was traced from Lucca to Pisa, Florence, Arezzo, Perugia, Foligno, Spoletto, and even to Terni;[a] but there all trace was lost. It appeared certain that she had never arrived in Rome; none of the priests had heard of her; every church and convent was examined; but no trace of her could be found. Every exertion was vain: it appeared as if she had sunk into the bowels of the earth.

During the period occupied by these researches, a great change had taken place in the mind of Euthanasia. Before, though her atmosphere had been torn by storms, and blackened by the heaviest clouds, her love had ever borne her on towards one point with resistless force; and it seemed as if, body and soul, she would in the end be its victim. Now the tide ebbed, and left her, as a poor wretch upon one point of rock, when the rising ocean suddenly subsides, and restores him unexpectedly to life. She had loved Castruccio; and, as is ever the case with pure and exalted minds, she had separated the object of her love from all other beings, and, investing him with a glory, he was no longer to her as one among / the common herd, nor ever for a moment could she confound him and class him with his fellow men. It is this feeling that is the essence and life of love, and that, still subsisting even after esteem and sympathy had been destroyed, had caused the excessive grief in which she had been plunged. She had separated herself from the rest as his chosen one; she had been selected from the whole world for him to love, and therefore was there a mighty barrier between her and all things else; no sentiment could pass through her mind unmingled with his image, no thought that did not bear his stamp to distinguish it from all other thoughts; as the moon in heaven shines bright, because the sun illumines her with his rays, so did she proceed on her high path in serene majesty, protected through her love for him from all meaner cares or joys; her very person was sacred, since she had dedicated herself to him; but, the god undeified, the honours of the priestess fell to the dust. The story of Beatrice dissolved the charm; she looked on him now in the common light of day;[b] the illusion and exaltation of love was dispelled for

---

[a] The last three were on the route over the Apennines to Rome traversed by the Shelleys, who, in November 1818, started out from Este. The spelling 'Spoletto' (for 'Spoleto') probably derives from Mary Shelley's manuscript (cf. *MWSJ*, I. p. 237).

[b] cf. 'the light of common day' (William Wordsworth, 'Ode: Intimations of Immortality from Recollections in Early Childhood' in *Poems, in Two Volumes* (1807), l. 76).

ever: / and, although disappointment, and the bitterness of destroyed hope, robbed her of every sensation of enjoyment, it was no longer that mad despair, that clinging to the very sword that cut her, which before had tainted her cheek with the hues of death. Her old feelings of duty, benevolence, and friendship returned; all was not now, as before, referred to love alone; the trees, the streams, the mountains, and the stars, no longer told one never-varying tale of disappointed passion: before, they had oppressed her heart by reminding her, through every change and every form, of what she had once seen in joy; and they lay as so heavy and sad a burthen on her soul, that she would exclaim as a modern poet has since done:

> Thou, thrush, that singest loud, and loud, and free,
> Into yon row of willows flit,
> Upon that alder sit,
> Or sing another song, or choose another tree!
> Roll back, sweet rill, back to thy mountain bounds,
> And there for ever be thy waters chained!
> For thou dost haunt the air with sounds
> That cannot be sustained.
>   *   *   *   *
> Be any thing, sweet rill, but that which thou art now[a] /

But now these feverish emotions ceased. Sorrow sat on her downcast eye, restrained her light step, and slept in the unmoved dimples of her fair cheek; but the wildness of grief had died, the fountain of selfish tears flowed no more, and she was restored from death to life. She considered Castruccio as bound to Beatrice; bound by the deep love and anguish of the fallen prophetess, by all her virtues, even by her faults; bound by his falsehood to her who was then his betrothed, and whom he carelessly wronged, and thus proved how little capable he was of participating in her own exalted feelings. She believed that he would be far happier in the passionate and unquestioning love of this enthusiast, than with her, who had lived too long to be satisfied alone with the affection of him she loved, but required in him a conformity of tastes to those she had herself cultivated, which in Castruccio was entirely wanting. She felt half glad, half sorry, for the change she was aware had been operated in her heart; for the misery that she before endured was not without its momentary intervals, which busy love filled with dreams / and hopes, that caused a wild transport, which, although it destroyed her, was still joy, still delight. But now there was no change; one steady hopeless blank was before her; the very energies of her mind were palsied; her imagination furled its wings, and the owlet, reason, was the only dweller that found sustenance and a being in her benighted soul.[b] /

---

[a] William Wordsworth, 'Tis said, that some have died for love' in *Lyrical Ballads with Other Poems* (1800), ll. 25–32, 36.

[b] See Endnote 4 on the possible position of the Luparo episode at the end of this chapter.

CHAPTER IX.

Castruccio plots the Assassination of Robert King of Naples. – Made Prince of Lucca. – Declares War against Florence. – Plot for a Revolution in Lucca defeated. – Castruccio summons Valperga.

The ambitious designs of Castruccio were each day ripening. The whole Ghibeline force in Italy was now turned to the siege of Genoa, which was defended by Robert, king of Naples, at the head of the Guelphs. Castruccio had never actually joined the besieging army.[a] But he had taken advantage of the war, which prevented the Genoese from defending their castles on the sea-coast, to surprise many of them, and to spread his conquests far beyond the Lucchese territory; and he was ever attentive to the slightest incident that might contribute to the exaltation of the / Ghibelines. He aided his Lombard friends, by annoying the enemy as much as was in his power, and did not hesitate in using the most nefarious arts to injure and destroy them. He now fully sub-scribed to all the articles of Pepi's political creed, and thought fraud and secret murder fair play, when it thinned the ranks of the enemy.

Robert, king of Naples, was at the head of the Guelph army at Genoa. The siege had now lasted with various fortune for two years; and every summer the king visited this city to conduct the enterprizes of the campaign. Castruccio, urged by Galeazzo Visconti, and by his own belief in the expediency of the scheme, conspired to destroy the king: a foolish plan in many ways; for a legitimate king, like a vine, never dies; and when you throw earth over the old root, a new sprout ever springs up from the parent stock.

The king of Naples had fitted out a fleet to go and attack the king of Sicily, who was a protector of the Ghibelines. Castruccio sent two desperate, but faithful fellows, to set fire to the ship in which the king himself sailed. / The men got admittance on board the royal galley, which, swifter than the rest, sped on through the waves, while the rest of the fleet hung like a cloud on the far horizon. At night the smell of fire was perceived in the vessel, and a small flame issued from one of the windows: the affright and confusion were terrible, when they found that they were burning thus on the desert sea, while the other vessels were too distant to afford them aid. All hands were at work to

---

[a] Mary Shelley follows Tegrimi (1742 Chronology) in recording Castruccio's involvement with the siege of Genoa in 1320. Sismondi (ch. xxix), mentions Castruccio's participation in 1318 only; the siege went on for four years.

extinguish the flames; and it was then that the hired incendiaries were perceived, as they tried to fire another part of the ship. It was found that they were provided with floats of cork, by which they hoped to preserve themselves in the water, until by some accident they might be rescued.

The fire was seen by the galley, in which the eldest son of king Robert was embarked, and which bore down to his relief. The youthful prince, in an agony of terror, lent his own hand to the oar that they might arrive more speedily. The whole crew was saved; and the criminals were reserved for torture and death. /

The news of this detestable plot was spread through all Italy, nor was it much blamed. It was then that Euthanasia, the living spirit of goodness and honour, amidst the anguish that the unworthiness of Castruccio occasioned her, felt a just triumph, that she had overcome her inclinations, and was not the bride of a suborner and a murderer. Even now, remembering that it was known that she once loved Antelminelli, she was penetrated with shame, and her cheeks burned with blushes when she heard the tale. But, careless of an infamy which he shared with many of his countrymen, and sorry only that his design had not succeeded, Castruccio did not attempt to conceal the part he had taken in the plot, and loudly declared that all his enemies might expect the same measure as king Robert, while in return he permitted them to try the like arts against him.[a]

In the mean time he prosecuted the war with redoubled vigour. In the winter of the year 1320, the Ghibelines reinforced their armies before Genoa, and called upon their allies for their utmost assistance;[b] and Castruccio / among the rest was to advance to their aid with all his forces. But the Guelphs were not idle: Florence had sent soldiers every campaign to reinforce the Genoese, and entered with spirit into all the enterprizes undertaken against the imperial party; although a wish to preserve their territory free from the horrors of war, and to repair by a long peace the injury done to their[4] vines and olive woods, had caused them to preserve a shew of peace with Lucca.

Castruccio considered all his present successes as preliminaries only to his grand undertaking; and, having now reduced not only the territory of Lucca, but many castles and strong holds, which before had either been independent, or had paid tribute to Genoa, or to the lords of Lombardy, he planned a more vigorous system of warfare for the ensuing campaign. His first step was to increase his security and power in Lucca itself.

Having grown proud upon his recent successes, he began to disdain the name of consul, which he had hitherto borne. He assembled the senate; and, at the instance[c] of his friends, who had been tutored for the purpose, this /

---

[a] This incident was interpolated at 'rough transcript' stage (see Endnote 4) and may be Mary Shelley's invention; the known sources report only that the king sent an armada to Sicily (Villani, IX, cap. 112).

[b] i.e. the beginning of the year 1320.

[c] Urgent solicitation.

assembly bestowed upon him the government of Lucca for life, with the title of prince. He afterwards caused this grant to be confirmed by an assembly of the people; his warlike atchievements, joined to the moderate expenditure of his government, had made him a great favourite with the inferior classes of the community, and they cordially entered into the projects of his ambition. Soon after, through the mediation of his friend Galeazzo Visconti, he obtained from Frederic, king of the Romans, the dignity of Imperial Vicar in Tuscany.[a]

All this passed during the winter; and in the spring he assembled his troops, intent upon some new design. He had now been at peace with Florence for the space of three years, although, fighting under opposite banners, the spirit of enmity had always subsisted between him and them. Now, without declaring war, or in any way advising them of their peril, he suddenly made an incursion into their territory, burning and wasting their land as far as Empoli, taking several castles, and carrying off an / immense booty; he then retreated back to Lucca.[b]

This violation of every law of nations filled the Florentines at first with affright, and afterwards with indignation. They had sent their best troops to Genoa; and they found themselves attacked without warning or time for preparation. When the Lucchese retreated, anger and complaint succeeded. Castruccio replied to the reproaches of the Florentines by a declaration of war, and then immediately marched with his forces to join the besieging army before Genoa.

When the Florentines found that they could obtain no redress, they turned their thoughts to revenge. They raised what fresh troops they could among the citizens; and wishing to assist their small army by other measures which were then rife in the Italian system of warfare, they endeavoured to foment a conspiracy among the Lucchese for the overthrow of their prince's government. Castruccio received in one day letters from Giovanni da Castiglione, the general who commanded the few troops which / he had left to guard his own principality, to inform him, that the Florentines had entered the Val di Nievole, burning and spoiling every thing before them; and from Vanni Mordecastelli, his civil lieutenant at Lucca, with information of a plot for the destruction of his power which was brewing in that city.[c] Castruccio immediately left the Lombard army, and returned with his troops to disconcert these designs.

Of the castles which were situated within a circuit of many miles round Lucca, all were subject to Castruccio, except the castle of Valperga and its

---

[a] Castruccio was given his titles on 26 April and 1 May 1320 (Tegrimi, 1742 Chronology). Frederick (c.1286–1330), Hapsburg King of the Germans, had irregularly acquired the title of King of the Romans, the title of emperors-elect. With Henry VII's death in 1313, Frederick and his cousin Louis of Bavaria both claimed the Empire. Each was elected by supporters, but Louis was eventually (1326) to crush Frederick and become Emperor (1328).

[b] The account of hostilities is taken from Sismondi, ch. xxix. Empoli is a town about twenty miles from Florence, on the road to Pisa.

[c] Giovanni da Castiglione and Vanni Mordecastelli, the latter named as Castruccio's 'Princivalle Veglio', are both taken from Tegrimi (p. 45); see p. 73.

dependencies. He had often solicited Euthanasia to place her lordship under the protection of his government; and she had uniformly refused. The castle of Valperga was situated on a rock, among the mountains that bound the pass through which the Serchio flows, and commanded the northern entrance to the Lucchese territory. It was a place of great strength, and in the hands of an enemy might afford an easy entrance for an hostile army into the plain of Lucca itself. The Florentines, trusting to the affection which / the countess bore their city, sent ambassadors to her to intreat her to engage in an alliance with them against Castruccio, and to admit a party of Florentine soldiers into her castle; but she rejected their proposals, and positively refused to enter into any league injurious to the existing government of Lucca. The ambassadors had been selected from among her intimate friends; and her *Monualdo*, Bondelmonti, was at the head of them: they were not therefore intimidated by one repulse, but reiterated their arguments, founded upon her own interest, and the service she would render to her native town, in vain. She felt that the liberty in which she had been permitted to remain, while, one after another, all the castles around her had been reduced, could only have arisen from the friendship and forbearance of the prince; and she judged that it would be a sort of treason in her, to take advantage of his moderation to introduce devastation into his country; at the same time she promised, that no threats or intreaties should induce her to ally herself with, or submit to, the enemy of Florence.

The ambassadors, who had been bred in / the Italian school of politics of that age, little understood, and by no means approved her scruples; they found her however invincible to their arguments, and were obliged to give up all expectation of her assistance. But they made the hope of overcoming her objections the pretext for their protracted stay in her castle; for they had other designs in view. The vicinity of Valperga to Lucca, and the intercourse which took place between it and that town, gave them an opportunity of becoming acquainted with several of the discontented nobles, the remnants of the faction of the *Neri*, who had been permitted to remain. Euthanasia, being a Guelph, had of course much intercourse with the few of that party who were to be found in Lucca; and from the conversation of these men the Florentine ambassadors conceived the hope of weaving some plot which would produce the downfal of Castruccio. And they believed, that in one of them they had found a successor to his dignity, and a chief who would prove as faithful to the papal party, as Castruccio had been to the imperial.

Among those of the faction of the *Neri* who / had remained in Lucca, was a branch of the family of Guinigi, and one of the youths of this house had married Lauretta dei Adimari, a cousin of Euthanasia. This connexion had caused great intimacy between the families; and Leodino de' Guinigi,[a] the

---

[a] For Leodino, see the note to Guarino, p. 101.

195

husband of Lauretta, was a young man of talent, spirit and ambition. Being refused a command in the army of Castruccio, he was however forced to expend his love of action and his desire of distinction, in hunting, hawking and tournaments. He was a man of large fortune, and greatly respected and loved in Lucca; for his manners were courteous, and his disposition generous, so that every one blamed the prince for neglecting a person of so much merit on account of his party. Every year however added to the discontent of Leodino; and he used frequently at the castle of his cousin Euthanasia, to bemoan his fate, and declare how he longed for a change which should draw him from idleness and obscurity. Lauretta was a beautiful and amiable girl; but party feelings ran so high in Lucca, that she was shunned as a Guelph and a Florentine, and therefore she / also entered eagerly into the complaints of her husband; while the fear of the confiscation of his property withheld Leodino from serving under some leader of his own party. Euthanasia esteemed him highly; his mind was greatly cultivated; and the similarity of their tastes and pursuits had given rise to a sincere affection and sympathy between them. The Florentine ambassadors saw Leodino and his wife at the castle of Valperga; they easily penetrated his character and wishes; and Bondelmonti undertook to work on him to co-operate with them in their design. Leodino required little instigation, and immediately set to work in Lucca to gain partizans: every thing promised well. All this had been carefully concealed from Euthanasia; who was too sincere of disposition to suspect fraud in others. But their plot was now ripe; and the ambassadors were on the eve of returning to Florence to lead their troops to the attack; when the conspiracy was betrayed to Mordecastelli, and Castruccio suddenly appeared in Lucca.

Bondelmonti and his associates instantly quitted Valperga; and several of the conspirators, / struck with affright, fled from Lucca: but Leodino, trusting to the secrecy with which he had enveloped his name, resolved to brave all danger and to remain. This imprudence caused his destruction; and, the morning after the return of Castruccio, he and six more of his intimate associates were arrested, and thrown into prison. Lauretta fled in despair to the castle of Valperga; she threw herself into the arms of Euthanasia, confessed the plot that had been carried on with Bondelmonti, and intreated her intercession with the prince to save the life of Leodino. Euthanasia felt her indignation rise, on discovering that her hospitality had been abused, and her friendship employed as the pretence which veiled a conspiracy. But, when the weeping Lauretta urged the danger of Leodino, all her anger was changed into compassion and anxiety; and she ordered the horses to be brought to the gate, that she might hasten to Lucca. "I am afraid, my poor cousin," said she, "if the prince be not of himself inclined to mercy, that my intreaties will have little effect: but be assured that I will spare no prayers to gain the life of / Leodino. His life! indeed that is far too precious to be lightly sacrificed; I feel a confidence within me, which assures me that he will be saved; fear nothing, therefore; I will bring him back with me when I return."

She had covered her head with her veil, and folded her capuchin round her; when an attendant announced the arrival of Castruccio himself at the castle. This unexpected news made her turn pale; and again the blood, flowing from her heart, dyed her cheeks and even her fingers with pink; she hardly knew what caused her agitation; but she trembled, her eyes filled with tears, her voice faultered; – Castruccio entered.

He was no longer her lover, scarcely her friend; no joy sparkled in the eyes of either at this meeting after a separation of months; she had loved him passionately, and still dwelt with tenderness on the memory of what he had been; but she saw no likeness between the friend of her youth, beaming with love, joy and hope, and the prince who now stood before her; his brow was bent, his curved lips expressed disdain, his attitude and gesture were / haughty and almost repulsive.[a] Euthanasia was not to be daunted by this shew of superiority; she instantly recovered her presence of mind, and advanced towards him with calm dignity, saying, "My lord, I was about to visit you, when I find that you prevent me by honouring my castle with your presence; I was coming as a suppliant for the life of a dear friend."

"Countess, perhaps my errand is of more serious import, – at least to yourself: and, since it may include an answer to your supplication, I intreat you to hear me before we enter on any other subject."

Euthanasia bowed assent, and Castruccio continued.

"Madonna, you may remember that I have often in friendly terms intreated you to place yourself under the protection of my government at Lucca; you have ever refused me, and I indulgently acceded to your refusal. I have subdued all the castles around, several stronger than this, but I have left you to enjoy the independence you prized. I did this, trusting to your promise, that, although you / were not my ally, you would not become my enemy, and that, in whatever war I might engage myself, you would preserve a strict neutrality. On my return from Genoa, forced to this hasty measure by the intimation of a plot being formed against me, I find that you are at the head of my enemies, and that, in violation of your faith, if you have not declared war, you have acted a more injurious part, in fomenting a conspiracy, and giving traitors those opportunities for maturing their plans, which, unless you had done this, they could never have dreamed of."

Euthanasia replied earnestly; "My lord, your mistake would be pardonable, had you not known me long enough to be assured that I am incapable of acting the part you attribute to me. But, although you have forgotten that treason and artifice are as foreign to my nature as darkness to that of the sun, you will at least believe me, when I give you my solemn assurance, that until this morning I knew nothing of the conspiracy entered into against you. And now"———

---

[a] Probably in the obsolete sense of 'unfriendly' rather than 'repellent'.

"But how can this be? Did not Bondelmonti / and his associates reside in this castle for two months?"

"They did; they came to urge me to enter into the Florentine war against you, which I refused."

"And was it necessary to hesitate during two months for your answer? or, did it now rather enter into your plans, that they should remain as spies and plotters for my destruction? but enough of this"——

"Enough, and far too much, my lord. You doubt my faith, and disbelieve my word: these are outrages which I did not expect to receive from you, but to which I must submit. And now permit me to ask to you on the subject of my intended visit."

"Pardon me, but you may remember that we agreed I should be the first heard; and I have not yet mentioned why I intrude myself into your castle. I am at war with Florence; you are not; and you believe yourself permitted, not only to hold correspondence with my enemies, but also to afford them an opportunity through your means to carry on plots with my traitorous subjects. This may have been / done very innocently on your part; but I cannot permit a repetition of the same mime, or of any other, which, though differing in words, shall be the same in spirit. If you have not taken advantage of my forbearance, you have at least shewn yourself incapable of sustaining the trust I reposed in you. But, Euthanasia, if you are indeed innocent, I am unmannerly in being thus stern with you; and, since you deny that you entered into this plot, and I would fain believe you, it is with repugnance that I enter upon the subject of my visit. You must surrender your castle to me; prudence no longer permits me to suffer you to enjoy independence; and, however painful the alternative, you must submit to become my ally."

"It were of little moment to enter into a treaty with me," said Euthanasia, with a bitter smile: "since, if I am capable of treason, I may be more dangerous as an ally than an enemy."

"Not so; for the first article of our alliance must be the razing of this castle; in exchange you shall have a site afforded you in the plain / for the erection of a palace, nor shall you incur any loss in fortune or revenue; but you must descend to the rank of a private individual, and this castle, and your power in this country, must be resigned into my hands."

"My lord, I am afraid that we shall not agree on the first article of our intended treaty. I will persevere in the neutrality I promised, and endeavour to be more prudent than I was in this last unfortunate affair. But I cannot surrender my castle, or permit the seat of my ancestors to be razed to the ground. And now allow me to speak of what is nearer to my heart. Leodino de' Guinigi has conspired against you, you have discovered his plot, and have thrown him into prison. I know that you consider his life a forfeit to your laws; but I intreat you to spare him: if neither the generosity of your character, nor the impotence of your enemy will incline you to mercy, I intreat you by our

198

antient friendship. His wife, Lauretta dei Adimari, is my cousin, and my friend; Leodino, although your enemy, is a man distinguished by every virtue, brave, generous and wise. If you would obtain a / faithful and trust-worthy friend, pardon him, confide in him; and his gratitude will be to you as a guard an hundred strong: if you have not sufficient magnanimity to trust your enemy, banish him; but for my sake spare his life."

Castruccio appeared somewhat moved by her earnestness, but he replied; – "It cannot be; I am sorry to refuse you, but the example would be too dangerous. Put aside this from your thoughts, and let me intreat you to consider what I have just said. You answer me slightly; but be assured that I have not mentioned this alternative of war or peace between us, until my purpose was fixed: reflect seriously on the evils that resistance may bring upon you, and send me your answer tomorrow."

"Tomorrow, or today, it is the same. But you, Castruccio, reflect upon the misery you cause, if you refuse to spare my unfortunate friend."

"Do not torment yourself or me any more on the subject of Leodino; your intercession is fruitless; he is already dead; I gave orders for his immediate execution before I left Lucca. / – But why are you so pale? – What agitates you?"

Euthanasia could not speak; the horror that she felt on hearing the violent death of one she loved announced so coldly by his murderer, overcame her: she struggled violently not to faint; but, when Castruccio drew near to support her, he found her hand cold and lifeless; and her trembling limbs alone shewed that she still felt: her lips were pale; she stood as if changed to stone: –

"Euthanasia, speak!"

"Speak! What should I say? Leave me! You touch me, and your hands are covered with blood, your garments are dripping with gore; come not near me! – Oh! God, have pity on me, that I should know this misery! Leave me; you are not a man; your heart is stone; your very features betray the icy blood which fills your veins. Oh, Leodino!"

And then she wept, and her features relaxed from the rigid horror they had expressed into softness and grief. After she had wept awhile, and thus calmed her agitation, she said: "My lord, this is the last time that we shall ever / meet. You may attack my castle, if you will; you may tear it down, and leave not a stone to shew where it stood; but I will never voluntarily submit to a tyrant and a murderer. My answer is brief; – Do your worst: it cannot be so bad as that which you have already done! You have destroyed every hope of my life; you have done worse, far worse, than my words can express; do not exasperate me, or let me exasperate you, by a longer stay: I can never forgive the death of Leodino; farewell! – we are enemies; do your worst against me."

She left him, unable to retain any longer even the patience to behold him. But she had no leisure afforded her to indulge her grief or indignation. Lauretta had heard of the death of her husband; and her despair, and the convulsions it

199

occasioned, entirely engrossed Euthanasia's attention, so that she forgot her own feelings and situation; nor did she recur to the threats of Castruccio, until they were recalled to her recollection by other proceedings on his part.

He did not doubt in his own mind, that, / when pushed to extremity, the countess would surrender her castle. When he first heard that it had been selected by the conspirators as their rendezvous, he believed that she had had a principal share in the plot; but now, when assured of her innocence (for it was impossible not to believe her words, so clearly were truth and courageous sincerity painted on her noble countenance), he did not for that relent in his purpose of depriving her of the independence that she possessed, in the midst of a territory subject to himself. Like many of his predecessors and successors in usurpation, Castruccio had a method in his tyranny; and he never proceeded to any act of violence, without first consulting with his council, and obtaining their sanction to his measures. On his return from the castle of Valperga, he called together this friendly assembly, and represented to them the evil he incurred by permitting so violent a Guelph as the countess Euthanasia, to preserve her power, and erect her standard, in the very heart of his principality. His council replied to his representations with one voice, that the castle must be reduced. /

The following morning Castruccio bade Arrigo di Guinigi carry a message to Euthanasia. Arrigo had always been a favourite with the countess; and Castruccio thought that it would be more delicate and forbearing, to send one so young and unpresuming as the bearer of his most displeasing message. Euthanasia received the youth with kindness; they talked on various subjects; but she carefully refrained from mentioning Castruccio's name, or alluding to the late transactions at Lucca; and it was long before Arrigo could summon courage to introduce the topic himself; at length he said;

"Madonna, I bear a message to you from the prince."

Euthanasia changed colour when he was alluded to; he, whom she now feared, as formerly she had dwelt on his idea with love. She replied hastily; "What is Antelminelli's pleasure with me? Speak quickly, that there may soon be an end of a subject, which I cannot even think upon without agitation."

"Yet I must intreat your patience, for my message is neither short nor unimportant; and you must pardon me that I am its bearer: / you know by what ties I am bound to Castruccio; and if I now obey him, do not, dearest countess, condemn me too harshly. He intreats you to remember what he said when he visited you two days ago; he has since discussed the affair in council; and it is agreed that you can no longer be permitted to retain your independence. You know that the prince is all-powerful here; his army is well disciplined and formidable; his commands every where submitted to unquestioned. Look at every castle and village for miles around; they acknowledge his law; you cannot dream therefore of resisting; and, if you refuse to submit, it is because you believe that he will not proceed to extremities with you. My dear Euthanasia, this is a grievous task for me, and one which no earthly power but Castruccio could have persuaded me to undertake; pardon me, if I appear unmannerly when I repeat his words.

"He says, that he does not forget the friendship that once subsisted between you, and that he deeply regrets that your coldness and violence caused a division between you; but this / is a question of state, and not a private altercation; and he would be unworthy of the trust reposed in him, if he permitted his individual inclinations to interfere with his duty towards the public. He is commanded by the ruling powers of his country, to compel the submission of the castle and rock of Valperga; and he is resolved to obey them: he intreats you to spare both yourself and him the unhappiness you will inflict on him, and the blood that must be shed, if you resist. It would be absurd to attempt to defend yourself alone: to give your cause the least chance of success you must call in foreign aid; and, by bringing the Florentines into the heart of this valley, you not only introduce war and destruction into the abodes of peace, but you act a treasonable part (forgive me if I repeat his word), in taking advantage of the power which you hold through his indulgence, to endeavour to bring ruin upon him. But, whatever you determine upon, whether to hold out with your own small forces, or to call strangers to your assistance, he is resolved to spare no exertion, and to be stopped by no obstacle, until he has reduced into / his own hands Valperga and all its dependencies; at the same time that you, so far from being a loser, except in nominal advantages, shall be fully compensated for your present possessions."

Euthanasia listened attentively, although sometimes disdain hovered on her lips, and at times her eyes flashed fire at the words she heard. She paused a moment to collect her thoughts, and then she replied: "My dear Arrigo, I pardon most freely all the part you take in these unfortunate circumstances; I would that the prince had not so far degraded himself, as to veil his tyranny with hypocrisy and falsehood; his is the power, and not the senate's; to him I reply; and, casting away all the vain pretexts with which he would hide, perhaps to himself, his injustice and lawless ambition, I reply with plain words to his artful speech; and I beg that without any alteration you faithfully deliver my message to him.

"I will never willingly surrender my power into his hands: I hold it for the good of my people, who are happy under my government, and towards whom I shall ever perform my / duty. I look upon him as a lawless tyrant, whom every one ought to resist to the utmost of their power; nor will I through cowardice give way to injustice. I may be exasperated beyond prudence; but right is on my side: I have preserved the articles of my alliance with him, and I will hold them still; but, if he attack me, I shall defend myself, and shall hold myself justified in accepting the assistance of my friends. If I had not that right, if indeed I had pledged myself to submit whenever he should call upon me to resign my birthright, what an absurd mockery is it to talk of his moderation towards me!

I acknowledge that he might long ago have attempted, as now he threatens, to reduce this castle to a frightful ruin; but then I should have resisted as I shall now; resisted with my own forces, and those of my allies. Valperga stands on a barren rock, and the few villages that own its law are poor and unprotected; but this castle is as dear to me as all his dominion is to him; I inherited it from my ancestors; and if I wished to despoil myself of power, it would be to make / my people free, and not to force them to enter the muster-roll of a usurper and a tyrant.

"My dear Arrigo, do not endeavour to persuade me to alter my purpose; for it is fixed. I am not young nor old enough to be scared by threats, nor happy enough to buy life on any terms Castruccio may choose to offer. I am willing to lose it in a just cause; and such I conceive to be the preservation of my inheritance."

Arrigo was too raw and inexperienced to contend in words with Euthanasia; he was overcome by her enthusiasm, which, although serious and apparently quiet, was as a stream that runs deep and waveless, but whose course is swifter and stronger than that which wastes its force in foam and noise. /

CHAPTER X.

Castruccio reconnoitres for a Surprise. – Embassy of Tripalda.

Arrigo returned sorrowfully to Lucca. He found Castruccio playing at chess with Mordecastelli; while a priest, Battista Tripalda, sat observing the game, and spoiling it by his interference.

"Nay, Vanni, I shall check-mate you next move," said Castruccio; "think again if you cannot escape, and make better play. Well, Arrigo, is peace or war the word you bring?"

"You must choose that, my lord; the countess wishes for peace, but she will not submit."

"Not submit!" cried Tripalda, stalking with his tall, upright figure into the middle of the room. "The woman is mad! I see that there is something wrong in this, that I must set right."

"Aye," said Mordecastelli; "as you set / my game right for me, and made me lose two knights and a castle."

"I wish he could persuade Euthanasia to lose a castle, and then all would go well. Are there no hopes, Arrigo? tell me what she said."

Arrigo repeated her message, endeavouring to soften her expressions; but

Castruccio was too experienced in the management of the human mind, not to draw from the youth the very words she had uttered.

"A murderer and a tyrant! pretty words applied to me, because I put a traitor to death, who otherwise would have placed my head on a Florentine pike. To what extremities am I driven! I would give the world not to go to open war about her miserable castle; yet have it I must, and that quickly, before she can send for her Florentine friends. What a spirit she has! I do not blame her; but, by St. Martin, I must tame it! Vanni, send for Castiglione; I must give him instructions for the conduct of the siege: I will have nothing to do with it personally; so tomorrow I shall away to keep the Florentines in check, if not to beat them." /

"My lord," said Tripalda, drawing himself up before Castruccio with an air of the utmost self-consequence, "you have often found me of use in occasions of this sort; and I intreat you to authorize me to go and expostulate with the countess; I doubt not that I shall bring you a favourable answer: she must hear reason, and from no one is she so likely to hear it as from myself."

"You little know her disposition, friend Tripalda; but the most hopeless effort is worth making, before I declare war, and take her possessions by force. Go therefore to-morrow morning early; in the mean time I will give Castiglione my instructions; that, if your persuasions are vain, he may commence the attack the following day."

Tripalda then retired to meditate the speech by which he should persuade Euthanasia to yield; while Castruccio, desperate of any composition, gave his full directions for the conduct of the siege.

"If I were not in the secret of the place," said he to Castiglione, "I might well believe the castle of Valperga to be impregnable, except / by famine; and that would be a tedious proceeding; but I know of other means which will give you entrance before nightfall. Lead a detachment of your most useless soldiers to the pathway which conducts to the main entrance of the castle; that of course will be well guarded; and, if the defence is directed with common judgement, the disadvantages under which the assailants must labour would render the attempt almost insane. But, as I said, let your more useless troops be employed there; they will keep the besieged in play; while you will conduct a chosen band to sure victory. You remember the fountain of the rock, beside which we were feasted, when the countess held her court, and where she sustained the mockery of a siege; to be conquered in play, as she now will be in earnest. You remember the narrow path that leads from the fountain to the postern, a gate, which, though strong, may easily be cut through by active arms and good hatchets. I know a path which leads from this valley to the fountain; it is long, difficult, and almost impracticable; but I have scaled it, and so may you and your followers. / To-night before the moon rises, and it rises late, we will ride to the spot, and when you are in possession of this secret, the castle is at your mercy."

203

It was now the beginning of the month of October; the summer, which had been particularly sultry, had swiftly declined; already the gales which attend upon the equinox swept through the woods, and the trees, who know

> His voice, and suddenly grow grey with fear,
> And tremble and despoil themselves,[a]

had already begun to obey the command of their ruler: the delicate chesnut woods, which last dare encounter the blasts of spring, whose tender leaves do not expand until they may become a shelter to a swallow, and which first hear the voice of the tyrant Libeccio, as he comes all conquering from the west, had already changed their hues, and shone yellow and red, amidst the sea-green foliage of the olives, the darker but light boughs of the cork trees, and the deep and heavy masses of ilexes and pines. The evening was hot; for the Libeccio, although it shuts out the sun with / clouds, yet brings a close and heavy air, that warms, while it oppresses.

When evening came, Castruccio and his companion addressed themselves for their expedition. They muffled themselves in their capuchins, and, leaving the town of Lucca, crossed the plain, riding swiftly and silently along. Who can descend into the heart of man, and know what the prince felt, as he conducted Castiglione to the secret path, discovered by his love, now used to injure and subdue her whom he had loved? The white walls of the castle, half concealed by the cork and ilex trees which grew on the platform before it, stood quietly and silent; and she who dwelt within, whose heart now beat fast with fear and wretchedness, was the lovely and beloved Euthanasia, whose sweet and soft eyes, which shone as violets beneath a load of snow, had formerly beamed unutterable love on him, and whose gentle and modulated voice had once pronounced words of tenderness, which, though changed, he could never forget, – it was she, the beautiful, who had lived on earth as the enshrined statue of a divinity, adorning all / places where she appeared, and adored by all who saw her; it was she, whose castle he was about to take and raze, it was against her that he now warred with a fixed resolution to conquer. Castruccio thought on all this; he called to mind her altered mien, and the coldness which had changed her heart from a fountain of burning love to an icy spring: and this awakened a feeling which he would fain have believed to be indignation. "Shall this false girl," he muttered, "enjoy this triumph over me? And shall the love which she despises, save her from the fate to which her own coldness and imprudence consign her? Let her yield; and she will find the Castruccio whom she calumniates, neither a tyrant nor a monster; but, if she resist, on her be the burthen of the misery that must follow."

---

[a] P. B. Shelley, 'Ode to the West Wind', ll. 41–2 (adapted), composed October 1819 in Florence, published 1820, five hundred years after the historical events on which this part of the narrative is based; cf. journal entries descriptive of the weather made during October 1820 at the commencement of writing *Valperga* (*MWSJ*, I, pp. 336–7).

Yet still, as officious conscience brought forward excuses for her, and called on him again and again to beware, he rode along side Castiglione, and entered into conversation. "Tomorrow at this hour," he said, "you and your troop must come along this road, and hide yourselves in the forest which we are about to / enter. When morning is up, do not long delay to scale the mountain, and enter the castle, for the sooner you take it, the less blood will be shed: order the battle so, that the troops you leave for the false attack may be fully engaged with the besieged before you enter; and then, coming behind the garrison, you can drive them down the mountain among their enemies, so that they may all be taken prisoners, at small expence either of their lives or ours."

They now dismounted; and, leaving their horses to their servants, began to ascend the acclivity. They moved cautiously along; and, if there had been any to listen to their footsteps, the sound was drowned by the singing of the pines, which moaned beneath the wind. Following the path of a torrent, and holding by the jutting points of rock, or the bare and tangled roots of the trees that overhung them, they proceeded slowly up the face of the mountain. Then turning to the right, they penetrated a complete wilderness of forest ground, where the undergrowth of the giant trees, and the fern and brambles, covered every path, so / that Castruccio had need of all his sagacity to distinguish the slight peculiarities of scene that guided him. They awoke the hare from her form; and the pheasants, looking down from the branches of the trees, flew away with a sharp cry, and the whiz of their heavy wings, as their solitude was disturbed.

Their progress was difficult and slow; but, after their toil had continued nearly two hours, Castruccio exclaimed, "Yes, I see that I am right!" and he paused a moment beside a spring, near which grew a solitary, but gigantic cypress, that seemed, as you looked up, to attain to the bright star which shone right above it, and towards which its moveless spire pointed; "I am right; I know this place well; mark it, Castiglione; and now our journey is almost ended."

It was here, that in their childish days Castruccio and Euthanasia often played; their names were carved on the rough bark of the cypress, and here, in memory of their infantine friendship, they had since met, to renew the vows they had formerly made, vows now broken, scattered to the winds, more worthless / than the fallen leaves of autumn on which he then trod. The way to the rock which overlooked the fountain was now short, but more difficult than ever; and both hands and feet were necessary to conquer the ascent. At length they came to a pinnacle, which, higher than the castle, overlooked the whole plain; and immediately under was the alcove which sheltered Euthanasia's fountain.

"I see no path which may lead to the fountain, my lord," said Castiglione.

"There is none," replied the prince, "nor did I ever get into the castle this way; but I have observed the place, and doubt not of the practicability of my plan."

Castruccio drew from under his cloak a rope, and fastened it to the shattered stump of a lightning-blasted tree; by the help of this rope, and a stick shod with iron which he carried in his hand, he contrived with the aid of Castiglione to reach a projecting ledge in the rock about two feet wide, which ran round the precipice about ten feet from its base; the fountain flowed from a crevice in this ledge, and steps were hewn out of the rock, leading / from the source to the basin. Castruccio pointed out these circumstances to his companion, and made it fully apparent that, with a little boldness and caution, they might arrive by the means he had pointed out at the path which led to the postern of the castle. A few questions asked by Castiglione, which the prince answered with accuracy and minuteness, sufficed to clear all the doubts which the former had entertained, and to explain the whole of this proceeding.

As they returned, however, Castiglione said suddenly, "My lord, you understand this path so much better than I; why will you not undertake the attack?"

"I thank you," replied Castruccio, with a bitter smile; "but this business falls to your share; I must away to keep off the aid the countess expects from the Florentines."

They descended slowly; the moon had risen, which would have discovered their path to them, but that she was hid behind so thick a woof of dark and lightning-bearing clouds, that her presence sufficed only to dispel the pitchy blackness, in which, but for her, they / had been enveloped. Every now and then the growling of distant but heavy thunder shook the air, and was answered by the screeching of the owl, and the screams of the birds whom it awoke from their sleep among the trees. The two adventurers soon reached the valley; and, mounting their horses, crossed the plain at full gallop; and the strong Libeccio against which they drove, cutting the air with difficulty, warmed the spirits, and somewhat dissipated the melancholy, which, in spite of all his efforts, oppressed Castruccio. He arrived much fatigued at his journey's end; and, whatever might be the revolutions in his feelings, or the remorse which stung him when he reflected on the work for which he prepared, throwing himself on his couch, deep sleep quickly overcame all; nor did he awake, until an attendant came to announce to him, that the day was advanced, that the troops had long quitted Lucca, and that his principal officers waited only for him to join them in their march towards the Florentine camp. Castruccio then shook off sleep; and, having examined well that his esquire had omitted no / piece of his armour which another horse bore, and having visited his charger which was to be led unbacked to the field, he mounted a black palfrey; and, merely saying to Castiglione, as he passed him in the palace court, "You understand all," – he joined his officers, and they rode off on the road to Florence.

As they quitted the town, they met Tripalda, who, accosting the prince, told him, that he was now going to Valperga, and that he did not doubt that his arguments would induce the countess to surrender. Castruccio shook his head in disbelief, and, hastily wishing him good-success, put spurs to his horse, apparently impatient to quit every thing that reminded him of the odious task he had left his friends to perform.

Battista Tripalda, the ambassador of Castruccio on this occasion, was a canon of the cathedral of St. Ambrose at Perugia. By this time the colleges of canons, who had before lived in common like monks, had been dissolved, and each member was permitted to live privately, receiving his share of the yearly income / which was before employed as a common stock.[a] But the canons had offices to perform in the church, which obliged them to reside in the town, in which the cathedral to which they belonged was situated; Tripalda had however been long absent from his duties, nor did his bishop ever enquire after him, or require him to return. He had appeared at Lucca about a year before this time, unknown and unrecommended; but he had intruded himself into the palaces of the nobles, and been well received: his eccentric manners made them pardon his opinions, and the subtleties of his mind forced them to forgive his uncouth and arrogant demeanour. Yet, although received by all, he was liked by none, for there was a mystery about him that no one could divine; and we seldom like what we do not comprehend. He was an unbelieving priest, yet was permitted to exercise the clerical functions; he was a man who cried out against the simony and wickedness of the Roman religion, yet he was tolerated by all its members; he was equally severe against tyrants and lords, yet he was received at every court in Italy. / He was an earnest panegyrizer of republics and democracies; yet he was satisfied with no existing form of government, because none was sufficiently free: he contended that each man ought to be his own king and judge; yet he pretended to morality, and to be a strict censor of manners and luxury. He had a deep insight into artful and artificial character, and a kind of instinctive prudence in extricating himself from the most embarrassing circumstances; so that his penetration almost gave him the appearance of a tamperer in the forbidden arts, which however he held in supreme contempt.

He was equally well received by the opposite factions, allying himself with neither, but condemning both. When he first appeared at Lucca, he was humble and mild, pretending to nothing but uncorrupted and uncorruptible virtue, desiring none of the goods of fortune, except that which she could not withhold from him, namely, the esteem and friendship of all good men. But this was merely the prelude to what was to follow. He was as those dwarfs we read of in fairy tales, who at first / appear small and impotent, but who on further acquaintance assume the form of tremendous giants;[b] so, when he became familiar with his new friends, he cast off his modest disguise, and appeared vain, presumptuous and insolent, delivering his opinions as oracles, violent

---

[a] Details of this system were taken from Muratori, III, diss. 66, pp. 333–4; noted in adds. e. 17 (p. 234 rev.).
[b] Not identified.

when opposed in argument, contemptuous even when agreed with: there was besides something buffoonish in his manner, which he occasionally endeavoured to pass off for wit and imagination, and at other times, served him as a cloak for deep designs and dangerous opinions. The Guelphs declared that they believed him to be a Ghibeline spy; the Ghibelines, that he was under pay from the Pope; many said, that he tampered with both parties, and betrayed both. Worse stories had been whispered concerning him, but they were believed by few; it was said that the flagrant wickedness of his actions had caused him to be banished from Perugia; but this was disproved at once, for if so, why was he not deprived of his emoluments in the church?

The first conjecture concerning him was that he was a spy; but, however that might be, / he escaped detection, and contrived to maintain his confidence with the chiefs of the opposite factions, and among these was Euthanasia. She admired his talents, believed him to be honest, and refused to listen to the accusations advanced against him, since the manner in which they were brought forward stamped them with the show of unfounded calumnies. She was sometimes irritated by his impertinence, and shocked at his want of delicacy; but she had heard that early misfortunes had deranged his understanding, and she pitied and forgave him. Indeed she had known him a very short time; and he had not yet thrown off his mask of humility and virtue, which he ever wore on his first appearance on a new scene.

Euthanasia waited with impatience to hear the result of her message to Castruccio. She could not believe that he would put his threats in execution; but, in case of the worst, she resolved to oppose his pretensions, and to use every means to preserve her independence. She had sent, the same night of her interview with Arrigo, to intreat the Florentine general to dispatch / a brigade for her defence, and to request the assistance of an able officer in sustaining the siege she might encounter. She called together the few militia of her villages. She visited the works of the castle, and gave orders for the immediate demolition of all roads and bridges on the first advance of the enemy; and then, overcome by the sense of wretchedness which clung to her in spite of the exalted state of her mind, she shrunk to solitude, and tried to seek in the recesses of her own soul for the long-studied lessons of courage and fortitude.

She believed herself justified, nay called upon to oppose the encroachments of the prince of Lucca; she felt roused to resistance by his menaces, and the implied accusation of treachery with which he had endeavoured to brand her. Her innocence made her proud, her spirit of independence, bold; she had ever refused to submit to his usurpations; her castle had often been the asylum for his victims, and herself the aider of the persecuted. "I may fall," she thought; "but I will not stoop. I may become his victim; but I will never be his slave. I refused to yield to him when I / loved him, if he did not dismiss his ambitious designs. Love, which is the ruling principle of my mind, whose power I now feel in every nerve, in every beating of my heart, I would not submit my conscience to the control of love; and shall fear rule me?"

She said this, and at the same moment Tripalda was announced. He advanced towards Euthanasia with a serious and important look, yet at the same time with an endeavour to appear courteous, if not humble. He kissed her hand, and having gravely asked after her health, he soon began to speak on the object of his visit, and to endeavour to persuade her that all resistance to the will of the prince was useless, and that in timely submission was the only hope left for her preservation. Euthanasia felt her cheeks glow as he spoke, and once her eyes seemed to flash lightning, when the word *Mercy* escaped from the orator, who talked on, appearing to observe little of what she felt, but to be wholly engrossed in the winding up of his periods. "Madonna," said he, "the prince has a true and sincere friendship for you, and he is infinitely grieved at the idea of / being at open hostility with you; but he must obey the will of the senate and the council, and you must ultimately submit to the forces sent against you. Listen then to one older than yourself, who has lived longer in the world, and has grown wise by experience: never, being weak, contend with the strong; for it is far more politic to yield at first upon conditions, than, falling after combat, to receive the law from the conqueror."

"I am afraid, *Messer Canonico*," replied Euthanasia, calmly, but somewhat haughtily, "that our opinions agree too little, to allow you to be a fitting arbiter between me and the prince of Lucca. This castle, and the power annexed to it, belonged to my ancestors; and when I received it from my mother's hands, I vowed to exercise and preserve it for the good of my people———"

"And is it for the good of your people to expose them to the desolation of war, when you might conclude a satisfactory peace?"

"Messer Battista, I listened patiently while you spoke; and it boots little to continue this discussion, if you will not also attend to me. / I will be very brief: Castruccio formed an alliance with me, and, as the condition of my independence, I promised not to join his enemies. I have preserved my part of the agreement; and, if he wishes to break his, I have friends and allies, who will not permit that my situation should be so hopeless as you imagine. It is the height of injustice to say that I bring war into this territory; since every prayer and every wish of my heart is for peace; but, if attacked, I will defend myself, and my right must become both my sword and shield."

"You speak proudly, but foolishly, countess Euthanasia; for right was never yet sword or shield to any one. It is well to talk in this manner to women and children, and thus to keep the world in some degree of order. You are a woman, it is true; but your rank and power have placed you in a situation to know the truth of things; and, if you have not yet learned the futility of the lessons of the priests, whose sole end to all their speeches is to find a way, shorter or longer, into your purse; learn it from me, who am both willing and able to teach you." /

209

"I shall make a sorry pupil, I am afraid; but, if you please, I will alter my phraseology, that my meaning may be more clear. I expect the aid of the Florentines; and I depend upon the courage with which the hatred of a usurper will inspire my soldiers, who love me, and will, I doubt not, defend me to the last drop of their blood: if my right cannot help me, my resolution shall. The prince of Lucca has called me, perhaps he believes me to be, a traitor; I am none to him, nor will I be to the party to which I belong. I promised my allies not to submit; and my word is sacred. Messer Battista, I doubt not that the motives which urged your visit, were honest, perhaps friendly; but cease to vex yourself and me with fruitless altercation."

"I do not intend altercation, Madonna; but I wished to expostulate with you, and to shew you the pit into which you seem obstinately resolved to fall. I know that the wisdom of all ages tells us, that women will have their will; I had hoped to find you superior to the foibles of your sex; and my mistake becomes my crime: for in truth you are as headstrong / as a girl of fifteen, who hopes to cover her head with the nuptial veil. But I have set my heart on carrying this point with you, and will not be discouraged by a woman's eloquence or obstinacy."

"This is going too far," said Euthanasia, half angrily; "you imagine perhaps that I am already the slave of your lord, that you no longer preserve the respect which even then would be due to me. My mind is too full both of grief and anxiety, to string sentences together in answer to your arguments; but my purpose is firm, and you cannot shake it. If you come from the lord Castruccio himself, my answer is the same. I am at peace with him; but, if he attacks me, I know how to defend myself."

Any man but Tripalda might have been awed by the dignity of Euthanasia, and the restrained indignation, that glistened in her eyes, and flushed her cheek. She rose to bid the priest farewel, and her serious manner made him pause for an instant in his address; but his accustomed impudence quickly overcame the momentary shame, and he said, "I came to / speak reason to the deaf, and to shew danger to the blind; but the deaf man says, I hear better than you, and the sound of arms and trumpets is yet far off; – and the blind man cries, Avaunt! I see my path better than you: meanwhile the one falls into the hands of the enemy, and the other tumbles into the pit round which I would have led him. You will repent too late, that you did not follow my counsel; and then who will medicine your wounds?"

"The God who inflicted them upon me. I fear not!"

Tripalda returned to Lucca. Castruccio had left the town; and Castiglione, hearing the result of the priest's embassy, instantly prepared for the attack. Heralds were sent in due form to demand the surrender of the castle; and, when refused, war was immediately declared.

In the mean time the Florentine army had advanced into the Lucchese territory; but, when they heard of the march of Castruccio, they fell back to

Fucecchio, and pitched their tents on the banks of the river Guisciana.[a] /
Castruccio came up to them with his troops; but, being on opposite sides of the
river, and not caring to cross it in face of the enemy, both armies remained
observing each other's motions, each preparing to attack the other on the first
shew of fear or retreat. The Florentine general had received the message of
Euthanasia, but he found it difficult to comply with her wishes; for any troops
sent to her aid must pass the Guisciana, and that was too well guarded to
permit of any but a general passage and attack. He communicated her situation
to the Florentine government, which sent her a small troop with Bondelmonti
at its head, who, making the circuit of Bologna and the Modenese mountains,
arrived on the eve of the attack, having with infinite difficulty surmounted the
fortified passages of the mountains; so that many of his followers being made
prisoners, and others left behind, he made his appearance at Valperga with not
more than fifty men. /

CHAPTER XI.

Valperga taken.

After the departure of Tripalda, Euthanasia remained long on the battlements
of her castle, watching the men who were employed in repairing and erecting
some outworks for its defence. Every now and then she heard a murmuring
near her, a slight noise, and then a voice which said – "Aye, that will do; this
helmet is still too large, I must find some way to cut it round the edges."

Looking up, she saw at a small window of one of the projecting towers the
Albinois, who appeared furbishing and repairing arms. "Are we so straitened
for men," she said, "that you are obliged to turn armourer, my poor Bindo?"

"Not an armourer, but a soldier, lady; tomorrow I gird on my sword for your
defence."

"You, and a sword! Nay, that is impossible; / you must not expose yourself
to danger, where you can do no good."

"Countess, have firm hope; I have learned from the stars, that tomorrow is a
fortunate day for us. I have visited the holy fountain; and, sprinkling its waters
three times around, I have called on its saints to aid us: tomorrow is named as
a lucky day for us, and I will be among your defenders."

He spoke earnestly; and so highly wrought were the feelings of Euthanasia,

---

[a] The modern Usciana, a continuation of the Nievole and a tributary of the Arno; Fucecchio is a
town nearby. The ensuing account follows Sismondi, ch. xxx.

that, although at another time she might have smiled, she could now with difficulty repress her tears. "If you would defend me," she replied, "wait then near me; I will not indeed have you risk your life to no end."

"Why, Madonna," said Bindo, "should you care more for my life, than for those of the brave fellows who will tomorrow die for you? We shall succeed; but death will be among us; and tomorrow many a child will lose its father, and many a wife her husband, fighting for this heap of stones which can feel neither defeat nor triumph. I will be among them; fear not, St. Martin has declared for us." /

There are moments in our lives, when the chance-word of a madman or a fool is sufficient to cause our misery; and such was the present state of Euthanasia's mind. She hastily retreated to solitude, and in earnest thought tried to overcome the effect of the conscience-stricken wound which the Albinois had inflicted. We are distrustful of ourselves; so little do we depend upon our human reason, that, on the eve of any action, even the most praiseworthy, it will sometimes assume another semblance, and that will appear selfish wilfulness, or at best a distorted freak of the imagination, which, when we first contemplated it, seemed the highest effort of human virtue. It had appeared to Euthanasia her first duty to resist the incroachments of Castruccio, and to preserve the independence of her subjects. Now again she paused, and thought that all the shows this world presents were dearly bought at the price of one drop of human blood. She doubted the purity of her own motives; she doubted the justification which even now she was called upon to make at the tribunal of her conscience, and hereafter before that of her / God; she stopt, and shivered on the brink of her purpose, as a mighty fragment of rock will pause shaking at the edge of a precipice, and then fall to the darkness that must receive it.

"The earth is a wide sea," she cried, "and we its passing bubbles; it is a changeful heaven, and we its smallest and swiftest driven vapours; all changes, all passes – nothing is stable, nothing for one moment the same. But, if it be so, oh my God! if in Eternity all the years that man has numbered on this green earth be but a point, and we but the minutest speck in the great whole, why is the present moment every thing to us? Why do our minds, grasping all, feel as if eternity and immeasurable space were kernelled up in one instantaneous sensation? We look back to times past, and we mass them together, and say in such a year such and such events took place, such wars occupied that year, and during the next there was peace. Yet each year was then divided into weeks, days, minutes, and slow-moving seconds, during which there were human minds to note and distinguish them, as now. We think of a small motion of the dial / as of an eternity; yet ages have past, and they are but hours; the present moment will soon be only a memory, an unseen atom in the night of by-gone time. A hundred years hence, and young and old we shall all be gathered to the dust, and I shall no longer feel the coil that is at work in my heart, or any longer struggle within the inextricable bonds of fate. I know this; but yet this moment, this point of time, during which the sun makes but one round amidst the many millions it has made, and the many millions it will make, this moment is all to me. Most willingly, nay, most earnestly, do I pray that I may die this night, and that all contention may cease with the beatings of my heart. Yet, if I live, shall I submit? Is all that we prize but a shadow? Are tyranny, and cruelty, and liberty, and virtue only names? Or, are they not rather the misery or joy, that makes our hearts the abode of storms, or as a smiling, flower-covered isle? Oh! I will no longer question my purpose, or waver where necessity ought to inspire me with courage. One heart is too weak to contain so overwhelming a contention." /

While her melancholy thoughts thus wandered, and she seemed to range in idea through the whole universe, yet no where found repose, it was announced to her that Bondelmonti and his soldiers had arrived, and that the chief desired to see her. There was something in the name of Bondelmonti that struck a favourable chord in her heart; he had been her father's friend; he was her guardian, and, although she had sometimes run counter to his advice, yet she always felt most happy when his opinion coincided with hers. His presence thus announced seemed to cancel half her care; she collected all the courage she possessed, and that was a mighty store, and descended, even smiling, to the hall; her cares and regrets were leashed like dogs by the huntsmen, but they neither bayed nor yelled, but cowered in silence. Bondelmonti was struck by the serenity of her aspect; and his countenance changed from the doubt it had before expressed, to a frank and gallant address.

"Madonna," said he, "the work we undertake is difficult; Castruccio keeps our army in check, and guards the passes; and the fifty / men that I bring you, is all out of three hundred that could pass the Serchio. Have good heart however, your castle walls are strong and will resist all the stones with which their *battifolle** can batter it, if indeed they can scale the rock, which we must make as impracticable as we can. But this is not fitting work for you, fair countess; do you retire to rest; I would indeed that we could place you in safety in Florence out of all danger, where you would not be able to hear the clash of arms that tomorrow will resound in this castle. But I know that you have courage; and I now see all the calm fortitude of your father shine in your clear eyes; you are a good girl, Euthanasia, a good and a wise girl, and be assured that every drop of blood that warms my heart, every faculty of my body or my mind, are devoted to your cause."

Euthanasia thanked him in the warm language her feeling heart dictated, and

---

* *Battifolle*, or *balestri*, machines for casting stones.[a]

[a] *Battifolle* were actually temporary wooden bastions (Muratori, I, diss. 26, pp. 369–71); *ballestri* (see p. 12) are described nearby in Muratori I, diss. 26, pp. 351 and 375 ff.; noted Ab. Dep. e. 274, pp. 74, 79.

he continued; "I should have much to say to you, much encouragement from your friends and / messages of praise and affection; but my time is short: believe then in one word, that all your Florentine friends love, approve and admire you; and if you fall, which this good sword forbid, we shall at least have this consolation, that our long absent Euthanasia will reappear among us. But now to the works of war; I will apply to your seneschal to know what food you have in the castle, and what possibilities there are of increasing your stock; and your principal officers shall shew me your works of defence, that I may concert with them the plan for to-morrow's combat."

Euthanasia however undertook this task herself: she was too much agitated, not to find some relief in the shew of composure which she preserved with Bondelmonti, and in the exertion of explaining and pointing out the various modes of defence which she had adopted, in addition to those with which nature had furnished her habitation. The castle was built, as I have before said, on the projecting platform of a precipitous mountain: the wall of the edifice itself was thick and strong; and but / a small way removed from it was a lower wall, built with corner towers and battlements, which at once defended the main building, and sheltered the besieged, who could shower stones and arrows on the assailants from the portholes, and be in no danger of retaliation. Before the gate of the castle was a green plot, about fifteen paces across, planted with a few cork and ilex trees, and surrounded by a barbican or low wall built on the edge of the precipice, which, high, bare, and inaccessible, hung over the plain below. Between the wall and the barbican, a path ran round one side of the castle, which was terminated by massy gates and a portcullis; and it was there that, crossing the chasm which insulated the castle, by means of a drawbridge, you found the path that conducted to the plain. This path was defended by various works; palisades, wooden towers to shelter archers, and more by nature herself, for the rock and the trees were all so many asylums whence the defenders could uninjured prevent the approach of an enemy.

"This is all excellent," said Bondelmonti, / "it is impossible that all the armies of Italy could force this pass, though it were defended only by a handful. But, Madonna, is there no other entrance to your castle? Is there no postern with a path up or down the mountain, whose secret your enemies may learn, and thus attack you unawares?"

"None; the only postern is that which opens on a path conducting to a small fountain about a hundred paces up the acclivity; but there it stops, and the rock rising precipitously behind forbids approach."

"It is well. I will now review your soldiers, appoint their various posts, and see that mine are refreshed; then, cousin, having tasted your wine, I will go to rest, that I may awake betimes to-morrow. I am resolved that all shall go well; Castruccio will be defeated; and you shall ever be, as you deserve, the castellana of Valperga."

The tables were spread in the great hall of the castle, and heaped with wine and food. After Euthanasia had seen every want of her guests supplied, she retired to her own room at the eastern angle of the castle, one window / of which overlooked the whole plain of Lucca; and she sat near this window, unable to rest or sleep, in that breathless and feverish state, in which we expect a coming, but uncertain danger.

The veil of night was at length withdrawn; first Euthanasia saw the stars wax faint, and then the western sky caught a crimson tinge from the opposing sun. It was long ere he climbed the eastern hill: but his rays fell upon the opposite mountains, and the windows of the castle of Valperga shone dazzlingly bright. A *reveillée* was sounded in the court below, and roused the young countess from her waking dreams, to the reality that yawned as a gulph before her. First, she composed her dress, and bound the wandering locks of her hair round her head; then for a moment she stood, her hands folded on her bosom, her eyes cast up to heaven. At first her countenance expressed pain: but it changed; her pale cheek began to glow, her brow became clear from the cloud that had dimmed it, her eyes grew brighter, and her whole form gained dignity and firmness. "I do my duty," she thought, "and in that dear belief do I place / my strength; I do my duty towards myself, towards my peasants, towards Castruccio, from whose hands I detain only the power of doing greater ill; God is my help, and I fear not."

Thinking and feeling thus, she descended to the hall of the castle; most of the soldiers had gone to their posts; but Bondelmonti, and some of those of higher rank in her party and household, were waiting her appearance. She entered not gaily, but serenely; and her beauty, the courage painted on her face, and her thrilling tone as she bade them good morrow, inspired them with a simultaneous emotion, which they almost expressed, and midway checked their voices. Bondelmonti kissed her hand; "Farewel, my friends," she said; "you risk your lives for me, and the sacrifice of mine were a poor recompense; my honour, my every hope rests upon your swords; they are wielded by those who love me, and I do not fear the result."

Bondelmonti addressed himself to the combat, ordered the men to their posts, and took his own station on the drawbridge of the castle. The winding path which led to the foot / of the mountain, was lined with archers and slingers, who were hid behind the projecting rocks or trees, or within small wooden towers, erected for the purpose. A chosen band armed with long spears was stationed in firm array at the most precipitous part of the path, who, drawn up in close rank, and advancing their arms, formed an outwork of iron spikes, impossible to be passed or driven back. The foremost in the combat were the dependents of Euthanasia; they were full of that loud, but undisciplined courage which anger and fear inspire; Bindo was among them, and he harangued them, saying, that every sign in the heavens, and every power of air, was propitious to their mistress; at other times they had derided his superstition;

but now it acted as another incentive to their indignation, and supporter for their courage.

In the mean time Euthanasia had retired to the apartment of Lauretta. This unfortunate lady had remained in the castle since the death of her husband; and such was the agony of grief she endured, that Euthanasia had not communicated to her the threats of / Castruccio, and the approaching siege. The noise of arms, and the sound of many voices alarmed her; and she wildly asked the cause. Her friend related to her the events of the few last days, and endeavoured to calm her; Lauretta listened in fear; she had suffered so much by the like contentions, that every thing presented itself to her in the gloomiest point of view. Grasping the countess's hand, she intreated her to submit; "You know not what a siege is," she cried; "my father's castle was stormed, and therefore I well know. Even if Castruccio were at the head of his troops, he would in vain endeavour to restrain their fury; a triumphant soldier is worse than the buffalo of the forest, and no humanity can check his thirst for blood and outrage; they will conquer, and neither God nor man can save us."

Euthanasia tried to soothe her; but in vain. She wept bitterly, and prayed so earnestly that the countess would spare them both the utter misery they would endure, that Euthanasia was for a moment startled by her adjurations; but then, recalling her thoughts, she replied with gentle firmness, and bade her lay aside / her fears which were unfounded, for there was nothing to dread save an easy imprisonment, if they should be overcome.

And now, as they were talking thus, a messenger came from Bondelmonti. "The general desires you to have good heart," he said; "the troops of the enemy advance; and, if we may judge by their appearance, they are few, and even those few the refuse of the prince's army."

Euthanasia listened incredulously; for she knew that however doubtful the decision of the combat might be, the contention must be fierce. Soon the war-cry arose from without the castle, and was echoed from the walls and mountains; when it ceased, it was answered by the Ghibeline cry from the assailants. But this only proved the truth of Bondelmonti's assertion, that they were few, and of no note; for the shout was not that exhilarating sound, that echoes the soul's triumph, and, borne along the line, raises responsive ardour in every breast; it was loud, but soon died away.

Wearied by the childish remonstrances of / Lauretta, Euthanasia descended to the platform of the castle, and leaned over the barbican; but she could see nothing, though her ears were stunned by the cries, and clash of arms, that rose from the valley. Returning to the inner court, she met some men who were bearing the wounded from the field, and bringing them for succour to the castle; for a moment her heart sunk within her, for a moment she was pierced with grief, as she thought – "This is my work!" But she recovered herself – "It must all be endured," said she; "I have undertaken a part, and will not faint on the threshold. Spirit of my father, aid me!"

Beds had been prepared in a large apartment of the castle, and Euthanasia mingled with the women who ministered to the wounded; she bound them with her own hands, cheered them with her voice, and endeavoured, by supporting their minds, to alleviate the sense of bodily pain. The men, who saw her flitting like an angel about them, aiding and ministering to their wants, felt all the love and / gratitude that such unwonted, but gracious kindness might inspire. "Fear not, lady," they said; "we are even more numerous than those who attack us; already they are tired, and out of breath; fear not, the day is ours."

A messenger also came from Bondelmonti, to say, that the imprudence of an under-officer had caused the few to fall who had fallen, but that her troops were now all sheltered, and, that without the loss of a man they would either destroy all the assailants, or drive them down the steep; and this assertion appeared confirmed, since no more wounded were brought in. Thus reassured, Euthanasia left the hall, and ascended to her own apartment; her spirit was lightened of much of its burthen; the first barrier had been passed; and she feared not, she would not fear, the rest.

As she thought this, a sudden scream echoed through the castle; for a moment she was transfixed; the scream was repeated, louder and nearer, and she hastened to the window that overlooked the outer court. Thence she saw a party of soldiers in the Lucchese uniform / issue from the gate, and run round the castle towards the drawbridge; as they came out in file she thought their numbers would never end, and she recognized several of the officers as those of the highest rank in Castruccio's army; the last at length disappeared, and she looked around for an explanation. The castle was silent; she stood alone in the room; and even the echo of footsteps reached her not: she paused a moment; and then, weary of further doubt, she hastened to the room of Lauretta, and found it full of soldiers, – the enemy's soldiers; while the poor girl, pale and trembling, sat bewildered and silent. Euthanasia entered from a small door, leading from a private staircase: her first words were addressed to her friend; "Fear not," she cried; "we are betrayed; but fear not."

The soldiers, seeing her appear, had sent for their chief officer, who came forward, saying, "The castle is ours; and, Madonna, it were well that you ordered your people to yield; for further resistance would be useless, and could only cause more bloodshed: we are commanded / by our general to act with the greatest moderation."

"It is enough," replied Euthanasia, quietly; "the commander will judge of the necessity of submission: but see, you frighten this lady, who is ill and delicate. I beseech you to leave this room awhile; if I find that indeed no further resistance can be made, I shall soon be prepared to obey what orders you may bring."

"Madonna, we withdraw as you desire: but permit me to add, that it is the general's orders that we escort you to Lucca this evening: until then we shall not intrude upon you."

217

The soldiers quitted the room; and Euthanasia, leaving Lauretta with her servant, retired to her own apartment. Here she found several of her attendants, who told with many tears that there was no longer any hope; that the enemy, entering at the postern, had attacked her soldiers from behind, and driven them down the mountain, and that the party left in the castle having raised the drawbridge, were / now in undisturbed possession. Euthanasia heard all this with an unaltered mien, and, when the melancholy tale was finished, she bade them leave her, and go to the commanding officer of the troop to receive orders for their further proceeding, but not to return to her, until she should command their attendance. /

CHAPTER XII.

Euthanasia at Lucca.

The castle bell tolled the *Ave Maria* for the last time, answering the belfries of the various convents in the vale below. "There is my knell!" cried Euthanasia. At first she thought that it would please her, in quitting for ever the abode of her ancestors, to array herself in mourning garments; but then the simplicity of her mind made her instinctively shun any thing that had the appearance of affectation; so she covered her head with a white veil, folded her capuchin about her, and returned to the chamber of Lauretta to prepare for her removal. Castiglione sent thither to desire admittance; when he came, he felt awed by the deportment of Euthanasia, who received him with that slight tinge of pride mingled with her accustomed dignity, which adversity naturally / bestows on the good. He announced that the escort had arrived to convey them to Lucca; Euthanasia bowed her head in acquiescence; and, supporting Lauretta, with an unfaltering step she left for the last time the castle of her ancestors; she supported her friend with one hand, and with the other folded her veil close to her face, that no rudely curious eye might read in its expression the sorrow that she felt in her heart. "My grief is my own," she thought; "the only treasure that remains to me; and I will hoard it with more jealousy from the sight and knowledge of others, than a miser does his gold."

She walked unhesitating through the hall, long the seat of her purest happiness. Her infant feet had trodden its pavement in unreproved gaiety; and she thought for a moment that she saw the venerable form of her father seated in his accustomed place. But she proudly shook the softening emotion from her, and looked with a tearless eye upon the hearth, round which the soldiers of her enemy stood, profaning its sacredness by their presence. The inner court of the castle was filled by a / number of women and children, the wives of the peasantry who depended on her, who, as they saw her advance, raised one cry of grief; she started, and said in a smothered voice, "Could I not have been spared this?"

"Impossible," replied Castiglione, who overheard her; "nothing but the most brutal force could have prevented them."

"Enough," said Euthanasia; "I am satisfied."

The women clung about her, kissing her hands, her garments, and throwing themselves on their knees with all the violent gesticulation of Italians. They tore their hair, and called on heaven to save and bless their mistress, and to avenge her wrongs; – "God bless you, good people!" cried their countess; "may you never be reminded of my loss by any misfortune that may befal yourselves!"

And, disengaging herself from their grasp, she walked on, while they followed crying and bewailing. She crossed the drawbridge, which was guarded at each end by soldiers; ere she put her foot on the opposite rock, Euthanasia paused for one moment; it seemed to her that / all was irretrievably lost, when once she had[5] passed the barrier which this bridge placed between her past and future life; she glanced back once more at the castle, and looked up to the window of her apartment; she had expected to find it desert and blank; but it was filled with soldiers, who stood looking from it on her departure; she sighed deeply, and then with quicker steps hastened down the mountain.

The idea that this path had been the scene of the morning's combat affrighted her; and she dared not look round, fearing that she might see some lifeless victim among the bushes and rocks on the road-side: and so it might easily have been; for, when Castiglione had ordered to the road to be cleared of the dead, many had been cast behind the projections of rock, or under the low wood, in their haste; and, as they passed, the vulture arose from among the grass, scared from his prey, and told too truly that he feasted upon limbs which that same morning had been endowed with life. The very path on which she trod was slippery with blood; and she felt as if she walked through / one of the circles of hell's torments*, until she reached the foot of the rock.

Lauretta was placed in a litter; Euthanasia mounted her horse; and they prepared to depart: but the women again raising a cry, threw themselves about the horse, seizing the reins, and vowing that she should not leave them. "God bless you!" cried the poor countess, who, although filled with her own grief, yet sympathized with these good people; "but now go; you may harm yourselves with your new master; you can do no good to me."

The soldiers interfered; and, opening the path before Euthanasia, she gave

---

* See Dante.[a]

[a] Reminiscent especially of the seventh circle of the *Inferno* where Dante comes to a chaos of shattered rocks; through it runs a boiling river of blood in which those who injure others by violence are placed.

the reins to her horse, and rode with speed out of the hearing of the cry, which her people again sent up, when they saw that she had indeed left them. She had outridden the rest of her party; and, finding herself alone, she drew up her palfrey to wait their arrival. She looked upon the castle, no longer hers; a few quick drops fell; she dried them again; and, seeing her escort approach, she turned her horse's head, and, / without a word, proceeded slowly on her way to Lucca.

The city-gates were shut; but, on the word being given by her escort, they were thrown open, and she entered the dark and narrow streets of the town. "My prison!" thought Euthanasia. Here the company divided: Lauretta, at her own request, was conveyed to the house of the mother of Leodino; and Euthanasia was led to the palace prepared for her reception. She took no notice of the streets through which she passed, and cared little whether they conducted her to a palace or a prison; indeed during the latter part of her ride, her strength both of mind and body so much forsook her, that she could hardly keep her seat on her horse, but rode like a veiled statue of despair.

Euthanasia was led to her chamber; her attendants came to her, but she dismissed them all; and, her mind confused, her spirits and strength quite exhausted by long watching during several of the preceding nights, and by the exciting circumstances of the day, she threw herself dressed as she was on a couch, / and, kindly nature coming to her aid, sank instantaneously into a heavy and dreamless sleep.

Day was far advanced, before she again awoke, and looked forth on the light, with a sentiment, as if the slight refreshment of spirit and strength she had received, were but a mockery of the sad weight that oppressed her heart. She lifted her heavy head, like a water lily whose cup is filled by a thunder shower: but, presently recalling her scattered faculties, she sat for some time in deep meditation, endeavouring to philosophize herself out of the unhappiness that she felt. The palace to which she had been conducted, was a large and magnificent one, near the outskirts of the town: it had belonged to one of the victims of Castruccio's despotism, and had the desolate and woe-begone appearance of a mansion which has lost its master. From the chamber where she sat, she looked upon the garden; a square plot of ground surrounded by four high walls, which had been planted in the Italian taste, but which now ran wild; the small flower-beds were overgrown with weeds, and / the grass, a rude commoner, had thrust itself into the untrod paths; the stone-pedestals for the lemon-pots were green with moss and lichens; and here and there the wind-borne seed of some delicate plant had sown a lovely flower in the midst of the moist, coarse herbage which could ill claim its fellowship. A few cypress and box trees, which had been cut into shape, now mocked the gardener's knife with the unpruned growth of three years; and ivy darkened the walls side by side with the orange trees, whose golden apples shone amidst the dark foliage. A few lizards had crept from beneath the stones to bask in the rays of the autumnal sun; and the frogs croaked in a reservoir or cistern, which had once played as a fountain, but which was now choked with weeds and dirt. Such was the desolate scene which arrested the eyes of Euthanasia, as she looked from her window. "The image of my fortunes;" she thought, and turned away, while a tear flowed down her cheek.

Her servant now entered; and, while she arranged her dress, the woman related the catastrophe of the siege. When the soldiers / of Castruccio had appeared behind her defenders coming down from the castle, they threw themselves first on those who guarded the bridge, and took Bondelmonti and the principal Florentines prisoners: but the dependents of the countess, transported with fury, and elevated by the promises which Bindo had held out of success, rushed out of their hiding-places, and charging those at the foot of the rock, drove them with desperate courage down the mountain path, unmindful of the enemies who pressed upon their rear. The battle was bloody; many fell on each side; the small troop of Valpergans were destroyed almost to a man, falling voluntary sacrifices for their mistress's preservation. A few were taken prisoners, and among them Bindo, who almost miraculously had escaped unwounded. But, if he were not wounded in body, his mind was almost frenzied with rage and disappointment, when he saw the Lucchese flag wave from the donjon of the castle; he tried to break from those who held him, and, weak as he appeared to be, he exerted such desperate strength, using both hands, feet, and teeth, / that the soldiers found it necessary to bind him. – As they fastened the cords, Castiglione came up: he remembered the Albinois; and, asking why it was that he was used so roughly, he ordered them to set him free. As soon as his bonds were loosened, without speaking or looking round, he darted off; and, running across the country as swiftly as a deer from the hounds, was quickly out of sight.

Euthanasia wept when she heard of the blood that had been spilt for her; and self-reproach, who is ever ready to thrust in his sharp sting, if he find that mailed conscience has one weak part, now tormented her that she had not yielded, before one human life had been lost in so unhappy a cause. "Do not evil that good may come," thought she. "Are not those the words of the Teacher? I have done infinite evil, in spilling that blood whose each precious drop was of more worth than the jewels of a kingly crown; but my evil has borne its fitting fruit; its root in death, its produce poison."

In the course of the day, Arrigo Guinigi came to visit her. He came with a message / from Castruccio, who intreated her to remain quietly in the palace provided for her, until he should return to Lucca, which would be in a few days, when he would learn from her own lips what her wishes were with regard to her future life. Arrigo said all this with downcast eyes and a heaving breast, hardly daring to speak, and much less raise his eyes upon the countess; who replied that she would obey; that she had much rather not see the prince; but that if he commanded it, she was ready to submit. "You see me, my dear

Arrigo, a prisoner, despoiled of my possessions, a slave to your lord's will. Yet I hope and trust, that these events would not have created the deep sorrow with which I feel that my soul is filled, did not bitter sentiments of lost affections, disappointed expectations, and utter hopelessness, fill up the measure of my infelicity. My good youth, we are born to misery; so our priests tell us, and there is more sooth in that lesson, than in early youth we are willing to believe; yet fortitude is the virtue with which my father endeavoured principally to imbue me, and I would fain not disgrace his counsels; but / indeed a poisoned barb has entered my heart, and I cannot draw it out."

Arrigo endeavoured to comfort her – "Your state is far from hopeless; the prince has promised, and intends to keep his promise, that your revenues shall not be injured by the loss of your castle. At Florence you will be surrounded by friends, and every luxury and pleasure of life; and there you may again be happy."

Autumn was now far advanced, and the rains came on. The Florentine and Lucchese armies, which had remained looking at each other from opposite sides of the river, were now further divided by the overflowing of its waters; so each retreated to their several towns, and the campaign of that year ended. Castruccio returned to Lucca. His first concern was a long and private conversation with Castiglione; and immediately after he dispatched Arrigo to prepare Euthanasia for a conference.

Poor girl! her heart beat, and the blood mounted to her before pale cheeks, when she heard that she was to see him whom she had loved, and to whose memory, as of what had / been, she clung with tenacious affection. It was a cruel task for her to behold his form, graceful as it had been when she gazed on it in happier days, and his countenance, which, but that more pride were mingled in the expression, was as gloriously beautiful, as when it beamed love upon her; and more than all, to hear his voice, whose soft and mellow cadences had wrapt her soul in Elysium, now to be heard as the voice of an alien. But indignation mingled itself with these feelings, and enabled her to support the coming trial with greater courage; so, calling up all of pride with which her delicacy might arm her, and all of fortitude which her philosophy had taught, she awaited with patience the expected moment.

She sat on a low sopha; her dress was dark; the vest, formed of purple silk, and fastened at her waist by a silken cord, fell in large folds to her feet; a cloak of sables hung on her shoulder; and her golden hair, partly clustered on her neck, and partly confined by a ribbon, covered with its ringlets her fair brow. When she heard the step of Castruccio approaching, / she became pale; her very lips lost their colour; and her serious eyes, shorn of their beams, were as the deep azure of midnight, where the stars shine not.[a] He entered. When he

---

[a] From 'her serious' is drafted in adds. e. 17, p. 231 rev.

had seen her last, he had been haughty and imperious; but now his manner was all softness, gentleness and humility; so that, when he spoke, in spite of the high nobility of her spirit, her eyes were weighed down by the unshed tears.

"Countess," he said, "pardon me, if my intrusion upon you appear ungenerous; but persons, that, like myself, are occupied in the affairs of government, are apt to leave too much to underlings, who never do or say that which it were exactly right to have said or done. Your future peace is too dear to me, to permit me to hear from any but yourself what are your wishes and your expectations."

He paused, waiting for an answer, and fixed on her his soft and full eyes, which seemed to read her soul, while a gentle smile of compassion and love played on his lips. After collecting her thoughts, she raised her eyes to reply, and met those of her former lover, whose expression / seemed fraught with all that affection he had once vowed to her. She was unable to speak; but then, angry at her own weakness, she rallied her spirits, and replied, – "I have but one favour to intreat, which is your permission to remove instantly to Florence."

"Your wishes in this respect, Madonna, are commands; yet I could have desired that you would consent to stay awhile in Lucca. I know the judgement that you have formed of me; you look on me as a wild beast ravenous for blood, as a lawless monster, despoiled of all the feelings of humanity. I could have desired that you would stay awhile, to find and to avow your injustice; I could wish you to stay, until the deep respect, and if you will permit the word, the love I feel for you, should make such impression on your heart, that you would allow me to assuage those sorrows of which I have unhappily been the cause."

"My lord, do not speak thus to me," replied Euthanasia, with a voice which at first trembled, but which gained firmness as she continued; "We are divided; there is an eternal barrier between us now, sealed by the blood of / those miserable people who fell for me. I cannot, I do not love you; and, if a most frivolous and reprehensible weakness could make me listen now, the ghosts of the slain would arise to divide us. My lord, I cannot reason with you, I can hardly speak; the blood of the slaughtered, the tears of the survivors, the scathed ruins of my castle, are all answers, louder than words, to your present offers. If these have been your acts of courtship, pardon me if I say, that I had rather woo the lion in his den to be my husband, than become the bride of a conqueror. But this is useless cavilling, painful to both of us; it awakens in me the indignation I would fain repress; and it may kindle resentment in your heart, which is already too apt to be inflamed with that sentiment. You came, you say, to learn my wishes; you have now heard them; let us part; we part in that peace every Christian believer owes to his brother; I forgive you from my inmost heart; do not you hate me; and thus farewell."

"You forgive me, Euthanasia? Is then your soul so pure? me, who indeed have grievously / wronged you; and, however necessary my actions have been, yet have they been destructive to you. But, if indeed you forgive me, and part in

223

Christian amity, allow me once more to take your hand, that I may know that it is not a mere form of words, but that you express a feeling of the heart."

Euthanasia held out her hand, which he took in both his, and holding it thus, he said: "Hear me, my loved girl; you whom alone in the world I have ever loved. You despise, repulse, and almost hate me; and yet, God knows, I still cherish you as tenderly, as when we told each other's love-tale first in yonder unhappy castle. I do not ask you to love me, you cannot; – but you are still young, very young, Euthanasia; and fortune yet may have many changes in store for you. Remember, that, through them all, I am your friend; and if ever in any misery you want a protector, one to save and preserve you, Castruccio, the neglected, mistaken, but most faithful Castruccio, will ever be ready to use his arm and his power in your service. Now, Euthanasia, farewel." /

"Oh God!" cried the unhappy girl, moved to her inmost heart, "could you not have spared me this? leave me; farewel for ever!"

He kissed her hand, and left her; while she, her delicate frame yielding under the many emotions she experienced, sank almost lifeless on the couch. She had suffered much, and borne up through all. But this last interview overcame her: her health, which had been weakened by watching, and agitation, and tears, now entirely gave way. A fever followed, – delirium, and utter deprivation of strength. The disease seemed to feed on her very vitals; and death already tainted her cheek with his fingers. But youth, and a constitution, nourished and strengthened among mountains, and healthful exertions of body and mind, saved her; and, after a confinement of several months, she again crept forth, to see the sun of spring smile on his children, who laughingly welcomed his genial beams.

Where during this time was the prophetess of Ferrara?

END OF VOLUME II. /

VALPERGA:

OR, THE

LIFE AND ADVENTURES

OF

CASTRUCCIO,

PRINCE OF LUCCA.

BY THE AUTHOR OF "FRANKENSTEIN."

IN THREE VOLUMES.

VOL. III.

LONDON:

PRINTED FOR G. AND W. B. WHITTAKER,

AVE-MARIA-LANE.

1823.

*The politics
are good in
this volume
comparatively.*

VALPERGA

CHAPTER I.

The Witch of the Forest.

When Bindo had been released by the command of Castiglione from the hands of the Lucchese soldiers, he fled across the country; and, possessed with horror and despair at the issue of all his predictions, hastened to the only human being to whom he ever spoke his real sentiments, or in whom he placed any confidence.

To the north of Lucca, where the mountains rise highest, and the country is most wild, there was, at the period those people lived concerning whom I write, an immense ilex wood, which covered the Apennines, and was lost to / sight in the grey distance, and among the folds and declivities of the hills. In this forest there lived a witch; she inhabited a cottage built partly of trunks of trees, partly of stones, and which partly was inclosed by the side of the mountain against which it leaned.[a] This hut was very old; that part of it which was built of stone was covered with moss, lichens and wall-flowers, whose beauty and scent appeared alien to the gloom around; but, amidst desolation and horror, Nature loves to place the lovely and excellent, that man, viewing the scene, may not forget that she, the Mother, dwells every where. The trees were covered with ivy, many of them hollow and decaying, while around them the new sprouts arose, and refreshed the eye with an appearance of youth. On a stone near the cabin door sat the witch; she was very old; none knew how old: men, verging on decrepitude, remembered their childish fears of her; and they all agreed that formerly she appeared more aged and decrepid than now. She was bent nearly double; there was no flesh on her bones; and the brown and wrinkled skin hung loosely about her cheeks and arms. She was / short, thin and small; her hair was perfectly white, and her red eyes, the only part about her that appeared to have life, glared within their sunken sockets; her voice was cracked and shrill.

---

[a] cf. the situation of the Creature's hovel in *Frankenstein*, vol. II, ch. iii; 'and which partly' is an emendation of 'and partly'.

227

"Well, son," said she, when she saw Bindo arrive, "What news? Are thine, or my predictions most true?"

Bindo threw himself on the ground, and tore his hair with rage, but he answered not a word.

"You would not believe my words," continued she, with a malicious laugh; "but the stars are not truer to their course, than I to fate; tomorrow not one stone will lie upon another of the castle of Valperga."

"This must not be," cried Bindo, starting up furiously; "it shall not be! Are you not a witch? and if you have sold your soul to the devil, will he not obey your will?"

"I sold my soul to the devil!" she replied in a tone, which bordered on a scream; "I tell thee, thou wert happy, if thy soul were as certain to be saved as mine. I rule the spirits, and do not serve them; what can angels do / more? But one thing I cannot do; I cannot impede the star of Castruccio: that must rise."

"Aye, – you are all alike; – you can lame cattle, strangle fowls, and milk cows; but, when power is wanted, you are as weak as this straw. Come, if you are a witch, act as one."

"What would you that I should do? I can cover the sky with clouds; I can conjure rain and thunder from the blue empyrean; the Serchio will obey me; the winds from the north and the south know my call; the mines of the earth are subject to me; I can call the dead from their graves, and command the spirits of air to obey me. The fortunes of men are known to me; but man himself is not to be ruled, unless he consent to obey. Castruccio is set above men; his star is highest in the sky, and the aspect of the vast heaven favours him; I can do nothing with him."

"Then farewel; and may the curses of hell cling to you, and blight you! I want no conjuror's tricks, – but man shall do for me what the devil cannot." /

"Stay, son," cried the witch; "now you say right; now you are reasonable. Though the star of Castruccio be high, it will fall at last, burst and fall like a dead stick upon the ground. Be it for us to hasten this moment; man may help you, and be that your task; watch all that happens, and tell me all; let no act or word escape your notice; and something will happen which I may wind to my purpose. We have both vowed to pursue the prince of Lucca to the death. There are no means now; but some will arise, and we shall triumph. Keep in mind one thing; do not let your mistress depart. I know that she desires to go to Florence; she must remain at Lucca, until the destined time be fulfilled; be it your task to keep her."

"I do not like these slow measures," replied the Albinois sullenly; "and, methinks, his waxen image at the fire, or his heart stuck full of pins, might soon rid the earth of him; surely if curses might kill a man, he were dead; tell me in truth is he not a fiend? Is he not one of the spirits of the damned housed in flesh to torment us?" /

"Seek not to enquire into the mysteries of our art. You tell your wishes; I direct their accomplishment; – obey – you can do no more. When death, the mower, is in the field, few plants are tough enough to turn the edge of his scythe: yet Castruccio is one of these few; and patience and prudence alone can effect his fall. Watch every thing; report all to me; and beware that the countess leaves not Lucca; our power is gone, when she goes."

Such was the scene that immediately followed the destruction of the castle of Valperga. Bindo had hitherto loved his mistress, with an affection whose energy had never been called into action; but he loved her, as the lioness in the desert loves her whelps, who day by day feeds them in peace, but, when aroused by the hunters, will defend them to the last drop of blood. He loved her, as we all love, and know not how fervently, until events awake our love to the expression of its energy. He had seldom thought upon Castruccio; when he came frequently to Valperga, and he saw his mistress happy in his visits, then these visits also made the Albinois joyful; yet he / sympathized too little in the course of daily life, to disapprove of him when he came no more: but, when he sought to injure the sole being whom Bindo loved and reverenced, then a hidden spring suddenly burst forth in the Albinois' mind; and hate, till then unknown, arose, and filled every conduit of his heart, and, mingling its gall with the waters of love, became the first feeling, the prime mover in his soul.

He had long associated with this witch. He felt his defects in bodily prowess; perhaps also he felt the weakness of his reason; and therefore he sought for powers of art, which might overcome strength, and powers of mind, which were denied to the majority of the human species. Bindo was a very favourable subject for the witch to act upon; she deceived him easily, and through his means spread far the fame of her incantations. What made these women pretend to powers they did not possess, incur the greatest perils for the sake of being believed to be what they were not, without any apparent advantage accruing to themselves from this belief? I believe we may find / the answer in our own hearts: the love of power is inherent in human nature; and, in evil natures, to be feared is a kind of power. The witch of the Lucchese forest was much feared; and no one contributed to the spread of this feeling more than Bindo.

She had no interest to preserve Euthanasia, or to destroy Castruccio; but she must feign these feelings in order to preserve her power over the Albinois. She resolved however not to be drawn into any action which might attract the hatred of the prince; for she knew him indeed to be a man out of her sphere, a man who went to mass, and told his beads as the church directed him, and who would have no hesitation in consigning to what he would call, condign punishment, all such as dealt with evil spirits, infernal drugs, and diabolical craft.

Bindo saw nothing of the motives which actuated her; and he really believed that the star of Castruccio had the ascendant: so after the first ebullitions of despair were calmed, he waited, with the patience of cherished hate, for the events which the witch told him might / in the course of time bring about the sequel he so much desired.

229

He had made calculations, and cast lots upon the fate of Valperga, whose results were contrary to the enunciations of the witch. These had proved false; and, when time had calmed his feelings, this disappointment itself made him cling more readily to the distant, but as he hoped, surer promises of the witch, and build upon her words the certain expectation of the overthrow of Castruccio, and the restoration of Valperga in more than its original splendour. He returned to Euthanasia, and watched by her sick chamber, as the savage mother of a wild brood tends upon her expiring young; the fear of losing her by this sickness, at once exasperated him against the man whom he believed to be the cause of the mischief, and by the mightiness of his fear filled him with that calm which is the consummation of wretchedness. He neither ate nor slept; his existence appeared a miracle. But his mistress recovered; and his exhausted frame was now as much shaken with joy, as before with grief; yet, pale, emaciated, trembling / as it were on the edge of life, but still living, he survived all these changes.

The summer advanced; and still Euthanasia remained at Lucca. A number of slight circumstances caused this: her health was yet weak; and her pale cheek and beamless eye shewed that life hardly sat firm upon his throne within her frame; they were menaced with a peculiarly hot season, and it was scarcely judged right that she should expose herself to the excessive heat of a Florentine summer. Lauretta also, her cousin, promised to accompany her, if she would delay her journey until autumn; so she consented to remain, although in truth she felt Lucca to be to her as a narrow prison, and cherished the hope of finding healthful feelings, and some slight return of happiness, at Florence. Yet the joyless state which was now her portion, was one reason why she cared not to change; it bred within her an indolence of feeling, that loved to feed upon old cares, rather than upon new hopes. A sense of duty, rather than any other sentiment, made her wish to remove; she believed, that she owed it to herself to revive / from the kind of moral death she had endured, and to begin as it were a fresh life with new expectations. But we are all such creatures of habit, that we cling rather to sorrows which have been our companions of old, than to a new-sprung race[a] of pleasures, whose very names perhaps are unknown to us.

Euthanasia loved to sit in the desolate garden of her palace, and to moralize in her own mind, when she saw a tender rose embraced and choked by evil weeds that grew in strength about it; or sometimes to visit the tower of her palace, and to look towards the rock where the castle of Valperga had once stood, now a heap of ruins. Could she endure to look upon the formless mass which had before constituted her shelter and home? where had stood the hall within whose atmosphere she had grown to womanhood; where she had

---

[a] 'new-sprung race' is a buried quotation from a then well-known drawing-room ballad, 'The Nabob' (c.1780) also cited in *Lodore*.

experienced all the joys that her imagination and heart (storehouses of count-less treasure) could bestow? Yet that was all gone, and she must begin life anew: she prayed for her father's spirit to inspire her with courage; but her mind was too subtle and delicate in its / feelings, to forget its antient attach-ments. There are some souls, bright and precious, which, like gold and silver, may be subdued by the fiery trial, and yield to new moulds; but there are others, pure and solid as the diamond, which may be shivered to pieces, yet in every fragment retain their indelible characteristics.

"I can never change." she thought, "never become other than I am. And yet I am told that this obstinate sorrow is weakness, and that the wise and good, like strong plants, shoot up with fresh vigour, when cut down even to the root. It may be so; and so it may perhaps be with me: but as yet I feel all dead, except pain, and that dwells for ever within me. Alas! life, and the little it contains, is not worth the misery I endure; its best joys are fleeting shadows; its griefs ought to be the same; and those are true philosophers, who trample on both, and seek in the grave for a wisdom and happiness, which life cannot bring us.

"Why was I born to feel sorrow? Why do I not die, that pain may expire with me? / And yet I now speak as a presumptuous caviller, unread in the lessons of the wise, and who vainly blunders over and misquotes their best learning. Life has more in it than we think; it is all that we have, all that we know.

"Life is all our knowledge, and our highest praise is to have lived well. If we had never lived, we should know nothing of earth, or sky, or God, or man, or delight, or sorrow. When our Creator bestowed on us this gift, he gave us that which is beyond all words precious; for without it our apparent forms would have been a blind atom in the mass, our souls would never have been. We live; and we learn all that is good, and see all that is beautiful; our will is called into action, our minds expand like flowers, till, overworn, they fade; if we did not live, we should know nothing of all this; and if we do not live well, we reap sorrow alone.

"What do we know of heroes and sages, but that they lived? Let us not spurn therefore this sum and summit of our knowledge, but, cherishing it, make it so appear that we value, and in some degree deserve, the gift of / life, and the many wonders that accompany it."

Euthanasia suffered much during the summer months; and all that she heard of Castruccio turned the fount of wholesome tears to drops of agony. He had in truth become a tyrant. He did not slay his thousands like Ezzelin of Padua; but he had received the graft of vain-glory into his soul, and he now bore the fruits. He put to death remorselessly those whom he suspected, and would even use torture, either to discover other victims, or to satisfy his desire of revenge. Several circumstances of this kind happened during this summer, which made Euthanasia more miserable than words or tears could express. If she saw his enemies, they uttered deep curses on his cruelty; if she saw those who had formerly been his friends, their talk was filled with bitter sarcasms on his ingratitude, and careless coldness of heart.[a] That heart had once been the garden of virtue, where all good qualities sprung up and flourished, like odorous and delicately painted flowers; but now ambition had become its gardener, and the weed-overgrown / inclosure of Euthanasia's palace was but a slight symbol of all of cruel and treacherous that sprung up there, which allowed no rose to blow, and hid the blooms of the jessamine in the coarse and broad leaves of worthless brambles. Sometimes she thanked Providence that she had not become the wife of this man: but it was a bitter thankfulness. She had not been wedded to him by the church's rites; but her soul, her thoughts, her fate, had been married to his; she tried to loosen the chain that bound them eternally together, and felt that the effort was fruitless: if he were evil, she must weep; if his light-hearted selfishness allowed no room for remorse in his own breast, humiliation and sorrow was doubly her portion, and this was her destiny for ever.

His military exploits of this year rather consisted in the slow laying of foundation-stones, than were distinguished by any peculiar glory. The Florentine army retreated in trepidation before him; he took several castles, made several new alliances, and consolidated more and more the power which he hoped one day to put to a mighty purpose.[b] Desire of dominion / and lordship was the only passion that now had much power in his soul; he had forgotten Euthanasia; or if he remembered her, he called her a peevish girl, and wasted no further thought upon her.

The summer had been tremendously hot; and all the fields were parched, and the earth baked and cracked from the long drouth. These were all signs of a wet autumn; and hardly had Euthanasia determined on her journey to Florence, before it was stopped by tremendous rains and tempests, that deluged the earth, and disturbed the sky. The lightning became as a shaft in the hands of an experienced warrior; so true it seemed to its aim, and destroying so many with its subtle fire: and the thunder, reverberating along the hills, sent up to heaven the shout, which proclaimed the triumph and desolation of its precursor. Then came the rain; and the earth gladly received these tokens of heaven's love, which blessed her with fertility. The torrents roared down the hills; and the rivers, no longer restrained within their banks, rose, and deluged the plain, filling even the streets of Lucca with water. /

Bindo looked on all this labour of the elements with a mind hovering between pleasure and fear. He believed that the witch of the forest had caused this inundation, to impede the journey of the countess; but, thinking thus, he trembled at the power she possessed, and at the strange company of unseen

---

[a] Castruccio's ingratitude at this point in his career is mentioned in Sismondi (ch. xxx) with special reference to the Pisans.

[b] 'This year' refers to 1321; the alliances were made among the Ghibellines of Milan, Piacenza, Parma, Pisa and Arezzo (Sismondi, ch. xxx).

spirits, which thus, unknown to mortals, interfere with their destinies. The devil, he knew, was called prince of the air; but there is a wide difference between our belief of an hearsay, and the *proof* which he now thought was presented to him. When he repaired at the mysterious hour of midnight to a running stream, and saw, as the witch uttered her incantations, and lashed the waters with her rod, – that a tempestuous wind arose from the south, and the dark clouds among which the lightnings played, advanced over their heads, and then the rain in quick big drops, accompanied by hail, fell on the earth;[a] – when he saw this, his limbs trembled, his heart beat quick with fear; he dared not cross himself, nor mutter a *pater-noster*; and, if love and hate had not possessed him so entirely, he would never have ventured again to witness the magical powers of his friend. /

A cold and early winter followed the flood, and froze the waters before they retreated from the inundated fields. For many years so terrible a season had not been known in Italy; and, in the Lucchese states particularly, it occasioned a great loss of fruit-trees and vines. The mountains were covered with snow; the torrents were arrested in their course by the subtle nets which winter cast over them; it was a strange sight for an Italian to see. "And this," thought Euthanasia, "is what the Transalpines mean, when they talk of the fearful cold of winter. Oh! indeed, no hunter is like him, when he comes down from the north, bringing frost, his bride, along with him; he hunts the leaves from the trees, and destroys the animals which inhabit the earth, even in their holds and fastnesses. He casts bonds upon the rivers and streams; and even the 'sapless foliage of the ocean,'[b] and the mighty monsters and numberless spawn that rove through its wastes, are all subdued by his fierce and resistless ravages."

Thus she thought, as she saw the country, late so beautiful, the Earth, lovely as a young mother nursing her only care, now as wild and / forlorn as that mother if she be ruthlessly bereft of her infant. The fields were hardened by frost; and the flood lay moveless and white over the plain; the hills were covered with snow. It was a grievous change from the smiles of summer; but it did not last long; and thaw quickly reversed the scene. The earth was again alive; and the rivers and floods again filled the air with sound. Euthanasia resolved to wait only until the season should be somewhat more advanced, to make her long delayed journey to Florence. /

---

[a] From notes on witches' rain-making rites taken from an unidentified source (in adds. e. 17, p. 122 rev.).

[b] P. B. Shelley, 'Ode to the West Wind', l. 40. The imagery of the onset of winter and of the weed-choked garden is reminiscent of his 'The Sensitive Plant', published in 1820 with the 'Ode'.

CHAPTER II.

Beatrice in the Inquisition at Lucca. – Freed by Castruccio, at the Intercession of Euthanasia.

While Euthanasia yet remained at Lucca in this uncertain manner, a circumstance occurred which caused her to suspend the preparations for her journey. Late one night (it was nearly twelve o'clock), the visit of a stranger was announced; a man, they said, so wrapt up in his capuchin, that his physiognomy could not be distinguished. Why did Euthanasia's heart beat fast, and the colour desert her warm lips? What could she hope or fear? The man was admitted, and one glance sufficed to satisfy her curiosity, and to quiet her trembling expectation. He was one of the meaner class; and, when he threw back his cloak, Euthanasia perceived that he was an entire / stranger to her; but there was a kindness, a rough sensibility in his face, that pleased her, and she gently enquired what he had to say to her.

"Noble countess, I come on a work of charity, which would ruin me for ever if my superiors were to discover it. I am the jailor of the Lucchese prison; and this morning the Dominican inquisitors put under my custody a Paterin woman*, whom it would move any soul but theirs to behold. She has touched me with the greatest pity by her tears and heart-breaking intreaties: she denies her heresy, and says that you can prove her faith; but she must see you first; and I, at peril of all that I am worth, am come to conduct you to her dungeon, for I can admit you only by night. Surely you will come; poor thing, she is very young and fearful, and is now lying on / the floor of her prison panting with terror and expectation."

"Unfortunate creature! Did she tell you her name?"

"She says that you do not know it; but she intreats you to remember a

---

* These heretics were long a principal subject of hostility to the Inquisition; and in 1290 a particular community was erected at Florence by San Pietro di Verona, for the express purpose of their extermination.[a]

    [a] The Paterini, a sect of Manicheans known also as Albigensians or Cathars, gradually spread into Western Europe from the Eastern Church after persecutions of the ninth century. Sismondi presents their chief tenets as: that the creator of the material universe is an evil spirit; that man is a fallen angel; that the individual is free to investigate religious questions. For him they prefigure the Puritan wing of Protestantism. Muratori is less sympathetic (Sismondi, ch. xiii; Muratori, III, diss. 60, p. 255; noted in Ab. Dep. e. 274, p. 96); the 'particular community' was called the Milizia Sacra (Lastri, I, p. 94; noted in adds. e. 17, p. 225 rev.).

pilgrim girl, whom you once received at your castle, and whom you pitied; a sun-burnt, way-worn creature who said that she was on the way to Rome."

"I do not recollect; but if she is unhappy, and desires to see me, it is enough, I follow you."

Euthanasia wrapt her capuchin around her, and followed the man through the dark, wet streets of Lucca: the thaw had not yet completed its work; the snow was deep and miry under their feet; while the melting collections of several days dripped, or rather streamed from the house-roofs on their heads: the Libeccio blew a warm, cloud-bringing wind, that made the night so black, that they could not avoid the standing pools that interspersed the streets. At length they arrived at the prison; the jailor entered by a small, low door which he carefully closed after them, and then / struck a light. He led Euthanasia through the bare and mildewed vaults, sometimes unlocking a massy gate, drawing back the harsh bolts which grated with rust and damp; sometimes they emerged into a passage open to the sky, but narrow, with tall black walls about it, which dropt their melted snow with a continual and sullen splash upon the pavement: small, glassless, grated windows looked into these strait passages; these were the holes that admitted light into the dungeons. At length they ascended a small, broken, staircase of wood; and, opening a door at the head of it, and consigning his lamp to the countess, the jailor said: "She is here; comfort her; in two hours I shall come to conduct you back."

Euthanasia entered the prison-chamber, awe-stricken and trembling; for the good ever feel humiliated at the sight of misfortune in others: the poor prisoner was seated crouched in a corner; she looked wildly towards the door; and, seeing Euthanasia, she leaped up, and, throwing herself at her feet, clinging to her knees, and clasping them with convulsive / strength, she cried, "Save me! You alone on earth can save me."

Poor Euthanasia was moved to tears; she raised the sufferer, and, taking her in her arms, tried to soothe her: the prisoner only sobbed, leaning her head upon Euthanasia's hand: "Fear not, you shall be saved; poor sufferer, calm yourself; speak, what would you with me? fear not, no harm shall reach you; I will be your friend."

"Will you indeed – indeed – be my friend? and go to him, and bid him save me? He alone can do it."

"Who? Speak calmly, dearest; pause awhile; reassure yourself, and then speak. Look, you are safe in my arms; I clasp them round you, do not fear!"

The prisoner sunk in Euthanasia's embrace: she was chilled, icy-cold; – and she lay panting, as a bleeding fawn who gazes on its death's wound. The warmth of Euthanasia's arms somewhat restored her; and she said, dividing the entangled strings of her hair with her thin fingers; "You do not remember me, nor / would he; I am as unlike what I was when he saw me, as is the yellow, fallen leaf to the bright-green foliage of May. You do not remember me?"

"Yes, now it flashes on my memory; are you then indeed———" Euthanasia paused; the name of Beatrice hovered on her lips, but a feeling of delicacy prevented her from speaking it: she continued; "Yes, I recollect the pilgrim, your refusal to remain at Valperga, and the deep interest I took in your sorrows."

"You were very, very kind; are you not so now? Will you not go to him, and ask him to order my release?"

"To whom am I to go? and from whom do I come?" asked Euthanasia, half-smiling; for, notwithstanding the prisoner recalled to her memory a scene, which made it appear that she was certainly Beatrice; yet so long had all trace of her been lost, that she wished for some confirmation from her own lips.

"Alas!" replied the unhappy girl, "I would not have him know, if I could help it. Do you think that, if you were to tell him that a poor girl, who five years ago had just attained her / seventeenth year, who was then happy, loving and adored, – who is now pursued for heresy – falsely – or if you will – truly; one very unfortunate, who earnestly implores him as he loves his own soul, to save her; do you not think he would compassionate me?"

"Who? you speak in riddles."

"In riddles! Are you not Euthanasia? You must know whom I mean; why, Antelminelli, – Castruccio."

The prisoner hid her face with her hands. She blushed deeply, and her fast-falling tears trickled through her fingers; Euthanasia blushed also, a tremulous hectic, that quickly vanished, while her companion's cheeks still burned.

"Yes, I will go to him, or to any one on earth to save you. – Yet methinks I had better go to the father-inquisitors; I am known to them, and I think I could as easily move them as the prince; he is careless————"

"Oh! no – no; you must go to him: he knew me once, and surely would compassionate me. Try him first with the echo of my complaints, and a relation of my tears; surely / his eyes, which can look into the soul, would then be dimmed: would they not?"

Euthanasia thought of Leodino; and she was about to reply, that warriors, politicians, and ambitious princes, such as Castruccio, were accustomed to regard with contempt woes like hers. But she hesitated; she would not rob him, whom she had once loved, of the smallest mite of another's praise, however undeserved; besides, she felt that the name of Beatrice alone would move him to compassion, perhaps to remorse. She was therefore silent; and the prisoner continued, with a voice of trembling earnestness, "Try every argument first; but, if he is obdurate, then tell him that he once knew me, – that now my fortunes are changed, – he will guess the cause: yet perhaps he will think wrong, for *that* is not the cause. Tell him I am one Beatrice; – he saw me some years ago at the house of the good bishop of Ferrara."

The poor fallen prophetess now burst into a passion of weeping; she wrung her hands, and tore her hair, while her companion looked on her, unable to restrain her tears. Castruccio / had described his Beatrice, so bright, so ethereal in her loveliness, that it moved Euthanasia's inmost soul to see what a change a very few years had made. Perceiving the blushes and shame of the lost girl, she concealed her knowledge of her tale, and answered only by endeavouring to soothe her, and to assure her of her safety.

"Am I safe? I tell you that I fear, oh! how much I fear! I am very young; I was once happy; but, since that, I have suffered beyond human utterance; yet I dread death; and, more than all, do I fear pain. They call me a heretic; aye," (and her dark eyes beamed fiercely) "I am one; I do not belong to their maudlin creed; I feel my wrongs, and I dare curse——— But, hush, not so loud. – You pardon me, do you not? Alas! if you turn against me, they seize on me, tear me, burn me!"

The two hours had swiftly passed, while Beatrice thus wept with alternate passion. The jailor came to reconduct Euthanasia; but Beatrice clung to her, clasping her neck, and intwining her fingers in her long thick hair. "No! no! you must not go!" she cried; / "I shall die, if I am again left alone. Oh! before you came, I sometimes felt as if I did not know where I was, and madness seemed to fall on me: you are good, consolatory, kind; you must not leave me."

"Then I cannot see the prince; I cannot intercede for your liberation."

"But that is many hours hence, and the comfortable day-light will be come; now it is quite dark; hark to the splashing water, and the howling of the Libeccio; I had forgotten all that; and now they come upon me with tenfold horror; do not leave me!"

Euthanasia could hardly distinguish the suppliant's features by the light of the jailor's small lamp; but she saw her eyes bright with tears, and felt her bosom throb against her own; again she strove to console her; reason was thrown away; – when the jailor urged his, her own, every one's safety – she shook her head.

"I thought you were kind; but you are not: my cheeks are pale with fear; put up your lamp to them that you may see. She can go early, the moment day dawns, – indeed she shall go then, but now she must not." /

Euthanasia tore herself away; though her heart was pierced by the wild shriek of Beatrice, as she threw herself on the floor. The jailor led her through the melancholy passages of the prison, and then along the wet streets, until she reached her home: and she retired to meditate during the remaining hours of night on the words she should employ in her representations to Castruccio the following morning.

The expectation of this meeting flushed her cheeks, and made her deep eyes beam, while every limb trembled. She had not seen him so long that his assumed power, his tyrannies, and mean politics, were lost in her recollection; she felt as if she should again see him honest, passion-breathing, and beautiful, as when they took sweet counsel together at Valperga. Valperga! that was now a black and hideous ruin, and he the author of its destruction. But she thought, "This is a dream; – I shall see him, and it will vanish; there is a coil wound

237

round me of sorrow and distrust, which will snap beneath his smile, and free me, – I shall see him!

"Why do I think of myself? I go to free / this poor girl, whom he has wronged, and to whom he belongs far more than to me; this unhappy Beatrice, who sheds tears of agony in her dungeon. I am nothing; I go as nothing; would that he should not recognize me! I go a suppliant for another, and I must tame my looks: they are not proud; but I must teach them humility; I must school my heart not to speak, not to think of itself – I go for her; and, having obtained my request, I will come away, forgetful that I am any thing."

Day dawned; day, cold, wet, and cloudy, but ever cheerful to one weighed down by the sense of darkness and inaction: day did not dawn this dreary winter morning, until seven o'clock, and the period had arrived when it was fitting that Euthanasia should seek Castruccio. She threw a veil over her shining hair, while she hid her form in a rich cloak of sables; then she stole out alone; for she could not endure that any one should know of this strange visit. When she arrived at the *Palazzo del Governo*, her rich attire and distinguished mien won her easy entrance, and she penetrated to the cabinet of the prince. /

Her heart beat audibly; she had entered with rapid, though light steps; now she paused; and, as it were gathering up the straggling feelings of her mind, she endeavoured to bind them in a firm knot; she resolved to calm herself, to still the convulsive motion of her lips, to remember nothing but Beatrice. She entered; Antelminelli was alone; he was at a table reading a paper, and a smile of light derision played upon his features; he raised on her his dark, piercing eyes, and seeing a lady before him, he rose; in a moment Euthanasia was self-possessed and resolved; and casting back her cloak, and throwing aside her veil, her eyes lifted up, yet not fixed on him, she began in her silver voice to say, "My lord, I come———"

But he was too much thunderstruck to listen; his cheeks glowed with pleasure; all the anger and indifference he had nourished vanished in her presence, and he broke forth in a torrent of wonder and thanks.

She waved her hand, – "Do not thank me, but listen; for I come on a message, an errand of charity; and if you can, hear me, and forget who it is that speaks." /

He smiled, and replied: "Certainly it were easy not to see the sun when it shines: but, whatever your errand may be, speak it not yet; – if you come to make a request, I shall grant it instantly, and then you will go; but pause awhile first, that I may look on you; it is a whole year since I saw you last; you are changed, you are paler, – your eyes – but you turn away from me, as if you were angry."

"I am not angry – but I am nothing. – There is a heretic, at least a girl accused of heresy, confined in your prisons, whom I wish you to free, and, for the love of Heaven, not by the shortest delay to add another moment of sorrow to her heap: she has suffered much."

"A heretic! that is beyond my jurisdiction; I do not meddle with religion."

"Yes you do; – you see priests every day: but I intreat you not to oblige me to argue with you; listen to me a few moments, and I shall say no more. She is very unfortunate, and fears death and pain with a horror that almost deprives her of reason; she is young; and it is piteous to see one scarcely more than twenty years of age, under the fangs of these / bloodhounds; she was once happy; alas! pity her, since she feels to the very centre of her heart the change from joy to grief."

"Yet no harm will happen to her, at most a few months' imprisonment: if she dread death and pain, she will of course recant and be freed; what will she suffer for so short a time?"

"Fear; the worst of evils, far worse than death. I would fain persuade you to throw aside this hard-heartedness, which is not natural to you; moments are years, if they are lengthened out by pain; every minute that she lives in her dungeon is to her a living death of agony;[a] but I will tell you her name, – at her request I wished to conceal it: but that will win you, if you are not already won by the sweet hope of saving one who suffers torments you can never know."

"Euthanasia, do not look so gloomily; I am not thinking of your heretic; I hesitate, that I may keep you here: you have your will; I will never refuse a request of yours."

A smile of fleeting disdain passed over her countenance. "Nay, when you know who / she is, you may grant my prayer for her own sake. I come from Beatrice, the daughter of Wilhelmina of Bohemia."

If the ghost of the poor prophetess had suddenly arisen, it could not have astounded Castruccio more, than to hear her name thus spoken by Euthanasia, coupled with the appellations of heretic and prisoner. The tide of his life ebbed; and, when it flowed again, he thought of the celestial Beatrice, her light step, her almost glorious presence; and the memory of her pale cheek and white lips when he last saw her, thrilled his heart. Years had passed since then; what had she suffered? What was she? A heretic? Alas! she was the daughter of Wilhelmina, the nursling of Magfreda, the ward of a leper, the adopted child of the good bishop of Ferrara.

Euthanasia saw the great confluence of passions, which agitated Castruccio, and made him alternately pale and red; she was silent, her quiet eyes beaming upon him in compassion; for a long time his heart could not find a voice, but at length he spoke, – "Hasten! hasten! free her, take her to you! Euthanasia, / you are the angel itself of charity; you know all her sad story – all that relates to me; calm her, console her, make her herself again, – poor, poor Beatrice!"

"Farewell then; I go, – send one of your officers with the order; I will hasten to her, as quickly as you can wish."

---

[a] From 'moments' to 'agony' is a free adaptation of P. B. Shelley, *Julian and Maddalo* (1824), ll. 415–19.

"Yet pause, stay one moment; shall I never see you again? You have cast me off utterly; yet, I pray you, be happy. Why should you be pale and sorrowful? you have other friends; must all that love me, mourn? Surely I am not a devil, that all I touch must wither. Beware! tear the veil from your heart; read, read its inmost secrets, the eternal words imprinted in its core; you do not despise me, you love me, – be mine."

The pale cheek of Euthanasia was flushed, her eyes flashed fire, – "Never! tie myself to tyranny, to slavery, to war, to deceit, to hate? I tell thee I am as free as air. But I am hurried far beyond the bounds I prescribed for myself, and now not a word more."

"Yes, one word more; not of yourself, wild enthusiast, but of Beatrice. I destroyed her; not that I knew what I did; but heedlessly, / foolishly, destroyed her; do you then repair my work; I would give half my soul that she should be as when I first saw her. You have heard a part of her story, and you will now perhaps learn those sufferings which she has endured since we parted; it is doubtless a strange and miserable tale; but do you be the ministering angel of mercy and love to her."

Sorrow and even humiliation were marked on Castruccio's countenance; Euthanasia looked at it, almost for the first time since she had entered; she sighed softly, and said nearly in a whisper, "Alas! that you should no longer be what you once were!"

Pride now returned and swelled every feature of Castruccio; "Enough, enough: whatever wine of life I drain, I mingled it myself. Euthanasia, if we never meet again, remember, I am content; can you be more?"

Euthanasia said not a word; she vanished, her bright presence was gone; and Castruccio, to whom, as to the fallen arch-angel, that line might be applied,

> Vaunting aloud, though rack'd with deep despair,[a] /

tearless, his lips pressed together, sat recalling to mind her words and looks, until, remembering his boast, he looked up with angry defiance; and, shaking from his heart the dew of tenderness he plunged amidst the crowd where he commanded, where his very eye was obeyed.

Euthanasia hastened to the prison, where the kind-hearted jailor led her with a face of joyful triumph to the dungeon of Beatrice; the poor thing was sleeping, the traces of tears were on her cheeks (for like a child she had cried herself to sleep), and several times she started uneasily. Euthanasia made a sign to the jailor to be silent, and knelt down beside her, looking at her countenance, once so gloriously beautiful; the exquisite carving of her well shaped eyelids, her oval face, and pointed chin still shewed signs of what she had been; the rest was lost. Her complexion was sun-burnt, her hands very thin and

---

[a] *Paradise Lost*, I. 126 (with 'though' for 'but').

yellow, and care had already marked her sunken cheeks and brow with many lines; her jet black hair was mingled with grey; her long tresses had been / cut, and now reached only to her neck; while, strait and thin, they were the shadow merely of what they had been; her face, her whole person was emaciated, worn and faded. She awoke and beheld the eyes of Euthanasia, like heaven itself, clear and deep, gazing on her. – "Arise, poor sufferer, you are free!"

Beatrice looked wildly; then, starting up, she clapped her hands in a transport of joy, she threw herself at the feet of her deliverer, she embraced the jailor, she was frantic. "Free! free!" for some time she could repeat no other word. At length she said, "Pardon me; yesterday I was rude and selfish; I tormented and reproached you, who are all kindness. And you, excellent man, you will forgive me, will you not? What was it that I feared? Now that I am going to leave my dungeon, methinks it is a good cell enough, and I could stay here always well content; it is somewhat dark and cold, but one can wrap oneself up, and shut one's eyes, and fancy one's self under the sun of heaven."

She continued prattling, and would have / said much more, but that Euthanasia with gentle force drew her from the dungeon, out of the gloomy prison; and they hastened to her palace, where Beatrice was quickly refreshed by a bath and food. But, when the first joy of liberation was passed, she sunk to melancholy: she would not speak, but sat listlessly, and her tears fell in silence. Euthanasia tried to comfort her; but many days passed, during which she continued sullen and untractable.

In the mean time Euthanasia received several billets from Castruccio, with earnest enquiries concerning the welfare of this poor girl. "God knows," he wrote, "what has happened to this unfortunate being since we parted. My heart is agonized, not only for what she suffers, but for what she may have suffered. She is now, they say, a heretic, a Paterin, one who believes in the ascendancy of the evil spirit in the world; poor insane girl! Euthanasia, for her soul's sake, and for mine which must answer for hers, reason with her, and convert her; be to her as an affectionate sister, an angel of peace and pardon. I leave the guidance / of her future destiny to your judgement: but do not lose sight of her. What do I ask of you? And what right have I to bring upon you the burthen of my faults? But you are good, and will forgive me." /

241

CHAPTER III.

Beatrice, her Creed, and her Love.

Euthanasia was meditating on this letter, when Beatrice entered, and sat down beside her. She took her hand, and kissed it, and then said, "How can you forgive my ingratitude? I am self-willed, sullen, and humorous;[a] alas! sometimes the memory of the evils I have suffered presses on me, and I forget all my duties. Duties! until I knew you I had none; for five years my life has been one scene of despair: you cannot tell what a fall mine was."

"Forget, I do intreat you, poor sufferer, all your past unhappiness; forget every thing that you once were."

"Aye, you say right; I must forget every thing, or to be what I am must torture me to despair. Poor, misled, foolish, insensate Beatrice! I can accuse myself alone for my many / ills; myself, and that power who sits on high, and scatters evil like dew upon the earth, a killing, blighting honey dew."

"Hush! my poor girl, do not talk thus; indeed I must not have you utter these sentiments."

"Oh! let me speak: before all others I must hide my bursting feelings, deep, deep. Yet for one moment let me curse!"

Beatrice arose; she pointed to heaven; she stood in the same attitude, as when she had prophesied to the people of Ferrara under the portico of the church of St. Anna; but how changed! Her form thin; her face care-worn; her love-formed lips withered; her hands and arms, then so round and fair, now wrinkled and faded; her eyes were not the same; they had lost that softness which, mingling with their fire, was as something wonderful in brilliancy and beauty; they now, like the sun from beneath a thunder-cloud, glared fiercely from under her dark and scattered hair that shaded her brow: but even now, as in those times, she spoke with tumultuous eloquence:

"Euthanasia, you are much deceived; you / either worship a useless shadow, or a fiend in the clothing of a god. Listen to me, while I announce to you the eternal and victorious influence of evil, which circulates like air about us, clinging to our flesh like a poisonous garment, eating into us, and destroying us. Are you blind, that you see it not? Are you deaf, that you hear no groans? Are you insensible, that you feel no misery? Open your eyes, and you will behold all

---

[a] Subject to changes of mood.

of which I speak, standing in hideous array before you. Look around. Is there not war, violation of treaties, and hard-hearted cruelty? Look at the societies of men; are not our fellow creatures tormented one by the other in an endless circle of pain? Some shut up in iron cages, starved and destroyed; cities float in blood, and the hopes of the husbandman are manured by his own mangled limbs: remember the times of our fathers, the extirpation of the Albigenses; – the cruelties of Ezzelin, when troops of the blind, and the lame, and the mutilated, the scum of his prisons, inundated the Italian states. Remember the destruction of the templars. Did you never glance in thought into the tower of famine of / Ugolino; or into the hearts of the armies of exiles, that each day the warring citizens banish from their homes? Did you never reflect on the guilty policy of the Popes, those ministers of the reigning king of heaven? Remember the Sicilian vespers; the death of the innocent Conradin; the myriads whose bones are now bleached beneath the sun of Asia: they went in honour of His name, and thus He rewards them.[a]

"Then reflect upon domestic life, on the strife, hatred and uncharitableness, that, as sharp spears, pierce one's bosom at every turn; think of jealousy, midnight murders, envy, want of faith, calumny, ingratitude, cruelty, and all which man in his daily sport inflicts upon man. Think upon disease, plague, famine, leprosy, fever, and all the aching pains our limbs suffer withal; visit in thought the hospital, the lazar house; Oh! surely God's hand is the chastening hand of a father, that thus torments his children! His children? his eternal enemies! look, I am one! He created the seeds of disease, maremma,[b] thirst, want; he created man, – that most wretched of slaves; oh! know you not / what a wretch man is? and what a store house of infinite pain is this much-vaunted human soul? Look into your own heart; or, if that be too peaceful, gaze on mine; I will tear it open for your inspection. There is remorse, hatred, grief – overwhelming, mighty and eternal misery. God created me: am I the work of a beneficent being? Oh, what spirit mingled in my wretched frame love, hope, energy, confidence, – to find indifference, to be blasted to despair, to be as

---

[a] In 1215 Pope Innocent III first gave permission to St Dominic to persecute the Albigensians (Sismondi, ch. xiii, ch. xv); in an atrocity of 1259, Ezzelino da Romano punished the Paduans with terrible mutilations, and turned them out of the city to beg (Sismondi, ch. xix); the Order of Knights Templar (founded in 1128 by Crusaders) was, according to Sismondi (ch. xxvi), a model of Christian chivalry. Templars were accused of heresy and immorality, tortured, burnt, and finally suppressed by Pope Clement V between 1307 and 1311, on the orders of Philippe-le-Bel who wanted their wealth. For this cruelty, Dante calls Philip the 'new Pilate', re-crucifying Christ (*Purgatorio*, XX. 91–3); the 'Sicilian Vespers', which resulted in the House of Anjou losing Sicily, was the massacre of 4000 French, men, women and children, during vespers on Easter Monday 1282, by the citizens of Palermo; see also Dante, *Paradiso*, VIII. 74–5; Sismondi (ch xxi and ch. xxii) regarded the vespers as the reaction of the Sicilians to French tyranny and as delayed retribution upon King Charles I of Naples and Sicily (Charles of Anjou) for his execution of Conradin; 'the myriads' refers to the Crusaders.
[b] Pestilential marsh.

weak as the fallen leaf, to be betrayed by all! Now I am changed, – I hate; – my energy is spent in curses, and if I trust, it is to be the more deeply wounded.

"Did not the power you worship create the passions of man; his desires which outleap possibility, and bring ruin upon his head? Did he not implant the seeds of ambition, revenge and hate? Did he not create love, the tempter: he who keeps the key of that mansion whose motto must ever be

Lasciate ogni speranza voi che intrate.[a]

And the imagination, that masterpiece of his malice; that spreads honey on the cup that / you may drink poison; that strews roses over thorns, thorns sharp and big as spears; that semblance of beauty which beckons you to the desart; that apple of gold with the heart of ashes;[b] that foul image, with the veil of excellence; that mist of the maremma, glowing with roseate hues beneath the sun, that creates it, and beautifies it, to destroy you; that diadem of nettles; that spear, broken in the heart! He, the damned and triumphant one, sat meditating many thousand years for the conclusion, the consummation, the final crown, the seal of all misery, which he might set on man's brain and heart to doom him to endless torment; and he created the Imagination. And then we are told the fault is ours; good and evil are sown in our hearts, and ours is the tillage, ours the harvest; and can this justify an omnipotent deity that he permits one particle of pain to subsist in his world? Oh, never.

"I tell thee what; there is not an atom of life in this all-peopled world that does not suffer pain; we destroy animals; – look at your own dress, which a myriad of living creatures / wove and then died; those sables, – a thousand hearts once beat beneath those skins, quenched in the agonies of death to furnish forth that cloak. Yet why not? While they lived, those miserable hearts beat under the influence of fear, cold and famine. Oh! better to die, than to suffer! The whale in the great ocean destroys nations of fish, but thousands live on him and torment him. Destruction is the watchword of the world; the death by which it lives, the despair by which it hopes: oh, surely a good being created all this!

"Let me tell you, that you do ill to ally yourself to the triumphant spirit of evil, leaving the worship of the good, who is fallen and depressed, yet who still lives. He wanders about the world a proscribed and helpless thing, hooted from the palaces of kings, excommunicated from churches; sometimes he wanders into the heart of man, and makes his bosom glow with love and virtue; but so surely as he enters, misfortune, bound to him by his enemy, as a corpse to a living body, enters with him; the wretch who has received his influence, becomes poor, helpless and deserted; happy if he / be not burnt at the stake, whipt with iron, torn with red-hot pincers.

---

[a] 'Abandon Hope all ye who enter here', the inscription over the gate of Hell (*Inferno*, III. 9).
[b] cf. *Paradise Lost*, X. 547–70, where the devils in Hell eat a deceitful semblance of the fruit of the Tree of Knowledge.

"The Spirit of Evil chose a nation for his own; the Spirit of Good tried to redeem that nation from its gulph of vice and misery, and was cruelly destroyed by it; and now, as the masterpiece of the enemy, they are adored together; and he the beneficent, kind and suffering, is made the mediator to pull down curses upon us.

"How quick and secure are the deeds of the evil spirit; how slow and uncertain those of the good! I remember once a good and learned friend of mine telling me, that the country about Athens was adorned by the most exquisite works man had ever produced; marble temples traced with divine sculpture, statues transcending human beauty; the art of man had been exhausted to embellish it, the lives of hundreds of men had been wasted to accomplish it, the genius of the wisest had been employed in its execution; ages had passed, while slowly, year by year, these wonders had been collected; some were almost falling / through exceeding age, while others shone in their first infancy. Well: – a king, Philip of Macedon, destroyed all these in three days, burnt them, razed them, annihilated them.[a] This is the proportionate energy of good and evil; the produce of ages is the harvest of a moment; a man may spend years in curbing his passions, in acquiring wisdom, in becoming an angel in excellence; the brutality of a fellow creature, or the chance of war, may fell him in an instant; and all his knowledge and virtues become blank, as a moonless, starless night.

"Euthanasia, my heart aches, and my spirits flag: I was a poor, simple girl; but I have suffered much; and endurance, and bitter experience have let me into the truth of things; that deceitful veil which is cast over this world, is powerless to hide its deformity from me. I see the cruel heart, which lurks beneath the beatiful skin of the pard; I see the blight of autumn in the green leaves of spring, the wrinkles of age in the face of youth, rust on the burnished iron, storm in the very breast of / calm, sorrow in the heart of joy; all beauty wraps deformity, as the fruit of the kernel; Time opens the shell, the seed is poison."

The eyes of Beatrice shot forth sparks of fire as she poured out this anathema against the creation; her cheeks were fevered with a hectic glow; her voice, sharp and broken, which was sometimes raised almost to a shriek, and sometimes lowered to a whisper, fell on the brain of Euthanasia like a rain of alternate fire and ice; she shrunk and trembled beneath the flood of terror that inundated and confounded her understanding: but the eloquent prophetess of Evil ceased at last, and, pale and exhausted, she sank down; clasping Euthanasia in her arms, she hid her face on her knees, and sobbed, and wept: "Forgive

---

[a] The story is told in Livy, XXXI. xxiv-vi; this is not Philip II of Macedon, father of Alexander, but the almost equally famous Philip V (c.237–c.179 BC), who intrigued with Hannibal against Italy during the 2nd Punic War. The destruction took place in 198 BC. Both Philips present parallels to Castruccio; in summing up his career, Machiavelli compares him to Philip II.

245

me, if I have said that which appears to you blasphemy; I will unveil my heart to you, tell you my sufferings, and surely you will then curse with me the author of my being."

Euthanasia spoke consolation alone; she bade her weep no more; that she need no longer fear or hate; that she might again love, hope and trust; and that she as a tender sister / would sympathize with and support her. The undisciplined mind of poor Beatrice was as a flower that droops beneath the storm; but, on the first gleam of sunshine, raises again its head, even though the hail-stones and the wind might have broken and tarnished its leaves and its tints. She looked up, and smiled; "I will do all that you tell me; I will be docile, good and affectionate; – I will be obedient to your smallest sign, kindest, dearest Euthanasia. Trust me, you shall make me a Catholic again, if you will love me unceasingly for one whole year, and in the mean time I do not die. I am very teachable, very, very tractable; but I have suffered greatly, as one day you will know; for I will tell you every thing. Now, good bye; I am very tired, and I think I shall sleep."

"Sleep then, poor creature; here is a couch ready for you; I will watch near you; and may your dreams be pleasant."

"Give me your hand then; I will hold it while I rest; how small, and white, and soft it is! Look at mine, it is yellow and dry; once it was like yours; I think it was rather smaller, / but never so well shaped; the tips of my fingers and my nails were never dyed by so roseate a tint as this, nor was the palm so silken soft. You are very beautiful, and very good, dear Euthanasia; I hope you are, and will be happy."

Euthanasia kissed the forehead of this child of imagination and misery; and soon she slept, forgetful of all her sufferings. Euthanasia felt deeply interested in her; she felt that they were bound together, by their love for one who loved only himself; she thought over her wild denunciations; and, strange to say, she felt doubly warmed with admiration of the creation, and gratitude towards God, at the moment that Beatrice had painted its defects. She thought of the beauty of the world and the wondrous nature of man, until her mind was raised to an enthusiastic sentiment of happiness and praise. "And you also shall curb your wild thoughts," whispered Euthanasia, as she looked at the sleeping girl; "I will endeavour to teach you the lessons of true religion; and, in reducing the wandering thoughts / of one so lovely and so good, I shall be in part fulfilling my task on the earth."

For several days after this conversation Beatrice became peaceful and mild, saying little, and appearing complacent, almost content; she attended mass, told her beads, and talked of going to confession. Euthanasia was astounded; she was herself so steady in her principles, so firm in opinion and action, slow to change, but resolute having changed, that she was at a loss to understand the variable feelings and swift mutations of the poor, untaught Beatrice.

"Confess!" she repeated; "you promised that I should convert you in a year; but you have already forsaken your Paterin opinions!"

"No, indeed, I have not; but it is of so little consequence; I would please you, dearest, by seeming what I am not; not that I am sure that I am not what you desire. You know, if God is good, he will forgive my errors: if he is evil, I care not to please him; so I shall endeavour to please the virtuous and kind of this world, and you are one of those, my best / friend. Besides, now I think of it, this world seems too beautiful to have been created by an evil spirit; he would have made us all toads, the trees and flowers all mushrooms, and the rocks and mountains would have been huge, formless polypi. Yet there is evil; but I will not trouble myself more about it; you shall form my creed; and, as a lisping infant, with clasped hands, I will repeat my prayers after you."

"Why so, dearest Beatrice? Why will you not recal the creeds of your childhood, as your adoptive parents taught them you? I cannot school you better than they."

"My childhood!" cried the prophetess; her eyes becoming dark and stormy, "what to become again a dupe, a maniac? to fall again, as I have fallen? Cease, cease, in mercy cease, to talk of my childhood; days of error, vanity and paradise! My lessons must all be new; all retold in words signifying other ideas than what they signified during my mad, brief dream of youth. Then faith was not a shadow: it was what these eyes saw; I clutched hope, and found it certainty; I heard the angels of / heaven, and saw the souls of the departed; can I ever see them again?"

"Sweetest and most unfortunate, drive away memory, and take hope to you. Youth is indeed a dream; and, if I spent it not in your extacies, yet believe me I was not then as I am now. I am older than you, and know life better; I have passed the fearful change from dream to reality, and am now calm. I have known all your throes; sometimes indeed they now visit me; but I quench them, cast them aside, tread on them; – so may you."

"Never! never!" replied Beatrice: "I was born for wretchedness. When the fates twined my destiny, they mingled three threads; the first was green hope, the second purple joy, the third black despair; but the two first were very short, and soon came to an end; a dreary line of black alone remains. Yet I would forget all that; and for many days I have been as calm as a bird that broods, rocked on her tree by a gentle wind; full of a quiet, sleepy life. Should this state continue longer, I might become what you wish me to be; but I find my soul awakening, and I fear a / relapse; I fear the return of tears and endless groans. Oh! let me wrap myself round you, my better angel, hope of my life; pour your balmy words upon me; lay your cool, healthful cheek near my burning one, let our pulses beat responsive! Oh! that once I could become less feverish, less wild, less like a dark and crimsoned thunder-cloud, driven away, away, through the unknown wildernesses of sky."

Euthanasia was glad to hear her suffering friend talk, however wildly; for she observed that, when she had exhausted herself in speech, she became calmer and happier; while, if she brooded silently over her cares, she became almost insane through grief. Occasionally she sought consolation in music; there was something magical in her voice, and in the tones she could draw from the organ or the harp: in her days of glory it had been said, that she was taught to sing by angelic instructors; and now those remembered melodies remained, sole relics of her faded honours. The recollection of this sometimes disturbed her; and she would suddenly break off her / song, and peevishly exclaim, that music, like the rest of the world's masks, contained the soul of bitterness within its form of beauty.

"Not so, dear girl," said Euthanasia; "Euterpe[a] has ever been so dear a friend of mine, that I cannot permit you to calumniate her unjustly; there is to me an unalloyed pleasure in music. Some blessed spirit, compassionate of man's estate, and loving him, sent it, to teach him that he is other than what he seems: it comes, like a voice from a far world, to tell you that there are depths of intense emotion veiled in the blue empyrean, and the windows of heaven are opened by music alone. It chastens and lulls our extacies; and, if it awakens grief, it also soothes it. But more than to the happy or the sorrowful, music is an inestimable gift to those who forget all sublimer emotions in the pursuits of daily life. I listen to the talk of men; I play with my embroidery-frame; I enter into society: suddenly high song awakens me, and I leave all this tedious routine far, far distant; I listen, till all the world is changed, and the beautiful earth becomes more beautiful. Evening and / all its soft delights, morning and all its refreshing loveliness; – noonday, when the busy soul rests, like the sun in its diurnal course, and then gathering new strength, descends; all these, when thought upon, bring pleasure; but music is far more delicious than these. Never do I feel happier and better, than when I have heard sweet music; my thoughts often sleep like young children nestled in their cradles, until music awakens them, and they open their starry eyes. I may be mistaken; but music seems to me to reveal to us some of the profoundest secrets of the universe; and the spirit, freed from prison by its charms, can then soar, and gaze with eagle eyes on the eternal sun of this all-beauteous world."

Beatrice smiled. – Since her days of happiness had ended, Euthanasia's enthusiasm had become more concentrated, more concealed; but Beatrice again awoke her to words, and these two ladies, bound by the sweet ties of gratitude and pity, found in each other's converse some balm for their misfortunes. Circumstances had thus made friends of those whom nature seemed to separate: they were / much unlike; but the wild looks of Beatrice sometimes reflected the soft light of Euthanasia's eyes; and Euthanasia found her heart, which was sinking to apathy, awake again, as she listened to Beatrice. And, though we may be unhappy, we can never be perfectly wretched, while the mind is active; it is inaction alone that constitutes true wretchedness.

---

[a] The muse of music.

In the mean time her own journey to Florence was put off indefinitely. She was too much interested in the fate of Beatrice, and already loved her too well, to desert her; the poor prophetess appeared little capable of the journey, since the most trifling circumstance would awaken her wildest fancies, and fever and convulsions followed. Once indeed Euthanasia had mentioned her wish to go thither; Beatrice looked at her with flashing eyes, and cried, "Did you not promise never to desert me? Are you faithless also?"

"But would you not accompany me?"

"Do you see that river that flows near Lucca?" exclaimed Beatrice. "I fancy that it has flowed through the self-same banks these many thousand years; and sooner will it desert / them, than I this town. See you that cypress, that grows towering above all its neighbour trees in that convent-garden? I am as firm to this soil as that; I will never leave this place but by force, and then I die."

She said these words in her wildest manner; and they were followed by such an annihilation of strength, and such symptoms of fever, that Euthanasia did not again dare mention her removal to Florence. She also suffered less by her continued stay at Lucca; for the feelings of her heart were so completely absorbed in pity and love for Beatrice, that the painful ideas of many years' growth seemed rooted out by a new and mightier power. She was so little selfish, that she could easily forget her own sorrows, deep as they were, in her sympathy for the unhappy prophetess, who had suffered evils tremendous and irremediable.

Castruccio often sent to learn of the welfare of this poor girl, and Euthanasia answered his enquiries with exactness. She did this; for she thought that perhaps the future destiny of Beatrice was in his hands, and that he might / engraft life and even happiness on the blighted plant.

One day Beatrice went out. It was the first time she had quitted the palace; and Euthanasia was vexed and anxious. After an absence of some hours she returned; she was clothed in a great coarse cloak that entirely disguised her; she put it off; and, trembling, blushing, panting, she threw herself into the arms of her protectress.

"I have seen him! I have seen him!"

"Calm yourself, poor fluttering bird; you have seen him: well, well, he is changed, much altered; why do you weep?"

"Aye, he is changed; but he is far more beautiful than ever he was. Oh, Euthanasia, how radiant, how divine he is! His eyes, which, like an eagle's, could outgaze the sun, yet melt in the sweetest love, as a cloud, shining, yet soft; his brow, manly and expansive, on which his raven curls rest; his upturned lips, where pride, and joy, and love, and wisdom, and triumph live, small spirits, ready to obey his smallest will; and his head, cinctured / by a slight diadem, looks carved out by the intensest knowledge of beauty! How graceful his slightest motion! and his voice, – his voice is here,——"

Beatrice put her hand upon her heart; her eyes were filled with tears; and the

249

whole expression of her face was softened and humanized. Suddenly she stopped; she dried her eyes; and, fixing them on Euthanasia, she took her two hands in hers, and looked on her, as if she would read her soul. "Beautiful creature," she said, "once he told me that he loved you. Did he not? does he not? Why are you separated? do you not love him?"

"I did; once I did truly; but he has cast off that which was my love; and, like a flower plucked from the stalk, it has withered – as you see it."

"Aye, that is strange. What did he cast off?"

"Why will you make me speak? He cast off humanity, honesty, honourable feeling, all that I prize."

"Forms, forms, – mere forms, my mistaken Euthanasia. *He* remained, and was not that / every thing? Methinks, it would please me, that my lover should cast off all humanity, and be a reprobate, and an outcast of his species. Oh! then how deeply and tenderly I should love him; soiled with crimes, his hands dripping blood, I would shade him as the flowering shrub invests the ruin; I would cover him with a spotless veil; – my intensity of love would annihilate his wickedness; – every one would hate him; – but, if all adored him, it would not come near the sum of my single affection. I should be every thing to him, life, and hope; he would die in his remorse; but he would live again and again in the light of my love; I would invest him as a silvery mist, so that none should see how evil he was; I would pour out before him large draughts of love, that he should become drunk with it, until he grew good and kind. So you deserted this glorious being, and he has felt the pangs of unrequited affection, the helpless throes of love cast as water upon the sand of the desert? Oh, indeed I pity him!"

"Believe me," cried Euthanasia, "he has other affections. Glory and conquest are his / mistresses, and he is a successful lover; already he has deluged our vallies in blood, and turned our habitations into black and formless ruins; he has torn down the banners of the Florentines, and planted his own upon the towers of noble cities; I believe him to be happy."

"Thank God for that; I would pour out my blood, drop by drop, to make him happy. But he is not married, and you have deserted him; I love him; he has loved me; is it impossible – ? Oh! foolish, hateful wretch that I am, what do I say? No creature was ever so utterly undone!"

Beatrice covered her face with her hands; her struggles were violent; she shrunk from Euthanasia's consoling embrace; and at length, quite overcome, she sank in convulsions on the pavement of the hall. Her paroxysm was long and fearful; it was succeeded by a heavy lethargic sleep; during the first part of which she was feverish and uneasy; but, after some hours, her cheeks became pale, her pulse beat slower, and her breath was drawn regularly.

Euthanasia watched beside her alone: when / she found that she was sleeping quietly and deeply, she retired from her bedside; and, sitting at some distance, she tried to school herself on the bitter feelings that had oppressed her since the morning. Euthanasia was so self-examining, that she never allowed a night to elapse without recalling her feelings and actions of the past day; she endeavoured to be simply just to herself, and her soul had so long been accustomed to this discipline, that it easily laid open its dearest secrets. Misfortune had not dulled her sense of right and wrong; her understanding was still clear, though tinged by the same lofty enthusiasm which had ever been her characteristic. She now searched her soul to find what were the feelings which still remained to her concerning Castruccio; she hardly knew whether it was hate or love. Hate! could she hate one, to whom once she had delivered up all her thoughts, as to the tribunal of her God, whom she had loved as one to whom she was willing to unite herself for ever? And could she love one, who had deceived her in her dearest hopes, / who had lulled her on the brink of a precipice, to plunge her with greater force to eternal unhappiness? She felt neither hatred, nor revenge, nor contempt colder than either; she felt grief alone, and that sentiment was deeply engraven on her soul. /

CHAPTER IV.

Beatrice's Narrative.

She was awakened from this reverie by the voice of Beatrice, who called to her to come near. "I am quite recovered," she said, "though weak; I have been very ill to-day, and I am frightened to think of the violence of my sensations. But sit near me, beloved friend; it is now night, and you will hear no sound but my feeble voice; while I fulfil my promise of relating to you my wretched history."

"Mine own Beatrice, do not now vex yourself with these recollections; you must seek calm and peace alone; let memory go to its grave."

"Nay, you must know all," replied Beatrice, peevishly; "why do you balk me? indeed I do best when I follow my own smallest inclinations; for, when I try to combat them, I / am again ill, as I was this morning. Sit beside me; I will make room for you on my couch; give me your hand, but turn away your soft eyes; and now I will tell you every thing.

"You know that I loved Castruccio; how much I need hardly tell: I loved him beyond human love, for I thought heaven itself had interfered to unite us. I thought—— alas! it is with aching pain that I recollect my wild dreams, – that we two were chosen from the rest of the world, gifted with celestial faculties. It appeared to me to be a dispensation of Providence, that I should have met him at the full height of my glory, when I was burning with triumph and joy. I do not think, my own Euthanasia, that you can ever have experienced the vigour

251

and fire of my sensations. Victory in an almost desperate struggle, success in art, love itself, are earthly feelings, subject to change and death; but, when these three most exquisite sensations are bestowed by the visible intervention of heaven, thus giving security to the unstable, and eternity to what is fleeting, such an event fills the over-brimming / cup, intoxicates the brain, and renders her who feels them more than mortal.

"Victory and glory I had, and an assurance of divine inspiration; the fame of what I was, was spread among the people of my country; then love came, and flattered, and softened, and overcame me. Well, that I will pass over: to conceive that all I felt was human, common, and now faded, disgusts me, and makes me look back with horror to my lost paradise. Castruccio left me; and I sat I cannot tell how long, white, immoveable, and intranced; hours, I believe days, passed; I cannot tell, for in truth I think I was mad. Yet I was silent; not a word, not a tear, not a sound escaped me, until some one mentioned the name of Castruccio before me, and then I wept. I did not rave or weep aloud; I crept about like a shadow, brooding over my own thoughts, and trying to divine the mystery of my destiny.

"At length I went to my good father, the bishop; I knelt down before him: 'Rise, dear child,' he said; 'how pale you are! what has quenched the fire of your brilliant eyes?'

"'Father, holy father,' I replied, 'I will / not rise till you answer me one question.' – My looks were haggard with want of rest; my tangled locks fell on my neck; my glazed eyes could scarcely distinguish any object.

"'My blessed Beatrice,' said the good old man, 'you are much unlike yourself: but speak; I know that you can ask nothing that I can refuse to tell.'

"'Tell me then, by your hopes of heaven,' I cried, 'whether fraud was used in the *Judgement of God* that I underwent, or how I escaped the fearful burning of the hot shares.'

"Tears started in my father's eyes; he rose, and embraced me, and, lifting me up, said with passion, – 'Thank God! my prayers are fulfilled. Beatrice, you shall not be deceived, you will no longer deceive yourself; and do not be unhappy, but joy that the deceit is removed from you, and that you may return from your wild and feverish extacies to a true and real piety.'

"'This is all well,' I replied calmly; 'but tell me truly how it happened.'

"'That I cannot, my child, for I was myself kept in the dark; I only know that fraud was / most certainly practised for your deliverance. My child, we have all of us much erred; you less than any; for you have been deceived, led away by your feelings and imagination to believe yourself that which you are not.'

"I will not repeat to you all that the bishop said; it was severe but kind. First he shewed me, how I had deceived myself, and nourished extacies and transports of the soul which were in no way allied to holiness; and then he told me how I must repair my faults by deep humility, prayer, and a steady faith in that alone which others taught, not what I myself imagined. I listened silently; but I

252

heard every word; I was very docile; I believed all he said; and although my soul bled with its agony, I accused none, none but myself. At first I thought that I would tell my countrymen of their deception. But, unsupported by my supernatural powers, I now shrunk from all display; no veil, no wall could conceal me sufficiently; for it could not hide me from myself. My very powers of speech deserted me, and I could not articulate a syllable; I listened, my eyes bent on the earth, my cheek pale; I / listened until I almost became marble. At length the good old man ceased; and, with many words of affectionate comfort, he bade me go and make firm peace with my own heart, and that then he hoped to teach me a calm road to happiness. Happiness! surely I must have been stone; for I neither frowned in despite, nor laughed in derision, when that term was applied to any thing that I could hereafter feel. I kissed his hand, and withdrew.

"Did you ever feel true humility? a prostration of soul, that accuses itself alone, and asks pardon of a superior power with entire penitence, and a confiding desertion of all self-merit, a persuasion intimate and heartfelt of one's own unworthiness? That was what I felt; I had been vain, proud, presumptuous; now I fell to utter poverty of spirit; yet it was not poverty, for there was a richness in my penitence which reminded me of the sacred text, that says 'Oh, that my head were water, and mine eyes a fountain of tears!'[a]

"Then succeeded to this mental humiliation, a desire to mortify and punish myself for my / temerity and mistakes. I was possessed by a spirit of martyrdom. Sometimes I thought that I would again undergo the *Judgement of God* fairly and justly: but now I shrunk from public exhibition; besides, the good bishop had strongly reprobated these temptations of God's justice. At other times I thought that I would confess all to my excellent father; and this perhaps is what I ought to have done; what would really have caused me to regain a part of the calm that I had lost; but I could not; womanly shame forbade me; death would have been a far preferable alternative. At length an idea struck me, that seemed to my overstrained feelings to transcend all other penitence; a wretchedness and anguish that might well redeem my exceeding sins.

"Think you that, while I thus humbled myself, I forgot Castruccio? Never! the love I bore clung around me, festered on my soul, and kept me ever alive to pain. Love him! I adored him; to whisper his name only in solitude, where none could hear my voice but my own most attentive ear, thrilled me with transport. I tried to banish him my / thoughts; he recurred in my dreams, which I could not control. I saw him there, beautiful as his real self, and my heart was burnt by my emotion. Well; it was on this excess of love that I built my penitence, which was to go as a pilgrim and ask alms of you. Euthanasia! I only knew your name; the very idea of seeing you made me shiver. I was three

---

[a] Jeremiah 9: 1 (with 'water' for 'waters').

months before I could steel my heart to this resolve. I saw none; I spoke to none; I was occupied by my meditations alone, and those were deep and undermining as the ocean.

"Well; as I have said, I dwelt long and deeply upon my plan, until every moment seemed a crime, that went by before I put it in execution. The long winter passed thus; my poor mother, the lady Marchesana, watched me, as a child might watch a favourite bird fluttering in the agonies of death. She saw that some mysterious and painful feeling oppressed me, that I no longer appeared in public, that I shunned the worship of my admirers, that the spirit of prophecy was dead within me; but I was silent, and reserved; and her reverence for me (Good angels! her reverence / for me!) prevented any enquiries. In the spring the bishop Marsilio was promoted to another see, and he was obliged to go to Avignon to receive the investiture. Excellent and beloved old man! he blessed me, and kissed me, and with words of affectionate advice departed. I have never seen him more.

"When he was gone, the labour of my departure was lightened; and in gentle and hesitating words I told my best and loved mother that I had vowed a pilgrimage to Rome: she wished to accompany me. Those were heart-breaking scenes, my Euthanasia, when I left all my friends, all who loved me, and whom I had ever loved: I knew that I should never see them again. How did I know this? In truth, after having performed my vow with regard to you, I intended to visit the sepulchres at Rome; and I might then have returned. I was no prophetess; and yet I felt that mine was not a simple pilgrimage, but an eternal separation from all former associations, from every one I had ever known. Thus, hopeless of future good, I deserted all that yet rendered life in any degree sufferable: I did / this to satisfy my sense of duty, to do homage to the divinity by some atonement for his violated laws: I did this; and henceforward I was to be an outcast, a poor lonely shrub on a bleak heath, a single reed in a vast and overflowing river.

"I had known too much luxury in my youth; every one loved me, and tended on me; I had seen about me eyes beaming with affection, smiles all my own, words of deep interest and respect, that had become to me a second nature. I departed alone at four in the morning from Ferrara by the secret entrance of the viscountess's palace, on a clear and lovely day in the spring. I was dressed as the meanest pilgrim, and I carefully hid my white hands and fair cheeks, which might have betrayed my way of life during the past; except indeed when I was alone, – then I loved to throw off my cloak, to bare my arms, my face, my neck to the scorching sun-beams, that I might the sooner destroy a delicacy I despised: the work was quickly done; a few hours exposure to the sun of noon burnt up my skin, and made it red and common. /

"The first day was one of unmixed pain; the sun parched my frame; my feet were blistered, my limbs ached; I walked all day, until bodily fatigue lulled my mental anguish, for I was unhappy beyond all words. Alone, deserted by God and man, I had lost my firm support, my belief in my own powers; I had lost my friends; and I found, that the vain, self-sufficing, cloud-inhabiting Beatrice was in truth a poor dependent creature, whose heart sunk, when in the evening she came to a clear brook running through a little wood, and she found no cup to drink, and no dainties to satisfy her appetite. I dragged my weary limbs three miles further, to an hospital for pilgrims, and repined over my coarse fare and coarser bed: – I, the ethereal prophetess, who fancied that I could feed upon air and beautiful thoughts, who had regarded my body but as a servant to my will, to hunger and thirst only as I bade it.

"Alone! alone! I travelled on day after day, in short, but wearisome journeys, and I felt the pain of utter and forced solitude; the burning sun shone, and the dews fell at evening, / but there was no breeze, no coolness to refresh me; the nights were close, and my limbs, dried with the scorching of the day, and stiff with walking, burned all night as if a furnace had glowed within them. Were these slight evils? Alas! I was a spoiled child, and I felt every pain as an agony.

"I fell ill; I caught cold one evening, when just after sunset I threw myself down to rest under a tree, and the unwholesome dew fell upon me. I got a low fever, which for a long time I did not understand, feeling one day well, and the next feverish, cold, and languid. Some attendant nuns at an hospital found out my disorder, and nursed me; I was confined for six weeks; and, when I issued forth, little of the fire of my eyes, or of the beauty the lady Marchesana used to dwell upon, out-lived this attack. – I was yellow, meagre,—— a shadow of what I had been.

"My journey to your castle was very long. I crossed the Apennines during the summer, and passing through Florence I arrived at Pistoia in the beginning of June. But now my heart again failed; I heard of your name, your / prosperity, your beauty, the respect and adoration you every where excited: it was a double penance to humble myself before so excelling a rival. If you had been worthless, a self-contenting pride would have eased my wounds, but to do homage to my equal – oh! to one far my superior, – was a new lesson to my stubborn soul. I remained nearly three months at Pistoia, very unhappy, hesitating, – cast about, as a boat that for ever shifts its sail, but can never find the right wind to lead it into port.

"I visited you in September; do you remember my coming? do you remember my hesitating gait, and low and trembling voice? I was giddy – sick – I thought that death was upon me, for that nothing but that great change could cause such an annihilation of my powers, such an utter sinking of my spirit. A cold dew stood upon my forehead, my eyes were glazed and sightless, my limbs trembled as with convulsions. Castruccio loved you! Castruccio! it is long since I have mentioned his name: during this weary journey never did his loved image for a moment quit its temple, / its fane, its only home, that it still and for ever fills. Love him! it was madness; yet I did; – yet I do; – put your hand upon my heart, – does it not beat fast?"

255

Euthanasia kissed poor Beatrice's forehead; and, after a short pause, she continued:

"My penance was completed, yet I did not triumph; an unconquerable sadness hung over me; miserable dreams haunted my sleep; and their recollected images strayed among my day-thoughts, as thin and grim ghosts, frightening and astounding me. Once, – I can never forget, – I had been oppressed for several days by an overpowering and black melancholy, for which I could in no manner account; it was not regret or grief; it was a sinking, an annihilation of all my mental powers in which I was a passive sufferer, as if the shadow of some mightier spirit was cast over to darken and depress me. I was haunted as by a prophecy, or rather a sense of evil, which I could neither define nor understand. Three evenings after, as I sat beside a quiet spring that lulled me almost to insensibility, the cause of my mournful reveries suddenly flashed across me; it / stalked on my recollection, as a terrific and gigantic shadow, and made me almost die with terror. The memory of a dream flashed across me. Again and again I have dreamed this dream, and always on the eve of some great misfortune. It is my genius, my dæmon. What was it? there was something said, something done, a scene pourtrayed. Listen attentively, I intreat; there was a wide plain flooded by the waters of an overflowing river, the road was dry, being on the side of a hill above the level of the plain, and I kept along the path which declined, wondering if I should come to an insurmountable obstacle; at a distance before me they were driving a flock of sheep; on my left, on the side of the hill, there was a ruined circuit of wall, which inclosed the dilapidated houses of a deserted town; at some distance a dreary, large, ruinous house, half like a castle, yet without a tower, dilapidated, and overgrown with moss, was dimly seen, islanded by the flood on which it cast a night-black shade; the scirocco blew, and covered the sky with fleecy clouds; and the mists in the distance hovered low over the plain; a bat above / me wheeled around. Then something happened, what I cannot now tell, terrific it most certainly was; Euthanasia, there is something in this strange world, that we none of us understand.

"Euthanasia, I came to that scene; if I live, I did! I saw it all as I had before seen it in the slumbers of the night. Great God, what am I? I am frailer than the first autumnal leaf that falls; I am overpowered."

She paused sobbing with passion; a clinging horror fell upon Euthanasia; they were for a long time silent, and then Beatrice in a low subdued voice continued:

"I had returned to Florence; I had passed through Arezzo; I had left Thrasymene to the north; I had passed through Perugia, Foligno, and Terni, and was descending towards the plain surrounding Rome; the Tiber had overflowed, the whole of the low country was under water; but I proceeded, descending the mountains, until, having passed Narni, I came to the lowest hill which bounds the Campagna di Roma;[a] the scirocco blew; the mists were on the hills, and half concealed the head / of lone Soracte;[b] the white waters, cold and dreary, were spread far, waste and shelterless; on my left was a high dark wall surrounding a ruined town – I looked, – some way beyond I saw on the road a flock of sheep almost lost in the distance, – my brain was troubled, I grew dizzy and sick – when my glazed eyes caught a glance of an old, large, dilapidated house islanded in the flood, – the dream flashed across my memory; I uttered a wild shriek, and fell lifeless on the road.

"I again awoke, but all was changed: I was lying on a couch, in a vast apartment, whose loose tapestries waved and sighed in the wind; – near me were two boys holding torches which flared, and their black smoke was driven across my eyes; an old woman was chafing my temples. – I turned my head from the light of the torches, and then I first saw my wicked and powerful enemy: he leaned against the wall, observing me; his eyes had a kind of fascination in them, and, unknowing what I did, hardly conscious that he was a human creature, (indeed for a time it appeared to me only a continuation of my dream,) I gazed on / his face, which became illuminated by a proud triumphant, fiendlike smile. – I felt sick at heart, and relapsed into a painful swoon.

"Well: I promised to be brief, and I go on dwelling on the particulars of my tale, until your fair cheek is blanched still whiter by fear. But I have said enough, nor will I tell that which would chill your warm blood with horror. I remained three years in this house; and what I saw, and what I endured, is a tale for the unhallowed ears of infidels, or for those who have lost humanity in the sight of blood, and not for so tender a heart as yours. It has changed me, much changed me, to have been witness of these scenes; I entered young, I came out grey, old and withered; I went in innocent; and, if innocence consist in ignorance, I am now guilty of the knowledge of crime, which it would seem that fiends alone could contrive.

"What was he, who was the author and mechanist of these crimes? he bore a human name; they say that his lineage was human; yet could he be a man? During the day he was absent; at night he returned, and his roofs / rung with the sounds of festivity, mingled with shrieks and imprecations. It was the carnival of devils, when we miserable victims were dragged out to——

"Enough! enough! Euthanasia, do you wonder that I, who have been the slave of incarnate Evil, should have become a Paterin?

---

[a] A path through wild scenery and Italian history. Lake Thrasymene was the site of one of Hannibal's most crushing victories; Terni was famous for its waterfall; Narni (ancient Roman Narnia) was the stronghold against Hasdrubal's threatened march on Rome.

[b] A mountain near the Tiber, twenty-six miles north of Rome; in ancient times it was sacred to Apollo, God of poetry. The Soractian priests were fabled to walk over burning coals with impunity (Lemprière).

"That time has passed as a dream. Often my faculties were exerted to the utmost; my energies alive, at work, combating; – but I struggled against victory, and was ever vanquished. I have seen the quiet stars shine, and the shadow of the grated window of the hall lie upon the moon-enlightened pavement, and it crawled along silently as I had observed it in childhood, so that truly I inhabited the same world as you, – yet how different! Animal life was the same; the household dog knew, and was at last obedient to my voice; the cat slumbered in the sun; – what was the influence that hung alone over the mind of man, rendering it cruel, hard and fiendlike?

"And who was the author of these ills? There was something about him that might be called beautiful; but it was the beauty of the / tiger, of lightning, of the cataract that destroys. Obedience waited on his slightest motion; for he made none, that did not command; his followers worshipped him, but it was as a savage might worship the god of evil. His slaves dared not murmur; – his eyes beamed with irresistible fire, his smile was as death. I hated him; and I alone among his many victims was not quelled to submission. I cursed him – I poured forth eloquent and tumultuous maledictions on his head, until I changed his detested love into less dreadful, less injurious hate. Yet then I did not escape; his boiling and hideous passions, turned to revenge, now endeavoured to wreak themselves in my misery. These limbs, my Euthanasia, have been wrenched in tortures; cold, famine and thirst have kept like blood-hounds a perpetual watch upon my wearied life; yet I still live to remember and to curse.

"But, though life survived these rending struggles, my reason sank beneath them! – I became mad. Oh! dearest friend, may you never know what I suffered, when I perceived the shadow of a false vision overpower me, and my sickening throes, when the bars of my / dungeon, its low roof, and black thick air, would, as it were, peer upon me with a stifling sense of reality amidst my insane transports. I struggled to recall my reason, and to preserve it; I wept, I prayed; – but I was again lost; and the fire that dwelt in my brain gave unnatural light to every object. But I must speak of that no more; methinks I again feel, what it is madness only to recollect.[a]

"I told you that I remained for three years in this infernal house. You can easily imagine how slowly the days and nights succeeded one to another, each adding to my age, each adding one misery more to my list. Still I was the slave of him, who was a man in form alone, and of his companions, who, if they did not equal him in malice, yet were more vile, more treacherous, than he. At length the Pope's party besieged the castle. The many crimes of its possessor had drawn on him the hatred of the country round; and the moment that a leader appeared, the whole peasantry flocked as to a crusade to destroy their oppressor. He was destroyed. I saw him die, calm, courageous and unrepenting.

---

[a] cf. P. B. Shelley, *The Cenci*, III, i. 14–25.

I stood alone near his couch of blood-stained cloaks thrown / in a heap upon the floor, on which when he staggered into the room he had fallen; he asked me for a cup of water; I raised his head, and gave him to drink; he said – 'I feel new strength, I shall be better soon.' And, saying those words, he died.

"I was now free. I arose from the floor on which I knelt; and dividing from my eyes my hair dabbled in his blood, I cut off with his dagger the long and dripping locks, and threw them on his body. I disguised me in the clothes of one of his pages, and hid myself, until by the submission of his followers the outlet from my prison should be free. As I said before, it was more a vast palace than a castle, being without towers or battlements; but it was fortified by numberless ditches and other obstacles, apparently small, yet which, defended by slingers and archers, became almost impregnable. But when the chief died, these were deserted; and the partners of his rapine and his feasts filled the air with their savage lamentations. The fortress was taken; and I escaped to the mountains, the wild, / wild mountains, – I sought them as a home after my long and painful imprisonment.

"I was now free. The ilex trees shaded me; the waters murmured beside me; the sweet winds passed over my cheeks. I felt new life. I was no longer a haggard prisoner, the despairing victim of others' crimes, the inhabitant of the dark and blood-stained walls of a house, which hedged me in on all sides, and interrupted the free course of my health even in sleep. I was again Beatrice; I again felt the long absent sensations of joy: it was paradise to me, to see the stars of heaven, unimpeded by the grates of my dungeon-windows, to walk, to rest, to think, to speak, uninterrupted and unheard. I became delirious with joy; I embraced the rough trunks of the old trees, as if they were my sisters in freedom and delight; – I took up in my hand the sparkling waters of the stream, and scattered them to the winds; – I threw myself on the earth, I kissed the rocks, I raved with tumultuous pleasure. Free! free! I can run, until my strength fails; I can rest on a mossy bank, until my strength / returns; I hear the waving of the branches; I see the flight of the birds; I can lie on the grassy floor of my mother-earth so long unvisited; and I can call nature my own again. It was autumn, and the underwood of the forest had strewn the ground with its withered leaves; the arbutus-berries, chesnuts, and other fruits satisfied my appetite. I felt no want, no fatigue; the common shapes of this world seemed arrayed in unusual loveliness, to welcome and feast me on my new-found liberty.

"I wandered many days, and penetrated into the wild country of the Abruzzi.[a] But I was again lost: I know not what deprived me of reason thus, when I most needed it. Whether it were the joy, or the sudden change, attendant on a too intense sensation of freedom, which made me feel as if I interpenetrated all

---

[a] Area of the southern continuation of the Apennines.

nature, alive and boundless. I have recollections, as if sometimes I saw the woods, the green earth, and blue sky, and heard the roaring of a mighty waterfal which splashed me with its cold waters: but there is a blank, as of a deep, lethargic sleep; and many weeks / passed before I awoke again, and entered upon the reality of life.

"I found myself in a cavern lying on the ground. It was night; and a solitary lamp burned, fastened to the wall of the cave; the half-extinguished ashes of a fire glimmered in a recess; and a few utensils that appeared to have been intended for the preparing food, seemed to mark this as a human habitation. It was dry, and furnished with a few benches and a table, on which lay bread and fruits. I felt as if I had become the inhabitant of the dwelling of a spirit; and, with a strange, half-painful, half-pleasurable feeling, I raised an apple to my lips, that by its fragrance and taste I might assure myself that it was earthly. Then again I looked around for some fellow-creature. I found a narrow passage from my cave, which led to an inner apartment much smaller and very low; on the ground, on a bed of leaves lay an old man: his grey hairs were thinly strewn on his venerable temples, his beard white, flowing and soft, fell to his girdle; he smiled even in his sleep a gentle smile / of benevolence. I knelt down beside him; methought it was my excellent father, the lord Marsilio; but that there were greater traces of thought and care upon the fallen cheeks and wrinkled brow of this old man.

"He awoke: 'My poor girl,' he said, 'what would you?'

"'I wish to know where I am, and what I do here?'

"My words convinced my good protector, that the kindly sleep into which his medicines had thrown me, had restored my reason; and, it being now day-break, he arose, and opened the door of his cave. It was dug under the side of a mountain, covered by ivy, wild vines, and other parasites,[a] and shaded by ilex trees; it opened on the edge of a small grassy platform, with a steep wall of rock behind, and a precipice before: the mountain in which it was scooped, was one of many that inclosed a rugged valley; and, from one spot on the platform, I could distinguish a mass of waters falling with a tremendous crash, which were otherwise hidden by the inequalities of the mountain, / and then were seen, a turbid and swift river, at the bottom of the valley. The lower sides of the mountain were covered with olive woods, whose seagreen colour contrasted with the dark ilex, and the fresh-budding leaves of a few chesnuts. I felt cold, and the mountain had just begun to be tipped by the rising sun; it seemed as if no path led to or from the platform, and that we were shut out from the whole world, suspended on the side of a rocky mountain.

"This cavern had been an hospital for me during the long winter months. The old man had found me straying wildly among the forests, complaining of the heavy chains that bound me, and the wrongs and imprisonment that I

---

[a] Climbing plants.

suffered. He, poor wretch, was an outcast of his species, a heretic, a Paterin, who hid himself in the woods from the fury of the priests who would have destroyed him. He led me to his cave; he tended me as the kindest father; he restored me to reason, and even then did not desert me. He lived here quite alone; no one was intrusted with the secret of his retreat; / at night, muffled up and disguised, he often went to seek for food, and again hastened back to peace and solitude.

"I partook his solitude for many months: at sunrise we quitted our dwelling, and enjoyed the fresh air, and the view of the sky and the hills, until the sight of the first countryman in the vale below warned us to retire. On moonlight nights, we sat there; and, while she, lady of the night, moved slowly above us, and the stars twinkled around, we talked, and, in our conversations of faith, goodness and power, his doctrines unveiled to me, what had before been obscure, and from him I learned that creed which you hold in detestation, but which, believe me, has much to be said in its behalf.

"Look, dear Euthanasia, daylight has made dim the glimmer of your lamp, and bids me remember how often I have forgotten my promise to be brief in my relation; it is now almost finished. I soon greatly loved my kind guardian; he was the gentlest and most amiable of mortals, wise as a Grecian sage, fearless and independent. He died in torture: the bloodhounds hunted him from his den; they / bound his aged limbs; they dragged him to the stake. He died without dread, I would fain believe almost without pain. Could these things be, oh, my preserver, best and most excellent of men? It were well befitting, that thou shouldst die thus, and that I lived, and still live.

"It were tedious to relate how all this passed; how I wept and prayed; how I escaped, and, half maddened by this misery, cursed the creation and its cruel laws. The rest is all uninteresting; I was returning from the task of carrying the last legacy of this old man to his daughter at Genoa, when I was seized in this town by the Inquisitors, and cast into prison,—— you know the rest.

"And now, dearest friend, leave me. Having related the events of my past life, it makes me look on towards the future; it is not enough to rise every day, and then lie down to sleep; I would look on what I may become with firmness; I know that no creature in the whole world is so miserable as I; but I have not yet drained the cup of life; something still remains to be done. /

"Yet one word, my Euthanasia, of Him who is the law of my life; and yet I dare not say what I thought of saying. You write to him about me sometimes; do you not? You may still; I would not check you in this. In truth he is the master of my fate; and it were well that he knew all that relates to me."

Poor Beatrice then wept bitterly; but she waved her hand in sign that she would be left alone; and Euthanasia retired. She had not slept the whole night, but she felt no inclination to rest. The last words of Beatrice seemed to imply that she wished that Castruccio should know her story; so she sat down, and wrote an abstract of it, while her eyes often filled with tears, as she related the wondrous miseries of the ill-fated prophetess. /

CHAPTER V.

Beatrice resolves to take the Veil. – Euthanasia visits Florence.

On the following day Beatrice seemed far more calm. Euthanasia had feared, that the reviving the memory of past sorrows, might awaken the frenzy from which she had before suffered; but it was not so. She had pined for confidence; her heart was too big to close up in secrecy all the mighty store of unhappiness to which it was conscious; but, having now communicated the particulars to another, she felt somewhat relieved. She and Euthanasia walked up and down the overgrown paths of the palace-garden; and, as Beatrice held her friend's hand, after a silence of a few minutes she said:

"I do not like to pry into the secrets of my / own heart; and yet I am ever impelled to do it. I was about to compare it to this unweeded garden; but here all is still; and the progress of life, be it beautiful or evil, goes on in peace: in my soul all jars, – one thought strikes against another, and produces most vile discord. Sometimes for a moment this ceases; and would that that state of peace would endure for ever: but, crash! – comes in the stroke of a mightier hand, which destroys all harmony and melody, alas! that may be found in your gentler heart; in mine all recollection of it even is extinct."

"I will tell you how this is, my sweet Beatrice," replied Euthanasia playfully. "I will tell you what the human mind is; and you shall learn to regulate its various powers. The human soul, dear girl, is a vast cave, in which many powers sit and live. First, Consciousness is as a centinel at the entrance; and near him wait Joy and Sorrow, Love and Hate, and all the quick sensations that through his means gain entrance into our hearts.

"In the vestibule of this cavern, still illumined by the light of day, sit Memory with / banded eyes, grave Judgement bearing her scales, and Reason in a lawyer's gown. Hope and Fear dwell there, hand in hand, twin sisters; the first (the elder by some brief moments, of ruddy complexion, firm step, eyes eagerly looking forward, and lips apart in earnest expectation,) would often hurry on to take her seat beside Joy; if she were not held back by Fear, the younger born; who, pale and trembling, would as often fly, if Hope held not her hand, and supported her; her eyes are ever turned back to appeal to Memory, and you may see her heart beat through her dun robe. Religion dwells there also, and Charity, or sometimes in their place, their counterfeits or opposites, Hypocrisy, Avarice and Cruelty.

"Within, excluded from the light of day, Conscience sits, who can see indeed, as an owl, in the dark. His temples are circled by a diadem of thorns, and in his hand he bears a whip; yet his garb is kingly, and his countenance, though severe, majestical.

"But beyond all this there is an inner cave, difficult of access, rude, strange, and dangerous. Few visit this, and it is often barren / and empty; but sometimes (like caverns that we read of, which are discovered in the bosoms of the mountains, and exist in beauty, unknown and neglected)[a] this last recess is decorated with the strangest and most wondrous devices; – stalactites of surpassing beauty, stores of unimagined wealth, and silver sounds, which the dropping water makes, or the circulation of the air, felt among the delicate crystals. But here also find abode owls, and bats, and vipers, and scorpions, and other deadly reptiles. This recess receives no light from outward day; nor has Conscience any authority here. Sometimes it is lighted by an inborn light; and then the birds of night retreat, and the reptiles creep not from their holes. But, if this light do not exist, oh! then let those beware who would explore this cave. It is hence that bad men receive those excuses for their crimes, which take the whip from the hand of Conscience, and blunt his sharp crown; it is hence that the daring heretic learns strange secrets. This is the habitation of the madman, when all the powers desert the vestibule, and he, finding no light, makes darkling, fantastic combinations, / and lives among them. From thence there is a short path to hell, and the evil spirits pass and repass unreproved, devising their temptations.

"But it is here also that Poetry and Imagination live; it is here that Heroism, and Self-sacrifice, and the highest virtues dwell, and here they find a lore far better than all the lessons of the world; and here dwells the sweet reward of all our toil, Content of Mind, who crowned with roses, and bearing a flower-wreathed sceptre, rules, instead of Conscience, those admitted to her happy dominion."

Euthanasia talked thus, trying to give birth in the mind of Beatrice to calmer ideas; but it was in vain; the poor girl listened, and when her friend had finished, she raised her eyes heavy with tears. "Talk no more in this strain," she said; "every word you utter tells me only too plainly what a lost wretch I am. No content of mind exists for me, no beauty of thought, or poetry; and, if imagination live, it is as a tyrant, armed with fire, and venomed darts, to drive me to despair."

A torrent of tears followed these words; / and no caresses or consolation could soothe her.

Soon after, Euthanasia received an answer from Castruccio to the letter in which she had sketched Beatrice's unhappy story. He lamented the misfortunes, which through his means had overwhelmed the poor prophetess. "I know," he continued, "of no refuge or shelter for her, if it be not in your

---

[a] Euthanasia may be supposed to have read of these in a work such as the *Natural History* of Pliny the Elder. Mary Shelley herself noted from her reading of Targioni (I, pp. 360–63; adds. e. 17, p. 221 rev.) that there were 'beautiful caves' at the nearby town of Noce.

protecting affection. If she were as when I knew her, her own feelings might suggest a cloister, as the last resource for one so outraged and so miserable as she is. But she is a Paterin; and, until she be reclaimed from this detestable heresy, she is shut out from the consolations of our religion."

"And he writes thus coldly of this ruined temple, which was once all that is fair and beautiful! Ah! I wonder not," thought Euthanasia, "that he cast away my affections, since he can spare no deeper sympathy for Beatrice. She does not interfere with his ambition or his designs; it is therefore hardness of heart alone which dictates his chilling councils."

At this moment Beatrice entered. To see that / beautiful creature only (for beautiful she still was in spite of calamity and madness), was to behold all that can be imagined of soft and lovely in woman, soft and lovely, yet wild, so that, while you gazed with delight, you feared. Her low brow, though its fairness were tarnished by the sun, still gleamed beneath her raven-black hair; her eyes, which had reassumed some of their ancient gentleness, slept as it were beneath their heavy lids. Her angry look, which was lightning, her smile, which was as paradise, all elevated her above her fellow creatures; she seemed like the incarnation of some strange planetary spirit, that, robed in flesh, felt uneasy in its bonds, and longed to be away on the wings of its own will.

She spoke with trepidation: "Do not blush, my friend, or endeavour to conceal that paper; I know what it is; and, if you care for my peace of mind, if you love me, if the welfare of my almost lost soul be dear to you, let me see that writing."

"There is no consolation for you in it," replied Euthanasia, sadly.

"Nay, of that I alone can judge; look, I / kneel to you, Euthanasia; and do you deny me? I intreat you to give me that paper."

"My own Beatrice, do not torture me thus: if I do not shew it you – Never mind: here it is; read it, and know what Castruccio is."

Beatrice read it with a peaceful air; and then, folding it up, said composedly; – "I see no ill in this; and his will shall be done. It is a strange coincidence, that I had already decided on what he advises; and I trust he will be glad to find that the wandering prophetess again seeks her antient path of religion and peace. I must explain these things to you, my Euthanasia. I know that you wish to remove to Florence: I can never leave this town. I shall never see him again, hear him speak, or be any thing to him; but to live within the same walls, to breathe the air of heaven which perhaps has hovered near him, this is a joy which I will never, never forego. My resolution is fixed: but you perish here; and would find loving and cherished friends there, where he can never come. I would not detain you; I have chosen the mode of my future destiny, and planned it all. The convent nearest to his / palace is one of nuns dedicated to San Michele.[a] I have already sent for the confessor of that convent; through him I shall make my peace with the church;

---

[a] Mentioned in Muratori, III, diss. 66, p. 336; noted in adds. e. 17, p. 234 rev.

and, when he believes me sufficiently pure to become an inhabitant of those
sainted walls, I shall enter myself as a novice, and afterwards become a nun of
that order. I intreat you, dearest, to stay only till my vows are made, when, wholly
dedicated to heaven, I shall feel less an earthly separation."

She spoke in a hurried, faltering voice, and closed her speech in tears; she
threw herself into Euthanasia's arms, and they both wept. – "Oh! no, unhappy,
but dear, dear Beatrice, indeed you shall not leave me. I can be of little use now
in the world to myself or others: but to cheer you, to teach you, as well as my
poor skill will permit, the softest path to heaven, these shall be my tasks; you
shall never leave me."

Beatrice disengaged herself from the arms of Euthanasia; and, casting up her
eyes, with that look of inspiration which seemed to seek and find converse with
the powers above, she said: "I thank you from the depth of my / heart, and may
God bless you as you deserve, divine Euthanasia; but I am fixed. Alas! my mind
is as the waters, now lashed into waves by the winds of circumstance, now coldly
dark under a lowering heaven, but never smiled upon by the life-giving sun. And
this perishable frame is to my soul as a weak, tempest-beaten promontory,
against which the Libeccio impels the undermining sea. I shall soon perish: but
let my death be that of the holy; and that can alone be in the solitude of a cloister:
that is the consummation of my fate. Oppose me no more: has not he pronounced? And I will obey his word, as if he were my king, my lord, my——
Speak not; contradict me not; you see what a fragile being I am."

And now this Beatrice, this Paterin, who had so lately with heartfelt hatred
told the tale of all the miseries that are suffered under the sun, and cursed the
author of them, became as docile to the voice of the priest, as a seven-years-old
child. The confessor for whom she had sent, found it no difficult task to turn
her mind to the reception of his tenets; and prayer / and penitence became
again for her the law of the day. She never went out; she remained secluded in
Euthanasia's palace; and, with her beads in her hand, her wild eyes turned
heavenwards, she sought for peace, and she found at least a respite from some
of the dreadful feelings that had hitherto tormented her.

In the mean time "the mother of the months"[a] had many times waned, and
again refilled her horn; and summer, and its treasure of blue skies, odorous
flowers, merry insects, and sweet-voiced birds, again bade the world be happy.
The peasant prepared the threshing floor, choosing a sunny spot which he
carefully cleared of grass and weeds, and pouring water on it, beat it, till it was
as hard as a barn-floor in the north. The ploughs, whose rough workmanship
Virgil describes,[b] lay useless beside the tilth, now filled with the rising corn: the

---

[a] A poeticism for the moon; used by P. B. Shelley in 'The Witch of Atlas', l. 73.

[b] Virgil, *Georgics*, I. 169–75; John Martyn's *The Georgicks of Virgil* (1741), owned by P. B.
Shelley (*PBSL*, I, pp. 347, 549) discussed, with an illustration, the similarity of the modern Italian
plough to Virgil's.

primroses had faded; but one began to scent the myrtle on the mountains; the innumerable fireflies, loving the green wheat, made a second heaven of twinkling stars upon a verdant floor, or, darting among the olive copses, formed a fairy scene of the sweet Italian night; / the soft-eyed oxen reposed in their stalls; and the flowers of the chesnuts and olives had given place to the young, half-formed fruit. This is the season that man has ever chosen for the destruction of his fellow-creatures, to make the brooks run blood, the air, filled with the carolling of happy birds, to echo also to the groans and shrieks of the dying, and the blue and serene heaven to become tainted with the dew which the unburied corpse exhales; winter were Bellona's[a] fitting mate; but, no; she hangs about the neck of summer, who would fain shake her off, as might well be expected for so quarrelsome a bride.

Castruccio now possessed the whole territory of Lucca and several other circumjacent provinces, in peace and obedience. But his eyes were always turned towards Florence; and his most ardent wish was to humble, if not possess himself of, that city. He made another step towards it during the summer. The abbot of Pacciana got by popular favour entire power in Pistoia; he used this in behalf of Castruccio, turning out the Florentine ambassadors, and giving up to the prince of Lucca / many of the strong-holds and towers of the Pistoian territory.[b] Castruccio was possessed of the fortresses placed on the mountain which overlooked the town, where he hovered, like a hawk over his prey, ready to pounce, delaying only for the destined minute.

During this summer also he conceived some hopes of taking Pisa. The head of the government there, who reigned entirely through the affections of the people, suddenly offended his masters; he was decapitated; and the various parties in the town, running to arms, entered into a bloody warfare. At this moment Castruccio appeared with his army on the hill of St. Giuliano: this sight pacified the combatants; they elected a new lord, and turned their powers towards resisting the common enemy.[c] Castruccio retreated to Lucca; but he was so moved by the overthrow of the Pisan chief, that, resolving to trust no more, as he had hitherto done, to the affections of his people, he erected in the same year a strong fortress within the walls of his city, which he called Agosta. He spared no expence or labour in it; and it was considered by all as the most / magnificent work of those days: it was situated in that part of the town which looks towards Pisa, surrounded by a strong and high wall, and fortified by

---

[a] The Roman goddess of war.

[b] Ormanno de Tedici, the Abbot Pacciana, expelled the Florentine ambassadors on 10 April, 1322 (Sismondi, ch. xxx).

[c] The leader was Coscietto delle Colle, a 'populario huomo di grande valore' (Villani, XI, cap. 153), beheaded by order of Ranieri della Gherardesca, head of the military forces. Coscietto, however, had come to power only shortly before, during a period of internecine warfare between patricians and plebeians (Sismondi, ch. xxx); the sudden appearance of Castruccio on San Giuliano is taken from Villani.

thirty towers. The inhabitants of a whole quarter were turned out of their dwellings, to make room for this new symbol of tyranny; and here he, his family, and followers, lived in proud security.[a]

Towards the end of the month of June, Euthanasia, who had hitherto been occupied in attending to the sorrows of Beatrice, received information, that one of her most valued Florentine friends was dangerously ill, and earnestly desired her attendance. She mentioned this to her guest; and Beatrice, ever variable, was then in a docile mood. She had long listened with deep and earnest faith to the lessons of Padre Lanfranco,[b] the confessor of the convent to which she was about to retire. It would seem that this old man humoured warily and wisely her disturbed understanding; for she appeared at peace with herself and others: if she now wept, she did not accuse, as she had before done, Him who had created the fountain of her tears. /

"Go, kind friend," said she to Euthanasia; "go; but return again. Remember, I claim your companionship, until I take the veil, – then you are free. Methinks, I should like to be left now in utter solitude, I could commune more intensely with the hopes and heavenly gifts that I entertain. Go; blessed spirit of Good, guardian Angel of poor Beatrice, poor in all but gratitude, – you shall not see your work marred on your return; you will still find me the good, obedient child, which I have been, now, I think, for more than a month."

Euthanasia left her with pain, and with a mournful presentiment; but, as all wore the aspect of peace, she thought herself bound to obey the voice of friendship, and to see, perhaps for the last time, one who had been the friend and companion of her early youth; and she departed for Florence. There were for her too many associations allied to the Val di Nievole, to permit her to choose that route. Besides Castruccio's army occupied the passes, and she feared to meet him. She accordingly went round by Pisa.[c] Nothing could be more beautiful than the country; the low Pisan hills / covered with chesnut and olive woods, interspersed with darker patches of pine and cork (while, among all, the cypresses raised their tapering spires), and, crowned by castles and towers, bounded in a plain of unparalleled fertility. The corn was cutting, and the song of the reapers kept time as it were with the noisy cicale in the olive trees, and the chirping birds. Peace, for the first time for several years, sat brooding with outspread wings over the land; and underneath their blessed shade sprung joy and plenty.

---

[a] Villani (IX, cap. 154) gives the fullest account of the building of the citadel of Agosta in 1322; spelled 'Augusta' in Tegrimi (p. 49) and Sismondi (ch. xxx); sometimes called 'La Gusta' in Villani.

[b] Not found as a historical character; the name may be suggested by the famous Pisan family of Lanfranchi.

[c] In 1820 two main routes, probably of ancient origin, led from Lucca to Pisa, both through the Bagni di Pisa; the less direct one, further to the west, skirted the banks of the Serchio and went through Ripafratta and Pugnano, the other went over the Monte San Giuliano; evidently the latter was intended here.

Euthanasia arrived at Florence. She found her friend recovered; but all her acquaintance, who had eagerly expected her arrival, were much disappointed when they heard that it was her intention to return to Lucca. She however both loved and pitied Beatrice too much, to be wanting in any of the duties of friendship towards her. After a month's residence in her natal and beloved city, she again departed from Florence. In the mean time what had become of the ill-fated prophetess? /

CHAPTER VI.

Beatrice meets Tripalda – is led by Bindo to the Witch's Cave.

The Albinois Bindo had been greatly struck by the appearance of Beatrice. There was a wildness in her countenance and gestures that excited his curiosity; and he seemed to feel instinctively that she had about her the marks of one who dealt with unembodied spirits. He had ventured to speak to his mistress concerning her; but he learnt nothing except that Ferrara was her native town. With this slight information he visited his friend, the witch, and they canvassed the subject together.

"Her eye sees beyond this world," said Bindo; "if you were to look on her, you would find a companion in your art. I have discovered that there is a mysterious connexion between her and the prince: he liberated her when she was imprisoned by the Dominican / fathers, as a Paterin, they say, but I suspect that it was for magic."

"At any rate," replied the witch, "there is a mystery in this that I will clear up. I will go to Ferrara, and learn who and what she is. Expect me back in less than a month; in the mean time watch her; watch every word and action; something may come of this."

The witch went to Ferrara. She traversed the hills, and went by unknown paths, and across the untrodden mountains, guided either by her former experience, or by the arch fiend himself; for it required almost supernatural knowledge to trace her way among the heaped and confused range of the Apennines. She walked at night, and rested during the day, and saw the sun many times rise and set among the wild forests that covered the hills. At Ferrara she learnt what she desired: Beatrice, the *Ancilla Dei*, the prophetess, was not forgotten; even her connexion with Castruccio had been guessed at; and some even dared assert, that she had never quitted Lucca, or the palace of the prince, during her pretended pilgrimage to Rome. The witch returned, / joyful to think that she had now obtained an instrument for some of her projects.

268

What were her projects? They had not that settled aim and undeviating course which one object might inspire. Her desire was malice; and her present hope, to impress upon Bindo some notion of the powers to which she pretended. She had been young once; and her nature, never mild, had been turned to ferocity by wrongs which had been received so long ago, that the authors of them were all dead, and she, the victim, alone survived. Calumny had blasted her name; her dearest affections had been blighted; her children torn from her; and she remained to execrate and to avenge.

Her evil propensities had long exhausted themselves in acts of petty mischief among the peasantry; but her connexion with Bindo gave her hopes of a wider scope for wickedness. To injure Castruccio, or to benefit Euthanasia, was alike indifferent to her. She saw and understood more of the human heart than Bindo did: she knew, that Euthanasia had once loved the prince; and injury to him she hoped would carry a double sting. She was old, perhaps / about to die; and she thought that there would be a pleasure in expiring amidst the groans of the victims of her malice.

In these days, when the passions, if they are not milder, are more restrained, and assume a more conventional appearance, it will be doubted if such fiendish love of mischief ever existed; but that it did, all tradition and history prove. It was believed, that the witch loved evil as her daily bread, and that she had sold her soul to the devil to do ill alone; *she* knew how powerless she was; but she desired to fill in every part the character attributed to her.

As she returned over the Apennines, she planned her future conduct; she thought she saw one mighty ruin envelop three master-spirits of the human kind, plotted by her alone. It was a dangerous experiment. "But I must die," she cried; "and what death will be sweeter, even if it be in the midst of flames, if so many share the torments with me? And thou, puny abortion, who darest with trembling hands meddle in work beyond thee, thou also shalt taste the poison so long withheld! / A canker cling to you all! I have long sought for labour suited to my genius; and now I have found it."

It was on the day previous to the departure of Euthanasia for Florence, that the witch returned: she met Bindo with a ghastly smile. "All," she cried, "is as you wish; the star of Castruccio will be extinguished behind the murky cloud which this same Beatrice will raise. Bring her to me; in time you shall know all: but be wary; the countess must be blind and deaf to our machinations."

Euthanasia had departed, leaving Beatrice far calmer than she had before been since her release from prison. But no feelings were more fluctuating than those of the poor prophetess. The day after she had parted from her protectress, Padre Lanfranco had been called upon urgent business to Sienna; and she was left without a guide to the workings of her own mind. She could not stand this; the consolations of Euthanasia, and the exhortations of the priest were alike forgotten; and Beatrice, turned out, as it were, without shelter, fell into repinings and despair. /

269

She had ardently desired to see Castruccio; but her confessor had commanded her to avoid all occasions of meeting him, if she wished to fit herself for the holy life to which she said she felt herself called. Beatrice was easily led; but she had no command over herself; and, the moment she was left to her own guidance, she was hurried away by the slightest impression.

Castruccio had just returned from Pistoia on the news of the insurrection of Pisa; and it was said that he would again quit Lucca on the following morning. "Now or never," thought Beatrice, "I may have my will unreproved; if this day escape, I am again surrounded, enchained; I might see him, hear his voice; oh! that I had courage to make the attempt! Yet I fear that this may be the ⌞suggestion of some evil spirit; I must not, dare not see him."

She wept and prayed; but in vain. In her days of extatic reverie she had sanctified and obeyed every impulse as of divine origin; and now she could not withstand the impressions she felt. She wrapped a coarse capuchin / around her, and sallied forth, with trembling steps, and eyes gleaming with tears, to go and gaze on the form of him for whom she had sacrificed her all. Hardly had she proceeded two paces from Euthanasia's palace-gate, before a form – a man – passed before her, and with a loud shriek she fell senseless on the pavement. She was brought back to the house, and carefully nursed; but several days elapsed, while, still possessed with fever, she raved of the most tremendous and appalling scenes and actions, which she fancied were taking place around her. The man whom she had seen was Tripalda; and from what she said in her delirium, it might be gathered, that he had been an actor in the frightful wrongs she had endured during her strange imprisonment in the Campagna di Roma. She was attended on with kindness, and she recovered; and such was the effect of her delirium, that she persuaded herself that what had so terrified her, was a mere vision conjured up by her imagination. She thought that the vivid image of this partner of her enemy's crimes, thus / coming across her while she was on the point of disobeying her confessor's injunction, was a warning and punishment from heaven.

Euthanasia was away, and Beatrice dared not speak to any: she brooded in her own mind over the appearance, mysterious as she thought it, of this man; until her fancy was so high wrought, that she feared her very shadow on the wall; and the echo of her own steps as she trod the marble pavement of her chamber, made her tremble with terror; the scenes she had witnessed, the horrors that she had endured in that unhallowed asylum of crime, presented themselves to her in their most vivid colours; she remembered all, saw all; and the deep anguish she felt was no longer mitigated by converse with her friend.

"Oh, cruel, unkind Euthanasia!" she cried, "why did you leave me? My only hope, my only trust was in you; and you desert me. Alas! alas! I am a broken reed, and none will support me; the winds blow, and I am prostrated to the ground; and, if I rise again, I am bruised, almost annihilated.

"Oh! that I could die! and yet I fear / death. Oh! thou, who wert my teacher and saviour, thou who expiredst smiling amidst flames, would that thou wert here to teach me to die! What do I in this fair garden of the world? I am a weed, a noxious insect; would that some superior power would root me out utterly, or some giant-foot tread me to dust! Yet I ask for what I do not wish. Was he a good God that moulded all the agonizing contradictions of this frail heart?

"Yet hush, presumptuous spirit! recall no more those lessons, which I hoped had been forgotten. Father! God! behold the most miserable and weakest of thy creatures; teach me to die; and then kill me!"

She sat in the neglected garden of the palace, on one of the pedestals which had been placed as a stand for the pots containing lemon trees; she leaned her head upon her hand, while the tears trickled down unheeded. It had been her delight, ever since her arrival at Lucca, to rove in this wild garden; and sometimes, when the sun had been long set, and the sound of the *Ave Maria* had died away, she would sit there, and, fixing her eyes on / the brightest star of the heavens, would sing the remembered melodies of her childhood. Nothing recalls past feeling so strongly as the notes of once-loved music; the memory was almost too much for her; and her eyes streamed tears, as she sang the sweetest lay that mortal ear had ever heard. Euthanasia had listened, she loved to listen, to her wild airs; and, as Beatrice saw her own deep emotions reflected in the beaming eyes of her friend, she felt soothed. But she was now alone; she felt the solitude; she felt, that she sang, and that none heeded her song: but, as the violet breathes as sweet an odour on the indifferent air, as when the loveliest creature in the world bends over it to inhale its fragrance; so did Beatrice now sing in solitude, while, her heart warmed, her imagination expanded, and she felt a transport which was pleasure, although a sea of black despair was its near boundary.

As she sang, Bindo came near her unperceived. He had never addressed her before; and she had never observed him: she was one of those persons, who feel their own life and identity so much, that they seem to have no / spare feeling and sense for the uninteresting events and persons that pass around them. He now spoke in a loud voice, arousing her from her deep reverie:

"Awake, prophetess; it is not well that you should sleep; the spirits of the air have work for you; all Tuscany feels your superhuman presence."

Beatrice started, and gazed with surprize on the being who thus addressed her: his dwarfish stature, his white hair and eyelashes, his pale and wrinkled face, and his light reddish eyes gave him a strange appearance; he looked indeed like one of the spirits whose existence he asserted; and she shuddered as she beheld him.

"I come," continued Bindo, "from one, whose eye can see the forms that pass, to me viewless, through the air; from one, who has thunder and tempest like dogs in a leash, and who can wind and unwind the will of man, as the simple girl spins thread from her distaff. I bear a message to you."

"Of whom do you speak? I do not understand you." /

"You will understand her words; for between the gifted there are signs, which none else know, but which bind them fast together."

"Are you one of those?" asked the wondering girl.

"I am not," replied Bindo; "you know that I am not, though I did not tell you. Are you not Beatrice, the prophetess of Ferrara? But my words are weak. There is one who lives in a cavern not far off, who was called, when young, Fior di Ligi, and now she calls herself Fior di Mandragola;[a] she rules the spirits who live about us, and is powerful over the seasons, and over the misfortunes and sorrows of life. She bade me tell you to awake; this night I will lead you to her; and she will by her incantations take off the veil which spirits of darkness have thrown over you."

"You talk of nothing; who are you?"

"I am a servant of the countess of Valperga; nothing more; a poor, ignorant, despised dwarf, a blight, a stunt: but I am more powerful in my weakness, than they with their giant limbs and strong muscles; – at least I have that strength, as long as I am obedient to her of / whom I spoke. These are the words she bade me to say to you, – 'There is a cloud over you which words of power can dispel; you are that which you seemed, and not that which you believe; – come to the cavern of Fior di Mandragola; and she will restore you to that height, from which the ignorance of others, and your own want of faith have precipitated you."

"And who is Fior di Mandragola?"

"A witch, – a woman with grey hair and decrepid limbs; she is clothed in rags, and feeds upon acorns and wood-nuts; but she is greater than any queen. If she were to command, this blue sky would be covered with clouds, the Serchio would overflow, and the plain of Lucca heave with earthquake; she makes men fear they know not what; for by her command spirits tug them by the hair, and they shiver with dread. One only she cannot command; one will, one fortune, one power cannot be controled by her; but your star surmounts his. – So, come, that you may know how to rule him."

"Whom?" /

"The prince of Lucca."

"Away! you know not what you say."

"I obey; speak not of this to the countess; I will be at your chamber-window by midnight."

Bindo retreated, leaving Beatrice startled and trembling. She did not rely on his wild creed; but she felt as if it might be true. She had once believed in the command of man over supernatural agency; and she had thrown aside that

---

[a] Lily flower, flower of the mandrake (a narcotic plant related to the nightshade, associated with witchcraft). The lily is the emblem of Florence. No clear reference has been found to Machiavelli's comedy *Mandragola*, which may nevertheless have suggested the name.

creed, when she lost her faith in her own powers. She ran rapidly in her thoughts over all that had occurred to her of this nature, her extacies, her delirious and joyous aspirations, – they were more dead and cold, than the white ashes of a long-extinguished fire; – but other events had occurred, and she had felt inexplicable emotions which seemed to link her to other existences. She remembered her dream; and, covering her eyes with her hands, she endeavoured to recal what words and forms had been revealed to her on that occasion—— vainly; the attempt served only more to shake a reason already tottering. It awoke her however from her unbelief; and she again felt those / deep and inquisitive thoughts, that had for many years been the life of her being. She resolved to visit Fior di Mandragola; she knew not why, but curiosity was mingled with the desire of change and freedom; she thought that it would be delightful to visit at midnight the witch's cave, guided by the strange Albinois. Beatrice was left alone to her own reflections for the whole evening; they were ever dreadful, except when the vivacity of her imagination mingled rainbows with the tempest.

Night came; and, wrapping a capuchin around her, she mounted the horse that Bindo had brought, and followed him across the country, towards the mountains which divide the Lucchese from the Modenese territory;[a] the dark forests extended into the valley, contrasting their black shadows with the dun hues of the low country; the stars shone keenly above. They rode swiftly; but the way was long; and it was two o'clock before they arrived at the witch's cave. It was a dreary habitation: and now, as the shades of night fell upon it, it appeared more desolate than ever; the pines made a sorrowful singing above it; the / earth around was herbless; and a few pine cones lay about, mingled with the grey rock that here and there peeped above the soil.

The witch sat at the door of the hovel. She was a strange being: her person was short, almost deformed, shrivelled and dried up, but agile and swift of motion; her brown and leathern face was drawn into a thousand lines; and the flesh of her cheeks, thus deformed, seemed hardly human; her hands were large, bony, and thin; she was unlike every other animal, but also was she unlike humanity, and seemed to form a species apart, which might well inspire the country people with awe. When she saw Beatrice, she arose, and advanced towards her, saying, "What do you here, child of a sleeping power? Come you here to teach, or to learn the secrets of our art?"

"I come at your own request," replied Beatrice, haughtily; "if you have nothing to say to me, I return."

"I have much to say to you," said Mandragola; "for I would awaken a spirit from lethargy, that can command us all. You are the mistress of those, of whom I am the slave; / will it, and a thousand spirits wait your bidding; look, like

---

[a] The region called the Pistoian Mountains by Tuscan writers, according to Sismondi (ch. xxx).

273

subdued hounds they now crouch at your feet, knowing that you are their superior. It is my glory to *obey* them, – how far do *you* transcend me!"

"You talk in riddles, good mother; I see no spirits, I feel no power."

"And if you did, would you be here? Here, at the cavern of a poor witch, who, spelling her incantations, and doing such penance as would make your young blood freeze but to hear it, just earns a power hardly gained, quickly to be resigned. But you could ride the winds, command the vegetation of the earth, and have all mankind your slaves. I ask you whether you did not once feel that strength? For a moment you were eclipsed; but the influence of the evil planet is well nigh gone, and you may now rule all, – will you accept this dominion?"

"Your words appear idle to me; give them proof, and I will listen."

"Consult your own heart, prophetess; and that will teach you far more than I can. Does it not contain strange secrets known only to / yourself? Have you never owned a power, which dwelt within you, and you felt your own mind distinct from it, as if it were more wise than you; so wise that you confessed, but could not comprehend its wisdom? Has it not revealed to you that, which without its aid you never could have known? Have you not seen this other self?"

"Stop, wonderful woman, if you would not madden me," screamed the poor terrified Beatrice. "That is the key, the unbreakable link of my existence; that dream must either place me above humanity, or destroy me."

"You own this power?" cried the witch triumphantly.

"Send away the Albinois, and I will tell you all. [At the beck of the witch Bindo withdrew.]ᵃ Yet I gasp for breath, and fear possesses me. What do you tell me of power? I feel that I am ruled; and, when this dream comes over me, as it now does, I am no longer myself. I dreamed of a flood, of a waste of white, still waters, of mountains, of a real scene which I had never beheld. There was a vast, black house standing in the midst of the water; / a concourse of dark shapes hovered about me; and suddenly I was transported into a boat which was to convey me to that mansion. Strange! another boat like to mine moved beside us; its prow was carved in the same manner; its rowers, the same in number, the same in habiliment, struck the water with their oars at the same time with ours; a woman sate near the stern, aghast and wild as I; – but their boat cut the waves without sound, their oars splashed not the waters as they struck them, and, though the boats were alike black, yet not like mine did this other cast a black shadow on the water. We landed together; I could not walk for fear; I was carried into a large room, and left alone: I leaned against the hangings, and there advanced to meet me another form. It was myself; I knew it; it stood before me, melancholy and silent; the very air about it was still. I can

---

ᵃ The square brackets and the sentence they enclose are probably Godwin's insertion.

tell no more; – a few minutes ago I remembered nothing of all this; a few moments, and I distinctly remembered the words it spoke; they have now faded. Yes; there is something mysterious in my nature, which I cannot fathom." /

Beatrice shivered; her face was deadly pale, and her eyes were glazed by fear. The witch had now tuned her instrument, and she proceeded to play on it with a master's hand.

"Heavenly girl," she said, "I acknowledge myself your slave. Command me and my powers, as you will; they will do all you bid them; – but that is little. There are other spirits, which belong not to the elements, but to the mind and fortunes of man, over which I have no sway, but which are attendant upon you. Fear not! The revelations you have received are almost too tremendous for your weak human frame; but gather strength; for your body and your spirit may master all the kings of the earth. That other self, which at one time lives within you, and anon wanders at will over the boundless universe, is a pure and immediate emanation of the divinity, and, as such, commands all creatures, be they earthly or ethereal. As yet you have seen it only in a dream; have faith, and the consciousness of its presence will visit your waking reveries."

Beatrice sighed deeply, and said: "I was in hope that my part was done, and that I / should die without more agitation and fear; but I am marked, and cannot combat with my destiny. Strange as is the tale which I have just related, I cannot believe what you say: and, though doubtless there are other existences, of which we know nothing, yet I do not believe that we can have communication with, and far less power over them. I would fain preserve the little reason I have still left me; and that tells me that what you say is false."

"But if I can prove it to be true?"

"How?"

"Ask what you will! Would you see the cloudless sky become black and tempestuous? Would you hear the roaring of the overflowing waters, or see the animals of the forest congregate at my feet? Or, would you exert your own power? Would you draw towards you by your powerful incantations, one whom you wish to see, and who must obey your call? If you speak, all must obey; the prince himself, the victorious Castruccio, could not resist you."

The burning cheeks, and flashing eyes of the prophetess, shewed the agitation that this / proposal excited in her heart. Poor girl! she still loved; that wound still festered, ever unhealed. She would have risked her soul, to gain a moment's power over Castruccio. She paused; and then said, "In three days I will tell you what I wish, and what I will do."

"In the mean time swear never to reveal this visit, this cavern, or my name: swear by yourself."

"A foolish vow, – by myself I swear."

"Enough; you dare not break that oath."

The witch retreated into her cave; and Bindo came forward to conduct

Beatrice home. She was faint and tired; and day dawned before they arrived at the palace of Euthanasia.

The three following days were days of doubt and trepidation for the unfortunate Beatrice. At one moment she utterly discredited the pretensions of Mandragola; but then her imagination, that evil pilot for her, suggested, *Yet, if it should be so!* and then she would picture forth the scenes she desired, until she gasped with expectation. At last, she thought, – "There will be no harm in the experiment; if her promises are vain, no injury will result; – / if true – To be sure I know they are not; but something will happen, and at least I will try.

"I know that Euthanasia, and more than she, Padre Lanfranco, would tell me, that, if true, this woman deals with the devil, and that I, who have lately saved my soul from his grasp, should beware of trusting myself within his reach. All this is well to children and old women; but I have already tempted the powers above me too far to flinch now. Am I not, was I not, a Paterin? Euthanasia, who has never wandered from the straight line of her duty, and Lanfranco, who has learned his morality in a cloister, cannot know what it most becomes an excommunicated wretch like me to do.

"Yet I am very ungrateful and wicked, when I say this; ungrateful to their prayers, wicked in transgressing the laws which God has promulgated.

"What does this woman say? that I shall see him, that he will obey my voice, and that, not by magic art, but by that innate power, which, by the order of the universe, one spirit possesses over another: – that I shall see him, / as I have seen him! – Oh, saints of heaven, suffer me not to be tempted thus! But no, – the heavenly powers deign not to interfere; they know my weakness, my incapacity to resist, – but, like most careless guardians, they permit that to approach which must overcome me. I am resolved; she shall guide me; if nothing come (as most surely nothing will come), it imports not. And, if I am destined for one moment more in this most wretched life to taste of joy, others may (but I will not) dash the intoxicating draught away."

She thought thus, and spoke thus to her secret mind; but every hour her resolution fluctuated, and remorse, hope, and dread possessed her by turns. She feared to be alone; but the presence of an indifferent person made her nerves tremble with the restraint she was obliged to keep upon herself. There seemed some link of confidence between her and Bindo; and she called for him to dispel the appalling sensations with which solitude inspired her. He came; and his conversation only tended to increase her chaos of conflicting thoughts. He related the wonderful exploits of Mandragola; / how he had seen her call lightning and cloud from the south, and how at her bidding the soft western wind would suddenly arise, and dispel the wondrous tempests she had brewed; how the planet of night obeyed her, and that, once during the full moon, this planet had suddenly deserted the sky, but that, while the heavens were blank and rayless, its image continued to lie placidly in the stream near which they stood. He related the strange effects she had produced upon the minds of men, forcing them most unwillingly to do her pleasure; at other times depriving them of their senses, so that for many hours they wandered about like madmen, until at her command their faculties were restored to them.

Beatrice listened, half in disdain, half in fear; her conclusion still was, – "The experiment is worth trying; if her words be false, there is no harm done; if true" – and then her imagination pictured forth happiness that never should be hers. /

CHAPTER VII.

Euthanasia returns. – Beatrice meets the witch, and encounters Castruccio and Tripalda. – Dies.

On the third night she returned to the witch. "You need not speak," said Mandragola, "I know your thoughts; you hardly believe my words, yet you are determined to make the trial. It is well; I should be surer of success, if you had implicit faith in my powers and your own; but it is enough. What do you wish to effect?"

"First mother, I must know what I can do."

"Your power is almost illimitable; but that of which I spoke, and that power which you prize most, is the power which you possess over the prince of Lucca. Do you wish to / see him? Do you wish in solitude, with none but me near, to see him come, to hear him renew his antient vows?"

"He never made vows to me," cried Beatrice angrily; "He was bound to me, I thought, by stronger ties than mortal oaths; that is past for ever; but, except the salvation of my soul, I would sacrifice every thing to see him once again, divested of the ceremonial power, listening to what will never be told, consoling her who can never be consoled."

"That is easy work," said the witch, with alacrity; "but first swear, swear by all that you hold sacred in the world, by your life, by his, that you will never disclose this conversation, or what I shall now reveal to you, or hint in any manner the work we shall undertake."

Beatrice shivered; she could no longer stand, she sunk to the ground: the witch went into the hut, and brought her a bowl of water; Beatrice put it to her lips; then suddenly withdrawing it, she cried, – "You have given me a poisonous drug, either to kill me, or undermine my understanding; – dare you thus trifle with me?" /

The witch took the bowl from her hand, and drank the liquid it contained: "Take shame for your mistrust," she said; "this was pure water from the spring;

277

and, except that the charmed moon-beams sleep on it, even when you see not the moon in the sky, it does not differ from the waters of any other fountain. Now speak; do you swear secrecy?"

Again the prophetess paused. But curiosity and hope hurried her beyond discretion; and with folded hands placed between the dry and skinny palms of the witch, she pronounced the vow that was dictated.

Mandragola then said: "This satisfies me. The moon is now on the wane: when she fills again, I will send Bindo to inform you what is to be done. Fear not, but that all will be well."

Beatrice returned to Lucca. Her glazed eyes and pale cheeks told that the spirit which animated her now found nor rest nor hope. She dreaded to look forward to the fearful trial she was about to make; and yet she could think of nothing else. Her rosary was thrown aside; her prayers were forgotten; and love / again reassumed his throne in her heart. Her reason was disturbed by doubt and fear; and she often sat whole hours, her eye fixed upon the earth, her parted lips pale, her hands closed with convulsive strength, as she tried to reason herself into disbelief concerning the promises and assertions of Mandragola. It was too much for her weak frame; if the witch had been near her to mark the wasting of her faculties, she might have wound her plot so as to inspire her with some courage: but no one was near except Bindo; and he by his tales, and his own fears and belief, only increased the combat of feelings to which the prophetess was a prey.

Euthanasia returned to Florence. She was much disappointed, much grieved, to find her friend far worse both in body and mind, than when she left her. More than all wildness of words and manner, she feared her silence and reserve, so very unlike her latest disposition. If the convent, or her future plans were named, she listened calmly, but did not reply; no intreaties could persuade her to give words to that which preyed upon her mind. / She would weep; and then, flying from the affectionate reproaches of her protectress, she would shut herself up to grieve alone, or far more dangerously to dream of the return of love and joy. Euthanasia reasoned, persuaded, intreated, but vainly: accustomed to the caprices of this unfortunate girl, she saw nothing in what now occurred, that appeared to arise from any external impulse; and she hoped that indulgence and kindness would in time restore her to her former calm. She reproached herself for having left her; and she resolved that, unless indeed Beatrice took the veil, which now seemed doubtful, she would never again separate herself from her. She loved her tenderly, and pitied her so truly, that she was willing to sacrifice all her own hopes of future peace to soothe and restore her to some degree of happiness.

Her endeavours were useless. The melancholy of poor Beatrice was undissipated by the slightest gleam of tranquillity: for five days she had not spoken, and had hardly touched any food. Euthanasia tried in vain to console her, and, hopeless of good, sought to excite any / passion that might rouse her from her mute reveries; she spoke not, but wandered restlessly from room to room, or among the wild paths of the garden; and thence she would have escaped into the open country, but that her weak limbs sunk beneath her. One night Euthanasia slept, when Beatrice suddenly entered the room; and, twining herself round her neck, and wrapping the long and thick hair of her friend around her brows——

"Save me!" she cried, "save me from madness, which, as a fiend, pursues and haunts me. I endeavour to fly him; but still he hovers near: is there no escape? Oh! if God be good, surely he will redeem my soul from this curse. I would fain preserve my reason; my lips are bloodless, and my hair quite grey; I am a skeleton without flesh or form; I am to what lives, like the waning moon at noonday, which floats up as a vapour, and the blue air seems to penetrate its pale and sickly form. Happiness, beauty, love have passed away; but I would fain preserve that without which I am as a poor hunted beast, whose sole repose is on the spear of the huntsmen. Breathe on / me, Euthanasia, breathe on my hands, my eyes; perhaps some portion of calm may flow from your bosom to mine. I only wish not to be mad; yet, if what is said be true, these wonderful things may be, and I still sane. There, there, your hand is cool; press my head. I know you well; you are Euthanasia; I am Beatrice; I may still be preserved from madness."

Euthanasia wept; she folded Beatrice in her arms; she placed her cool hand on her brow, and her pale cheek close to the flushed one of the poor sick girl. Beatrice rested a few moments in silence; and then again she spoke. "It has been said, that I am a witch, one who has power over the elements, and still more over the mind of man. I do not believe this: once, I know, a very long time ago, I fancied myself a prophetess; but I awoke from that dream many years since. Why then do they madden me with these insinuations? I will tell you, Euthanasia (sweet name, dear, much-loved friend), that sometimes I fancy this is true. – Oh! that I could tell the heavy secret that weighs upon my soul! I have sworn – / they did not well, that made me swear: – yet there is some truth in what they say, doubtless there is some truth, and it shall be *proved*. Well, well; I have sworn, and I will not tell – Good night, dearest; I shall sleep now; so not a word more; I have reasoned with myself, and am content."

Beatrice crept back to her chamber; but Euthanasia could not again rest. She was amazed at her friend's strange words, and tried to divine whether they proceeded from the heated imagination of the prophetess, or from some real event of which Euthanasia was ignorant; but she had no clue to guide her in her conjectures; and it appeared to her most probable, that Beatrice was moved by the suggestions of her own heart; she could not guess the dreadful and maniac thoughts that really disturbed her, or the frightful incitements that had been employed to deceive her.

A fortnight passed thus; when the Albinois brought a message from Mandra-gola, bidding Beatrice repair that same night at twelve, to a wood about four miles from Lucca. At this time Castruccio was employed in building the / tower of Nozzano, on a small hill which was surrounded by the wood chosen by the witch.[a] The weather (it was in the month of July) was exceedingly hot; the cattle panted beneath the sun; the earth was herbless; all life decayed: but delicious nights succeeded these oppressive days; and Castruccio was accustomed to repair, as early as two in the morning, to visit the fortress. Mandragola knew the spot near which he passed; and she so planned her scheme, that her incantation should be wound to the desired pitch, at the moment when he should ride through the wood: and thus, to the simple mind of the Albinois, and the exalted imagination of Beatrice, afford a proof of the extent of her power.

It is impossible to say what her object was in all this; she might be merely instigated by the desire to excite respect and terror, and have trusted that this apparent confirmation of her assertions would enable her to acquire unlimited power over the mind of her victims. She did not intend on this occasion that Beatrice should speak to the prince;—— that she should call for him, and he appear, was sufficient / mummery for one day: another time more might be done, and another step taken in the labyrinth of error and fraud.

That same night Bindo tapped at the door of Beatrice's chamber. The prophetess opened it; – she looked aghast and wild, but spoke not. – "This is the hour," said the Albinois.

"Wrap your cloak round you," he continued, "that you may not be known." Beatrice did as he desired, moving her arms like inanimate machines, and turning her eyes around, as if she saw nothing. Bindo led her down-stairs; they quitted the palace by a small back door; he made her mount a horse; and they rode out of the town. All passed in silence; Beatrice hardly appeared to know whither she was going, or why she went; the bridle fell from her hands, and hung loosely on the horse's neck; but the animal mechanically followed Bindo's horse, which led the way.

They arrived at the wood, and dismounted. Bindo tied the horses to a tree, and proceeded cautiously through the intricate paths of the forest. It was an ilex wood; and the dark / foliage canopied them above, while the moonbeams penetrated through the interstices of the leaves, and made a chequered shadow upon the ground, which was despoiled of its grassy covering through long drouth. At length they came to a more trodden road; and this led to a kind of woody amphitheatre, an open space in the midst of the trees, one of the corners of which the path traversed, and all around the ilexes formed a circular boundary of ample circumference. At one of the extremities, farthest from the

---

[a] The Rocca di Nozzano, a fortress of Uguccione overlooking Ripafratta on the north bank of the Serchio, restored by Castruccio (Tegrimi, p. 49). '[From the Guinigi tower in Lucca] towards the west you will see a dark wood where they will tell you there are the ruins of a castle which Castruccio built – & that wood is the scene of the incantations where Castruccio & Tripalda appear' (Mary Shelley to Leigh Hunt, 7 August 1823, *MWSL*, I, p. 364).

path, was a fountain, which kept a soft murmuring all the still night through. Near this fountain the witch sat: she was weaving two coronals of ivy, and muttering as she wove; Beatrice and the Albinois were before her, but she appeared not to notice them. Beatrice stood, her arms hanging down, her head fallen on her bosom in a mute lethargy, her cloak had dropt from her shoulders, and fallen to her feet; she was dressed, as the witch had commanded, in white: several years had passed since she had been thus habited, and her attire displayed the thinness of her form and the paleness of her wasted / cheeks; her hands were skinny and yellow, her hair perfectly grey; a few weeks ago, although mingled with white, its antient colour was preserved; but since then it had quite changed; her eyes were sunken, ringed with black, and rayless.

When the witch had finished her work, she rose; and, taking some of the water of the fountain in the hollow of her hand, she threw it over Beatrice, and then crowned her with one of the chaplets; she placed the other on her own head; and then she said to Bindo: – "I am about to sanctify this place; you must depart."

Bindo bowed assent, and disappeared. She took up a curiously fashioned ewer of brass; and, filling it at the fount, she walked round the amphitheatre of trees, sprinkling the ground as she went, and muttering her incantations, till she came round again to the spot, where Beatrice stood, white, motionless, and silent. "You appear faint, daughter," she said; "drink of this water." – She put it to the lips of her victim, who drank it eagerly; and immediately a change took place in her appearance; / her eyes lighted up, her cheeks were flushed, the heavy chain of mortality seemed to fall from her, she became active and even gay; by degrees a kind of transport seized her, a drunkenness of spirit, which made her lose all constraint over her words and actions, although it did not blind her to what was passing around*.

"Aye, mother," she said, "I know what I come for; now let us begin; I am an enchantress, you say; I can conjure him to appear, who before defied my powers? be it so; – let us begin."

"Listen," replied Mandragola, "no art requires so much patience as ours. We will make our incantations; and you will see him pass on horseback along that road: do not now seek to speak to him. Exercise your power moderately at first; and it will be greater afterwards: bind him now with a straw; in time he will be inextricably enthralled. To night be it enough that you see him." /

"Enough! oh! I would lay down my life for one, one moment's sight!"

---

* Jusquiamo [henbane: hebenon, *Shakespear*] was the principal ingredient in these intoxicating draughts. They had the property of producing madness.[a]

---

[a] An adaptation of Targioni, I, p. 126; noted in adds. e. 17, p. 221 rev.; the phrase in square brackets is probably Godwin's insertion. The reference is to *Hamlet*, I. v. 62. (The much-debated identification of the Folio reading 'hebenon' with 'henbane' was first conjectured in 1754 by the antiquarian Zachary Grey.)

The night was perfectly still; the air was sultry, and not a leaf moved: the trees, bathed as it were in the cold moonshine, slept; and the earth received their moveless shadows on her quiet bosom. The fountain murmured on; beside it stood the witch and Beatrice; – Beatrice, her eyes lifted to heaven, her arms crossed on her bosom, her hair clinging round her faded neck. Mandragola was full of business; she piled a small heap of wood, walking often around it, singing or chanting strange verses, and scattering water and oil about her; she drew, with a wand formed of a peeled chesnut-bough, a circle which surrounded the pile and the spot whereon Beatrice stood, and commanded her not to pass the line till she should give permission; since that circle would preserve her from the spirits that their terrible incantations had called around them. She then turned to the pile again, and placed on it incense and odoriferous gums, and plants, and strange devices, cut in wood, or moulded in wax, which no one might understand: then to crown the work / she cut off a lock of Beatrice's hair, and threw it on the heap.

She had just accomplished this work, when a slight sound struck her ear; "Now is the time!" she exclaimed; and she set up a wild song to drown the trampling of the approaching horses; she lighted a torch, and cried – "This is your work, mistress of the powers of air; light the pyre, and call thrice on the name of the prince of Lucca!"

Beatrice started forward with frantic haste; she seized the torch, thrust it into the pile, which caught the flame, and blazed up as she cried aloud, "Castruccio! Castruccio! Castruccio!"

And then, unable to restrain her impatience, she ran towards the path in which Mandragola had said he would appear. The witch called on her to stay; but she was too decrepid to follow swiftly to stop her: the sound of coming horsemen was now distinctly heard; Beatrice threw herself on her knees, in the midst of the path by which they must pass; with flashing eyes and outstretched arms, she gazed eagerly forwards: the dark wood covered / her; the moon beams fell on her; and there she, once the loveliest, now the most lost, the most utterly undone of women, kneeled in frantic expectation. The horsemen approached; a turn in the path concealed them, until they were full upon her; and then she saw Castruccio and Tripalda advance. Her brain, already on fire with impatience, and her spirits exalted by the drug administered to her, could no longer sustain the sensations that overpowered her. The presence of Tripalda was to her the sign of diabolical interference; she believed him dead; that it was his spirit which then appeared; and, if so, it was also an unreal form, the resemblance of Castruccio alone, that she beheld.—— She sunk in convulsions on the road.

Castruccio, surprised at what he saw, leaped from his horse; and his example was followed by his attendants. The witch, who had hitherto hobbled towards Beatrice, seeing them dismount, endeavoured to escape; but Tripalda, who, judging of others by himself, was ever ready to suspect knavery, cut off her retreat, and ordered two of the servants to hold / her. She submitted quietly, but remained invincibly silent to all the questions that were put to her. Beatrice was carried to the fountain; and they endeavoured, by chafing her temples, and rubbing her hands, to bring her to life: the prince himself supported her head; but he did not recognize her; so utterly was she changed from what the prophetess of Ferrara had been. Once she opened her eyes; she saw the face of Castruccio leaning over her, and she smiled. Castruccio thought that he knew that smile; but Tripalda, leaving the witch, pressed in among those who were about her. – No one who had seem him could ever forget him; she saw what she believed to be the evil genius of her life; and she again sunk into insensibility.

In the mean time the Albinois, who had been lurking near the spot, hearing the trampling of horses, and the sound of men's voices, ventured forward. Mandragola saw him first, as he came into the moonshine from under the dark covert of trees. She darted forward, and cried aloud – "Fly! fly!" Her words and gesture attracted the notice of her guards, as Bindo / turned about to obey her orders. They pursued him, and easily took him prisoner.

He was brought to Castruccio, who instantly recognized him. "What do you here?" he demanded. "Are you not the servant of the countess of Valperga?"

"I am."

"Who then is this lady? and how came you here?"

"That is Beatrice of Ferrara. I can tell you no more until she" (pointing to the witch) "gives me leave."

The name of Beatrice was sufficient to transfix the prince with pity and remorse. "Beatrice!" he cried, and throwing himself on the earth beside her, he kissed her hand passionately. Her faintness began now to dissipate; but her reason did not return. The first words she uttered were those of madness; she raved of that which ever haunted her thoughts in delirium, her prison in Romagna. Tripalda heard the words, and started, as if he had trodden on a viper; his sallow complexion became paler, – but Castruccio did not attend to this, or make out her speech. He / perceived her frenzy; and, unable any longer to endure his remorse, or the sight of his hapless victim, he gave hasty orders that she should be conveyed slowly and carefully to the palace of the countess of Valperga, and her companions be detained as prisoners; and then he rode off. He rode towards Lucca; and, reflecting on the fright that Euthanasia might sustain if she saw her unhappy friend brought home in so miserable a state, he resolved to go first to her palace, and inform her of what had passed.

"And are you come to this, lovely Beatrice?" he thought. "And is this the same creature, who, radiant with beauty and joy, formerly gave me her benediction at the palace of the good old Marsilio? I remember that day, as if it were yesterday; and now I find her with grey hairs and a wasted form, a young fruit utterly blighted, and, worse than all, her reason fallen the victim of her misery. Am I the cause of this?"

He rode on swiftly, and soon arrived at the palace. He did not reflect that he was going to behold Euthanasia, the beautiful and beloved; / and thinking of nothing but Beatrice, and finding the gates open, he entered. It was about three in the morning. During the night Euthanasia had thought that she heard a groan come from the chamber of Beatrice; and she hastened thither, to discover if any new sorrow disturbed her unfortunate guest. The chamber was empty; the bed unslept upon; she sought her in the adjoining rooms; and, not finding her, she became terrified, and, rousing the house, had the palace searched, but in vain; no trace of her was left. She sent several messengers to different gates of the town to learn whether she had been seen, and waited with inexpressible anxiety for their return.

The prince found men consulting together in the great hall; and the first words he heard was the name of "Madonna Beatrice."

"Do not be alarmed," he said, coming forward. "I know where she is, and she will soon be here; some of you see that her couch be prepared, and seek a physician, for she is very ill. Where is the countess?"

Appearing thus unexpectedly and alone, the / men did not recognize the prince; but the quick ear of Euthanasia caught the sound of his voice; and, coming out of an adjoining room, she cried, "Do you then know where my friend is, Castruccio?"

"I do indeed," he replied: "and it is fortunate; since I may have saved her from evil hands. But I am perfectly ignorant how and why she came to a spot so far from the town."

He related in a few words where and in what manner he had found her, and concluded by saying, "I leave her to your care; I know how kind and generous you are. If she recover, I intreat you to inform me without delay of so favourable a change."

As he said this, the trampling of horsemen was heard in the streets; – he cried, "I dare not see her again; farewell, Euthanasia; pity her and me!"

He hastened from the palace, and in a few minutes after Beatrice was brought in; her countenance was deadly pale, and her arms hung lifelessly over the shoulder of one of the men who supported her; her hair was dank, and her garments wetted with the dew of / morning; her eyes were open, and glared meaninglessly around. They laid her on a bed; and Euthanasia, approaching, took her hand; Beatrice did not notice her; she seemed to have lost all sensation, and the rolling of her eyes, and the convulsive gaspings of her breath, were all the signs of life that she gave.

Why should I describe the scenes that ensued during the following days? Descriptions of unmixed horror cannot be pleasing; and what other feelings could mingle to soften that sensation, on beholding the declining state of poor Beatrice? She never again had any return of reason, nor did she ever sleep; generally she lay, as I have described, pale and motionless; if ever she woke to sensation, it was to rave and scream, so that the hardest heart might have been penetrated with excess of pity. Some have seen, most have read the descriptions of, madness. She called upon Euthanasia, upon Castruccio; but, more than all, she fancied that she was chained to her dungeon-floor in her tremendous prison, mocked and laughed at by her keepers; and sometimes she imagined that these beloved friends / were chained beside her, suffering those torments which she had herself endured. She never in her wildest sallies uttered a reproachful word against Castruccio, although it appeared that she sometimes thought that he accused himself; and then with the tenderest accents, and most winning sweetness, she bade him not to grieve, and assured him that he had committed no fault.

These intervals of raving were short and rare; and, as she became weaker, she still seldomer emerged from her state of insensibility. She was evidently dying; the physicians gave no hopes of her life; and the priests crowded about her. Padre Lanfranco was among them; and he bitterly reproached himself for having left her, and endeavoured to compensate for his neglect, by watching day and night for some return of reason, when he might ask whether she died in the faith of the church. This never arrived: but the priests were lenient; they placed the crucifix on her breast, and she seemed to press it; once, when the name of her Redeemer was mentioned, / her eyes lighted up, and a smile seemed to play upon her lips. She was so perfectly senseless, that this could have had no connexion with the words that had been used; but the charitable priests chose to construe it into an external[a] assurance of the salvation of her soul; and they administered the sacraments. She never spoke afterwards; but day by day she grew weaker; Castruccio sent continually to inquire of her state; but he dared not come. Euthanasia hardly ever left her bed side; and she became as pale, and almost as weak, as the dying Beatrice.

Such had been the effect of the witch's incantations. Beatrice had needed the tenderest nursing; and she had received instead, a shock which saner nerves than hers could hardly have sustained. Yet her death was smoothed to her by the affectionate ministry of her friend; and she at last lost all sense even of pain. She died, peacefully, and calmly as a child; and her many sorrows and wrongs no longer filled her with anguish and despair. She died: Euthanasia was beside her when she / heard a gentle sigh, followed by a fixedness of feature and rigidity of limb, which shewed that the mighty change had taken place in her frame.

Tears and lamentation succeeded to her death. Euthanasia wished that her funeral should be private and unnoticed; but Castruccio insisted that it should be attended with every circumstance of pomp used in those days. The room was hung with black cloth, and made as dark as night, to give brightness to the many torches by which it was illuminated. Beatrice was laid on a bier, arrayed in costly apparel, and canopied with a pall of black velvet embroidered with

---

[a] Corrected from 'enternal'; 'internal' is an alternative possibility.

gold: flowers, whose beauty and freshness mocked the livid hues of the corpse, were strewn over her, and scattered about the room; and two boys walked about, swinging censers of incense. The chamber was filled with mourning women; one, the chief, dressed in black, with dishevelled hair, knelt near the head of the bier, and began the funeral song; she sang a strain in monotonous, but not unmelodious voice: the verses were / extempore, and described the virtues and fortunes of the deceased; they ended with the words:

*Oime! ora giace morta sulla bara!**

And the other women, taking up the burthen, cried in shrill tones:

Oime! ora giace morta sulla bara!

Again they were silent: and the *Cantatrice*, renewing her song, repeated another verse in praise of poor Beatrice. Castruccio had told her in part what ought to be the subject of her song. The first verse described her as beautiful, beloved and prosperous, among her friends and fellow citizens: "Then," cried the singer, "the spoiler came; she lost all that was dear to her; and she wandered forth a wretch upon the earth. Who can tell what she suffered? Evil persons were abroad; they seized on her; and she became the victim of unspoken crimes: worse ills followed, madness and heresy, which threatened to destroy her soul."

The woman wept, wept unfeigned tears as / she sang; and the hired mourners sympathized in her grief; each verse ended with the words,

Oime! ora giace morta sulla bara!

which were echoed by them all, and accompanied by cries and tears.[a]

She ended; and, night being come, the hour for interment arrived. The censers were replenished with incense; and the priests sprinkled holy water about the room. Four lay-brothers raised the bier, and followed a troop of priests and monks, who went first with the crucifix, chaunting a *De profundis*.[b] The streets through which they passed, were rendered as light as day by the glare of torches; after the priests, came the bier on which the body lay exposed, covered with flowers; many of the young girls and women of the city followed, each carrying a wax taper; a troop of horse closed the procession. It was midnight when they entered the church; the moon threw the shadow of the high window on the pavement; but all shadows were effaced by the torches which filled the church. Beatrice was laid in her peaceful grave; and, mass being said for the repose of her soul, the ceremony closed. /

---

* Alas! she now lies dead upon the bier!

---

[a] Invented from Muratori's account of ritual *lamentatrici* (hired mourners) at funerals (Muratori, I, diss. 23, pp. 278–80; noted in Ab. Dep. e. 274, p. 69); see also p. 61.

[b] 'Out of the Deep', the opening words of the penitential Psalm 130, used in the mass for the dead.

Euthanasia had not been present: and, although she longed for solitude to weep in peace over the fate of her hapless friend, she was obliged to receive the visits of the Lucchese ladies, who came to condole with her on this occasion, and perhaps to satisfy their curiosity concerning its object. The funeral feast was sumptuous and well attended, though few knew in whose honour it was given. Euthanasia shrunk from their questions, and was angry with Castruccio, that he should have placed her in so disagreeable a situation. It seemed to her better to befit the hapless fate of Beatrice, that she should have been permitted to depart unmarked, wept only by those, who knew her worth, and who lamented her unequaled misfortunes. It was the false pride of Castruccio, that made him think differently; and such were the prejudices of the times, that his contemporaries would have agreed with him, that he had in some degree compensated for the injuries that Beatrice had received from him, by the magnificence of her funeral.

After the ceremony was ended, Castruccio first thought of the two individuals whom he / had found in the forest with their victim. Mandragola had preserved an uniform silence; and no threats, nor torture itself, could induce her to speak. Bindo was formed of frailer clay; she had charged him not to reveal what had passed, and had imprecated the most terrible curses on his head, if he disobeyed. He trembled; but the sight of the instruments of torture overcame him, and he confessed all. Mandragola was condemned by the laws which then existed in every country against the dealers in the black art, and suffered death as a witch. Euthanasia endeavoured to procure the freedom of the Albinois; but in vain. He was confined to the dungeons of the Dominican convent; he pined for liberty; and in a few months he died.

The tie which bound Euthanasia to Lucca, was now broken. For many days she sorrowed, forgetful of herself, over the fate of her friend. By degrees however the feelings of actual life returned to her; and she longed to quit a town, which had been for her the theatre of tremendous misfortune. Two months after / the death of Beatrice she returned to Florence; where she found, in the society of her friends, and in the cultivation of her mind, some alleviation for her sorrow, and some compensation for the many evils she had endured. /

287

CHAPTER VIII.

Castruccio's Progress in Arms. – He brings Devastation to the Gates of Florence.
– A Conspiracy formed against him.

Castruccio had now been lord of Lucca for six years,[a] and had attained his thirty-third year; his character was formed; and his physiognomy, changed from its youthful expression, had become impressed by his habitual feelings. Constant exposure to the sun and weather had tinged his cheek with brown; which, but for that, had been deadly pale; for care, and the strong emotions to which he was subject, had left their mark on his countenance; his eye had grown hollow, and the smooth lustre of his brow was diminished by lines, which indeed looked gracefully at his years, since they marked the progress of thought; but some, more straggling and undefined, shewed that / those passions whose outward signs he suppressed, yet preyed upon the vital principle; his eyes had not lost their fire, but their softness was gone.

He was kind and even grateful to his friends, so long as he considered them as such; but he was quick to distrust; and cold looks and averted favour followed suspicion: if these were answered by aught but patience and submission, hatred quickly came, and that never failed to destroy its object. If he only suspected, that was sufficient cause, that he who had become thus obnoxious to his prince should be told that it was his will that he should instantly depart from Lucca; and the confiscation filled the public coffers. If he thought that he had reason to fear, the doom of that man whom he feared was sealed: he was cruel and unrelenting; and the death of his victim did not satisfy him; several were starved to death by his command, and worse tortures were inflicted upon others: – something of this was to be attributed to the usage of the times; but cruelty had become an elemental feature of Castruccio's character. /

If he were feared by his enemies in open war, his secret policy was still more dreaded. He had not forgotten the lessons of Alberto Scoto; and, as his attempt on the life of the king of Naples might prove, his measures had perhaps been influenced by the counsels of Benedetto Pepi. He had many spies in each town, and collected intelligence from every court of Lombardy. Women and priests were his frequent instruments; and even the more distinguished among the citizens were induced through his largesses to betray the counsels of their country.

---

[a] i.e. since 1316; upon his being acclaimed Lord of Lucca after his expulsion of the Della Faggiuola.

Such was Antelminelli, the some time lover of Euthanasia; daring, artful, bounteous and cruel; evil predominated in his character; and, if he were loved by a few, he was hated by most, and feared by all. His perpetual wars, which impoverished the neighbouring states, did not enrich his own; his artful policy sowed distrust among dear friends, and spies and traitors abounded during his reign. In Lucca he was as an eagle in a cage; he had a craving that seemed to demand the empire of the world; and, weak as he was / in means and hopes, he made the nations tremble.[a6]

The object of Castruccio's present policy was Florence. He proceeded by measured steps; but he was perpetually gaining some advantage against the rival state, improving his military discipline, and preparing for the last assault. His first attempt was upon Pistoia, and he carried this place by a double treachery.[b] The Florentines took the alarm upon so disastrous an event; and the pope sent to them Raymond de Cardona, one of the most eminent generals of the times, whom they immediately placed at the head of their armies.[c] Cardona crossed the Guisciana, and ravaged the plain of Lucca, which had for many years been unspoiled by the hostile sword; but, when it became necessary for him to retreat, Castruccio by masterly movements intercepted his march, obtained a complete victory, and, after a short, but severe contest, took Cardona and all his army prisoners.

The battle of this day was called the field of Altopascio.[d] Arrigo Guinigi was among the / slain; and his loss was grievously felt by Castruccio. The prince of Lucca had ever looked on him as a treasure consigned to him by his late father; and, amidst all his faults, Castruccio preserved his gratitude for the lessons of that admirable man, and a sweet remembrance of the days of peace he had passed with him among the Euganean hills. He had loved Arrigo, as a dear brother, or a son; childless himself, he sometimes thought, that, although there was small difference between their ages, Arrigo would succeed him, that his children would be his heirs, and that, if not bound to him by the ties of blood, yet they would look back to him with the same gratitude and respect, than an honoured posterity regard the founder of their house.[e] Ambition hardens the

---

[a] The 'long detail' of battles following the death of Beatrice, excised by Godwin, probably occurred here, as the narrative moves abruptly from late 1322 to 1325. Events in the interval include Castruccio's suborning of *condottieri* under Fontabuona hired by the Florentines, his incursions into and ravaging of Florentine territory, his attempts on Pisa and internal dissessions within Florence (Sismondi, ch. xxx).

[b] After the Abbé Pacciana's initial treachery of 1322, he himself was displaced by his nephew, who sold Pistoia to Castruccio in May 1325 (Sismondi, ch. xxx).

[c] Cardona, an Aragonese, had an inglorious military career in Italy (1322–5).

[d] 23 September 1325 (Villani, IX, cap. 305). Altopascio was a fortified castle in marshland northeast of Lake Bientina, now drained, but navigable in 1821. The lake was visited by P. B. Shelley and Edward Williams by boat on 31 May 1821 (*MWSJ*, I, p. 368).

[e] Castruccio's childlessness is taken from Machiavelli. The historical Castruccio married and had children.

heart; but such is the texture of the mind of man, that he is constantly urged to contemplate those days, when his once over-awing sceptre shall have fallen from his nerveless grasp; the worst usurper, as he advances in years, looks with tenderness on his children, who, in the peaceful exercise of power, are to efface the memory of the lawless deeds by / which he had acquired it. Castruccio saw the son of Guinigi in this light, and he felt a pang of sincere and deep grief, when it became his turn to heap his grassy tomb, amidst the many others with which the plain around Altopascio was crowded, and to order the place where the remains of Arrigo reposed, to be marked with a sepulchral pillar.

From Altopascio, Castruccio advanced with his army to the very gates of Florence. The peasants fled before him, and took refuge, with what property they could save, in the city; the rest became the prey of the Lucchese army, who marked their progress by fire and devastation. All the harvests had been brought in; but Castruccio's soldiers wreaked their vengeance upon the fields, tearing up and burning the vines, cutting down the olive woods, seizing or burning the winter-stock, and reducing the cottages of the poor to a heap of formless ruins. The country about Florence was adorned by numerous villas, the summer abodes of the rich citizens, ornamented with all the luxury of the times, the grounds laid out in the most delicious gardens, where beautiful / trees and flowers adorned the landscape, and natural and artificial rills and waterfalls diffused coolness in the midst of summer. These became the prey of the soldier; the palaces were ransacked, and afterwards burned, the cultivated grounds covered with ruins, the rivulets choked up, and all that, a few days before, had presented the show of a terrestrial paradise, now appeared as if an earthquake, mocking the best cares of man, had laid it in ruin.[a]

The army encamped before the gates of Florence. The remnant of the troops of Cardona and the remainder of the citizens capable of bearing arms, would have formed a force sufficient to cope with the army of Antelminelli. But more than their declared enemies, the Florentines feared domestic traitors; so many of their first citizens were prisoners to the prince of Lucca, that they dreaded lest their relations might endeavour to secure for them their freedom even by the betraying of their native city. Day and night they guarded the walls and gates, and patroled the streets, each regarding the other with suspicious eyes, and / listening with fear and horror to the sounds of rejoicing and riot that issued from the camp of Castruccio.

The prince, in contempt and derision of the besieged, encouraged every kind of pastime and insulting mockery, that might sting his proud, though humbled enemies: he instituted games and races, coined money, and sent continual defiances to the citizens to issue from their walls and encounter him in battle. the men, too ready to seize the spirit of hatred and ridicule, amused themselves

---

[a] The account is developed from Villani (IX, cap. 316) and Sismondi (ch. xxx); according to the latter, Castruccio carried off art-works to Lucca.

with casting by means of their *balestri*, the carcases of dead asses and dogs into the town.[a] Woe to the Florentine who fell into their hands; if a female, no innocence nor tears could save her from their brutality, and, if a man, if their insults were less cruel, they were hardly less cutting and humiliating; to lead a prisoner naked through the camp, seated on an ass, with his face turned towards the tail, was a common mockery. Castruccio perhaps did not perceive the full extent to which the brutal ferocity of his soldiers, made drunk by victory, carried them; if he did, he winked at it; for / he had not that magnanimity which should lead him to treat with respect and kindness a fallen enemy.

While the Lucchese soldiers rioted in plenty, filling themselves even to satiety with the delicate wines and food of the Florentine nobles, and consuming in a few weeks the provision of years, the inhabitants of the besieged city presented a far different spectacle. The villagers, driven from their cottages, had taken refuge in Florence, whose gates jealously closed, permitted not the means of subsistence to be increased. In consequence of this, of the supernumerary population of the town, and of the unwholesome food on which the poorer classes were forced to subsist, pestilence and other contagious fevers declared themselves: the streets were filled with mournful processions, the bells tolled a perpetual knell of death; the citizens invited their friends to the funeral feasts, but the seats of many of the guests were vacated by death, and the hosts who celebrated them had been invited to several similar commemorations. Every face looked blank and fearful. The magistrates / were obliged to interfere; they issued an order that the relations of the dead were no longer to celebrate their funerals by assemblies of their friends, or to toll the bell during the ceremony, so that the numerous dead might go to their long homes without terrifying the survivors by their numbers. Yet this law could not hide the works of death that were so frequent in the town; the streets were almost deserted, except by the monks, who hurried from house to house carrying the cross and sacrament to the dying; while the poor, almost starving, and often houseless, fell in the streets, or were carried in terrifying troops to the hospitals and convents of charity. And this was the work of Castruccio.[b]

Euthanasia saw and felt this; and she felt as if, bound to him by an indissoluble chain, it was her business to follow, like an angel, in his track, to heal the wounds that he inflicted. Dressed in a coarse garb, and endeavouring to throw aside those feelings of delicacy which were as a part of her, she visited

---

[a] Details of the taunting of the besieged city derive mostly from Tegrimi (p. 43) and are here combined with some details of Castruccio's later triumph. The coins were small tokens known as 'castrucani', mentioned also in Villani (IX, cap. 319), Muratori (II, diss. 29, p. 24; noted in Ab. Dep. 274, p. 84). Sismondi mentions that the Florentines had indulged in similar sports when besieging Milan under Cardona two years previously.

[b] This paragraph incorporates details from Boccaccio's description of the plague of Florence, with which the *Decameron* opens; also taken from Villani, IX, cap. 317.

the houses of the poor, aided the sick, fed the hungry, and would perform offices that even wives and mothers / shrunk from with disgust and fear. An heroic sentiment possessed her mind, and lifted her above humanity; she must atone for the crimes of him she had loved.

Bondelmonti one day visited her; she had just returned from closing the eyes of an unhappy woman, whose husband and children had fled from their mother and wife, in the fear of infection; she had changed her garments on entering the palace, and lay on a couch, exhausted; for she had not slept for the two previous nights. Bondelmonti approached her unperceived, and kissed her hand; – she drew it away: "Beware!" she said. "If you knew from whence I came, you would not touch a hand that may carry infection with it."

Bondelmonti reproached her for the carelessness with which she exposed her health and her life: but Euthanasia interrupted him: "I thank you, dear cousin, for your anxiety; but you know me of old, and will not attempt to deter me from doing that which I regard as my duty.—— But what would you now say to / me; for I perceive weighty thought in your overhanging brow?"

"Am I not like the rest of our townsmen in that? You see, Madonna, perhaps better than any of us, to what straits our city is reduced, while this Lucchese tyrant triumphs; you perceive our miseries too well not to pity them; and I trust that you are too good a patriot not to desire most earnestly to put an end to them."

"My dear friend, what do you say? I would sacrifice my life, and more than life, to be of use to my fellow citizens. God knows how deeply I lament their defeats and their unhappiness. But what can be done? An angel alone could inspire our troops with that spirit and courage, which would fit them to cope with the forces of the prince."

"You say true; but there are other means for overthrowing him. Consider, Euthanasia, that not only he conquers and despoils us, but that he is a cruel and bloody tyrant, execrated by the chiefs of our religion, feared and hated by all who approach him, one / whose death would spread joy and exultation over all Italy."

"His death!" Euthanasia's pale cheek became still paler.

"Nay, you are a woman; and, in spite of your superior strength of mind, I see that you are still to be frightened by words. Do not let us therefore talk of his death, but only of his overthrow; we must contrive that."

Euthanasia remained silent. Bondelmonti continued:

"Call to mind, Madonna, the many excellent and virtuous persons whom he has murdered. I need not mention your friend Leodino, or any other individual; his enemies have fallen beneath his axe like trees in a forest; and he feels as little remorse as the woodman who fells them. Torture, confiscation, treachery and ingratitude have gone hand in hand with murder. Before he came, Lucca belonged to the Guelphs, and peace hovered over Tuscany. Now the first nobles of the land have either fallen victims to his jealousy, or wander

as beggars in Italy. All that is virtuous and worthy under his dominion send /
up daily prayers for his downfall; and that is now near at hand; the means are
ready, the instruments are preparing——"

"For his death?" cried Euthanasia.

"Nay, if you intercede for him, he may be saved: but it must be upon one
condition."

"What is that?"

"That you join our conspiracy, and aid its accomplishment; thus Antelminelli
may be saved, otherwise his fate is sealed. Consider this alternative; you may
take a week for reflection on what I have said."

Bondelmonti left her. The sleep that had been about to visit her wearied
senses, fled far away, – scared by the doubts and anguish that possessed her
heart.

She felt with double severity this change from the calm that she had enjoyed
for the three preceding years, into the fears and miseries of a struggle to which
she saw no end. The tyranny and warlike propensities of Castruccio were so
entirely in opposition to every feeling of her heart, that she would not have
lamented his fall; especially as then perhaps she would have conceived it her
duty to stand near him / in misfortune, to console his disappointed hopes, and
to teach him the lesson of content in obscurity. But to join the conspiracy, to
become one of those who plotted against him, to assist in directing the blow
which should annihilate, if not his life, at least all that he regarded as necessary
to his happiness, was a task she shuddered at being called upon to fulfil.

No one can act conscientiously up to his sense of duty, or perhaps go even
beyond that sense, in the exercise of benevolence and self-sacrifice, without
being repaid by the sweetest and most secure happiness that man can enjoy,
self-approbation. Euthanasia had devoted herself for some weeks to the nursing the sick, and the feeding of the hungry; and her benevolence was repaid by
a return of healthful spirits and peace of mind, which it seemed that no passing
circumstance of life could disturb. It was in vain that she witnessed scenes of
pain and wretchedness; she felt that pity which angels are said to feel; but so
strange is the nature of the human mind, that the most unblemished serenity
reigned in her soul. Her sleep, when she found time to sleep, was deep / and
refreshing; as she moved, she felt as if she were air, there was so much elasticity
and lightness of spirit in her motions and her thoughts. She shed tears, as she
heard the groans and complaints of the sufferers; but she felt as if she were
lifted beyond their sphere, and that her soul, clothed in garments of heavenly
texture, could not be tarnished with earthly dross. All this was now changed.
She fell again into weak humanity, doubting, fearing, hoping.

When Castruccio's army removed from before the walls of Florence, the
gates were thrown open, and its inhabitants were relieved from the pressure
and burthen of supernumerary inhabitants. But where did the peasant go? he
found his cottage burnt, his vines, his next year's hope, destroyed, ghastly ruin

293

stared him in the face, and his countenance reflected back the horrors of a long train of misery that he saw was preparing for him. Euthanasia could do little good amidst the universal devastation; what she could do, she did. She restricted her own expenditure, and all the money she could collect, was expended on the / relief of these poor people; but this was a small pittance, a drop of water in the ocean of their calamities.

She was returning from one of these visits to the country, where she had been struck with horror to perceive the inadequacy of her aid to the miseries around her. A whole village had been laid waste, the implements of husbandry destroyed, the cattle carried off, and there was neither food for the starving inhabitants, nor hope of an harvest for the ensuing year. She had heard the name of Antelminelli loaded with such imprecations as a father's mind suggested, when his children called on him vainly for food, and Castruccio the cause of this misery. "If God fulfils," she thought, "as they say he does, the curses of the injured, how will *his* soul escape, weighed down by the imprecations of thousands? Yet I will not consent to the hopes of his enemies, nor be instrumental in dragging him from his seat of power. I have loved him; and what would be just vengeance in another, would be treachery and black ingratitude in me. Ingratitude! And yet for what? For lost hopes, / content destroyed, and confidence in virtue shaken. These are the benefits I have received from him; yet I will not join his enemies."

On her return to her palace, she found Bondelmonti waiting for her. "Have you decided?" he asked.

"I have. I cannot enter into your conspiracy."

"Do you know, Madonna, that in deciding thus you sign his death-warrant?"

"Nay, cousin, it is ungenerous and unmanly to use such a menace with me. If he be doomed to death, which indeed cannot, must not be,—— how can I save him? how can I, a woman, turn aside the daggers of the conspirators? if it be not indeed by betraying your plot to him, a deed you may perhaps force me to at last."

"I hope not, Euthanasia. For your own sake – for the sake of all the virtue that ever dwelt beneath the female form, I hope that you will not be led to commit so base an action. You cannot harm us. If you inform Antelminelli that there is a conspiracy formed against him, and that I am at the head of it, you tell / him no more than he already knows. He does not need the lessons of history; his own experience teaches him sufficiently, that the sword is suspended over the tyrant's head by a single hair.[a] He knows that he has enemies; but he has too many to arrest them all: he knows that his friends are treacherous; but he will never guess who on the present occasion will turn traitor. He

---

[a] Alluding to the story of Damocles, who, granted his wish to become a tyrant for a period, asked for it to be revoked on seeing the suspended sword; the story is told in the *Tusculan Disputations*, V. 21, of Marcus Tullius Cicero (106–43 BC).

cannot be surprised, nor can it do him any good to know, that I am the chief conspirator; I have ever been his open and determined foe; and this is not my first attempt to accomplish his downfal.

"As to what you say concerning my childish menace, you much misunderstand me when you call it a threat. The persons who must act in this business are Lucchese; I may direct their exertions; but they are the actors. And, if you heard the appalling curses that they heap upon Castruccio's name, if you beheld the deep hate their eyes express when he is mentioned, their savage joy when they dream that one day they may wreak their vengeance upon him, you would feel that his life is indeed at stake. I do not wish him to die. Perhaps I / am wrong in this; if his life be preserved, it is probable that no good will arise from his downfal, and that no blood will in reality be spared. But I have eaten at his board, and he has been my guest within these walls, so that I would preserve his life; and I have pitched upon you as the person who can best assist me in this. What else can I do? I cannot go to Lucca to watch over and restrain the fury of his enemies; nor can I find one Lucchese to whom I dare disclose the secret of the conspiracy, and whom I may trust with the protection of his person. Indeed this task seems naturally to devolve to you. You hate tyranny and war; you are a Guelph, and would fain see the enemy of your country, the author of the innumerable evils under which we groan, removed from his government: but antient friendship, the reciprocal interchange of hospitality render his person dear to you, and your female softness, and perhaps weakness, would come in aid of these feelings. You are free to go to Lucca; you may mix the voice of humanity with the bloody machinations of these men; you may save him, and you alone." /

Euthanasia was deeply moved by the representations of Bondelmonti. But her thoughts were still confused; she saw no steady principle, on which to seize, and make it her guide from out the labyrinth. She paused, hesitated, and asked again for a few days for consideration. And this Bondelmonti reluctantly granted.

In the mean time Castruccio was engaged in exhibiting the pomp of a triumph, which was conducted with unparalleled splendour; and in which, like a merciless barbarian, the prince of Lucca, led along Cardona and all the most eminent of his prisoners as the attendants of his chariot.[a] /

---

[a] Villani (IX, cap. 320), Tegrimi (p. 43), Muratori, II, diss. 29, p. 24 all dwell on Castruccio's triumph. Sismondi (ch. xxx) gives a detailed account, mentioning that the ransoms provided Castruccio with money to continue the war.

CHAPTER IX.

Euthanasia joins the Conspiracy. – Tripalda a Member.

During this festivity at Lucca, every thing wore the face of sorrow and depression at Florence. The only circumstance that raised them from their ruin, was the commerce of the city; for, by means of the merchants, corn was brought from the neighbouring states, and the magistrates distributed it among the poorer peasantry.

Euthanasia had listened to the intelligence of Castruccio's triumph with unwilling ears. It seemed to her like the pomp of his funeral; and she dreaded lest his person, exposed during the ceremonial, should be attempted by some of his bolder enemies. But they worked with a closer design.

The tide of her sensations turned, when the conclusion of that day's pomp brought nothing / with it, but the account of its splendour and success; and, when she heard that the prince was personally safe, she found fresh reason for regret, in the want of that delicate and honourable feeling on his part, which above all her other virtues characterised her own mind.

But, if she were disgusted by the low pride that Castruccio manifested in his treatment of Cardona, her feelings of horror and of hatred were called forth by the occurrences that followed. Four days after this scene Bondelmonti entered her apartment: his manner was abrupt; his face pale; he could not speak. – When he had somewhat recovered, his first words were a torrent of execrations against Antelminelli.

"Oh, cease!" cried Euthanasia, "you hate, and would destroy, but do not curse him!"

"Bid me rather add tenfold bitterness to my weak execrations; but all words man can pronounce are poor. He has done that which, if he had before been an angel, would blot and disfigure him for ever. He is the worst of tyrants, the most cruel and atrocious wretch that breathes! But earth shall soon be rid of the monster. Read that writing!" /

He put into her hand a dirty scrap of paper, on which she deciphered these words:

"For holy Jesu's sake, save me! My mother does not send my ransom. I was put to the torture this morning. I suffer it again on Thursday, if you do not send six hundred golden florins.

"Pity your FRANCESCO BONDELMONTI."

The paper dropt from her hands. "This comes from my cousin Francesco," said Bondelmonti; "others are in the same situation. Those who have not been ransomed, he has thrown into the most loathsome dungeons, and starves and tortures them to quicken their appetite for freedom. Shall such a one reign?"

"No," cried Euthanasia, her cheek burning with indignation, and her lips quivering with excessive pity; "No, he shall not reign; he were unworthy to live, if it be not to repent. Bondelmonti, here is my hand; do with me what you please; let his life be saved; but let him be torn from the power which he uses more like a fiend than a human creature."

"Thank you, dear cousin, for this generous feeling: now I know you again. I know my Euthanasia, who had forgotten herself awhile, / only to awake again with new vigour. Call up all your spirits, Madonna; recollect all of noble, and wise, and courageous, that your excellent father taught you. This is no may-day trick, or the resolution of momentary indignation; it is the firm purpose of those, who see an evil beyond imagination pregnant with destruction and horror. Your quick concession merits my utmost confidence; and you shall have it. To-night I will see you again. Now I must endeavour to borrow money to liberate Francesco. My purse has been emptied by the ransom of my three brothers, and his mother has three hundred florins only."

"I can supply the rest," said Euthanasia. "Poor fellow, send them immediately; that with the shortest delay he may be rescued from the power of one more remorseless than the rack on which he suffers. To night I see you again."

Euthanasia spent the intervening hours in great agitation. She did not shrink from her purpose; she had given her word, and she did not dream of recalling it. But all was turmoil and confusion in her mind. She figured to / herself the scenes that would ensue; she imagined the downfal of him she had loved, his life saved only through her intervention,—— and he perhaps, knowing that she also had joined the conspiracy to despoil him of the power he had laboured to attain, would turn from her in abhorrence.

As she thought of this, a few natural tears fell; she cast her deep blue eyes up to heaven; and tried to collect all her fortitude. Night came, and with it the hour when she expected Bondelmonti; but all was tumult and uneasiness in her heart: and to all other regrets she added the startling doubt whether she were not on the present occasion quitting the path of innocence, for the intricate and painful one of error. Then she knelt down, and prayed fervently for a wisdom and judgement that might guide her aright.

Euthanasia was now advanced to the very prime of life. Ten years had elapsed since she had first interchanged vows with Antelminelli in her castle of Valperga; but her mind was of that youthful kind, that, ever, as it were, renewing itself from her own exhaustless treasure / of wisdom and sentiment, never slept upon the past, forgetful of the changes that took place around her. Her character was always improving, always adding some new acquirements, or strengthening those which she possessed before; and thus for ever enlarging her sphere of knowledge and feeling. She often felt as if she were not the same being that she had been a few years before; she often figured to herself, that it was only from such or such a period that she obtained a true insight into the affairs of life, and became initiated in real wisdom; but these epochs were continually changing, for day by day she experienced the acquisition of some new power, the discovery of some new light which guided her through the labyrinth, while another of the thousand-folded veils which hide the sun of reality from the ardent spirit of youth, fell before her piercing gaze. Yet the change that she felt in her faculties was greater than that which had really taken place; it was only the disclosure of another petal of the blowing rose, but the bud had contained the germ of all that appeared as if new-created. /

With this matured judgement and depth of feeling, she was called upon to take an arduous part in a most doubtful and perilous undertaking. The enthusiasm that distinguished her, had ever induced her to place a great confidence in her own sentiments, and the instantaneous decision of any doubtful point; and now she did not hesitate in resolving to become one in the conspiracy: her refusal would not stop its progress; her consent would enable her to judge of, and regulate its measures. She no longer loved the prince; his cruelty had degraded him even from the small place that he had still kept in her heart. But such was the force of early feeling, that she desired to restore her affections to him, when he should again become gentle and humane, as he appeared when she first knew him. Adversity might bring about this change.

Bondelmonti appeared. He appeared with a face of satisfaction and even of joy, as he claimed her promise of the morning. She renewed it solemnly, while her serious countenance, and the touching modulation of her voice, told how from the depth of her heart she / felt the extent and force of the engagement into which she entered. Bondelmonti then detailed to her the circumstances of the conspiracy.

The family of the Quartezzani had been that which had most assisted Castruccio in his rise to power, and had stood by him long with fidelity.[a] But, as his tyranny became more secure, he feared their power, more than he was pleased by their support, and suspected that they only looked upon him as an instrument to fight their battles awhile, and then to be put aside at the first opportunity. He changed his demeanour towards them, from that of friendliness, to the coldest distrust, and took the earliest opportunity to banish the chief among them from Lucca. Disgusted by this ingratitude, they withdrew from court, and tempted by the emissaries of Bondelmonti, now entered into a conspiracy against him, joining with the Avogadii,[b] his professed enemies, to despoil him of power, perhaps of life.

---

[a] Tegrimi (1742 Chronology) gives the date of the conspiracy of the Quartezzani (also spelled Quartergiani and Quartigiani in other sources) as 1326; Mary Shelley places it indeterminately in the winter of 1325/6; Villani (X, cap. 25) and Sismondi (ch. xxxi) place it in 1327.

[b] Mary Shelley uses the Latin plural because she is here following the Latin of the chronology in the 1742 Tegrimi, rather than Dati's Italian or Sismondi (ch. xxx).

Bondelmonti explained to Euthanasia all the circumstances of the plan they had concerted to get the city into their hands. The / present governor of Pisa, who remembered, and hated the prince on account of the treason he had fomented against him, was to advance in a hostile manner to Ripafrata; and, while the shew of force on that side should attract Castruccio and his army, a detachment was to cross the hill of St. Giuliano, and come suddenly on the city, whose gates would be opened to them by one of the conspirators. The Florentine force would hover on the banks of the Guisciana; and, taking advantage of the confusion which the seizure of Lucca would occasion, would pass the river, and march directly towards the city, declaring liberty to the peasant, and attacking the partizans of the tyrant alone. King Robert of Naples had a fleet already in the gulph of Spezia, which, on the news of the breaking out of the conspiracy, would disembark its soldiers on the Lucchese territory, and thus add to the general confusion.

This was the outline of the plan; there were many smaller circumstances which Bondelmonti detailed. He then named their associates / in the plot. In calling over the list he mentioned Tripalda; Euthanasia's eyes flashed angrily at the sound of that name.

"Tripalda!" she cried, "Battista Tripalda! Is he one of your associates? Nay then, I am truly sorry that I am now numbered among you."

"Why this passion, my fair cousin? Tripalda is a man of infinite talent: his counsels have been of the greatest benefit to us. I do not think that our plot would ever have ripened into maturity, had it not been for him. Of what consequence is the virtue or vice of a man on such an occasion? Edged tools are what we want; it matters little the evil name with which they may be branded."

"You reason ill, my friend; and, if you persist, I foresee the failure of our plan, and the destruction of those engaged in it. I have promised my assistance, nor will I shrink from the task imposed upon me; but I can no longer have faith in our success, if one so treacherous and unprincipled as Tripalda be admitted into a participation of our counsels. Accident has made me acquainted with the full extent of / his crimes; it is the knowledge of them that has caused his expulsion from the palace and society of the prince, his crimes alone impel him to associate in this conspiracy, and they also ought to induce us to reject him; that cause must be bad, which requires the assistance of one so wicked as this infidel priest."

"You are strangely prejudiced, methinks, against this man," replied Bondelmonti, "but indeed, my dear cousin, such as he is, we must now tolerate him. He is not only acquainted with every circumstance of the conspiracy, but has been its most active member. Many of our most valuable partizans have been gained over by him alone; he is the tie which binds those who are personally at variance one with the other, and the stay which fixes the fluctuating."

"And this then is the trap into which we are about to fall? This man hates the

299

prince, because Castruccio is fully acquainted with the extent of his iniquity; for the same reason he detests me———"

"This expression of yours," interrupted Bondelmonti, "proves the excess of your misapprehension. / So far from disliking, he esteems and admires you, and it was at his instigation that I first named our purpose to you."

"All that you say, unfortunately increases my distrust. But, if, as I believe, I have done well in promising my assistance, fear shall not withhold me from exerting my powers, and giving my whole heart to the undertaking. My dear Bondelmonti, you are the oldest of my friends, you were the friend of my father, I trust much to your judgement; I confide greatly in the sense of right which nature has implanted in my own heart; I hope no false view, no veiled passion, misleads me now, when most I desire to act well, justly towards others, and towards myself: the catastrophe is in the hands of that irresistible Power which guides us all; and, if we fail, no weakness, no vain reproach, or worse treachery, shall tarnish my defeat. Trust in me to the death." /

CHAPTER X.

Euthanasia removes to Lucca. – Conference with Tripalda. – Tripalda turns Informer.

One of the first effects of Euthanasia's entrance into the conspiracy of Bondelmonti, was a journey from Florence to Lucca. It was necessary for her to be there some time before the breaking out of the plot, that she might be able to take the part allotted to her. She quitted her native city with a heavy heart. It was at the end of the month of November; and the lowering skies portended rain, and the bare earth, stripped of its summer ornaments, appeared chilled by the cold blast that passed over it. The olive and ilex woods, and the few cork trees and cypresses, that grew on the declivities of the hills, diversified the landscape with their sober green: but they had a funereal appearance; they were as the pall of the dying / year, and the melancholy song of their waving branches was its dirge.

Euthanasia's mind was no store-house of blithe thoughts. She felt deeply the danger of the project in which she had embarked; and yet its danger was one of the considerations that reconciled her to it. To have encountered Castruccio with superior force, and to have despoiled him of all power with security to herself, would have been hateful to her feelings; and it appeared to her that in acting such a part she would have merited the disapprobation of mankind. But she approached the foundations of his power by a path encompassed with

danger; she groped through the murky air of night, and owls and bats flitted
before her, and flapped their wings in her eyes; her footing was unsteady; – a
precipice yawned on each side, and the probable result of her undertaking was
ignominy and death. She felt all this. The name of Tripalda had extinguished in
her bosom every hope of success. She felt that the purity of her intentions
would excuse her in her own eyes; and she could then endure with patience all
of bitter and evil / that might befal her. She could not say in the words of the
poet,

> Roll on, the chariot-wheels of my dear plots,
> And bear mine ends to their desired marks!
> As yet there's not a rub of wit, or gulph of thought,
> No rocky misconstruction, thorny maze,
> Or other let of any doubtfulness:
> As yet thy way is smooth and plain,
> Like the green ocean in a silent calm*.

No! the course she followed was a slippery path, that overhung a chasm terrible
as death: the sea on which she sailed was rife with quick-sands, and its breakers
threatened instant destruction.

Sometimes the memory of her peaceful life at Florence obtruded itself upon
her, and more than that, her charitable occupations when she attended the sick
in that city, and whence, as from a rough-hewn chalice containing nectarian
drink, she had quaffed happiness. Sometimes she reproached destiny that she
had not fallen a victim to her perilous exertions; but she endeavoured to shut
out these remembrances / from her mind, to look before her and not behind.
What though dense clouds hid the future, and thunder muttered above? she
was borne on by a virtuous purpose, which would be to her as the wings of an
eagle, or the sure foot of the precipice-walking chamois.

And then, if the enterprise succeeded, she would save Castruccio. But for
her he would be sacrificed by his insatiable enemies. But her hand would avert
their daggers, her voice bid them "Hold!"—— Her imagination pictured the
whole scene. He would be seized by his enemies, and expect death; he would
be conveyed aboard one of the vessels of the king of Naples; and she would be
there, to watch over and tend upon him. At first he might repulse, perhaps
spurn her: but patient forbearance, and her meek demeanour would soften
him; he would see the tears of her devotion; he would hear her defence; and he
would forgive her. They would disembark on some lovely island on the sea of

---

* The Dumb Knight by Machin: Act iv.[a]

[a] Lewes Machin and Gervase Markham, *The Dumb Knight*, (1608) (undivided acts); probably
one of the 'Old Plays' read by Mary Shelley between 14 June and 17 July, 1821 (*MWSJ*, I, pp. 370–
74; also ibid., p. 396, where she quotes from the beginning of Act IV); from a soliloquy of the Iago-
like Duke of Epire, whose plot to incite the King of Cyprus to kill his innocent queen appears at
this point to be successful. *Valperga* inverts certain situations in this play, which is set in Sicily.

Baiæ[a] – his prison. A resting-place, whose walls would be the ocean, and whose bars and locks the all-encompassing air – would be allotted to him / on the island of Ischia. Thence he would survey the land where the philosophers of past ages lived; he would study their lessons;[b] and their wisest lore would descend into his soul, like the dews of heaven upon the parched frame of the wanderer in the Arabian deserts. By degrees he would love obscurity. They would behold together the wondrous glories of the heavens, and the beauty of that transparent sea, whose floor of pebbles, shells and weeds, is as a diamond-paved palace of romance, shone on and illustrated as it is by the sun's rays. He would see the flame arise from Vesuvius, and behold afar off the smoke of the burning lava, – such was the emblem of his former life; but he would then have become, like the land he trod, an extinguished volcano; and the soil would prove more fertile, more rich in beauty and excellence, than those cold natures which had never felt the vivifying heat of mighty and subdued passions.

Thus she dreamed; and thus she cheated herself into tranquillity. She arrived at Pisa, where she was met by Orlando Quartezzani,[c] who explained to her much of the minutiæ of / the plot, and besought her to hasten its execution. "I pine, in exile," he said, "still to behold that ungrateful tyrant seated on a throne, which, if it be not formed of our skulls, yet exists only to torture and destroy us. My brothers are tardy, those Avogadii, lazy and inert. They are still at Lucca; they see its fertile vallies; they live among its mountains. Sometimes indeed I dare go to the top of the hill of San Giuliano, and behold its towers almost at my feet: but I long to make one with my fellow-citizens, to enter again into the lists of life."

Euthanasia quitted Pisa. She crossed the plain to the foot of the hills, and passed along through Pugnano and Ripafrata.[d] She was very melancholy. How could it be otherwise? She had entered upon a race, whose penalty was death, whose prize was yet hidden in the mists of futurity; – it might turn out even more blighting and terrible than death itself. But there was no room for retreat; the path was narrow, and her chariot could not turn; she must fix her eyes upon the goal, for be the consequence good or evil, she must arrive / there, she must there seek and find the fulfilment of her destiny.

She entered Lucca at the beginning of the month of December; and she went immediately to the palace which had been assigned her by the Lucchese

---

[a] The north-western end of the Bay of Naples.

[b] The lessons would be found in the stoicism of Cicero and Pliny the Elder (Gaius Plinius Secundus, AD 23–79), both of whom had owned villas on the western coast of Italy. Both died prematurely, Cicero, assassinated by Mark Antony's soldiers, and Pliny on the beach at Stabiae of volcanic fumes from the eruption of Pompeii.

[c] 'Ugo' and 'Lando' Quartezzani are mentioned by Tegrimi.

[d] The Bagni di Pisa lay on this route; Pugnano is a small town about two miles away on the road to Ripafratta, frequently visited in the summer of 1821 by Mary Shelley, whose friends, the Williams, had taken a villa there.

government, in compensation for her demolished castle. The same evening that she arrived, the two chiefs of the conspiracy, Ugo Quartezzani and Tripalda, visited her. The name of Tripalda, so often and so fearfully repeated by the dying Beatrice, made her shrink from all communication with one who had tarnished his life with the foulest crimes. On this occasion she was obliged however to smother her indignation; and he, from a sense of his own importance, was more presumptuous and insolent than she had ever seen him.

"Madonna," said he, stalking forward with an erect mien, and half shut eyes, which, although they were not bent on the ground, yet ever avoided the direct gaze of those to whom he spoke; – "Madonna, I must praise your wisdom in entering into this conspiracy. We all know that, when you choose to exert your abilities, / you are the cleverest woman in Tuscany. This is a period which will shew you in your true colours."

"Messer Battista, let us leave to speak of me and my poor talents: we come to talk of far weightier matter; and I bear a message to Messer Ugo from his brother Orlando."

They now began to speak of the future; but Tripalda would allow no one to talk but himself; and he walked up and down the room delivering his opinion in a loud voice.

"Hush, for Jesu's sake!" cried Ugo, "some one will overhear us, and we are all lost."

Tripalda looked suspiciously around, approached on tiptoe the sopha on which Euthanasia and Ugo sat, and, speaking in a whisper, he said, – "I tell you we shall succeed. Look! I have already sharpened the dagger which is to stab the tyrant to the heart."

"Now the Mother of God defend him!" cried Euthanasia, turning pale: "that is beyond my contract. Bear witness, Ugo, that I entered into this plot on condition that his life should be saved."

"Women! women!" said Tripalda, contemptuously. / "By the body of Bacchus! I wonder what Bondelmonti meant by introducing a woman into the plot. One way or another they have spoiled, and ever will spoil, every design that the wisdom of man has contrived. I say he must die."

"I say he shall not, sir priest. And remember, you are not one who dares place your warrant on the life of Antelminelli. That is guarded by spirits of whose very existence you are ignorant; it is guarded by devoted love and disinterested virtue; and you shall not endanger it."

"You indeed talk of spirits, of which I and all the wise among men know nothing. In the present case I do not exactly see what devoted love has to do with a conspiracy to overthrow the party beloved; and as for disinterested virtue, all the virtue I know any thing about bids me stab the tyrant. He shall die."

"Nay, as you say that you understand me not, you may well leave to speak of what dwells without the circle of your intelligence. Are you not a priest? a man

303

of peace? and dare you avow such thoughts? They shame your profession; / and, if any spark of virtue dwelt within you, you would now blush as deep a red, as your hands would shew, stained with that blood you think to shed."

"Madonna," said Ugo, "you are now animated beyond all prudence. Speak mildly; and Messer Tripalda will yield."

"That will I not!" cried Tripalda, compressing his thin lips, and elevating his high brows. "I have doomed him to death; and he shall die. By my soul's salvation, he shall!"

"Then is your soul lost, for he shall live."

The gentle modulation of Euthanasia's voice, now first attuned to command, carried with it an irresistible force, while she extended her fair arm in earnest gesture; then, calming herself, she continued: "I entered into this conspiracy on one condition; and I might well say, 'If you keep not your words with me, neither will I keep mine to you; if you betray me, so will I betray you.' But I say not this; I have other means of silencing this man. I know you, Tripalda; and you are well aware, that I can see through the many folds which / you have wound round your heart. You oblige me to menace you. I can tell a tale, Tripalda, a tale the knowledge of whose exceeding horror is confined to your own polluted heart; but whose slightest sketch would fill mankind with detestation, and your destruction would quickly follow. Dare not even to imagine the death of Castruccio; while he is safe, you are safe; otherwise you know what will follow."

"So far from knowing, I cannot even guess your meaning," replied Tripalda; but with a subdued voice and a humble manner. "In truth, Madonna, you speak enigmas to me. But since you are resolved to save the life of the prince, so let it be. But I suppose you will allow us to secure his person."

"We have a plan for that," said Euthanasia, turning to Ugo, "a plan to which I hope you will accede: for Castruccio must be saved; Bondelmonti entered into that engagement with me, before I became a party to your plot."

"It shall be as you command," replied Tripalda, who had shifted his place several times, / and seemed to stand as uneasily before the now softened looks of Euthanasia, as a hypocrite well might before the eyes of the accusing angel. "I will leave you now," continued he, "for I promised to be with Nicola dei Avogadii[a] at eight o'clock, and seven struck some time ago. Good night, Madonna; when we again meet, I hope you will be better pleased with my intentions, and thank me for my exertions in favour of your friend, the prince."

He quitted the room. Euthanasia followed him with her eyes until he had closed the door; and then she said to Ugo, "I distrust that man; and if my purpose did not lift me alike above fear and hope, I should dread him. But do you have a care, Ugo; and, if you regard your own safety, watch him, as you

---

[a] A historical Nicolao degli Avvocati did revolt against Castruccio, but in 1317 (Tegrimi, 1742 chronology; Green, p. 93).

would one whose sword you must parry, until the deed you meditate be accomplished."

"You judge hastily, Madonna; he is the sworn enemy of Castruccio; and I believe him to be, on this occasion at least, trust-worthy. I cannot divine what you know concerning him; it is surely something black, for he cowered beneath your words. But a man may be / one day wicked, and good the next; for self-interest sways all, and we are virtuous or vicious as we hope for advantage to ourselves. The downfal of Antelminelli will raise him; and therefore he is to be trusted."

"That is bad philosophy, and worse morality, Ugo: but we have no time to dispute now; remember, that I tell you to beware of Tripalda. Now let us occupy ourselves in worthier considerations."

After a long conversation, in which all was concluded except the exact period for the breaking out of the conspiracy, Ugo retired, to prepare messengers for Pisa and Florence, that they might, with the concurrence of their associates, determine the conduct of this last act of the tragedy. Euthanasia was left alone. She had been roused to the expression of anger by the insolent cruelty of Tripalda; but her nature, mild as it was, quickly forgot the feeling of indignation, and now other thoughts (oh, far other thoughts!) possessed her. She was again in Lucca. She ascended to the tower of her palace; and the waning moon, which shone in the east, shed its yellow and / melancholy light over the landscape: she could distinguish afar the abrupt and isolated rock on which the castle of Valperga had stood; it formed one of the sides of the chasm which the spirits of creation had opened to make free the course of the Serchio.[a] The scene was unchanged; and even in winter the soul of beauty hovered over it, ready again to reanimate the corpse, when the caducean wand[b] of spring should touch it. The narrow, deep streets of Lucca lay like the allies of a prison around her; and she longed for the consummation of the deed in which she had engaged, when she might fly for ever from a scene, which had been too dear to her, not to make its sight painful in her altered situation.

In the mean time, while in deep security of thought she brooded over the success of her attempt, the hour which lingered on the dial was big with her ruin; and events which threatened to destroy her for ever, already came so near, that their awful shadow began to be thrown on the path of her life.

Tripalda had left her, burning with all the malice of which his evil nature was so amply / susceptible. He had learned that the prisoner of the castle in the Campagna di Roma had survived, and had fallen into the hands of Euthanasia: and he knew that his fate depended upon disclosures that she was enabled to

---

[a] cf. the chasmic imagery of P. B. Shelley's description of the Ripafratta gorge in 'The Boat on the Serchio'.

[b] The caduceus was the serpent-entwined wand by which the god Mercury could revive the dead.

make. The prisoner was now dead; but both Castruccio and Euthanasia had become in part the depositaries of her secret; Euthanasia had heard his name pronounced, mingled with shrieks and despair, by the lips of the lovely maniac; and, after her death, she had revealed her suspicions to the prince, while he in anger forbade the priest ever again to approach his palace or his person. In disgracing and banishing him from his presence, Castruccio had incurred the penalty of his hate; and he was overjoyed to think, that in destroying the man who had injured him, he should also free himself from one who was conscious of the most perilous secrets concerning him. He had been loud in his abuse of the prince; but none had listened to him, except those who sympathized in his feelings; and Antelminelli despised him too heartily to take heed to what he said. /

Thus, with the wily heart and wicked design of a serpent beneath a magpie's exterior, this self-named Brutus[a] of modern Italy, whose feigned folly was a cover for pride, selfishness and all uncharitableness, fomented a conspiracy in Lucca to overthrow a tyrant, who well deserved to fall, but who was as pure as the milk-white dove, if compared with the sable plumage of this crow. He had endeavoured to entice Euthanasia to participate in the plot, he hardly knew why, secure that, if she were persuaded to enter into it, it would be pregnant with nothing but misery and suffering for her. The scene which had taken place in her palace, overturned all his ideas. Castruccio despised and banished him; but he had never menaced the disclosure of those secrets, whose smallest effect would be to immure him for ever within the dungeons of some convent. He therefore hated, rather than feared him; but the words of Euthanasia had terrified his soul, and with his terror awakened all those feelings of hellish malignity with which his heart was imbued. To destroy her, and save himself, was now the scope of his desire. / To betray the conspiracy, and deliver over his confederates to death, was of little moment in his eyes, compared with the care he had for his own preservation, and the satisfaction of his new-born revenge. All night he slept not; he walked up and down his room, easing his heart with curses, and with images of impending ruin for his enemies. When morning dawned, he hasted to Agosta, and made his way into the private cabinet of Vanni Mordecastelli.

Castruccio was at Pistoia, and would not return until the following day; in the mean time Mordecastelli was the governor of Lucca. He was seated in his cabinet with his secretary when Tripalda entered: like a true courtier, he hardly deigned to look on the man who was disgraced by his prince.

"Messer Tripalda," said he, "are you still in Lucca? I thought some one told me that you had returned to your canonicate. Have you any business with me? Be brief; for you see that I am occupied."

---

[a] Lucius Junius Brutus, founding father of republican Rome, who, after the murder of his father by King Tarquin the Proud, successfully feigned imbecility so as to preserve his life and eventually expel the Tarquins (Livy, I. lix–lx).

"Messer Vanni, I have business with you; but it must be private. Do not look thus contemptuously / on me; for you know that I have been useful to you before; and I shall now be so again."

"I do not much care to trust myself alone with you; for they say that you have sworn destruction to all the prince's friends. However, I am armed," he continued, taking a dagger from his bosom, and drawing it from it's sheath; "so, Ubaldo, you may leave us alone."

"And, Ubaldo, do you hear," cried Tripalda, "it is as much as your life is worth to tell any one that I am with the governor. The very walls of the palace must not know it."

"And are you the lord to threaten me, Messer Canonico? though you have a fool's head, pray keep a discreet tongue."

"Silence, Ubaldo," said Mordecastelli. "Go, and remember what he says: you shall answer for it, if it be known that this visit has taken place.——— And now, Sir Priest, what have you to say to me? if it be not something well worth the hearing, you shall pay a rich penalty for this impertinence of yours."

"Remember, Messer Vanni, who put you / on the right scent in Leodino's plot; remember the golden harvest which that brought you in. Remember this; and put aside your pride and insolence."

"I remember well the detestable part that you then played, and it had been well that your head had been struck off instead of Leodino's. But you trifle now, and I have no time to waste; if you have any fresh scene of villainy to disclose, be quick."

"I have discovered a plot of the highest consequence. One that counts among the conspirators the first citizens of the principality. But I must make my conditions before I tell you further: I hold the life of your lord in my grasp; and, before I part with any advantage, I must be paid its full worth."

"Conditions! Aye, they shall be generous and ample ones; if you fairly tell all, you shall be believed on your word, and not be put to the torture, to extort that which craft may make you conceal: these are all the conditions a villain, such as you, deserves. Come, waste no more time; if your plot be worth the telling, you well know that you will not go unrewarded; / if this is all smoke, why perchance you may be smothered in it; so no more delay."

Tripalda opened each door, peeped behind the hangings, under the tables, and chairs; and then, approaching as softly as a cat who sees a mouse playing in the moonshine, or a spider who beholds his prey unconsciously cleaning his wings within an inch of him, he sat down beside Mordecastelli and whispered:

"The Avogadii."

"Well, what of them? I know that they hate Antelminelli; but they are not powerful enough to do any mischief."

"The Quartezzani."

"Nay, then this is of deeper interest. Have they turned vipers? By St. Martin! they have a sting!"

307

Tripalda in a low and solemn voice entered into a detail of the plot. "And now," said he, when he had nearly concluded, "except for one circumstance, you had not heard a word of this from me."

"You are a villain to say so; – but what is / this circumstance? the love you bear your prince?"

"The love I bear him might have made me bring the Pope to Lucca with thirty thousand Gascons at his heels, but not betray a plot against him. No truly it was not that; but they have admitted a woman into it; and, as there is neither safety nor success where they are, I made my retreat in good time."

"A woman! What, Berta Avogadii?"

"One of far higher rank; the countess of Valperga."

"Nay, then, it is all a lie, Tripalda, and, by the Virgin, you shall repent having amused me with your inventions! The countess of Valperga! She is too wise and too holy to mingle in one of your midnight plots: besides, once upon a time, to my knowledge she loved Castruccio."

"The old proverb tells us, Vanni, that sweetest love turns to bitterest hate. Remember Valperga! Do you think she has forgotten it? Remember her castle, her power, the state she used to keep, when she was queen of those / barren mountains! Do you think she has forgotten that? She might carry it humbly; but she, like the rest of those painted ruins, is proud at heart, proud and revengeful; why she has vowed the death of her quondam lover."

"I would not believe it, if an angel were to tell me; do you think then that I will credit such a tale, when it is given out by a devil like you? Nay, do not frown, Sir Priest; the devil loves to clothe himself in a holy garb; and report says that you have more than once shewn the cloven foot."

"You are pleased to jest, Lord Governor," replied Tripalda, with a ghastly smile, "do you know the hand-writing of Orlando Quartezzani?"

"As I know my own."

"Read then that letter."

It was a letter from Orlando to Tripalda, conjuring him to be speedy in his operations, and saying that, since the countess of Valperga appeared to enter into the plot with a willing heart, all difficulties would now be easily removed.

Vanni put down the letter with a look of / mingled contempt and indignation. "And who else have ye among you? I expect next to hear that some of the saints or martyrs, or perhaps the Virgin herself has come down to aid you."

"Here is a list of the conspirators; and here are letters which will serve as further proofs of the truth of my disclosures."

"Give them to me. And now let me tell you, my excellent fox, that I by no means trust you, and that, knowing your tricks of old, I may well suspect that, after trying to get all you can from us by betraying your associates, you will endeavour to get all you can out of them by assisting them to escape; so, my good fellow, you must for the present remain under lock and key."

"I hoped that I had deserved better――"

"Deserved! Aye, you deserve the torture, as much as the vilest heretic who denies the passion of our Redeemer. You know yourself to be an arch-traitor, and, by the saints! you shall be treated like one. Come, there is a better room for your prison than you deserve: go in peaceably; for if you oblige me to use / force, you shall lodge for the next week in one of those holes under ground, of which I believe you have some knowledge, since your fiendish malice contrived them."

"Well, Vanni, I yield. but I hope that your future gratitude———"

"Oh! trust to my gratitude. I know my trade too well not to encourage such hell-hounds as you are." /

CHAPTER XI.

Euthanasia in Prison.

Having thus disposed of Tripalda, Vanni sat down to study the list of conspirators that he had given him. It contained three hundred names. "What a murderous dog this priest is!" he cried. "Why every noble family has one or more of its members engaged in this plot. I shall take the liberty to curtail it exceedingly, before it meets the eyes of the prince. The ringleaders are enough for him: the rest I shall punish on my private account; a few fines will bring them to reason, and they are better subjects ever after. But Valperga! I would as soon have believed that an ass could drink up the moon,[a] as that that villain could have drawn her from her illustrious sphere, to be swallowed up among the rest of the gulls, when he wants to make merry with a few murders. / But, by St. Martin! as she has sown, so must she reap; and I hate her ten times the more for her hypocritical, angel face. Conspire against Castruccio! He used her ill; but a meek and forbearing woman's love that forgave all injuries, is what she ever boasted, if not in words, at least in looks and manners. For thy sake, thou goodly painted saint, like the rest of them, well looking outside, but worms and corruption within, I will never trust more to any of thy sex! – Nor shalt thou escape. Others will pay a fearful penalty for their treason; and thine, which merits much more than theirs, shall not go free. I could have staked my life upon Euthanasia; I knew her from a child; I remember her a smiling cherub

---

[a] According to a story from an unidentified source, noted (April-June 1821) in adds. e .17, p. 221 rev., an ass drank water in which the moon was reflected; the moon was covered by a cloud; the ass was cut open in the superstitious belief that it had drunk the moon. The vituperation against women's hypocrisy is reminiscent of the speeches of Epire in *The Dumb Knight*, Act III.

309

with deep blue eyes and curly tresses; and her very name seemed to carry a divinity with it. I have many sins on my head; and, when my death comes, many years of purgatory may be tacked on to my absolution; but methought that, when I contemplated and almost adored the virtues of Euthanasia, my soul was half-way through its purification; – and she to fall!" /

Vanni, who, in the common acceptation, was truly faithful to his master, was struck with disgust at what appeared to him the depth of treachery on her part. He knew little of the human heart, its wondrous subtlety and lawyer-like distinctions; he could not imagine the thousand sophistries that cloaked her purpose to Euthanasia, the veils of woven wind, that made her apparent treachery shew like purest truth to her. He could not judge of the enthusiasm, that, although it permitted her to foresee the opprobrium and condemnation which would be attached to her conduct, yet made her trample upon all. She walked on in what she deemed the right path; and neither the pangs of doubt, nor the imminent risque that awaited her perseverance, could arrest her; or, worse than all, the harsh opinion of man, his ever ready censure of ideas he cannot understand, his fiery scorn of virtue which he might never attain. She passed on to her goal, fearless of, and despising "the barbed tongues, or thoughts more sharp than they,"[a] which threatened to wound her most sacred feelings. /

But Vanni could not penetrate the inner sanctuary of her heart, which throned self-approbation as its deity, and cared not for the false gods that usurp the pleasant groves and high places of the world. After having vented his spleen with that sceptred infallibility men assume, and condemned her and her whole sex unheard, Mordecastelli proceeded to more active business, and before night the chiefs of the conspiracy were thrown into prison.

Early the following morning Castruccio returned to Lucca. Mordecastelli met him with a countenance, in which the falcon-eye of the prince could read uncommon tidings. "Why do you look thus, my friend?" said he. "Either laugh or cry; or tell me why you do neither, although on the verge of both."

"My lord, I have cause. I have discovered a conspiracy which threatened your power, and that not a mean one; so that I must wish you joy, that you have again escaped from these harpies. But, when you hear the names of the conspirators, you also will be sorrowful; several of your friends are among them; and names, which have been repeated in your daily / prayers with blessings joined to them, are now written in the list of traitors."

"When I took power upon me, my dear Vanni, I well knew that I wrapt suspicion about me as a robe, and wedded danger, and treachery, and most other evils. So let it be! I was yet a boy, when I prayed to be a prince, though

---

[a] P. B. Shelley (1821), *Adonais*, l. 213 (adapted); Mary Shelley read the very recently printed *Adonais* on 12 July (*MWSJ*, I, p. 374) while working on the third volume of *Valperga*.

my crown were of thorns. But who are these? Which of my old friends are so blind, as to see their own interest in my downfal?"

Mordecastelli gave the list of the ringleaders which he had prepared, and watched the countenance of Castruccio as he read it. He observed contempt and carelessness on his countenance, until the name of the countess of Valperga met his eyes; he then saw the expression change, and a slight convulsion on his lips, which he evidently strove to suppress. Vanni could contain himself no longer.

"You see, my lord, you see her name. And, as true as there is a sun in heaven, as true, as she is false, this saintlike Euthanasia has spotted her soul with treason. I have proofs, here they are. It would make one doubt one's salvation, to see her with her Madona[a] / face creep into this nest of traitors. There they must have been, closeted in a cellar, or hid in some dark hole; for else my spies would have earthed them out long ago. And I figure her to myself, with her golden hair, and eyes which illumined even the night, they were so dazzling, – entering a room made dark enough to hide treason; – and to think that the hellish bat did not take wing out at the window when she appeared! but no, she cherished him in her bosom."

"You are eloquent, Vanni."

"I am, my lord. I took her for an angel, and I find her a woman; – one of those frail, foolish creatures we all despise———"

"Peace, peace, my dear Vanni; you talk insufferable nonsense. Let us proceed to more serious business. What have you done with these people?"

"They are all in prison."

"The countess among them?"

"Why, my lord, would you have had her spared?"

"She is in prison then?"

"She is." /

"Vanni, you must look to these people. I assure you that I by no means find myself mercifully inclined towards them. These continual plots, and this foolish ingratitude, to give it no worse name, disturb our government too much. I will tear it away root and branch; and the punishment of these fellows shall be a terrible warning to those who may think of treading in the same steps."

Castruccio fixed his eyes upon Mordecastelli; but there was an expression in them that made the confident cast his upon the ground. They glared; and his pale face became paler, so that his very lips were white. He looked steadily on Mordecastelli for some minutes; and then said:

"They must all die."

"They shall, my lord."

"Yet not by an easy death. That were a poor revenge. They shall die, as they

---

[a] Obsolete spelling, the possible effect of Mary Shelley's recent reading of Jacobean drama.

have lived, like traitors; and on their living tombs shall be written, Thus Castruccio punishes his rebel subjects.[a] Have I toiled, exposed my person to danger, become the fear and hope of Tuscany, to stain with my best blood the / dagger of one of these miserable villains? Do you see that they die so, Vanni, as that I may be satisfied."

"I will, my lord. And the countess?" –

"Leave her to me. I will be her judge and executioner."

"Castruccio?"

"Do not look so pale, Vanni; you do not understand. A few hours hence I will tell you more. Now leave me."

Solitude is a coy companion for a prince, and one he little loves. But Castruccio had much to occupy his thoughts, much that agonized him. "Revenge!" He clenched his hand, and, throwing his eyes upward, he cried: "Yes, revenge is among those few goods in life, which compensate for its many evils. Yet it is poor: it is a passion which can have no end. Burning in pursuit, cold and unsatisfactory in its conclusion, it is as love, which wears out its soul in unrequited caresses. But still, it shall be mine; and these shall suffer. They shall feel in every nerve what it is to have awakened me. I will not fear; I will not feel my life depend alone upon the word / of these most impotent slaves. They shall die; and the whole world shall learn that Castruccio can revenge."

Thus he thought: yet there was an inner sense, that betrayed to him the paltriness of his feelings, when he imagined that there was glory in trampling upon the enemy beneath his feet. He would not listen to this small still voice; but, turning from these ideas, he began to reflect on that which filled him with a bitterness of feeling to which he had long been a stranger.

"So, she has conspired against me; and, forgetful of all those ties that bound us notwithstanding her coldness, she has plotted my death! She knew, she must have known, that in spite of absence and repulse, she was the saint of my life; and that this one human weakness, or human virtue, remained to me, when power and a strong will had in other respects metamorphosed me. Does she forget, that I have ever worn near my heart a medallion engraven with her vows of childhood? She has forgotten all. And not only has she forgotten to love, but she has cast aside the uprightness / of her understanding, and stained the purity of her soul.

"It is well for me to speak thus, who, instead of the virtues that once were mine, have as ministers, revenge, and hate, and conquest. But, although I choose to be thus, and although I have selected these hell-hounds to drag my car of life, I have not lost the sense of what is just and right; and, in the midst of all my wilful errors and my degradation, I could discern and worship the pure loveliness of Euthanasia. By the saints! I believed, that, if she died, like

---

[a] Their fate is specified in Villani, X. cap. 25 and Sismondi, ch. xxxi.

Dante's Beatrice, she would plead for me before the throne of the Eternal, and that I should be saved through her. Now she is lost, and may perdition seize the whole worthless race of man, since it has fallen upon her!

"But SHE MUST BE SAVED. My hands shall not be stained with her blood, nor my soul bear the brand of that crime. But she must not stay here; nor shall she remain in Tuscany. She shall go far away, so that I never more may hear her name: that shall be her punishment, and she must bear it. Now I / must contrive the means; for she shall not remain another night in prison."

Euthanasia in prison! Yes; she had become the inhabitant of this abode of crime, though her mind was as far above fault as human nature could soar; hers, if it were an error, was one of judgement. But why should I call it error? To remove a cruel tyrant from his seat of power, – to devote those days, which she might have spent in luxury and pleasure, to a deep solitude, where neither love nor sympathy would cheer her; – to bear his anger, perhaps his hate, and in the midst of all to preserve a firmness and sweetness, that might sustain her, and soften him, – to quit all her friends, and her native country for ever, to follow in the steps of one she had ceased to love, but to whom she felt herself for ever bound by her wish to preserve him from that misery which his crimes would ultimately occasion him: these were her errors.

After Quartezzani had quitted her on the night of her arrival in Lucca, she had not slept; she was too full of various thought, of / dread and breathless expectation, to compose her spirits to rest. She felt eternity in each second; and each slow hour seemed to creep forward, stretching itself in a wide, endless circle around her. When day dawned, it found her, not sleeping, but with open eyes looking on the one last star that faded in the west, calling to mind a thousand associations, a thousand hopes, now lying dead in the ashes of that pyre time had heaped together and consumed; she looked forward; yet then she paused; she dared not attempt to penetrate into futurity; – all was so tempestuous and dark.

She arose at sun-rise, and had descended into the garden, to breathe the bleak, but, to her feverish spirits the refreshing air of a December morning; when, at noon, Quartezzani rushed in; he was deadly pale, and his hair seemed to stand on end with fear.

"Holy saints! what has happened?" cried Euthanasia.

"We are all lost! dead, or worse than dead! We are betrayed!"

"Tripalda has betrayed us?" /

"He has."

"And there is no escape?"

"None. The gates are shut, nor will they be opened, until we are all seized."

"Then most certainly we die?"

"As sure as that Christ died upon the cross! so surely shall we perish."

"Then courage, my friend, and let us cast aside, with all mortal hopes, all mortal fear. I have the start of you, Ugo; I was prepared for this; but you would

313

not believe me, until now my predictions are sealed by the event. Let us die, as we would have lived, for the cause of freedom; and let no trembling dismay, no coward fear, make us the mock of our enemies.

"Other men in various ages had died by untimely death, and we will dare to imitate them. Others have sustained their fate with fortitude; and let faith and submission to the will of heaven be to us, instead of that dauntless spirit of inbred virtue that supported the heroes of antiquity."

Euthanasia raised her own spirits as she spoke; and fearless expectation, and something / like triumph, illuminated her countenance, as she cast her eyes upward, and with her hand clasped that of her friend. He received no warmth from the pressure; chilly fear possessed him; and he stood utterly dejected before her – he wept.

"Aye, weep," she continued, "and I also, did not the tempest of my soul bear all clouds far away, I also might shed tears. You weep to leave those whom you love,——— that is a bitter pang. You weep to see your associates suffer; but each must relieve the other from that sorrow by cheerfulness and courage. But," she continued, seeing him entirely subdued by fear, "is there no hope of escape? Exert your ingenuity; once past the gates, you would soon be out of the territory of Lucca. And Castruccio———"

"Oh, that most hated name! Bloody, execrable tyrant! Curse him! May the fiends———"

"Cease! know you not that a dying man's curse falls more on himself, than on him against whom he imprecates the wrath of heaven? This is childish; Ugo, collect yourself; you have a wife; – woman's wit is ready; consult / with her; she may devise some plan for your safety."

"You are an angel of consolation, Euthanasia. Heaven bless you! and do you also reflect on your own danger."

He left her: and she (without giving a thought to vain regret; her moments were too precious) sat down and wrote a long letter to Bondelmonti. It was calm and affectionate: she felt raised above mortality; and her words expressed the exceeding serenity of her soul. She gave a last farewell to her friends. "It may seem strange to you," she wrote, "that I express myself thus: and indeed, when I reason with myself, methinks I ought not to expect death from the hands of Antelminelli. Nor do I; and yet I expect some solemn termination to this scene, some catastrophe which will divide me from you for ever. Nor is it Italy, beloved and native Italy, that I shall leave, but also this air, this sun, and the earth's beauty. I feel thus; and therefore do I write you an eternal farewell."

She had scarcely finished her letter, when a messenger arrived from Morde-castelli. He / told her that the conspiracy was divulged, and that she must in a prison await the orders of Castruccio. She started at the word *Prison*; but, recovering herself, she made a sign that she was ready to follow the messenger; so, without a word, without a sigh, she quitted her palace, and, ascending her litter, was conducted to her place of confinement. She passed through the same streets, through which the jailor had conducted her to the dungeon of Beatrice. A small and curiously carved shrine of the Madona with a lamp before it, chanced to recal this circumstance to her mind. "Thou art at peace, blessed one," she said, "there where I hope soon to be."

The jailor of the prison, who was the same that had besought her to come and comfort poor Beatrice, received her with a sorrowful countenance, and led her to his most decent apartment, high in the tower, that overlooked the rest of the building. There she was left alone to ruminate on her fortunes, and to imbue herself with that fortitude, which might carry her with honour through the trials that awaited her. The circumstance that pressed most painfully / upon her, was the death which her associates must suffer. She tried to forget herself; she did not fear death; she did not expect it at the hands of Castruccio; and her expectations and ideas were too vague to permit her to dread much the coming events as they regarded her. The window of her prison-chamber was not grated, and from it she could survey the neighbouring country. A thousand feelings passed through her mind, and she could put no order in her thoughts. Sleep refused to visit her; but her reflections became peaceful, and full of pleasant images and recollections.

Morning succeeded to a winter's night. It was clear, and sunshiny, but cold. The cheering beams poured into her room; she looked upon the azure sky, and the flock of giant mountains which lay crouching around, with a strange pleasure. She felt as if she saw them for the last time, but as if she were capable of enjoying until the latest moment those pleasures which nature had ever conferred upon her. She repeated some of Dante's verses where he describes in such divine / strains the solemn calm and celestial beauty of paradise. "When will it be my lot to wander there also," she said, "when shall I enjoy the windless air, and flower-starred meadows of that land?"[a]

Thus the whole day passed; but it was quickly dark; and she, who had watched for two nights, and was now quite overcome, looking out once upon the evening star, that star she had ever loved, and which was ever to her as the good genius of the world watching his children in their repose, repeated the Catholic ejaculation, "*Stella, alma, benigna, ora pro nobis!*"[b] then, crossing herself, she lay down to rest, and quickly slept, as peacefully and happily, as a babe rocked in its mother's arms. /

---

[a] cf. *Matilda*, ch. xii (*MWS Matilda etc*, pp. 62–3); this suggests that the Earthly Paradise of *Purgatorio*, XXVIII. 22–42 is alluded to, rather than *Paradiso*, XXIII. 70–84 or XXX. 46–69.

[b] 'Fostering, favouring star, pray for us!'; prayer addressed to the Virgin Mary.

CHAPTER XII.

Euthanasia sails for Sicily, and is lost.

A little before midnight Euthanasia's prison-chamber was unlocked, and the jailor entered, with a lamp in his hand, accompanied by one of majestic figure, and a countenance beautiful, but sad, and tarnished by the expression of pride that animated it. "She sleeps," whispered the jailor. His companion raised his finger in token of silence; and, taking the lamp from the man's hand, approached her mattress which was spread upon the floor, and, kneeling down beside it, earnestly gazed upon that face he had known so well in happier days. She made an uneasy motion, as if the lamp which he held disturbed her; he placed it on the ground, and shaded it with his figure; while, by the soft light that fell upon her, he tried to read the images that were working in her mind. /

She appeared but slightly altered since he had first seen her. If thought had drawn some lines in her brow, the intellect which its beautiful form expressed, effaced them to the eye of the spectator: her golden hair fell over her face and neck: he gently drew it back, while she smiled in her sleep; her smile was ever past description lovely, and one might well exclaim with Dante

> *Quel, ch' ella par quando un poco sorride,*
> *Non si puo dicer, ne tenere a mente;*
> *Si è nuovo miracolo, e gentile*.*

He gazed on her long; her white arm lay on her black dress, and he imprinted a sad kiss upon it; she awoke, and saw Castruccio gazing upon her.

She started up; "What does this mean?" she cried.

His countenance, which had softened as he looked upon her, now reassumed its severe expression. "Madonna," he replied, "I come to take you from this place." /

She looked on him, endeavouring to read his purpose in his eyes; but she saw there no explanation of her doubts: – "And whither do you intend to lead me?"

"That you will know hereafter."

She paused; and he added with a disdainful smile, "The countess of Valperga

---

* *Vita Nuova di Dante.*[a]

[a] Section XXI, sonnet 'Negli occhi', ll. 12–14, translated and adapted by P. B. Shelley, probably in 1815: 'What Mary is when she a little smiles/ I cannot even tell or call to mind,/ It is a miracle, so new, so rare.'

need not fear, while I have the power to protect her, the fate she prepared for me."

"What fate?"

"Death."

He spoke in an under tone, but with one of those modulations of voice, which, bringing to her mind scenes of other days, was best fitted to make an impression upon her. She replied almost unconsciously – "I did not prepare death for you; God is my witness!"

"Well, Madonna, we will not quarrel about words; or, like lawyers, clothe our purposes in such a subtle guise, that it might deceive all, if truth did not destroy the spider's web. I come to lead you from prison."

"Not thus, my lord, not thus will I be saved. I disdain any longer to assert my intentions, / since I am not believed. But am I to be liberated alone; or are my friends included in your merciful intentions?"

"Your friends are too dangerous enemies of the commonwealth, to be rescued from the fate that awaits them. Your sex, perhaps the memory of our ancient friendship, plead for you; and I do not think that it accords with your wisdom to make conditions with one who has the power to do that which best pleases him."

"And yet I will not yield; I will not most unworthily attend to my own safety, while my associates die. No, my lord, if they are to be sacrificed, the addition of one poor woman will add little to the number of your victims; and I cannot consent to desert them."

"How do you desert them? You will never see or hear of them more, or they of you. But this is trifling; and my moments are precious."

"I will not – I dare not follow you. My heart, my conscience tell me to remain. I must not disobey their voice."

"Is your conscience so officious now, and / did it say nothing, or did your heart silence it, when you plotted my destruction?"

"Castruccio, this I believe is the last time that I shall ever speak to you. Our hearts are in the hands of the father of all; and he sees my thoughts. You know me too well, to believe that I plotted your death, or that of any human creature. Now is not the time to explain my motives and plans: but my earnest prayer was that you might live; my best hope, to make that life less miserable, less unworthy, than it had hitherto been."

She spoke with deep earnestness; and there was something in her manner, as if the spirit of truth animated all her accents, that compelled assent. Castruccio believed all; and he spoke in a milder and more persuasive manner "Poor Euthanasia! so you were at last cajoled by that arch-traitor, Bondelmonti. Well, I believe, and pardon all; but, as the seal of the purity of your intentions, I now claim your consent to my offers of safety."

"I cannot, indeed I cannot, consent. Be merciful; be magnanimous; and pardon all, banish us all where our discontent cannot be / dangerous to you. But to desert my friends, and basely to save that life you deny to them, I never can."

317

The jailor, who had hitherto stood in the shade near the door, could no longer contain himself. He knelt to Euthanasia, and earnestly and warmly intreated her to save herself, and not with wilful presumption to cast aside those means which God had brought about for her safety. "Remember," he cried, "your misfortunes will be on the prince's head; make him not answer for you also. Oh! lady, for his sake, for all our sakes, yield."

Castruccio was much moved to see the warmth of this man. He took the hand of Euthanasia, he also knelt: "Yes, my only and dearest friend, save yourself for my sake. Yield, beloved Euthanasia, to my intreaties. Indeed you will not die; for you well know that your life is dearer to me than my own. But yield to my request, by our former loves, I intreat; by the prayers which you offer up for my salvation, I conjure you as they shall be heard, so also hear me!"

The light of the solitary lamp fell full upon / the countenance of Castruccio: it was softened from all severity; his eyes glistened, and a tear stole silently down his cheek as he prayed her to yield. They talk of the tears of women; but, when they flow most plenteously, they soften not the heart of man, as one tear from his eyes has power on a woman. Words and looks have been feigned; they say, though I believe them not, that women have feigned tears: but those of a man, which are ever as the last demonstration of a too full heart, force belief, and communicate to her who causes them, that excess of tenderness, that intense depth of passion, of which they are themselves the sure indication.

Euthanasia had seen Castruccio weep but once before; it was many years ago, when he departed for the battle of Monte Catini; and he then sympathized too deeply in her sorrows, not to repay her much weeping with one most true and sacred tear. And now this scene was present before her; the gap of years remained unfilled; and she had consented to his request, before she again recalled her thoughts, and saw the dreary prison-chamber, / the glimmering lamp, and the rough form of the jailor who knelt beside Antelminelli. Her consent was scarcely obtained, when Castruccio leapt up, and, bidding her wrap her capuchin about her, led her by the hand down the steep prison-stairs, while the jailor went before them, and unlocked, and drew back the bolts of, the heavy creaking doors.

At the entrance of the prison they found a man on horseback holding two other horses. It was Mordecastelli. Castruccio assisted Euthanasia to mount, and then sprang on his own saddle; they walked their horses to a gate of the town which was open; – they proceeded in silence; – at the gate Castruccio said to his companion – "Here leave us; I shall speedily return."

Vanni then turned his horse's head, slightly answering the salute of Euthanasia, which she had involuntarily made at parting for ever with one who had been her intimate acquaintance. A countryman was waiting on horseback outside the gate: "You are our guide?" said Castruccio. "Lead on then."

It was a frosty, cloudless night; there was / no moon, but the stars shone intensely above; the bright assemblage seemed to congregate from the far

318

wastes of heaven, and to press in innumerable clusters upon the edge of the visible atmosphere, to gaze upon the strange earth beneath. The party passed out of the city of Lucca by the Pisan gate, and at first put their horses to a gallop. As they approached the hills, Castruccio came up beside Euthanasia; they slackened their speed; she spoke thus:

"I have acceded to your request, and left the prison; indeed it were useless in me to resist one who possesses the absolute power that you do. But I intreat you now that I see you for the last time, to have pity on my companions in this conspiracy. I can think only of them; and if I am to live – if ever I am again to hear of the events which will pass within the walls of that town, reflect on the sharp pang you will inflict upon me, if I hear of their destruction."

"Madonna," replied the prince, "I will do that which I consider my duty: and let not these our last moments be employed in fruitless discussion." /

Euthanasia felt that it was in vain to speak. Her confederates, her friends, who were reserved instantly to die, stood in funereal groupe before the eye of her soul; her imagination made present to her all that they thought, and all that they were to suffer. She looked upon Castruccio; she saw that he was moulded of an impenetrable substance: her heart swelled to the confines of her bosom, and forbade her such degradation to the assured victims, as would be implied in her uttering one further word in their behalf to the unhearing, unrelenting being that stood before her. Castruccio continued:

"You are about to leave Tuscany, and to take up your abode in a foreign land. You are still young. I send you from your native country; but you may at a future period confess that I have done you a kindness. You have hitherto mingled in the embroiled politics of a republic, and seen conspiracies, heart-burnings, and war."

Euthanasia felt herself unable to reply.

They had crossed the plain of Lucca, and were arrived beneath those hills, which, crowned / with towers, and clothed with deep forests, were the beautiful romantic steeps that she best loved. They struck off here from the usual road, and, fording the Serchio, began to ascend the acclivities on the opposite side, proceeding one by one up the narrow path. At length they reached the summit, and viewed, stretched before them beneath the stars of night, a scene of enchanting beauty. The plain they had just crossed was dimly seen beneath, bounded by its hills; before them was another plain, desert and barren, through which the Serchio flows, bounded by the dark line of the sea; and the Lago di Macciucoli, a marshy lake, was close beneath.[a]

---

[a] The track would pass near Nozzano after the fording of the Serchio near the Lucca–Pisa border. One route from the crest of the hill overlooking Lake Macciucoli (or Maciucoli) down to the coast would have included the road between Montramita and Viareggio, said to have been built by Castruccio himself (Tegrimi, p. 53). (See the 'Charles the First' Notebook, p. xxxi, for a map showing early nineteenth-century routes in the area).

"Here I leave you," said Castruccio: "there is your destination," and he pointed to the sea; "remember one with whom you have passed your happiest days."

He took her hand, and kissed it. Her feelings were strange, and hardly to be described. She could not entirely forget what he had once been to her. She could at that moment have overlooked his tyranny, his lawless ambition, and his cruelty. But, no; the moment itself / was a bane to oblivion. She could have forgotten his past cruelties, but not those which were immediately to be perpetrated, to be perpetrated on individuals who had been united with her in a plot for liberty, and some of whom her name and her countenance had perhaps prompted to the desperate undertaking, and egged on to destruction.

Castruccio spoke to the guide, recommending haste as soon as they should reach the plain, and then turned his horse's head. Euthanasia and her conductor paused on the summit of the hill; and she heard the steps of Castruccio's horse, as it made its way back through the tangled underwood. Then she also began her descent on the other side.

Euthanasia, being now separated from her former connections, and from him who had been the evil genius of the scene, began to resume her wonted tone. The eternal spirit of the universe seemed to descend upon her, and she drank in breathlessly the sensation, which the silent night, the starry heavens, and the sleeping earth bestowed upon her. All seemed / so peaceful, that no unwelcome sensation in her own heart could disturb the scene of which she felt herself a part. She looked up, and exclaimed in her own beautiful Italian, whose soft accents and expressive phrases then so much transcended all other European languages – "What a brave canopy has this earth, and how graciously does the supreme empyrean smile upon its nursling!"

"E Bellissimo," replied her guide, "ma figuratevi, Madonna, se è tanto bello sul rovescio, cosa mai sarà al dritto*."

Euthanasia smiled at the fancy of one so uncouth in manners and habits of life; and she replied, – "Who knows how soon it may be my destiny to see that other side, which you imagine outdoes this sublime spectacle in splendour?"

"Heaven preserve you long upon earth," / replied the man; "and make you as happy as you deserve, as happy as you have made others!"

"Do you know me then?"

"I dwell in the village of Valperga. I and my family have been Aldiani[a] there, since the time of the old count Goffredo, your great-grandfather. But, Madonna,

---

* I could not refrain from recording in their original language the words of a Florentine peasant. A poet might well envy the vivacity of this man's imagination.[b]

---

[a] Peasants intermediate between bondmen and freemen (Muratori, I, diss. 15, pp. 139–40); also called *Aldioni.*

[b] 'It is very beautiful, but think, my lady, if it is so beautiful on the wrong side, what it will be on the right side.'

please you to put spur to your horse; for we have little time, and I fear that before long the heavens will be overclouded; that last puff had something of the scirocco in it, and I see a mist in the west that foretels wind from that quarter."

They put their horses to the gallop. Euthanasia's was a noble steed, and bore her proudly on. She felt her spirits rise with the exhilarating motion; the wind gathered from the west, and scattered her hair, which, as she quitted her prison, she had slightly bound with a handkerchief; and, as she faced the breeze, its warm breath brought the lagging blood to her cheeks.

The approached the sea, and began to hear its roar; the breeze became stronger as they drew near. The beach was flat, and the small / line of sand that bordered the waters, was now beaten upon, and covered by the waves. As they came near, Euthanasia felt some curiosity to know her destination; but she saw nothing but the dim weed-grown field, and the white breakers of the troubled ocean. It was not until they were close upon the sand, that she discerned a large black boat drawn up on the beach, and several men near it. One of them came up, and asked the word, which the countryman gave; and then a man, who had the appearance of a leader, came from the boat, and welcomed Euthanasia. – "I am commanded," he said, "by the prince of Lucca to receive you, lady."

"And whither am I to go?"

He pointed to a vessel which rode hard by, – so near, that she wondered she had not seen it before. Its black hulk cast a deep shade upon the waters; and the dim sails, increased to an extraordinary size by the darkness, flapped heavily. She looked upon it with surprize, and wondered whither it was to bear her; but she asked no more questions: addressing herself for her departure, she took a / kind leave of the countryman, and gave him the little gold that she had with her. The man turned to the chief, and said, – "Sir knight, if it be not thought impertinent, have the courtesy to inform me whither that vessel is bound."

The man looked at him somewhat haughtily: but replied – "To Sicily." Sicily was then under the rule of the family of the kings of Arragon, who inherited from the daughter of Manfred, and were of course Ghibelines.[a]

"The Virgin Mother bless your voyage!" said her guide to Euthanasia. – "I am afraid that it will be rough, for an ugly wind is rising: but the saints will surely guard you."

Euthanasia stepped into the boat; its commander sat beside her; and the men took their oars; she waved her hand to her guide, saying, "Farewel, may God bless you!" she added in a low tone, half to herself – "They speak Italian also in Sicily."

These were the last words she ever spoke to any one who returned to tell the

---

[a] Frederick II, King of Sicily (reigned 1296–1337), son of Costanza, Manfred's daughter; he is mentioned in Dante, *Purgatorio*, III. 116 and VII. 115–20.

tale. The countryman stood upon the beach; – he saw the boat moor beside the vessel; he saw its / crew ascend the dark sides. The boat was drawn up; the sails were set; and they bore out to sea, receding slowly with many tacks, for the wind was contrary; – the vessel faded on the sight; and he turned about, and speeded to Lucca.

The wind changed to a more northerly direction during the night; and the land-breeze of the morning filled their sails, so that, although slowly, they dropt down southward. About noon they met a Pisan vessel, who bade them beware of a Genoese squadron, which was cruizing off Corsica: so they bore in nearer to the shore. At sunset that day a fierce scirocco rose, accompanied by thunder and lightning, such as is seldom seen during the winter season. Presently they saw huge, dark columns, descending from heaven, and meeting the sea, which boiled beneath; they were borne on by the storm, and scattered by the wind. The rain came down in sheets; and the hail clattered, as it fell to its grave in the ocean; – the ocean was lashed into such waves, that, many miles inland, during the pauses of the wind, the hoarse and constant / murmurs of the far-off sea made the well-housed landsman mutter one more prayer for those exposed to its fury.

Such was the storm, as it was seen from the shore. Nothing more was ever known of the Sicilian vessel which bore Euthanasia. It never reached its destined port, nor were any of those on board ever after seen. The centinels who watched near Vado,[a] a tower on the sea beach of the Maremma, found on the following day, that the waves had washed on shore some of the wrecks of a vessel; they picked up a few planks and a broken mast, round which, tangled with some of its cordage, was a white silk handkerchief, such a one as had bound the tresses of Euthanasia the night that she had embarked, and in its knot were a few golden hairs.

She was never heard of more; even her name perished. She slept in the oozy cavern of the ocean; the sea-weed was tangled with her shining hair; and the spirits of the deep wondered that the earth had trusted so lovely a creature to the barren bosom of the sea, / which, as an evil step-mother, deceives and betrays all committed to her care.

Earth felt no change when she died; and men forgot her. Yet a lovelier spirit never ceased to breathe, nor was a lovelier form every destroyed amidst the many it brings forth. Endless tears might well have been shed at her loss; yet for her none wept, save the piteous skies, which deplored the mischief they had themselves committed; – none moaned except the sea-birds that flapped their heavy wings above the ocean-cave wherein she lay; – and the muttering thunder alone tolled her passing bell, as she quitted a life, which for her had been replete with change and sorrow. /

---

[a] About fifteen miles south of Leghorn; the desolate scene of P. B. Shelley's *Mazenghi* (1824) (based on Sismondi, ch. lx, from which the spelling 'Vado' is taken; elsewhere usually 'Vada'). In this poem, a black ship also appears.

CONCLUSION.

The private chronicles, from which the foregoing relation has been collected, end with the death of Euthanasia. It is therefore in public histories alone that we find an account of the last years of the life of Castruccio. We can know nothing of his grief, when he found that she whom he had once tenderly loved, and whom he had ever revered as the best and wisest among his friends, had died. We know however that, during the two years that he survived this event, his glory and power arose not only higher than they had ever before done, but that they surpassed those of any former Italian prince.

Louis of Bavaria, king of the Romans, entered Italy in the month of February 1327. He found Castruccio, the scourge of the Guelphs, the first power of Tuscany, and the principal supporter of his own titles and pretensions. /

Louis of Bavaria was crowned with the iron crown at Milan.[a] But his proceedings were tyrannical and imprudent. He deprived Galeazzo Visconti of his power, and imprisoned him, and set up the shadow of a republic at Milan, which was in fact composed of a few Ghibeline nobles, who by their jealousies and dissentions served only to weaken his power.

He marched through Lombardy, crossed the Apennines at Parma, and was met by Castruccio at Pontremoli.[b] The prince, whose chief aim was to ingratiate himself with, and to raise himself to power through the favour of, the emperor, made his visit more agreeable through the magnificent presents by which he was accompanied; and his sagacity, warlike spirit, and agreeable manners gained for him an easy entrance into the councils, and afterwards into the friendship, of Louis. They proceeded together to Pisa. The Pisans at first refused entrance to the emperor, but yielded after he had besieged them a few days. Louis then visited Lucca, where he erected a dutchy composed of the towns and territory of Lucca, Pistoia, Volterra and Lunigiana, and created / Castruccio duke, honouring and exalting him as his best friend, and the firmest support of the imperial power.[c]

They went to Rome together, where the emperor knighted him, and he bore the sword of state in the procession from the Campidoglio to St. Peter's, where

---

[a] Used for the Lombard coronation. For the second coronation as emperor, the imperial crown was used.

[b] Near the northern boundary of what was by that time a vastly extended state of Lucca; Castruccio had built a tower there (Tegrimi, p. 47).

[c] Details of Louis of Bavaria's progress through Tuscany and his accommodation with Castruccio are taken from Villani, X, cap. 56 and Sismondi, ch. xxxi.

Louis received the imperial crown. He was created count of the palace, senator of Rome, and master of the court. He had arrived at the summit of his glory; he was more feared and obeyed than the emperor himself; and, in the expedition which Louis meditated against Naples, king Robert dreaded Castruccio alone, as his most formidable and craftiest enemy. It was then, that the proud Antelminelli invested himself in a robe of silk richly adorned with gold and jewels; and on the breast were embroidered these words – EGLIE È COME DIO VUOLE. And on the shoulders, È SI SARA QUEL CHE DIO VORRÀ.[a]

While he was thus enjoying the maturity of his glory, and partaking all the amusements and feasts of the capital of Italy, he received intelligence that the Florentines had possessed themselves of Lucca. Without a moment's / delay, he quitted Rome, traversed the Maremma with a small band of friends, and appeared, when he was least expected, in the midst of his enemies.

It was here that he again met Galeazzo Visconti. At Castruccio's request the emperor had released him from prison; and he came to serve under the ensigns of his more fortunate friend. Their meeting was an occasion of mutual joy; they embraced each other affectionately, and confirmed and renewed the vows of friendship and support which they had entered into more than ten years before. Castruccio enjoyed for a short time the unalloyed pleasure which the society of his friend afforded him; they recounted to each other their various fortunes; and, in recording the events which had passed since their separation, Galeazzo found, that, if he had lost sovereignty and power, Castruccio had lost that which might be considered far more valuable; he had lost his dearest friends; and on his pale cheek might be read, that, although he disdained to acknowledge the power of fortune, she had made him feel in his heart's core her poisoned shafts.[b] We know nothing of the / private communion of these friends; but we may guess that, if Castruccio revealed the sorrows of his heart, Galeazzo might have regretted that, instead of having instigated the ambition, and destroyed the domestic felicity of his friend, he had not taught him other lessons, through which he might have enjoyed that peace, sympathy and happiness, of which he was now for ever deprived.

His presence restored the state of his affairs. He possessed himself of Pisa, recovered Pistoia,[c] and again returned in triumph to Lucca. But this was the term of his victories. During the siege of Pistoia he had tasked his strength beyond human suffering; he was ever in the trenches on horseback, or on foot exposed to the hot sun of July, encouraging the soldiers, directing the pioneers, and often, in the ardour of impatience, he himself took the spade, and worked

---

[a] 'What is, is as God wills. What God shall will shall be'. Mainly from Sismondi, ch. xxx, which follows Villani, X, cap. 60, but with Machiavelli's 'quel' adopted by Mary Shelley for the former's 'quello'. Sources give the date variously as 16 and 17 January 1328.

[b] Tegrimi and especially Machiavelli both stress the role of Fortune in Castruccio's career.

[a] Castruccio repossessed Pistoia on 13 May, 1328 (Tegrimi, 1742 chronology).

among them. He neither rested nor slept; and the heats of noon-day, and the dews of night alike fell upon him. Immediately on his return to his native city, he was seized with a malignant fever. He knew that he was about to die; and, with that coolness and presence / of mind which was his peculiar characteristic, he made every arrangement necessary for the welfare of Lucca, and gave particular directions to his captains for the prosecution of the war.[a] But he felt, that he left behind him no fitting successor; and that, if he were the sole creator and only support of the Lucchese, so they would fall into their primitive insignificance when he expired. Lying thus on the bed of pain, and conscious that in a few hours he must surely die, he grasped the hand of Vanni Mordecastelli, who wept beside him, saying: *Io morrò, e vedrete il mondo per varie turbolenze confondersi, e rivoltarsi ogni cosa.*[b] This consideration cast a gloom over his last moments; yet he supported himself with courage.

Galeazzo Visconti had assisted Castruccio in all his labours, exposing himself with like imprudence, and labouring with equal energy. He was attacked at Pistoia with the same fever and the same symptoms. Hearing that the prince was ill at Lucca, he desired, although dying, to be conveyed to him. He was carried as far as Pescia, where he expired on the third of September 1328.[c] /

On the same day, and at the same hour, Castruccio died at Lucca.

His enemies rejoiced in his death; his friends were confounded and overthrown. They, as the last act of gratitude, conducted the pomp of his funeral with princely magnificence. He was buried in the church of San Francesco, then without, now included within, the walls of Lucca. The antient tombstone is still seen on the walls of the church; and its inscription may serve for the moral and conclusion of this tale.

---

[a] Castruccio gave orders that his death be kept secret until 10 September to permit time for the garrisoning of his cities against a possible uprising. He was buried on 14 September (Villani, X, cap. 87; Tegrimi, 1742 Chronology; Sismondi, ch. xxxi).

[b] 'I shall die, and you will see the world thrown into confusion by different upheavals, and all turned upside down.' Taken from Dati's translation of Tegrimi's Latin. Villani's version is 'Io mi vegio morire & morto me di corto vedrete disastroccato'. In Machiavelli, Castruccio makes a long dying speech to Pagolo Guinigi.

[c] Galeazzo died of fever shortly before Castruccio, according to Villani (X, cap. 87), 'wretched, excommunicated and dependent upon Castruccio'. Pescia is fifteen miles north-east of Lucca. Green notes that Oliver Cromwell also died on 3 September (a circumstance that both Mary Shelley and Godwin would have been aware of).

En vivo vivamque

fama rerum gestarum

Italicæ militiæ splen-

dor; Lucensium

decus Etruriæ

ornamentum Cas-

truccius Gerii An-

telminellorum stirpe

vixi peccavi dolui

cessi naturæ indigen-

ti animæ piæ benevoli

succurrite brevi memores

vos morituros.[a]

*Behold I live & shall live
By referr of my deeds*

THE END. /

---

[a] 'Lo, by the fame of my deeds, I live and shall live, the glory of Italian soldiery, the paragon of the Lucchese, the pride of Tuscany, Castruccio, son of Gerio, of the family of the Antelminelli. I lived, I sinned, I suffered; I yielded to Nature. Men of good will, help a devout soul in need, mindful that in a short while ye are to die.' (Editor's translation, with advice from Peter Fisher). Mary Shelley's letter to Leigh Hunt of 7 August 1823 describes the location of the memorial; the version of the inscription here printed differs in a few details but derives from her transcript in Ab. Dep. e. 274, p. 47; that in *CC Journals*, p. 170 is almost identical, and one may be copied from the other. For the most part the original lineation is preserved. A transcript in Targioni (VII, p. 69) has 'pie' ('in piety', qualifying 'help') for 'piae' and 'et vos' ('ye too') for 'vos'; these may be more correct readings.

ENDNOTES

With diplomatic transcripts of leaves from the 'rough transcript' of *Valperga* in the Pierpont Morgan Library, New York.

Information for this note concerning the relevant manuscripts has been supplied by Christine Nelson, Associate Curator of Autograph Manuscripts at the Pierpont Morgan Library and Dr Bruce C. Barker-Benfield, Assistant Keeper of Western Manuscripts at the Bodleian Library, but the editor is responsible for inferences and conclusions from the facts supplied.

Nine leaves comprising seven fragments of *Valperga* draft in Mary Shelley's hand, the size of the fragments ranging from one to six written pages, have survived. There is no obvious reason why they, and not others, should have done so. On internal evidence they appear all to derive from what Mary Shelley called 'rough transcript'. Palacio (pp. 635–6, 653–4), reported that they were exhibited by the Grolier Club in 1923 as item 117 (Ruth S Graniss, *A Descriptive Catalogue of the First Editions of the Writings of Percy Bysshe Shelley*), and auctioned in 1929 (*The Library of Jerome Kern* (New York: Anderson Galleries, 21–24 January 1929), II, p. 345, Lot 1063). The buyer was the Pierpont Morgan Library, New York, where they are shelf-marked MA 1067. The leaves were already bound up (by Kern or a previous owner) when auctioned. They had been sequenced (incorrectly) according to Mary Shelley's pagination in ascending numerical order, with the single non-paginated leaf placed before the rest. It was not appreciated that her numerals anticipated the division of the published novel into three volumes, each of which had autonomous pagination. Each leaf was mounted on a stub and the leaves bound together in a tan paper folder, which in turn was housed in a loose grey folder with four flaps bearing the Kern book-plate and the ticket of Harry F. Marks, Bookseller, 31 West 47th Street, New York City. The leaves were at some point foliated 1–9 in the order of binding-up.

The leaves appear to be strays from a manuscript that was written fairly continuously (but allowing for break-offs) using a type of paper frequently found in the Bodleian Library among Shelley MSS of 1820–21. It is Italian-made, deckle-edged, laid, with vertical chain-lines, with the watermark of an emblematic fish in a crowned shield on the right *or* left hand half of the sheet. (Italian papers were then frequently made with 'twin' moulds, the second mould often repeating the design of the first, but with left/right positioning switched round.) Various countermarks occupy the other half; one type is ANT.FORTI / C with small initials S.L.° in the lower right hand corner, and another JL GRAN / MASSO (the I of IL being the form J). Various initials also appear beneath the fish. Dr Barker-Benfield conjectures that the emblem is a visual pun on Pescia (fish), a city not far from Pisa, where a noble family called 'Forti' has been recorded, and which was known for its paper mills in the early nineteenth century (in *Valperga*, Galeazzo Visconti dies there). A sheet size with parameters of 313–18 x 432–42 mm has been identified, and sheets were frequently carefully torn by the Shelleys to make half sheets. As the *Valperga* leaves measure approximately 318 × 216 mm, each can be deduced to be just such a half-sheet. Only deckle edges are visible on the microfilm, but torn edges could have been concealed by the mounting. Half-sheets divided as described above would exhibit the watermark or the countermark, not both.

The nine *Valperga* leaves furnish one example of the fish, without initials, four of the fish, over initials 'J C', two of ANT.FORTI / C and two of JL GRAN / MASSO. This may comprise two variants only: the 'Fish' with an ANT.FORTI / C countermark and the 'Fish J C' with an JL GRAN MASSO countermark. While all inferences from such a small sample must be very tentative, it is worth noting that when sorted into their order of correspondence to the published book, the 'Fish' leaf and the ANT.FORTI / C leaves, with one exception, separate out from 'Fish J C' and JL GRAN / MASSO leaves. The exception, an example of 'Fish J C', is an unpaginated later insertion. Mary Shelley might have begun with a stock of ANT.FORTI / C paper and changed over to JL GRAN / MASSO paper at some point during the 'rough transcript' of volume II, using the new stock for insertions. Edward Williams's draft of *The Promise*, Act IV, a drama based on a story in the *Decameron* (Bodleian MS Shelley adds. d. 3 ff. 21–35, 38–40), is also written on half sheets of 'Fish J C' + JL GRAN / MASSO paper. As Williams was writing his play at Pugnano c.May–July, and Mary Shelley was writing the rough transcript of Volumes II and III in June–July, it is pleasant to speculate that they shared a batch of paper as well as an interest in Boccaccio during the summer of 1821. But without closely comparing the spacing of the letters in relation to the chain-lines in the MSS this cannot be supported (or refuted). Be that as it may, the Williams draft is the nearest match found to the *Valperga* leaves to date. Another possible match is Bodleian MS Shelley adds. c. 4, ff. 108–9, a folded half-sheet of the right size, containing a draft for part of 'The Aziola' with the mark JL GRAN / MASSO.

Superscript numbers in the text are keyed to endnotes describing each fragment. Each begins with Mary Shelley's pagination, her round bracket being retained to distinguish her manuscript numbers from printed ones. This is followed by the watermark, information about writing on the leaves, correspondence to the 1823 edition (Pickering & Chatto pagination in brackets), and commentary, if relevant.

Transcripts (taken from microfilm) follow all together, in exactly the same order as the endnotes; leaves are keyed to them through Mary Shelley's pagination. They are 'diplomatic', i.e. they translate the characters into print as far as possible without other editorial intervention. The library's foliation has been omitted, but Mary Shelley's writing, including sigla (but not blots, random pen-strokes and under writing, of which last there is very little), has been reproduced. It has not been possible to match all gradations of character size nor to imitate cancellation-scribbles exactly. Spelling errors (e.g. 'lanscape') are left uncorrected. Conjectural readings are placed in square brackets thus: [?word]. Brief notes about the few untranscribable features which are most likely to be significant are placed at the foot of the relevant page of transcript.

[1] 11) 95)/ 12) 96): 'Fish'; one leaf, writing on both pages; corresponding to vol. I, pp. 117–20 and 122 (pp. 52–3), 'them is to destroy both [. . .] abhorrence of this republic?'. The change of pagination from lower to higher numerals possibly indicates that this portion originally belonged to Volume II.

[2] 12): ANT.FORTI / C, one leaf, writing on one page, apparently the recto, and so positioned by the binder, verso blank; corresponding to vol. II, pp. 14–15 (pp. 126–7), 'The Bishop and Castruccio [. . .] deliberate on their projects. Castruccio'.

[3] Unpaginated: 'Fish J C'; one leaf, writing on both pages, but the verso is only a quarter filled; the marginal X on the recto indicates that this was written for insertion into the existing draft; corresponding to vol. II, pp. 135–6 (pp. 169–70), 'She remembered her vow [. . .] to complete the sacrifice.'

[4] 137)/ 138): ANT.FORTI / C; one leaf, writing on both pages, containing the end of a chapter and the beginning of the next; the chapter ending is the vestige of an episode excised from the printed version (the Luparo episode). This perhaps once ended either chapter vii (p. 184) or chapter viii (p. 191) of volume II; the first option would require chapter viii to be a later interpolation. The chapter opening on page 138) corresponds to vol. II, pp. 193–200 (pp. 192–3), from the opening of chapter ix up to 'by a long peace the injury done to their'.

The Luparo episode, taken from its sole source in Tegrimi (pp. 36–9), tells how Castruccio reneged on a loan from his friend Luparo by altering 'will [pay]' (*volumus*) to 'will not [pay]' (*nolumus*) on the agreement. Mary Shelley evidently intended to illustrate Castruccio's use of fraud and betrayal of friendship as parallelling his use of force and betrayal of love. The Dante allusion is to *Inferno*, XXI. 38 ('Lo! one of Santa Zita's elders'). The circle number left unfilled in the draft is the eighth, to which Dante consigns the barrators (peculators), in the fifth gulf. Santa Zita (c.1218–78), in Dante's day recently canonised, had been a humble servant at Lucca. The sarcasms referred to include a satirical sonnet supposedly written by Luparo himself, to which Castruccio retorted in kind (interpolated into Tegrimi's Latin narrative but in

Italian). The former was translated by P. B. Shelley as 'If the good money which I lent to thee' (Bodleian MS Shelley adds. c. 4 f. 139ʳ), and possibly intended for inclusion in *Valperga*. The holograph is reproduced in *Miscellaneous Poetry, Prose and Translations from Bodleian MS Shelley adds. c. 4*, transcribed and edited by E. B. Murray, XXI in *The Bodleian Shelley Manuscripts* (New York and London: Garland Publishing, 1995). Luparo's sonnet is reproduced in Italian in W. H. Lyles, 'Niccolò Tegrimi's *Vita di Castruccio*, The Source of Shelley's "If the good money which I lent to thee"', *Modern Language Notes*, XCIII (January 1978), 137–8. Lyles (who first identified the Tegrimi source) took his text from Muratori, *Rerum*, vol. XI; there are a few differences between it and the 1742 text that the Shelleys used, but these are not significant. The (1) on p. 138) marks an insertion point for material, probably a draft of the episode of the attempt to kill King Robert.

[5] 200)/ 201): JL GRAN / MASSO; 205)/ 206): 'Fish J C'; two leaves, writing on all pages. Page 200) was originally numbered 204) and opens with cancelled material intermediate between 201) and 205); the two leaves comprise, with gaps, a previous draft of vol. II, pp. 266–73 (spanning the latter part of ch. xi and the opening section of ch. xii) (pp. 217–19): 'she hastened to the window that overlooked the outer court [...] lost, when once she had'.

[6] 118)/ 119): 'Fish J C'; 120)/ 121): JL GRAN / MASSO; 122)/ 123): 'Fish J C'; three leaves, writing on all pages. A previous draft of Volume III, pp. 169–72 (pp. 288–9): 'Castruccio had now been Lord of Lucca for six years [...] made the nations tremble'. There is no exact correspondence at the break-off point to the printed version. The portrait of Castruccio is drawn largely from Tegrimi, but the detail of his pallor is taken from Villani. The (cancelled) allusion on p. 118) to Vittorio Alfieri, whose plays and memoirs Mary Shelley read during September–October 1818 (*MWSJ*, II, p. 632), has not been identified. 'Albert' on p. 123) could be an earlier name for 'Arrigo'.

11) 95)   them is to destroy both ~~and~~ ^{or} under the mask of friendship
to reserve to himself all that each posessed.
~~to be the conqueror of Italy —~~

Pèpi uttered this harangue with an energy &
vivacity that startled Castruccio – his black eyes sparkled
his brows elevated and drawing down the _{perpendicular} wrinkels of

his cheeks & contracting the horizontal ones of his
forehead he looked round with an air of triumph on
his companions —

prognostications   You say true – Messer Benedetto – said FeTadèo _{groaning at the dismal}
~~prophecy~~ of his friend and I fear greatly that this pretended justice is the
watchword for war & bloodshed – yet all now ~~is~~ wears

the appearance of peace & brotherhood –The Lords
of –Pavia Langusco – Pavia – Vercelli Novara & Lodi have
all resigned their tyrannies & given up the keys of their
respective towns _{to Henry} & Imperials vicars ~~he~~ are every where

established – Guido della Torre the proudest & most power
ful tyrant of Lombardy has submitted, & the Court of the
Emperor _{at} of Milan is crowded by the Lords of the East
of Italy and the ambassadors of the free towns of the south –

Has Florence submitted? asked Castruccio

No — That town and its league holds out
Siena Lucca & Bologna — yet when the Emperor
marches South we shall see these proud republi
cans bend their stiff knees —

Never - cried Pèpi - Bologna Lucca & Siena
may submit but Florence never will — they are
stiff kneed - stiff necked & ~~more obsti ate~~ party spirited
hate the ~~mo~~ name of Emperor more than _{& master} ~~that of the~~ Pope

Urban hated ~~it in the tim~~ the house of Souabia
These republicans whom from my soul I hate - have
asserting the   turned out the ~~E~~ Ghibelines & are now fighting with
power of vulgar   the nobles till every petty artizan of its meanest lane
fancies himself as great an ~~Emp~~ prince as the

331

12) 96

Emperor Henry himself – Besides ~~they will be~~

when all else fails they will buy him off – These

Florentines squander their golden florins & pay
to purchase
thousands ~~for~~ what w^d be a dear bargain

as a gift —Their watch word is that
laughing stock
echo of fools & that ~~curse~~ of the wise –Liberty –

Surely the father of lies himself invented that

bait that trap which the multitude catch at

as a mouse at a piece of cheese well w^d it X

be for the world if they found the same end ~~and~~
they

X and as the nibbling mouse
pulls down the iron on his
head ~~neck~~ they

as if they had one neck ~~it~~ were lopped off as

they seized their prize -but Florence flourishes.
  Pèpi ended his speech by a deep groan & con

tinued lost in thought while Taddèo & Castruccio

discussed the chances ~~of~~ that might arrise from
the new order of things established in Italy — &

Castruccio owned his intention of joining the
court of the Emperor and his hope of being by

his means reinstated in his native town.
The evening wore away during these discussions

X
  For some time they rode along
silent~~by~~ – for Castruccio was over
come a variety of feelings on
again visiting Italian ground
  being winter
although ~~round~~ ⊦ & the lanscape
  &
was stript bare ~~of~~ its vineyards
& cornfields alike appeared
waste yet Castruccio thought
no country ~~had ever appeared so~~
~~beautiful~~ could vie with this
in beauty - if it were not the
plain of Lucca such he remem
bered it the last time he beheld
it from the tower of his father's
  palace
~~house~~ girdled by hills &
the many-towered town set
~~Lucca~~ ∧as its eye ~~set~~ in the
middle. He longed for a com
panion to whom he could
pour out his full heart – for
his overflowing feelings had

and they retired early to rest – The next morning

Castruccio & Pèpi took leave of Tadèo and

departed together on the road to Milan X

he
Messer Benedetto - said ~~Castruccio as~~ they
last night
~~road rode along~~ - you seemed to groan under the
  ∧
weight of your hatred of Florentines –now I have

good reason to hate them since by their means

my party was exiled & Lucca ranks among

the Guelph_{ic} towns of Tuscany – but you are of

Cremona a town seperated from Florence

by many mountains & rivers – whence therefore

arrises your ~~hat~~ abhorrence of the republic

'laughing stock' in P. B. Shelley's hand.

12) The Bishop and Castruccio continued together

the whole day, both mutually delighted with each other.

Castruccio had a great taste for
knowledge
theological ~~discussions~~ , & the Bishop, as a

man of the world was delighted with the

conversations & remarks of one who had

experienced so many changes of fortune

as Castruccio. ~~Thus they mi~~ Confidence

quickly arose between them, and when
they felt
the evening came∧as if they had been

friends for years, so well did each seem

to understand the feelings & character of

the other. The Bishop was a Ghibeline, but

his motives were pure and his hatred for

the corruptions of the papal court and the

brawls which appeared to him inseprable ~~with~~

from   a republic attached him strongly to the
of
party of the Emperor & to those lords who reigning

peacefully over a people who loved

them seemed to him ensure the quiet
of Italy.
In the evening the partizans of the
deliberate on
Marquess of Este assembled to ~~discuss~~ their
projects
~~plans~~ at the episcopal palace Castruccio

[recto]

X

Euthanasia remembered her vow not to unite
herself to the enemy of Florence & she resolved
to abide by it: — Her residence of these few
weeks in her native city had endeared its
inhabitants to her — she ne-renewed her
early friendships — she was again among
them one of them & could she join with
one who w^d bring havoc among her best
friends? She deaded the reproachful voice of
her conscience & in her well regulated mind
the fear of her own self condemnation
w^d have been sufficient to deter her
from incurring its censures — but he all
the feelings of her heart here interposed
her gentle friendships — Why the girl
she had best loved was now married to
one who w^d be exposed foremost to
the arms of Castruccio's soldiers — The best
friend of her father w^d lead his troop
also against them — her marriage with
him on condition of viewing his victories
over the Florentines of rejoicing in the
death of those she loved w^d be as if she

[verso]

united herself to the wheel — bound her
self for life body & soul to the ever
moving renewing pangs of some tyrant-invented
torture — It could not be - her resolution
was made — and the energy of her soul befitted
her to complete the sacrifize

137) but his treason; A miser can never be ~~faithful or~~

good for anything; as long as he concealed his failing

he was very dear to me but when he shews

that he values his money more than he

does me it is necessary that I also should

value these miserable crowns more than

Luparo himself. When this poor man found that

no entreaties or threats could ~~co~~ obtain his money

he left Lucca in despair and joining himself

with ~~one~~ Tedici the lord of Pistoia against

caused
Castruccio he ~~made~~ several castles under
to ^
his jurisdiction rebel — but Castruccio going
^
against them reduced them, deprived Lu

paro of all that he possessed and pursueing

his life the old man retired to Bologna

where poor & miserable he soon died of a

broken heart.

There was in the whole of this transaction

a degree of fraud and tyranny in the conduct

of Castruccio that irritated Euthanasia. She

saw no trace of the hero she had worshipped

in the falsifier of a money bond & in the

oppressor of an ~~as~~ old man who_{se} avarice was
his only fault. She had before felt the

exquisite delight of loving one approved &

honoured by the whole world, & the change

was proportionably bitter to find the God of

her imagination spoken of with contempt by

335

138)

jests

his enemies, and with ~~mockery~~ even by his

friends — for the change of <u>Volumus</u> to <u>Nolu</u>

mus gave rise to innumerable sarcasms,
~~and~~ the

    Ecco un degli anzian di Santa Zita

of Dante was applied to Castruccio, ~~and~~

                in the

~~even~~ and his place ~~amon~~   circle
                ^ ^

of hell allotted to him.

Chapter

Castruccio heeded this little while his

own ambitious designs were ripening every day.

The whole Ghibeline force was now turned to
the siege of Genoa which was defended by
Robert king of Naples at the head of the
Guelphs. This siege had continued with
intervals for two years, Castruccio had never
actually entered the besieging army but he

                   war ~~impediment~~

had taken advantage of the ~~occasion~~ which
                        ^

hindered the Genoese from defending their
castles on the seacoast to take many of them
and to spread his conquests far beyond the

x
                          *(1)

Lucchese territory. In the winter of the begin

and entered with spirit
into all the enterprizes   ning of the year 1320 the Ghibelines reinforced
                           their allies for

undertaken against   utmost
  imperial   their powers, called upon ~~all~~ their assistance
the ~~inimical~~ party   ^   ^
although   ~~of all their allies~~ and Castruccio among the
but a wish to preserve

                 rest was to advance to their aid with
their territory free from   the whole army. But the Guelphs were
the horrors of war, and   sent soldiers
to repair by a long peace   not idle. Florence had ^ every campaign
the injury done to their   reinforce

              ~~sent soldiers~~ to the army of the Genoese x

204)- 200

and which would soon be reduced to an unshaped
heap
　　When night came on Castiglione sent to
her to desire to be admitted. Madonna, said
he, pardon me but you must leave the castle
a palace is prepared for your reception at Lucca

but seeing nothing from the place where she stood
　　　　　　　　　　a　　　　　　　　　　whence
she hastened to ~~the~~ window of the gallery ^ she ~~saw~~

perceived　　　~~she saw~~ a party of soldiers, whom she knew by their
　　　　　　　　　　　in a long & almost never-ending file
dress to be soldiers of Castruccio, ~~run a~~ come out of the
castle gate & ~~running~~ round the walls towards
the drawbridge raising as they went the Ghibeline
war cry. she then heard steps at the further end of
coridor and had only time to enter the chamber
　　　Lauretta
of ~~Theresa~~ & to exclaim, we are betrayed! When it
was filled with soldiers and the chief officer com
ing forward cried the castle is ours, and addressing
himself to Euthanasia he said Madonna, it were
well that you ordered ~~these~~ your people to yield,

*

The Commander will judge of for it is useless to resist & can only be the cause
the necessity of submission　　　　　　h
　　　　　　　　　　of bloodsed; we are commanded by our general to
　　　　　　　　　　　　　^
　　　　　　　　　　act with the greatest moderation.

　　　　　　　　　　　　　It is enough, replied Euthanasia quietly
* If I find that indeed　* but ~~now you I wou request that you~~ see you frighten
no further resistance　. this lady who is ill & delicate. I beseech you leave the
can be made　　　　　room awhile* I shall soon be prepared to follow you.
　　　　　　　　　　　Madonna, we obey you; but permit me
　　　　　　　　　　to add that by the generals' orders you will not be

The cancelled portion (lines 1–6) is written with a thicker quill than the rest.

201)

removed from the castle until the evening
soldiers
The ~~man~~ left the room and Euthanasia
~~said~~ saying to Lauretta
~~turning to Theresa~~, I will send some people to you
         ^
dear Cousin, I cannot stay now — she quitted the

*Here she found several   chamber by another door and hastened through
of her attendants who told a corridor which conducted to her own appart

with many tears that   ment*   Chapter XII   fearless
there was no longer any hope - And now she was alone, and the ^ counte
          enemy
That the ~~party~~ entering   nance that she had put on fell, and the
from behind had driven   exertion she had made only caused the first
~~the~~ her soldiers down the burst of sorrow to be more poignant. She wept
rock to those below

& raising the draw   Farewell, dear habitation of my early years
             farewel all ye associations which are as a part
bridge Were now in   of my life; the dearer & better part of it! I leave
undisturbed possession   to
of the castle – she heard you ~~in~~ the hands of the spoiler; and he will~~t~~
all with an ~~all~~ unaltered not value ye because you were the birth
mien, and when the   place & nursery of his sometime loved Euthana
melancholy tale was   sia. Loved ! How did that word intrude? this
finished -she bade them is the work of hate, and let me call up from
leave her & go to the   my soul all severe thoughts, all ideas as stern
commanding officer of
the troop to receive ord_{ers} harsh & unrelenting as his purpose, & clothing
as to their further proce_{edings} them in fitting words let me curse the author
but not to return to her of all these evils.
until she should com   Curse! alas I hardly know how to
mand their attendance   the ~~angriest~~
            _____ frame that speech, and surely ~~my hardest~~
       bitterest reproach which I ever heaped on any was a
          — "God mend you!" Oh I will not curse but only

205) he felt awed by the mien of Euthanasia who

received them with ~~simplicit~~ that slight tinge
which
of pride mingled with her accustomed dignity ~~that~~
up
adversity naturally bestows ʌ on the virtuous

He announced that the escort had arrived to
~~to~~ bowed her head in acquiescence & ˌ

*
Lauretta   convey them to Lucca — Euthanasia with an
~~rising~~ raising ~~Theresa~~ she whis   she   ʌ
ʌ

pered comfort to her while   unfaltering step ~~le~~ f.left for the last time
her poor friend
the castle of her ancestors; she supported ~~Teresa~~
ʌ

with one hand & with the other folded her

veil close to her face that no rudely

curious eye might read in its expression

the sorrow that she felt in her heart

My grief is my own, she thought, the only

treasure that remains to me and I will
with
hoard it more jealousy from the sight &
ʌ
knowledge of others than a miser does he loved

gold. She walked unfaltering through the

hall, long the seat of her pleasures & hap

piness — her infant feet had trodden ~~there~~

its pavement   in unproved gaiety and she thought for

a moment she saw the venerable form

of a her father seated in his accustomed

place — but she proudly shook the softening

emotion from her & looked with a tearless

eye upon the hearth round which stood

the soldiers of her enemy profaning its
round
sacredness by their presence — ~~near the doo~~

Line 25: ~~there~~ *upon* ~~this~~ *or vice versa; line 31:* r *of* hearth *upon* l

339

castle gate
round the ~~door~~ stood a number of women & children
the   ^

206)   ꝑ the wives of ~~her~~ peasantry who depended on her
who as they saw her advance raised one cry of grief – she

started & said in a smothered voice – Could I

not have been spared this ? – Impossible replied

Castiglione who overheard her - nothing but the

most brutal force could prevent them. Enough

said Euthanasia I am content.

As she left the hall these women

clung about her kissing her hands her garments

& throwing themselves on their knees with all

the violent gesticulations of Italians they tore
                    imprecated
their hair, & ~~cried called upon~~ heaven to save

bless their Mistress & to avenge her wrongs –

~~Oh holy virgin look down on us – holy St Mar~~
              and each called ~~each~~
tin   ~~They called~~   on their favourite saint
                      ^
to cause some miracle which might even

now arrest ~~their~~ her departure – God bless you

good people – May you never feel my loss by any

misfortune that may happen to you   and dis
                                     selves
engaging herself from their grasp she walked

on — while they followed urging & praying –

they crossed the drawbridge which was guarded

at each end by soldiers — ere she put her

foot on the opposite rock Euthanasia paused

for one moment — it seemed to her that

all was irretrievably lost when once she had

Line 13: -ees of knees upon -ews; line 25: k of walked upon l

118) Chapter Castruccio had now been Lord of Lucca six years

and had attained his thirty third year; his character

was formed and his phisiognomy, changed from its

youthful expression, had ~~been~~ become impressed by

his habitual feelings — Constant exposure to the

sun & weather had ~~burnt~~ tinged his cheek with

broown which but for that had been deadly

pale — for care and the strong emotions to which

he was subject had ~~im~~ left their mark on his

          had grown   ⊥
contenance; ~~and~~ his eye ~~more~~ hollow ~~that his~~

          of his brow was ~~was~~ ~~blemished~~ diminished
and the smooth lustre ~~cheek brow deep fur~~ by deep lines which indeed
                 since they marked the progress of ~~deep~~ thought
shewed gracefully at his years ~~more pale than~~ _ _ _Alfieri
          straggling & undefined
yet some ~~wo~~ more ᴧ shewed that ~~wit~~ those passions whose signs

               though slowly
he suppressed yet preyed ᴧ upon the vital prin

ciple — his eyes had not lost their fire

but their softness was gone & there was now a

severity in their glance which awestruck

those who beheld him — few c^d stand his

look which seem fold by fold to unwind

the coverings they had placed around their

hearts & in its very core to read their dearest

secrets—) his person was now formed – it had

lossed the youthful appearance of the Apollo, but
          it was
it was not Herculean - ᴧmajestic firm

      ~~aspect~~ demænour
           severe & almost arrogant
& free. H His ~~very look~~ was ~~terrible~~ to his
          apalling

Line 3: the second i *of* phisiognomy *is upon* o; *line 7:* broown *written partially upon* ?brood; *line 10: false start might be* f; *line 34:* His *was* He

119)   enemies but with his friends he was gay &

kind — his conversation was full of wit & in

terest — he did no although he appeared superior

to the crowd around him yet he did not disdain

the affairs of life — and his smile, for he

often smiled, was not that of contempt ~~yet~~ but

~~it~~ appeared as if he had a deeper meaning in

his look than those about him c^d read, a

lurking sense of somthing beyond that for which

he seemed to smile — He was kind & even

grateful to his friends as long as he considered

them such; but he was quick to ~~suspicion~~ distrust –&

cold looks & averted favour followed suspicion

~~&~~ if these were answered by aught but patience

& submission hatred quickly came & to of &

that never failed to ~~oppress~~ destroy its object — If

he suspected alone, that was suffiencient

cause that he who had become thus ob

noxious to his prince shd be told that

it was his will that he instantly ~~departed~~ should

from Lucca and the confiscation of his

fortune filled the public coffers — if he

thought he had reason to fear the doom

of that man whom he feared was sealed.

The 9 of 119 may have been written upon 8

120)   He was cruel & unrelenting and the death of

his victim did not alone satisfy him, several

                     command
were starved to death by him~~s~~ ^ & worse tortures

inflicted upon others — somthing of this was to
                     usage of those
be pardoned on account of the times - but cruel
               ^ feature
ty had now become an indelible ^ of Castruccio's

character.   was unvaried & prudent:
    His ~~In this~~ internal policy ^ he flattered the

poor at the expence of the rich — he lightened
                the necessary articles of life
all customs particularly those upon ~~food~~ — and
                 x
he often bought corn at a high price in Sicily

& Spain to sell it at a low rate to the poor

citizens of Lucca – The expences of his government

were defrayed by innumerable confiscations

~~& the~~ a few taxes & the spoils of war. He

built many castles & strongholds – he made

bridges cut roads, dug canals and in every way

improved the situation of his poorer subjects –

but the rich were kept in check by spies
                   held
oppressed by heavy contributions, ^ in perpetual

danger of disgrace & poverty — & except

a few favoured individuals the whole class
was degraded —

    He was adored by his soldiery — his cou

rage was undaunted. — he was ever the first

121)

in onset, the first to scale a wall — the first

to stand in the breach — the first to swim ~~the~~ ^a

river when a flood had rendered ~~their~~ ^{its} passage

dangerous; he assisted in toils of the camp – and

as he ever went bareheaded his sunny &

flowing locks ~~among~~ ^{rising above} the helmets of his followers

often pointed him out as a mak^r to the

enemy — He entered into the interests of the

soldiery & called them by those names of father

brother or son which most endears them to

the chief — he distinguished & rewarded

merit – but his praise which was warm

& publickly bestowed was as eagerly sought

by his ~~soldiers~~ ^{troops} as the money or advancement

which surely followed that praise — ~~and~~ his

displeasure was dreaded in an equal ~~manner~~ ^{degree}

~~and~~ when with ^a stern look he pointed ^{one} out

~~one~~ as a coward or disobedient his com

panions fell off from him ~~av~~ nor did the

offender dare lift his head until by some

deed of valour he had redeemed his fame

He often said that the goodwill of

the soldiers was the nerve of war – that

money was the means of obtaining this but

that there were others to heighten & secure

122)

it which might never be neglected — ~~And~~

(these arts) he excersised (with signal success:

affable ~~in~~ during leisure daring in action

~~He~~ his soldiers looked on him as their

preserver & his enemies regarded ~~thes~~ him

as their inevitable destroyer & his name
      had power to
alone ~~e~~^d blanch their cheeks & make

them turn to fly.

      But if he were feared by his enemies

in open war his secret policy was still more

dreaded — He had not forgotten the lessons of

Alberto Scotto — and, as his attempts on the

life of the king of Naples might prove, his
         perhaps
measures had ʌbeen influenced by the
counsels of Benedetto Pepi. He had many
      each
spies in ~~every~~ town and collected intelligence

from every court in Lombardy — Women

& priests were his frequent instruments

and even the more distinguished among

the citizens were conquered by his largesses

to betray the consels of their country – The

simple plan ~~th~~ on which he had regulated
      speedy
his army & the ~~swift~~ intelligence that he

received of the motions of the enemy made

him incredibly swift in all his motions

345

123)

So that as he bore the eagle on his banner

he was said to be the eagle of war &

with ~~strong pi~~ piercing eye to discover danger

& with strong pinions to hasten to overcome

it —

In private life among his friends he was

more than affable for he fogot all distinc

tions of rank & power & was to them as a friend

~~ho~~ and brother. Some he loved far above the

rest - he loved Albert as his son - and his

friendship for Galeazzo Visconti was ardent

& sincere – although so far & so long sepera

ted they acted upon consentaneous plans &

~~the news of victory to~~ Castruccio in the very

field of battle wd send news of victory to

his friend who sympathized in his triumph

with the joy of a partizan & the warmth of

a sincere friend.

Castruccio had been much untaught

except in chivalrous excercises and the arts

of war but he loved the society of learned

men & he sought the conversation of monks

& priests whose discussions & subtle disquisi

tions upon ~~that~~ _{subjects} which none of them un

erstood greatly delighted him, the order of their

346

SILENT CORRECTIONS

Three items, though mentioned in footnotes, have been added for completeness. The reading preceding the square bracket is the one given in this edition.

Page   line

22	4	de'] de
28	22	mowing] moving
33	6	consult it."] consult it.
44	25	Lombardo] Lombardi
49	6	and / tasted] and / and tasted
52	23	"Bologna] Bologna
59	23	Antelminelli."] Antelminelli.
60	1	Arrigo; I] ; Arrigo I
69	10	it were] is were
72	14	summer was] summerwas
73	10	he was] hewas
73	36	Faggiuola] Fagginola
76	8	Serchio] Secchio
90	5	Italians,] Italians;
91	10	Lucca."] Lucca.
92	34	Arrigo,] Arigo,
94	24	demanded Castruccio] demandedCastruccio
99	18	for peace] fo rpeace
100	37	of peace] ofpeace
108	7/8	Tesoretto] Teroretto
108	30	Aziolo] Agiolo
116	31	Charlemagne] Charlemage
130	30	Antichità] Antichristà
140	9	upon?] upon` [broken type]
140	28	Safe I hope;] Safe I hope,
149	21/2	her?" He fixed] her?" he fixed
153	25	to-morrow night] to-morrow-night
162	1	vengeance] vengance
171	40	succession] succesion
181	29	than it] that it

347

Page	line		
186	13	aziolo's]	agiolo's
186	27	bath;]	bath,
188	1	agony,]	agony.
206	14	better than I;]	better than I,
209	3	Tripalda]	Tripaldi
212	4	my life]	mylife
217	31	"we are]	we are
233	18/19	Euthanasia,]	Euthansia,
249	12	convent-garden?]	convent-garden,
252	25	tell.']	tell."
263	8	strangest]	strongest
273	36	haughtily; "if]	haughtily;" if
274	31	mansion.]	mansion
278	11	hope.]	hope
285	21	external]	enternal
288	6	youthful]	youhtful
297	1	same situation.]	samesituation.
298	31	suspected]	supected
302	20	Avogadii]	Avoggadii
303	14	Messer]	Mester